Miscellanies

OF

the Fuller Worthies' Library

IN FOUR VOLUMES

VOLUME 3

EDITED BY THE REV. ALEXANDER B. GROSART

AMS PRESS
NEW YORK

137540

Reprinted from a copy in the collections of the Harvard College Library
From the edition of 1870–1876, Blackburn
First AMS EDITION published 1970
Manufactured in the United States of America

International Standard Book Number:
Complete Set: 0-404-02670-2

Volume 3: 0-404-02673-7

Library of Congress Card Catalog Number: 70-129362

AMS PRESS, INC.
NEW YORK, N.Y. 10003

Miscellanies

OF

The Fuller Worthies' Library.

IN FOUR VOLUMES.

VOL. III.

CONTAINING

TUKE'S 'HOLY EVCHARIST' (1625)—
FRAUNCES'S 'COUNTESSE OF PEMBROKE'S EMANUEL'
(1591)—
NORRIS OF BEMERTON'S COMPLETE POEMS—
VISCOUNT FALKLAND'S COLLECTED POEMS—
DR. GILES FLETCHER'S 'LICIA OR POEMS OF LOUE'
(1593)
AND
LEVER'S 'CRUCIFIXE OR HOLIE PASSION' AND
'QUEENE ELIZABETH'S TEARES.' (1607.)

EDITED WITH

Memorial-Introductions and Notes:

BY THE

REV. ALEXANDER B. GROSART,

ST. GEORGE'S, BLACKBURN, LANCASHIRE.

PRINTED FOR PRIVATE CIRCULATION.

1872.

156 COPIES ONLY.

Preface

'GOOD wine' says the proverb, 'needs no bush', that is, needs no 'sign' to be hung out by way of invitation—passive or urgent — to step in and quaff; and I apprehend that the title-page of this third Volume of our Miscellanies is more than sufficient to gain and retain interest in its contents from capable Readers and book-lovers. TUKE and FRAUNCE, NORRIS and FALKLAND, DR. GILES FLETCHER and CHRISTOPHER LEVER have been sorrowfully too long excluded from collections of our English Poetry. Our Introductions may be here assumed to establish the claim of each Worthy on recognition, in the modest form of our limited reprints. NORRIS and FALKLAND and the elder FLETCHER have received very gratifying welcome in unlooked-for places, as separately issued.

With reference to the text and notes of all, I have again to acknowledge the unfailing help of those friends named in previous Prefaces: and I would specify in connection with NORRIS my laborious correspondent in London Mr. W. T. BROOKE, who even to supererogation worked on the ' various readings' of the different editions, &c.

As before, my endeavour has been faithfully to reproduce each Worthy's own text, and in the respective Memorial-Introductions to furnish all get-at-able at this late day, concerning their subjects. In the book-market the original editions of the present collection could not be purchased for twice as many pounds as their cost in shillings from us.

Our next Volume—the closing one—promises to exceed rather than come short of, its predecessors. But I close our Preface with LEVER's little Letter to the Reader: " It is the common custome to intreate favour from courteous Readers. The custome is not good and therefore I vse it not; but if the matter merit, and the men be courteous, the sute of fauour will be easily granted ; if otherwise, it is but needlesse shame to beg a commendation where it is not. And therefore I [shall] willingly leaue to euery man the liberty of his iudgement and expose these tracts to general censure ". ("To Heauen and Earth " 1608).

ALEXANDER B. GROSART.

St. George's,
Blackburn, Feby. 7th, 1872.

TO

JAMES CROSSLEY, ESQ., F.S.A.,

President of the Chetham Society.

TO WHOM I OWE THE SUGGESTION OF COLLECTING THE
POEMS OF

VISCOUNT FALKLAND

AND EVER-READY HELPFULNESS FROM HIS WELL-STORED LIBRARY
AND BETTER-STORED MEMORY:

This Volume of Miscellanies is Inscribed

WITH SINCERE REGARD BY

THE EDITOR.

MISCELLANIES

OF

The Fuller Worthies' Library.

CONCERNING

The Holy Eucharist

AND

The Popish Breaden God

(1625)

BY

THOMAS TUKE:

Reprinted and Edited with Introduction and Notes

BY THE

REV. ALEXANDER B. GROSART,

ST. GEORGE'S, BLACKBURN, LANCASHIRE.

PRINTED FOR PRIVATE CIRCULATION.

1871.

156 COPIES ONLY.

Introduction.

BEYOND its chance occurrence in Library or Sale or Booksellers' catalogues and in compilations from these, such as LOWNDES, the name of THOMAS TUKE is unknown to Bibliographers. Even LOWNDES (new edition) chronicles only two of his books and HAZLITT simply our present reprint. And yet no one can read his quaint, pungent, intense little volumes—each rarer than another and three of which now before us seem to have utterly escaped notice—without a sigh of regret that slight as our contribution must be *in memoriam* it far exceeds any extant.

The earliest trace that we have found is in his "Treasvre of Trve Love" (1608) as follows: "The Treasvre of Trve Love. Or a liuely description of the loue of Christ vnto his Spouse, whom in loue he hath clensed in his blood from sinne, and made a Royall Priesthood vnto his Father. By Thomas Tuke, Preacher of the word. London,

Printed by Thomas Creede, and are to be solde by
Thomas Archer. 1608 [12o]. The Epistle-dedicatory of this 'savoury' treatise, addressed to "The
right worshipfull, Master Edward Barrett, Esquire," is dated " Jan. 23. 1607 :" a second dedi-
catory-epistle to "the right vertuous gentlewoman,
Mistris Elizabeth Leueson" is prefixed to Part
III. " Preacher of the Word " was a description
general enough ; but in his next title-pages, a year
later (1609), even this is lacking. Take these two
successively : (*a*) " The High-way to Heauen ; or
The Doctrine of Election, effectuall Vocation,
Iustification, Sanctification and eternal Life.
Grounded upon the holy Scriptures, confirmed by
the testimonies of sundry iudicious and great
Diuinès, Ancient and Moderne. Compiled by
Thomas Tvke. London, Printed by Nicholas
Okes, dwelling neere Holborne bridge. 1609.
[12o.] (*b*) " The Picture of a true Prostestant, or
God's House and Husbandry : wherein is declared
the duty and dignity of all God's children, both
Ministers and People. Written by Thomas Tvke,
London, Printed by Nicholas Okes ; and are to be
sold by Thomas Archer in Popes head Pallace,
neere the Royall Exchange. 1609 [12o.]. The
former is dedicated finely to " John Leueson Esquire : the latter " to the right worshipfull Mais-

ter Gabriel Armestrong Esquire and to the vertuous gentlewoman Mistris Margaret Armestrong, his louing wife", having for text 1 Corinthians iii. 9. The " Picture " yields this bit of memorable dating : " Many, large and admirable are the benefits wherewith the Lord hath honoured us these fifty by-past years together." ' Fifty ' from 1608-9 carries us back to 1558-9. It gives us also an odd use of the word ' affected ', noticeable as shewing how Time reverses the meaning of words, albeit the words do not perish :" If " says he " we consider the transcendent profaneness and *affected* ignorance of the multitude." By ' affected ' he meant self-chosen or cherished : now, in such application, it would indicate ' *pretence* ' of ignorance or putting-on airs of it. His next book is " A Treatise against Painting and Tinctvring of Men and Women : against Murther and Poysoning : against Pride and Ambition : against Adulterie and Witchcraft, and the roote of all these, Disobedience to the Ministrie of the Word. Wherevnto is added, " The Pictvre of a Pictvre or the Character of a painted Woman " and bears to be " By Thomas Tvke, Minister of God's Word at Saint Giles in the Fields. London. 1616. [4to.]". He must have held some subordinate appointment at " St. Giles" under the Rector of the period, who was probably ROGER MANWARING ; for Brian Walton came afterwards. NEWCOURT (*s. n.*) makes no mention of him here. The " Treatise " is of the raciest in its style, drollest in its illustrations, most plain-speaking and fiery in its invectives. Beside it even THOMAS HALL is tame and reticent. From NEWCOURT (I. 515) we gather that in 1617 (19th July) he was 'presented' by the King (James I.) to the vicarage of St. Olave Jewry, which important post he held until 1642, when according to Mércurius Rusticus (p 256) he was " sequester'd, plunder'd, and imprison'd for his loyalty in the late Rebellion." WALKER in his " Sufferings " (though neglecting to enter his name in his folio's copious indices) has duly transferred to his pages what he found in the " Repertorium ". He adds " I do not find that he returned to his parish after the Restoration ; and therefore suspect that he died before it " (Part II. p 178). From the Registers of St. Olave, Old Jewry, COLONEL CHESTER has kindly gleaned these entries for me :

" Burials 1622-3 Jan. 28. Mary, dau. of Thomas Tuke, Minister.

Burials 1636. Nov. 10. Thos. eldest son of Thos. Tuke, Clerk and Rector of the Parish.

[1643 Nov. 7th. William Hignell, Minister of God's Word and Rector of this Parish.]

1654 June 17th. Mrs. Mary Tuke, wife of Thomas."

He thus survived his wife: and it is touching to find him laying her in the family-grave of the Church from which he had been " sequestered ". No other mention of him either under marriages or baptisms appears. Doubtless WALKER's suspicion is correct: and he must have been in a ripe old age even in 1654, seeing in 1607—8 he was "Preacher of the Word".

The Poem now reprinted, originally published in 1625—the title-page given in its place—passed into a second edition in 1636, the date on page 26 being "February 2. 1625". It corresponds almost literally with the other: save that the Postscript thus commences: " These lines subnexed, being brought me by a friend haue occasioned the second impression of this book, which had been before printed, Anno 1625 ". From this one would have thought the "lines subnexed" were new, but they are precisely the same with those of the 1625 edition. His meaning must have been a modest ascription of any vitality in his Poem to what he had worked into it from the "subnexed lines", which by-the-way in 1636 edition are signed "Io. Anteff". I have met with the "Lines" in several of the Harleian and Additional MSS.

I think it will be conceded that the ancient Poem

has characteristics deserving revival in our Miscellanies. It has keenness of insight into the contradictions of the ultra-Roman doctrine of the Mass, gleams of grim humour where perchance humour is scarcely in place, well-put dilemmas, resonant and even o'times melodious versification and towards the end a yearning after a deeper unity spite of apparent diversity. For myself, though I must as a thing of common sense regard the superstitious accretions that have gathered around the original simple memorial-Feast of our dying Lord, as very sorrowful and far aside from His intention, I nevertheless feel it painful to treat any religious conviction of others lightly (not that Tuke is ' light' : he is awfully in earnest and even softly pitiful) or without allowance in charity for long traditional observance and a grand faith, over-leaping every difficulty and really finding Christ in the '*things*'. Dear old RICHARD BAXTER'S words on the death of his passionate accuser, ought to speak trumpet-tongued to us all : " Whilst we are wrangling here in the dark, we are dying, and passing to a world that will decide controversies, and the safest passage thither is by peaceable holiness ".

ALEXANDER B. GROSART.

CONCERNING

THE HOLY

E V C H A R I S T,

and the Popish

BREADEN-GOD

TO

THE MEN OF ROME,

as well

LAIQVES AS CLERIQVES,

BY

THOMAS TUKE.

ANNO MDCXXV.   [4o].

To the Courteous Reader.

WHIL'ST sunne doth shine, and does not
burne,
   Men willingly to it doe turne :
But if it once wax hot, they fly,
And hide themselues from't by and by.
So truth,[1] that's pleasing, giuing light,
Is grieuous, if it once doe bite,
   And oftentimes procures a foe,
   Whereas base flattring does not so.
For man would haue full scope in's wayes,
And gladly haue of all men praise.   10
   He would not be suppos'd to stray,
   Although he be quite out of 's way ;
Truth's like hony, put to a sore,
Which makes the place to smart the more.

---

[1] Amat eam (id est veritatem) lucente : oderunt eam
redarguentem. Quia enim falli nolunt et fallere volunt,
amant eam, cum seipsam indicat et oderunt eam, cum se
ipsos indicat. August. confess. lib 10. cap. 23.   T.

Of carnall mindes such is the case,
  So faine they would hold on their race.
To be discover'd, fann'd,[1] and tried,
Grieues them as much, as to be tied ;
  Yet welcome medicine, that does heale,
  And welcome they that truly deale.   20
Sore eyes indeed the light do shunne,
And batts, and owles loue not the sunne :
  The thief delighteth in the night,
  But honesty does loue the light.
The honest heart, the single eye,
Is very loath to tread awry.
  And therefore deemes the light full deare,
  And him, that speaks the truth, will heare.
It studies to be truly wise,
And would not be abus'd with lyes.   30
  It therefore giuues it selfe to pray,
  To read, heare, search, both night and day.
And, when the truth it has found out,
To loue't, and own't, it does not doubt.
  Glory, and greatnesse, and fear, and shame,
  Gaine, that's so lou'd, and worldly fame,
Carnall pleasure, and contentment,
Friendship of men, to errors bent,
  The honest heart, the single eye,

---

[1] St Matthew iii. 12.   G.

To truth doeth these things vilifie.[1]   40
Yea life, that is so deare to man,
To keepe the truth, forgo it can.
   And that is trueth, to be belieued,
Which from the Scriptures is derived.[2]
For that in faith makes but a breach,
Which holy Scriptures do not teach.[3]
   All teachers should their teachings square
By them : for they God's will declare.
They fully shew the Church, and truth lay
   out :
To follow other guides is to stray out.   50
   They, they are Faith's perfit rule and mea-
   sure.
   The touch-stone of truth, and matchlesse
   treasure.[4]

      Thine in the trueth, truely,
          THO. TUKE.

---

[1] Amicus Socrates, amicûs Plato, magis amica veritas, dixit Aristoteles. T.

[2] Niladdēdum legi, nihil auferendum Scripturæ. Cyril Alex in Iohan. lib 11, cap. 28. T.

[3] Perscripturum Deus loquitur omne quod vult. Gregor. moral. li. 16. cap. 16. T.

[4] Chrisost. Scripturā vocat exactissimam trutinam et quomonem, ac regulam, in 2 Cor. homil. 13 in fine. T.

The men of Rome,

AS WELL

Laiques, as Cleriques.

PRIESTS make their Maker Christ, yee
　　must not doubt ;
　　They eat, drink, box Him vp, and beare
　　about.
Substance of things they turne : nor is this all ;
For both the signes must hold in severall.
　　Hee's whole[1] ith' bread, whole ith' cuppe.
　　They eat Him whole : whole they suppe ;
　　Whole ith' cake, and whole ith' cuppe.
　This with you all doeth goe for veritie ;
To hold contrary is meer heresie,
This is pure, pure Catholique, pure divine.　　10
And thus feast ye ; he with his Christ, thou with
　　thine,

---

[1] Under the shewes, as they talke of bread and wine. T.

15

Without bread and wine indeed :
 For this is your Roman Creed ;
 Whom ye make, on Him ye feed.
The bread and wine themselues away are gone,
Shewes of them tary still, but substance none.
They make their God, and then they eat Him vp.
They swallow downe His flesh, and blood vp sup.
They'll taste no flesh on Frydayes—that's not
 good—
But of their new made God, and of His blood. 20
And as the whale did Jonas, so they eat
Him vp aliue, body and soule, as meat.
As men eat oysters, so on Him they feed ;
Whole, and aliue, and raw, and yet not bleed.
This cookerie, voyed of humanitie,
Is held in Rome for sound divinitie.
 And is not this strange to heare,
  That God, whom, ye say, ye feare,
  Ye should eat, as belly cheare ?
The Graver, Painter, Baker, euen these three, 30
Your priests haue reason for to magnifie.
Perhaps the Baker thinks, he merits more :
Yet both advance their honor, and their store.
 For they with their gentle feat
  Help them to mony and meat,
  Making Gods, to begge and eat.
And now me thinks I heare old Laban say

See, they haue stolne and borne my gods away.[1]
Me thinks, I heare and see that mountineer,
Michah of Ephraim ; who did idols feare,   40
Chiding with the Danits, for that they had
Took's priest, and gods away, which made him
    mad.[2]
Mee thinks I see the Philistines bereft
Of their vaine Gods, which they to Dauid left :
And how that noble worthy made them bee
Destroyed of his souldjers presentlie.[3]
Both men and beasts—a thing to be deplored—
May bear away the things, of you adored.
The things yee worship with your heart and minde,
Men like your selues, can burne, can melt, can
    grinde.   50
Baruch's base things—a shame it is to think—
Can marre the things, ye worship, and make
    stinck.
       And is not this great folly,
       More then childish vanity,
       To dote on things so silly ?
The foolish Heathens were not all so mad :
For they devoured not the gods they had.
The wiser knew their vanities were wood,

---

[1] Gen. 3. 2. T.   [2] Judg. 18. 2: 24. T.
[3] 2 Sam. 5. 21 : 1 Chron. 14. 12. T.
[4] Bar. 6. 12. 22. T.

Or such like stuffe : not gods, nor flesh and blood.[1]
But yee, as if bewitcht, do count, and call   60
That poore thing God, Maker, and Lord of all,
Which is plaine bread; in substance, very bread,
Made of wheat-flower, ground, with man's hand,
        and knead.
This, which is bread, which all men so will say,
Which haue not lost all sense, or thrown't away,
This ye doe say, ye do belieue it is,
Not bread in trueth, but the true God of blisse ;
Euen Jesus Christ, God-Man, flesh, blood, and
        bones,
Wherein y'are stupider then they, then stones.
O God ! what is a man, euen at his best,   70
If not of Thee with heavenly wisedome blest ?
        Grievous errors doth he swallow,
        And in sin perversly wallow,
        Not regarding what may follow.
    Poore Laique ! there is one thing more for thee ;
The cuppe of blessing thou art forc'd to flee.
Eat thou mayest by law : but thou mayest not
        suppe ;[2]
The Priest is he, that's worthy of the cuppe.

---

[1] Vid. Basil schol in Psal 113. Lactan. lib. 2, cap. 2.
Aug. in Psal. 113. conc. 2.   T.
[2] Consil. Constant. sess. 13.   T.

Take Christ thou may'st under the breaden signe :
But not touch Him under the shew of wine.　　80
A prince perhaps by favour with his lippe
Is suffer'd after's priest to take a sippe.

　　　　And is this a priestly feat,
　　　　Thus the people for to cheat,
　　　　Who should drink as well, as eat?
　　But lay-men are not priests : —who sayes they
　　　　are ?—
And therefore ought not in that cuppe to share,
Why? Are not princes lay-men? yet they may,
And do drink of the cup, as men do say.
Th' eleuen, or twelue,—for chuse ye whether—90
When they first receiued altogether,
Their Maister being by, then were they all
As sheep : the text ' disciples ' does them call.
And furthermore, if lay-men may not drink,
Because th' are such, why may they not then think
It lawfull for them to refuse to eat,
For the selfe same reason, of that sacred meat?
Or, who can justly say, and not deluded,
That Laiques from the cuppe are quite excluded,
When Christ sayes, ' *Drinke ye All of this*,' as
　　　　tho　　　　　　　　　　　　　　　　100
He spake to priests alone, and to no moe ;
And yet that, when He sayd those words, ' *Take
　　　　Eate*,'

c　　　　19

To priests and people too He meant that meat?
At Rome no drink's allow'd, but only meat:
Yet Paul doth bid men drink as well as eat.

    There sits one brazen face,
    That usurps a bishop's place,
    Who dares thus Christ's flock disgrace.

 Now to the man of might, who sayes, he can
Doe that, which is not in the power of man;   110
Who can make Christ of bread—hee's so diuine—
As Christ of water once did make true wine.
Angell, nor king, nor artizan of skill
Can this; the priest alone, and he at's will.
Others, who can make bread out of their grist,
Must leaue their bread to him, to make it Christ.
Make stones to be men we know that God can:
And the priest braggs he can make bread a man.
Make a god of a man we know men can:
But his art lyes in making God a man,   120
So, as if Christ had not took flesh before,
Yet without flesh He should be now no more.
Nor can the nimblest Baker work a cake,
So soone, as he his cake a man can make.
Four words, repeated with a voyce submisse,
Will serue to make vp's man and God, I wisse.
These four alone, ' *Hoc est corpus meum.*'[1]

---

[1] Per verba cōsecrationis vere et realiter uti transsub-

Will work the feat : there needs no greater summe.
Indeed the priest's intention should concurre,
Or els the work moy chance to take a blurre.   130
For, as they do say, this most rare invention
Will scarcely take without the priest's intention.

    But yet here we must all know,
    That all priests can not thus doe ;
    The Roman can : but no moe.

Naturall parents, be they nee'r so good,
Are God's instruments only but of flesh and blood.
To get, or make a soule's not in their power :
But he a perfect soule can make each houer.
Both soule and body are alike to him :   140
That shall not want a power, nor this a limme.
Parents their children get : they make them not ;
They get them like themselues, with staine and
    spot.
But he no getter is allow'd to bee,
And wife he does by vow with horror flee ;

---

stantiatur panis, ita producitur et quasi generatur Christus
in altari adeo potenter et efficaciter ut si Christus necdum
esset incarnatus, per hæc verba Hoc est corpus meum....
incarnaretur corpusque humanum assumeret, ut graves
theologi docent. Cornelius cornelij a Lapide. Comment.
in Esai. 7. 14.   [It is marvellous that TUKE in quoting
'Hoc est corpus meum' did not recall the popular verdict
in the corruption of it, as 'hocus-pocus'. G.]

Hee's only a Maker, and but of one :
If he make not that one, he makes just none.
And, whereas children by degrees do grow,
That, which he makes, is made at once : not so.
Full holy also, pure, voyd of all sin,   150
Hauing no soyle without, no fault within.
Yet he that makes Him, is not without both :
Which if not he, yet others often loth.
And which is strange, he may not get a man :
But yet make God he may, and thinks he can.
And, whereas others works may be destroyed,
His, he belieues, is not to be annoyed.
I ask then of this man, this man of might,
Who does so farre surmount this mortall wight;
Is thy mouth the virgin's wombe ? is bread her
          seed ?   160
Are thy words the Holy Ghost ? Is this our
          Creed ?
That thou of bread thy Maker should'st erect ?
What ? Does a temple make the architect ?
Or does a servant vse to make his Lord,
That priest's to theirs a beeing do afford ?
          O presumptuous Vndertaker !
          Neuer cake could make a Baker :
          And shall a priest make his Maker ?
     Indeed, we see some men by priests made
          stones :

But who sees them make bread, flesh, blood, and
     bones ?   170
They rather merit fayth, that say, they can,
Sooner make a man bread, than bread a man.
That, though vnnaturall, has often been :
This, supernaturall, was yet neuer seen.
Tell me : Was not Christ before thy bearing ?
And hundreds of yeers before thy sheering ?
Was He not a man before thine annointing ?
And must He yet be made at thine appointing ?
Does He not still abide in humane flesh,
That yet He must be made of thee afresh ?   180
And sooner too, then thou thyself wast made,
Eyther man, or of this man-making trade.
       What a kinde of brow hast thou,
       That doest say, thou mak'st Him now,
       Since thou took'st thy priestly vow ?
  Hast thou priest's power from the man Christ
     receiu'd ?
So thou wilt say, or els I am deceiu'd.
With what face then dar'st thou say, Thou Him
     makest,
Of whom thy selfe and power, thou say'st, thou
     takest ?
As if a Justice should say, he makes a King,   190
Of whome he does receiue his justicing :
As if a childe should say, he makes his sire,

Or color'd clothes should say, they make their
      diar.[1]
    Thus ye dimme the noone-day-light,
    And 'gainst sense and reason fight,
    Holding writlesse, what's not right.
    Perhaps you'll say, Christ Jesus is not made
Of bread : but that the bread away does fade,
And that His body followes in it's stead,
It beeing onely there now, and not bread.   200
Well : be it so, yet thus His bodie's made
Here still on earth to be : which is gainsayd,
By Christ Himselfe, by Peter, and our Creed :[2]
To whom we could adde more, if there were need.
For Austin,[3] Vigill,[4] and others agree,
That Christ is not now on earth bodilie.
And vaine is to plead the power divine,
Which out of darknes can make light to shine :
Which of just nothing can make things to bee,
And can make dead things liue, and stone blinde
      see,   210
And most easily doe the things, which can
Be comprehended of no braines of man.
Make it appear by Holy Scriptures' light,

---

[1] Dyer. G.   [2] John 12 and 17, and Act 3. T.
[3] St. Augustine. G.   [4] Vigilantius (?) G.

That God does will and work these things, ye
      fight
For, with such earnestnesse, and then we will
Confesse your power, and applaud your skill.
    But till ye proue by written Word,
    That God to these things does accord,
    To make fayth of them were absurd.
  We read of Christ twice made : and that is
    all ;   220
Of woman, and vnder Law.[1] Is this small,
Vnlesse thou also make Him at thy will
By thine high creating power, and thy skill ?
Is't not ynough for Him, and for us all,
That He was once borne, and once vnder thrall,
But that He must yet also, day by day,
By you be made, and offred, as ye say ?
    So, for fayth ye fancy teach,
    And for truth mens dreames ye preach,
    Making in God's Church a breach.   230
  What a silly thing is this, thou makest,
Which for the Lord Jesus Christ, thou takest ?
Which, idol-like, can neyther heare, nor talk,
Nor see, nor feele, nor smell, nor one jott walk.
Which can do nothing for ought does appear :
But's fit all wrong, that's offer'd, for to bear.

---

[1] Gal. 4. T.

Which can not saue it self from catte, nor dogge,
From rat, nor mouse, nor from the grunting hogge.
    Fy that such a sorry thing,
      A mouse can in danger bring   240
      Should be counted for thy king.
  Hezekiah sayes[1] the Assyrian king
The Gentiles gods into the fire did fling,
Because they were not gods : for so he sayth ;
Which plainly shewes the fondnesse[2] of your fayth
For this, ye say the priest hath made, ye call
God Almightie : and yet the same may fall,
Or by plaine force be cast into the fire,
By Turks or Moores, or flung into the mire.
    May not men then boldly say,   250
      It does your handy-work bewray,
      When they see it hurl'd away ?
  What a kinde of vile servitude is this,
Thou mak'st Him serue, of whom thou look'st for
      blisse ;
To coop Him in a piece of bread in show,
Where He must stay a time, and must not goe ?
A pretty godlin[3] sure, now in thine hand,
Then boxed vp, to carry by sea, or land.
Now in thy mouth, and by and by ith'maw :

---

[1] Is. 37. 19. T.   [2] Folly. G.
[3] A noticeable diminutive. G.

Oth' Altar now, then in some solemne shaw,   260
Riding about ith' streets, to grace that man,
Who dares do that, which justly no man can.
Yet more; This God, ye seeme so to adore,
Ye basely prostitute to knaue and whore;
Teaching that the wicked His flesh may eat,
Whereas Christ Jesus is to such no meat.
For he, that eats His flesh and drinks His blood,
Shall liue[1]: and therefore sure he must be good.
Yea he, that eats Christ's flesh, in Christ doeth
    dwell:[2]
But they in Him do dwell, that's kept for hell.[3] 270
He must be of Christ's flesh, that eats His flesh:
And onely those with it He does refresh.[4]
Indeed, the sacrament thereof ill men
May eat:[5] but bane it is vnto them then.
But it it selfe whosoever does eat,
To him it is no bane, but wholesome meat;
Able to nourish, and preserue the spirit,
And to do that, which no man can by's merit.[6]
He, eats of this bread, that eats of Mee,
Shall liue by Me, sayth Christ, eternallie.[7]   280

---

[1] Joh. 6. 51. T.   [2] Joh. 6. 56. T.   [3] Aug. de civi.
dei li. 21. ca. 25. Beddain. [4] 1 Cor. 6   T.   [5] Aug. in
Joh. tract 26 T.   [6] Ambros. de sacram lib. 5. cap. 4.
T.   [7] Johan. 6. 57. T.

And he that eats Christ, that does aright belieue,
And being knit unto Him does receiue,
And draw forth of Him that by fayth, which may
Sustaine, preserue, and feed him night and day.[8]
Whereas your Christ, ye say, ye take and eat
With hand and mouth, both good and bad, as
    meat,
I ween, ye say not now, ye teare and grinde
Him with your teeth in pieces, as I finde.
But, that ye mouth him, that ye all professe,
All, all of you alike, both more and lesse.   290

       O the great stupidity
       In absolute foolery,
       And sencelesse impietie!

  What's become of all those Christs, priests haue
    made?
Doe all those hostes of wonder bide? or fade?
Doe they stay below? or ascend on high?
Or turne they back to bread, and wine? or die?
Or are any by digestion wrought,
And into mens spirits, or bodies, brought?
Or is not He, that yet in heauen does stay,   300
Able to feed and keep vs every way,
But that there must be still a new creation

---

[1] Aug. trac. 26. in Johan. et serm. circa sacr. fer.
pasc. T.

Of Him, after your strange imagination ?
    One Christ bides : but all those fly.
    One Christ liues : but all those dy.
    One is true : the rest a ly.
When ye haue eat them, ye may say, as of yore,
The eye, that hath seene them, shall see them no
    more.[1]
    He abides, that is aboue.
    Him we feare, and Him we loue   **310**
    These below doe nothing proue.
Alas, alas, there needs no fabrication
Of Him still by priests for man's sustentation.
Jesus Christ both yesterday, and to day,
Is our food, and rock, the selfe-same, for ay.
    Great need we haue all to take Him,
    And feare, least we should forsake Him.
    But can not, nor need not make Him.
Hony we read found in a lyon dead :[3]
But not of wormes in God incarnate bred.   **320**
Yet in this thing, for Christ ye doe adore,
And whose almightie ayd ye do implore,
Euen in this very thing a worme hath bred,
Euen on this very thing a worme hath fed.
The silly jentles may in these things breed :

---

[1] Exod. 14. Job. 20. T.   [2] Hebr. 13 . T.
[3] Judg. 14. T.

Plain cralling magots may on these things feed.
    For shame then forsake this toy,
    Which the Church does so annoy,
    And in truth delight and joy.
  Ye shew vs clothes, which, ye say, saints haue
    worne,   330
As ye would perswade vs, which are not torne
As yet with Time, but uncorrupt, as were
Th' Izraelites in their walk of fourty yere.[1]
And yet many an age is come, and gon,
Since the saints did last put them off, or on,
Whereof I finde your reason to be such ;
Forsooth, their sacred bodyes did them touch.
Why then should putrefaction at all
These accidents, ye talk so off, befall ?
How is't that vermine are in them ingendred 340
Seeing Christ's blessed body's in them tendred ?
How is't, that filthines is there discouer'd,
Where Jesus Christ, our Lord, God-Man lyes
    cover'd.
Is't, because His body can not them touch ?
Or for that of vertue it has not much ?
Or is't, because theirs His did farre exceed ?
Or els for that no other wonders need ?
Yet such a wonder, shewen vnto the eye,

---

[1] Nehe, 9, 21. T.

Would with men be of no small potencye,
Being voyd of fraud, and no forged tale :   350
Whereas your, so much talk'd of, wonders fayle;
Things which neyther sence, nor Scriptures doe
    teach :
But which even ye yourselves do feyne, and preach.
    Indeed, we would confesse you made,
    If sence or Scriptures lent you aid :
    But by both them ye are gainsayd.
Saint Austin writes[1] euen what himself belieued,
That the disciples Jesus Christ receiued,
That they that heauen-corne of life did eat,
Which is to true belieuers drinck, and meat. 360
Yet Judas, who to avarice was wed,
Ate not the Lord, but only ate His bread :
But by your learning, seeing that the bread
Is turn'd into Christ's flesh, on's flesh he fed.
For seeing Christ vnder those showes doth lye,
Eate Christ he must ; which Austin does denye ;
Saying that he ate the bread of the Lord
Against the Lord : a thing to be abhorr'd.
Neither are bare shewes of bread bread in kinde,
And therefore Austin was not of your minde. 370
For he held the traytor on bread did feed,

---

[1] Tract 59 in Johan.   T.

Whereas yee say, There's nought, but shewes,
    indeed.
Yet one word more, Because ye doe from hence
Send packing with disdayne all human sense.
Far be it from vs, sayes the selfe-same Father,
That we should be at all in doubt, or waver,
But rest assured that, what senses pure,
And vncorrupt, doe teach vs, that is sure,
And true, the very selfe-same things, they seem :
No other things, then those, we do them deem. 380
I pray you shew then, why we should not trust
Our senses here, as if they were accurst,
Sith that in other precepts of the Lord
They stand us in great stead, to keepe His word.
For by our sense we can put difference
'Twixt man and man : and so doe reverence.
By sense 'twixt man and beast discerne we can,
Betweene a father and an other man.
By sense we may perceiue they are but stocks,
Which fools adore, who are themselues but
    blocks.   390
By sense men are let see how for to keep
Their fingers from their neighbours oxe, and sheep
And finallie, by sense men learne much good,

---

[1] Absit a nobis vt ea, quœ per sensus corporis didici-
mus, vera esse dubtemus. Aug. trinit. lib. 15, cap. 12.   T.

And avoide the shedding of guiltlesse blood.
Now tell me, why should sense be trusted here,
And yet so vtterly denyed there ?

    For tho to sense it does appeare,

    That bread and wine are truely there,

    Yet ye say Nay, and nothing feare.

  We are not certayn that Christ's disciples
     did   400
Receiue the Eucharist, whiles He lay hid
In's sepulcher, starke dead : but yet they might,
Haue boldly took it then, and done but right.
And say they had : if that, ye hold, were good,
Then had they eate and drunke Him, flesh and
       blood,
Hot, and aliue, when as in trueth He lay,
Not quick but dead, as doe the Scriptures say.
Or, will ye say the sacrament did lack
Its virtue, as being for a time kept back,
Or quite extinct, vntill He rose againe ?   410
Or that His body, as voyd of life, as paine,
Was really, and substantially,
Presented in the sacred Mystery ?
Eyther of which ye shall as soone make cleere,
As make the sunne at midnight to shine here.
Whereas to fayth Christ absent present is,
And dead, might liue to fayth ; w'are sure of this,
Whilst here He was, He present was to sence :

But absent from it now He is gone hence.
His blessed body present was, from dayes   420
Of old, to true belieuers fayth alwayes.
He ever with them was by the power of fayth,
By which He dwelleth in them, th' apostle sayth.[1]
Not come in flesh, yet was He come to fayth,
Slayne from the beginning, as Scripture sayth.[2]
And hence it is, that they of old by Paul[3]
Are sayed the verie same spirituall
Both meat to eat, and drink to drink : which we
Our selues receiue by fayth, and carnallie.
For meat and drink, which are spirituall,   430
Are not to be eaten and drunck as carnall.
This food, they fed on, is that promiss'd seed,
Which they receiu'd by fayth, and so did feed.[4]
And still by fayth, if true, is to be ta'en,
And not with hand, or mouth, as ye would faine.
For fayth can see things a farre off with ease,
And on them, as vpon things present, seize.[5]
Faith for the soule is as much, as the eye,
Hand, mouth, throat, and mawe are for the body.
But some of you stick not to say,[6] The Lord   440

---

[1] Ephesians iii. 17. T.   [2] Reuelations xii. 1. 8. T.
[2] 1 Corinthians x. 3. T.
[4] Genesis 3, 15, and 22, 18. T.   [5] Gal. 3, 19. T.
[6] As one at Paul's crosse in Queen Maries Dayes. D.
Lessius de sum. bono, l. 4, c. 2, pag. 568, lin. 23. T.

Deceiu'd you, if deceiu'd ye be, with's word.
Forsooth, because He sayes, This is my body.
A bold conceipt it is: both blinde, and frothy.
For, if it please you to weigh this Scripture
With other Scriptures, or in peace endure
To see it for you done in loue by others,
—Who are, if ye be Christe's, in truth your
    brothers—
Ye may cleerely see, if ye will permit
Your will to be directed by your wit,
That these same words do beare an other sense, 450
Then that, ye go about to fetch from thence.
View well the places, ye see quoted here,
And ye may plainly see what IS. meanes there.
To put IS for SIGNIFIES is not rare,
As he soone may see, that to see does care.
Neyther is this exposition new,
But old: no youth, as that, that's brought by you.
    Forherein your Mother's wit,
    Neither sense, nor Holy Writ,
    Nor antiquitie does fit.   460
  As for that offering of Christ, ye hold,

---

[1] Genes. 17, 10 and 41, 26; Exod. 12, 11, and 13, 9, and
31, 13, 16 , Esay. 5, 7; Ezek. 37, 11; Zach. 1, 9; Math.
13, 37; Luke 8, 11; Gal. 4, 24; Rev. 1, 20, and 4, 5, and
5, 8, and 11, 4.

I wonder much wherefore ye are so bold.
Search the Scriptures : ye can not finde it there :
Or look to reason and y'are ne'erthe neare ;
His owne one's ynough, all-able and good,
Nor is sin pardon'd without shedding blood.[1]
And therefore yours, without such effusion,
Is nought els at all but mere delusion.
Yours eyther is the same with His, or not :   470
If it be not the same, then haue ye got
An other Gospell besides that He tought.[2]
But if it be the same with that He wrought,
Then doe ye offer Him in blood, and slayen,
Which ye can not, would ye never so faine,
Christ is no more on earth, but is aboue.
He says as much : and that doth you reproue.[3]
I say again, that must have consecration,
Which unto God is made a right oblation :
And who dare say that's not a divel's limme,
That Jesus Christ is consecrate by him.   480
By one offring hath He consecrated
For ever, them that are sanctified.
He consecrates vs, and His act is stable.
To consecrate Him we are all vnable.

---

[1] Heb. 10, 10, and 7, 27, and 9, 28.   T
[2] Heb. 9, 22.   T.
[3] Rom. 6, 1 ; John 12, 8, and 17, 11.   T.
[4] Heb 10, 14.   T.

See then the straits, whereinto ye are brought;
Whiles yee forsake the wayes inth' Scriptures
      tought.
    To the Scriptures then giue eare :
    And, what God speaks in them, heare ;
    Holding fast the truth in feare.
Now do I speak to all you men of fire,   **490**
Who hotter are, then reason does require ;
There's one thing, I would gladly haue you show,
Wherefore your choler should so strangely flow,
That nothing will suffice you, but the blood
Of such as think your doctrine is not good,
But new, and naught, concerning your Oblation
Of Christ, and of your Transubstantiation ?
And yet both yee and wee agree in this,
That Jesus Christ, our life, in heauen now is.
We both belieue He died vpon the tree,   **500**
And offer'd up Himselfe most willinglie.
We both acknowledge His owne one oblation,
Made on the crosse, is our propitiation.
We neither of vs doubt, but hold He is
A true and perfit man, God, Lord of blisse.
More, Both of vs affirme, and not deceived,
That Hee's giuen i'th Eucharist, and receiued,
Giuen of God, and reciu'd of the godly
Which come fitted for that sacred Myst'ry.
And yet, forsooth, this will not serue our turne, **510**

But that as heretiques we needs must burne.
And why as heretiques? Because we say,
There's no such offring of Him day by day.
—Yet confesse we that a representation
Is in the sacrament, of His oblation,
Who once did offer up Himselfe for sin,
But since that once hath never offer'd bin ;[1]
Not properly, but in a type, or figure,
Whereof we certain are : of yours not sure.
And for because we say, as sence does teach,   520
And as both Scriptures and old Doctors preach,
That bread and wine doe truly there remaine,
And not in shew onely, as ye do faigne,
Teaching men to belieue vnder a curse,
That their substance is gone : and which is worse,
Turn'd into the flesh and blood of our Lord :
Which ye presse vpon men with word and sword.
Now for because we do not hold this turning,
Ye hold vs, as heretiques, worthy burning.

      Well, what's past, let that suffice,   530
      Wake, and learne for to be wise,
      Hate not men for hating lies.

The great and mightie God, that hath made all,
Christians and others, both great and small,
Allowes you not to take away man's life

---

[1] Hebr. 9, 28, and 10, 12.   T.

Through bitter zeale and vnadvised strife :
Allowes you not His creatures blood to spill,
For crossing of your private thoughts and will.
Foule shame it is that mens owne fonde[1] opinions,
In Christendome should cause so great divisions. 540
A shame it is, such boasters of antiquitie
Should be so faultie in devising novitie.[2]
O that all humane vnderstanding might
Once become subject to the Scriptures' light !
That all would truly yeeld, and nothing grudge,
To make them their sole Rule of Faith, and judge,
O that charitie, so much talk'd off, might
Once among Christians obteyne her right !
O that God, whose great name we all confesse,
Were better serued, and offended lesse ! 550
If filthie lucre, pride and base ambition,
Which are the workers of so great confusion,
Were once abandon'd, and that men would go,
Roundly to work, the naked trueth to know,
Preferring it to all things els beside,
Then should our Lord be better glorified.

    Then factions soone would cease :
    They, that vex, would seek to please,
    And Christ's kingdome would increase.
Then they, that now the holy church do rend, 560

---

[1] Foolish. G.   [2] Novelty. G.

Would all their wits and labors for it spend,
Then factious nick-names soone would all be left,
Neyther should men of peace be so bereft.

> The trueth, that now is banish'd,
> True loue, which now is vanish'd,
> Would both be better cherish'd.

Now to the plaine, and wel-minded Romane,
Who is misled, I am returnd' againe.
The truth, ye should be taught, I will not tell
That which your learned priestes do knowe full
    well,   570
The cuppe is yours all as well as the bread,
As in the sacred Scriptures ye may read.[1]
The substance of the bread and wine remaine
After their consecration, that's plaine.
They are afterwards, what they were afore :
And yet afterwards they are something more.
Euen as the priest, now order'd will confesse,
Hee's what he was, yet more by this accesse.
As for theyr essence, they are the same, they were :
But for vse, an other nature they beare.[2]   580
Tho then their proper nature does endure,
Yet in their service they are chang'd it's sure.
For, once hallow'd, they are a sacrament

---

[1] Mat. xxvi, 27, Mar. xiv. 23, Cor. 1 xi· 28-29. T.
[2] I mean service, office, or condition. T.

Of Christ's body and blood, vpon vs spent.
The signes they are not : they are also seales
And exhibit the grace, the word reveales.
The signes thou tak'st at the hand of a man :
But God giues thee His Son ; for no man can.
And, when thou comm'st vnto this sacrament,
Belieuing, humbled, and true penitent ;   590
Thou art hereby put into sure possession
Of Jesus Christ, and of His blessed passion.
As truly as thou tak'st the bread and wine,
So truely are Christ's flesh and blood made thine.
His benefits alone thou doest not take
But Christ withall, Who dyed for thy sake.
The fruits are thine : the tree is also thine,
Euen as the substance of the bread and wine.
Yea fast thou art united to thy Lord
Who does Himselfe, and His to thee afford.   600
To say That men prepair'd doe eat His flesh,
And drinck his blood, their soules for to refresh,
Euen His very flesh, and His very blood,
May well be sayde, if't be well vnderstood.
And sauing fayth, by which we do belieue,
Is that, by which we eat Him, and receiue,
Or say, how this is done, we doe not know :
Yet the faithfull doe it, although no moe.
But, if thou doest not thither come prepared,

Then, though thou tak'st this holy cuppe and
    bread   610
Yet doest thou not the bread of life receiue :
But doest in truth thy foolish heart deceiue.
For, who so comm's without due preparation,
He eats and drinks vnto his own damnation ;
It being certeinly no small offence,
To rush on these things without reverence.
And yet too many doe, as may appeare
By their ill liues, after they haue been there;
Following the courses, they ran before,
Whereby they anger God so much the more.   620
Too many also themselues doe occupy
Not in themselues, but in this Mysterie,
Searching and sifting it with carnall wit :
Whereas to trye themselues were farre more fit :
But chiefly now, sith God has drawen His sword,
And does not to us speak alone by word.
The grievous judgments which make many cry,
Should moue us all our selues in time to trie.
But yet more, know that Holy Writ doeth teach,
—That which the holy men of old did preach— 630
That the signes themselues are dignified
With the names of the things signified.
And this is for their honor done, and more,
Euen for to raise our hearts, from things before
Our eyes, vnto the things, that are aboue,

Which here are tendred to us of free loue.
  This is trueth : it is no lie.
  This is true antiquitie,
  The other's new and silly.   639

 Glorie be to God on high, and to men truth,
 And loue, and peace, through Jesus Christ,
  by the mightie working of the
   Holie Spirit,
  Amen and Amen
March vij. 1624.   THO. TUKE.

A Postscript to the Reader.

HESE lines subnexed were brought me
by a friend some eighteene months agoe,
from an author vnknowne vnto us both.
Which occasioned me to write these, thou seest.
If I haue vsed, or abused any of them, or all,
I craue pardon of their Author, and giue him free
leaue to doe so with mine, if he be *in vivis*, as I
hope and wish, and be so pleased.

Priests make Christ's body and soule, you must
  not doubt.

They eate, they drinke, they box him vp, and
    bear about.
  One is too litle, bread and wine holds him sever-
    all.
  So we dine ; I with my Christ, thou with thine.
Is thy mouth the virgin's womb ? is bread her
    seed ?
Are thy words the Holy Ghost ? is this the Creed ?
    O presumptuous vndertaker,
    Never cake could make a baker,
    Yet the priest can make his Maker.
What's become of all those Christs which priests
    haue made ?
Doe all those hostes of Hoastes abide ? or do they
    fade ?
    One Christ bides, all these flye.
    One Christ lives, all these dye,
    One is true, the rest a lye.

Finis.

MISCELLANIES

OF

𝕿𝖍𝖊 𝕱𝖚𝖑𝖑𝖊𝖗 𝖂𝖔𝖗𝖙𝖍𝖎𝖊𝖘' 𝕷𝖎𝖇𝖗𝖆𝖗𝖞.

———

THE

COUNTESSE OF PEMBROKE'S
EMANUELL

TOGETHER WITH

CERTAINE PSALMES. ·

BY

ABRAHAM FRAUNCE:

(1591)

𝔈𝔡𝔦𝔱𝔢𝔡 𝔴𝔦𝔱𝔥 𝔍𝔫𝔱𝔯𝔬𝔡𝔲𝔠𝔱𝔦𝔬𝔫 𝔞𝔫𝔡 𝔑𝔬𝔱𝔢𝔰.

BY THE

REV. ALEXANDER B. GROSART,

ST. GEORGE'S, BLACKBURN, LANCASHIRE.

PRINTED FOR PRIVATE CIRCULATION.

1871.

Introduction.

LL are agreed that it was of our present Worthy—ABRAHAM FRAUNCE—SPENSER sung in "Colin Clout's Come Home Againe" (1591)

> ———"There is Corydon, though meanly waged,
> Yet HABLEST WIT OF MOST I KNOW THIS DAY."
> (lines 382-3.)

the name 'Corydon' being fetched from his "Lamentations of *Corydon* for the Love of Alexis." (1588). When we remember those who were 'known' by SPENSER at that 'day' and how choice and chary he was in his praise, the couplet becomes very memorable.

Further: the correspondence of SIDNEY and GABRIEL HARVEY, and PEELE's and NASH's books, shew that he was esteemed and loved of "Sir Philip" and admitted into the 'innermost circle' of the foremost men of that foremost age intellectually. One marvels that next to nothing has

B 47

come down to us concerning him notwithstanding.
Surely the light will come some day from presently-
sealed MSS.   One beshrews your compiling-
Historians of Shropshire knowing (or culpably
nknowing) Abraham Fraunce to have been a
Salopian, and yet putting forth no effort to get at
his life-story. As so often, we have in superfluity,
information on titled no-bodies (or 'bodies' only :)
but utter lack of pains (in the fine old sense) to
illumine such names as demand illumination.

I have done my best, though fruitlessly, to discover more than is furnished by OLDYS and by
MALONE and the "Athenæ Cantbrigiensis " of the
Messrs. COOPER and the Hunter MSS, after OLDYS
and MALONE and the authorities therein cited.

It is stated in all the notices that I have read, that
he was a' native of Shropshire ' and 'probably educated at Shrewsbury school '. DR. Moss informs me
his name does not appear in the Register of famous
' Shrewsbury.' I wish some son of Salop would
trace out birth-place and birth-date :   probably
the Shrewsbury muniments record both.   He
passed from Shrewsbury (or elsewhere) to the
University of Cambridge, where he matriculated
' as a pensioner of St. John's College, 20th May,
1575.'   He ' proceeded B. A. 1579-80, and took
a part in Dr. LEGGE's *Richardus Tertius*, which

was acted at St. John's College at the bachelor's commencement, in the latter year. He was ' elected a fellow in 1580 and commenced M. A. 1583, about which time he removed to Gray's Inn.' He originally proceeeded to the University—the Tradition so runs according to OLDYS—under the patronage and even at the expense of Sir Philip Sidney. In due course it would appear, he was called to the bar, and ' practised in the Court of Marches in Wales'—the last thing suggesting association with Fulke Greville, afterwards Lord Brooke. In 1590 he was recommended by Henry earl of Pembroke, to Lord Burghley, ' as in every respect qualified for the office of the Queen's solicitor in that Court.' Nothing further of outward-fact beyond his books survives : nor is the date of his death known. His career of authorship was short, extending only from 1582 to 1592. A MS. of his, without date, was sold among the BRIGHT MSS. (1844). It was entitled "Yeeld, Yeeld, O Yeeld : Omnia vincit amor. Venus dignissima pomo " (4to) and was addressed to Sir Philip Sidney. *En passant* it must be noted that certain Sonnets or lyrics by Fraunce appeared in ' Astrophel and Stella '—an honour beyond compare. In the Hunter MSS. British Museum, there is recorded a MS., "Epithalamium presented to

Sir Gervase Culler of Stainborough in Yorkshire
on his marriage with Lady Magdalene Egerton,
daughter of John, earl of Winchester, President
of the Marches of Wales in 1633." In an Epistle
to Sir Gervase the Author tells him that he had
paid the same compliment to all the Earl's daughters on their marriage. He calls the earl his
'lord' ; whence it is surmised that he obtained
some office from him in Wales. The Epithalamium thus links him with "Comus". He must
have been an old man in 1633.

Fraunce's books are somewhat numerous. The
Reader will find a pretty full record in the biblio-
graphical authorities, from RITSON to HAZLITT.
His "Lawiers Logike, exemplifying the Precepts
of Logike by the Practice of Common Lawe"
(1588) is notable in many ways. Its 'examples' like those in his 'Arcadian Rhetoricke
or the Precepts of Rhetoricke made plaine
by examples, Greeke, Latin, English, Italian,
French, Spanish........ (1588) are of rare
interest — the 'Rhetorike' quoting from the
unpublished MSS. of SPENSER's "Fairy Queene".
It appears from a MS. of the 'Lawier's Logike' extant, that the Author originally intended to ded-
icate it to SIR EDWARD DYER, the Poet, under the
title of "THE SHEPHEARDES LOGIKE" (*Brit. Bibl.*

ii. 276). The '*Arcadian* Rhetorike' goes out of the way to pay reverence to its patron's '*Arcadia*' in its title-page.

I do not here enter on the central matter of FRAUNCE's literary life—his cultivation of what he and HARVEY called 'English Hexameters.' Touching as the endeavour and controversy did upon SPENSER and SIDNEY and other great contemporaries, surely too little attention has been given to them. I have selected one of the most favourable specimens of our Worthy's achievement in his self-imposed art and task. I have endeavoured to reproduce the original with literal accuracy, even to the many capitals and somewhat arbitrary punctuation. The student of English Poetry must be glad of an opportunity to study these Hexameters. As a memorial of an epoch-marking experiment in English Verse, which might have robbed all Literature of the "Fairy Queen"— for Spenser was 'taken' captive a-while by the Hexameter—and as containing some gleams of noble thought and feeling nobly and gravely uttered, I have pleasure in giving "Emmanuel" and related Psalms, a place in the Fuller Worthies Miscellanies.

ALEXANDER B. GROSART.

⁎ A few Notes are added at close.

Note.

The following is the original title-page of Fraunce's "Emanuel":

COUNTESSE OF PEMBROKES
EMANUELL.

Conteining the Nativity, Pas
sion, Buriall, and Resurrection
of Christ: togeather with cer
taine Psalmes of Dauid
All in English Hex
ameters.
BY ABRAHAM FRAUNCE.
Imprinted at London, for
William Ponsonby, dwelling in
Paules Churchyard, at the
Signe of the Bishops
head.
1591.   [4to].

The Epistle-dedicatory is very brief: and is here given:

To the right excellent and most honorable Lady, the Lady Mary, Countesse of Pembroke.[1]

Mary the best Mother sends her best Babe to a Mary:
Lord to a Ladies sight, and Christe to a Christian hearing.
Your Honour's most
affectionate.
ABRAHAM FRAUNCE.

---

[1] The ' fair ladye' to whom this poem is addressed, was

53

Mary, daughter of Sir Henry Sidney, K. G.   She became
third wife to Henry, second Earl of Pembroke.   It was to
her Sir Philip Sidney dedicated the Arcadia.   She survived
her husband, and died in an advanced age, 25th September, 1621, at her house in Aldersgate Street, London, and
was buried near her husband in Salisbury Cathedral.
For a full Memoir see Ballard's British Ladies.   G.

The Countesse of Pembrokes's Emanuell.

THE NATIUITY OF CHRIST, IN RYMING HEXAMETERS.

CHRISTE euer-lyuing, once dying, only triumpher,
 Ouer' death by death; Christe Jesus mighty redeemer
Of forelorne mankȳnde, which led captyuyty captiue,
And made thraldome thrall; whose grace and mercy defensive
Mercyles and graceles men sau'd; Christe liuely reuiuer
Of sowles oppressed with sin; Christe louely reporter
Of good-spell Gospell, Mayds son, celestial ofspring,
Emanuel, Man-god, Messyas, euer abounding
With pity perpetuall, with pure love, charity liuely,
This Christe shalbe my song, and my meditation only,

O euerlasting, æternall, euer-abyding,
Euer-lyuing Lord : O life, and stil-pity-taking,
Stil-quicknyng Spyrite, which causedst God to be
 manly,
That true-God true-man might soe cause man to
 be godly;
Graunt mee a sounding voyce to recount these
 funeral horrors,
Which made vs t'enioy those sweete celestial
 harbors.
And thou Babe stil-borne, borne always from the
 begynning,
Whose sweete byrth in skyes causd angels for to
 be singing;
Looke, sweete Babe, from aboue, lend gracius eares
 to my prayers,
Soe shall these my lipps, this mouth, this tong, be
 thy praysers.
 When noe Sunne gaue light, noe Moone dis-
 tinctly apeared,
And noe twinckling starrs this lightsom Olympus
 adorned,
When noe world was made; then that most mighty
 Jehoua
That king omnipotent, that Lord and only
 Monarcha
Himself did meditate, enioyd his glorious essence,

Glorius, æternall, vnspeakable, infynit essence :
Liu'd and Lou'd himself, himself, felicity matchles,
All through all, chief good, chief blisse, perfection
    endles.
But this most good God, this simple Trinity blessed,
This most louing Lord, this three-fould Vnity
    sacred,
Would haue this goodnes manifest, this bounty
    declared,
This loue expressed, this wondrous mercy reuealed.
  In tyme conuenient therefore, this world he
    created,
And it, a large Theater to behould his glory,
    apoynted.
Which when he had with store of treasures richly
    replenisht,
And with abundant grace causd euery part to be
    furnisht ;
Man was made at length ; Adam was lastly created
Last woork, not least woork ; Adam was dayntily
    framed,
Most perfect creature, and like to the mighty
    Creator,
Good, wise, immortall, of mankynde onely beginner.
  But prowd ambition, but Serpent craftily cloak-
    ing

With curst bitter-sweete his cankred poyson
    abounding,
Adam dispossest of pleasant beautiful harbors,
Adams hart possest with most vnspeakable hor-
    rors:
Man was mard at length, Adam was fowly defaced.
Last woork, and lost woork, Adam was filthily
    fowled,
Most cursed creature, vnlyke to the mighty
    creator,
Bad, foolish, mortall, of mankinde only the
    murdrer.
  Yet that greatest God, pitying this fall of a
    sinner,
His manyfold mercies did againe most freely
    remember:
Gaue new grace to the world, and caused his only
    begotten,
Only beloued son to be sent vs downe fro the
    heauen:
Here to receaue our flesh, and here with thorns to
    be crowned,
Here to be mockt, to be whipt, and here at last to
    be murdred:
Murdred for mankynde, t'appease Gods infinit
    anger,

Guyltles for guylefull, man synles, for man a
    synner.
  And now that good tyme, that ioy full day was
    approaching,
Which by the liuing Lord was apoynted from
    the begynning :
  There was a man which came from Dauyds pro-
    geny noble,
Called iust Ioseph, but dwelt in a place very simple,
Nazzareth it was nam'de : himself had lately be-
    troathed
That most spotles spowse, that Mayden Mary
    renowmed : (sic)
Whoe to be Christs mother was a chosen vessel
    apoynted,
And by an Angels voyce from God thus friendly
    saluted ;
  Hayle, ô sacred Nymph, of woemens company
    greatest,
Blest with abundant grace, to the blessed Trynity
    dearest.
At these wondrous woords this mayde was some-
    what abashed,
And did meruayle much, by an Angel strangely
    saluted.
Which when Gabriel once perceaued, he myldly
    replyed,

Feare not blessed Mary, beleeue, and stand not
    amased :

Blessed Mary, beleeue, thou shalt be a mayd, be
    a mother,

Jesus thy son shall be a King, be a Lord, be a
    ruler :

Ruler, Lord, and King, almighty, without any
    ending,

His faythfull subiects with grace and mercy pro-
    tecting.

    Mary began thus againe : Good God, this seem-
        eth a woonder,

How can a mayd conceave ? can a mayd vntutcht
    be a mother ?

Gabryel added againe, this thy conception holy

Is not a woork of man, but Gods operation only,

Gods dyuine power shall woork this woonder upon
    thee,

And therefore this chylde soe borne is son to the
    mighty,

Mighty triumphant Lord : this Lords dyuynyty
    dreadfull

Thy cosyn Elizabeth made alsoe for to be fruytfull,

Which was barren afore : therefore geue eare to
    the Lords heast,

For there is noething impossible vnto the highest.

Mary resolu'd in mynde this message firmely
  beleeued,
And submytts herself, by the Angells woords to
  be guyded.
Then soone after that, to the hylls of Jury shee
  hastned,
And there, Elizabeth greate with Chylde, sweetly
  saluted.
At which chearefull woords from blessed Mary
  proceeding
Elizabeths yong babe this sound very strangely
  receauing,
Sprang in wombe for ioy, causd Maryes voyce to
  be sounding,
Elizabeth for to reioyce, dumbe Zachary for to be
  speaking.
Mary, with her kinsfolk, three moonths in Jury
  remayned
And then blessed Nymph to her husband home
  shee returned,
Husband iust Joseph, good-man, whoe thought
  it a wonder,
That new wife, vnknown, vntucht, should now be
  a mother.
Vnwilling therefore in publyke place to reproue her,
Good-natur'd Joseph meant pryuyly for to renounce
  her.

This man thus meanyng, in sleepe Gods Angel
    apeared,
And with chearefull woords this message fryendly
    delyured.
Feare not, iust Joseph, thy wife is a mayde, is a
    mother,
Pure, chaste, vnspotted, feare not therefore to re-
    ceave her,
This babe is Gods Chylde, this son cælestial of-spring,
Lambe of God, Gods heyre ordeyned from the be-
    gynning
For to redeeme lost Sheepe, to be mankynds sole
    mediator,
For to releeue poore sowles, to be mankynds
    mighty protector.
Joseph awak's from sleepe, Gods angel he gladly
    obeyeth,
And his matchles mate, mayd, mother, Mary, re-
    ceaueth,
    In those dayse, all warrs, and vproares fully re-
    pressed,
Augustus Cæsar caus'd man to be taxed,
Taxed in each mans towne : then Joseph quyckly
    remoued
Vnto the blest Beathleme, and brought home Mary
    beloued ;

62

Mary beloued he brought; whoe there, when tyme
    was apoynted,
Was mayd, was Mother, was most dyuynely de-
    lyured,
Bare her first borne Chylde, and layd him downe
    in a manger,
Wrapt in swadling cloaths, poore bed, for want of
    a better.
  Seelly Shepheards by the night theyr flocks
    were waryly watching,
And fro the skyes they sawe strange brightnes
    myghtily shynyng :
Downe to the ground they fall : but an Angel
    cheareful apeared,
And with ioyfull news theyr trembling harts he
    reuyued.
Feare not fryendly shepheards, for I bring good
    news from Olympus,
This day borne is a babe, his name is called Jesus,
Only Reconcyler, Mediator, mighty Redeemer,
Only the salue to the sick, and pardon free to
    the synner.
And take this for a signe : this babe is a sleepe in
    a manger,
Wrapt in swadlyng cloaths, sweete sowle, and
    cast in a corner.

Eu'n as he spake these woords, many thousands
    sweetly resounding

Immortall spyrites, cælestiall harmony making,

Sang and praysed God, lyfting theyr voyce to the
    heauen,

For this ioyfull birth, this blessed babe of a mayden,

Glory to God most high, good will to man and to
    his of-spring,

Peace to the earth itselfe, and all that on earth
    is abyding

  Seelly Shepherds ran downe to behould theyr
    only redeemer,

And found all to be true, and sawe Christe layd
    in a manger.

Then they praysed God, most chereful company
    keeping,

And gaue lawd to the Lord, that gracius harmony
    making,

Glory to God most high, good will to man and
    to his of-spring,

Peace to the earth itself, and all that on earth is
    abyding,

Soe that on euery side, this glorius eccho resounded,

Glory to God most high, which man-kynde freely
    redeemed,

Freely redeem'd man-kynde, yet man-kynde dear-
    ely redeemed,

In that his owne deare sonne for man was freely
    delyu'red.
  O blessed byrth day, ô starrs most luckyly
    shynyng,
O first day of ioy, and last of anoy to the of-spring,
Of sinfull man-kynde, ô great compassion endles,
O loue still fayntles, pyty peareless, Charyty
    matchles.
God that ruleth aboue in royall throane of Olympus,
Sent his blessed Babe, and only begotten among vs
And fro the bowre of blisse did abase him downe
    to the manger,
For to reconcile vs lost sheepe, that wandred in
    error.
Noe mans tong can tell, nor noe mans hairt can
    imagin,
That th' æternall God, should thus take flesh of a
    Virgin.
  Christe that in heauen sate with God most
    mighty coæquall,
From the beginning crownd with grace and glory
    supernall,
This God's made to be man, this King is come for
    the scepter,
This Christe is swadled, this Lord is laid in a
    manger :

Christe whoe fils each place, (ô Christe how are
    wee beholding ?)

Christe whome noe-place holds, in soe small place
    is abiding;

Christe noe-way-conteind, Christ first, last, Christ
    the Creator,

Infinit euery way, is now conteynd of a creture;

Christe noe-where-enclosd, Christe ender, Christe
    the beginner,

Euery-where, noe-where, is now enclosd in a corner,

And all this for man : soe that, where sin was
    abounding,

Grace did abound much more ; as man was cause
    for a falling

Man was a raiser againe ; as man made deadly be-
    ginning,

Soe true God, true man did make most gracius
    ending.

    Adam sinned first, and brought in death to
      reward it :

Christe by death kild death, and gaue his life to
    remoue it.

Adam lost Paradise, where pleasures earthly abyded;

Christe purchast heauen, where treasures greater
    abounded.

Serpent wyly beguyld Adam, by the meanes of a
    woeman.

Aspyring Adam was quite cast downe to the
    darcknes,
Humble-minded Christe hath lifted vs vp to the
    brightnes
Of stil lasting light, to the ioyful face, to the pre-
    sence,
Of God, there to behold his sacred ineffable essence.
  Sing then, friendly Shepherds, and lift your
    voyce to the heauen,
Glory to God most high, for blessed Babe of a
    Mayden,
Whom neither Sathan could daunt, nor company
    hellish,
Nor raging Pharisees, nor deaths vnspeakable an-
    guish :
Who by the crosse, by the nayles, by the spear,
    by the thorns, by the whipping,
Passed aloft to the skies, and there in ioy is abyding :
Whoe by the whipps, by the thorns, by the speare
    by the nayles, by the crossing;
Lifted vs vp to the skies, with his Angels stil to
    be dwelling.
Whoe to be blest, was curst ; whoe gaue himself
    for a ransome,
Whoe by the Crosse crost death, by death obteyned
    vs a kingdome,

67

Whose incessant pangs, whose grief and agony
  restles,
Whose bloody sweate did cause our sinfull soules
  to be spotles.
  Sing then, friendly Shepherds, and Angels all
  be a singing :
Come fro the East, you Kings, and make acceptable
  offring :
Come fro the East by the light of a blessed starre
  that apeareth,
And to the King of Jews your footsteps rightly
  directeth.
Loe, here lyes your Lord, bow downe, make
  peaceable offring,
Gold to the golden Babe, of golden time the beginning ;
Frankencense and Myrrhe, to be sweete perfumes
  to the sweetest
Chylde, that sweete sacrifice, acceptable vnto the
  highest,
Sweet-smelling sacrifice, once offered only for euer
For t'appease Gods wrath and his most infynit
  anger.
  Home to the East, you Kings, and bring this
  news to the godly,
God suffieth for man, guyltles condemnd for a
  guylty :

Home to the East, you Kings, and tell this
    abroade for a wonder,
Wee haue seene that Babe of a Virgin, layd in
    a manger.
Home to the East, you Kings, and shew that
    mighty resounding
Of those sweete angels cælestial harmony making :
Tell this abroade for a truth, and think, that from
    the beginning,
Noe such sight to an eye, noe such sound to a
    hearing.
Backe to the East, you Kings, but back by a con-
    trary passage,
Least ye be partakers of a most vnmercifull outrage.
  And get away Joseph, get away, and haste thee
    to Ægypt,
Herode seekes thy sonne to be murdred, not to be
    worshipt :
Merciles Herodes to be sole and only triumphant,
Seeking one infant, wil murder a number of infants.
Beathlem's red with blood, sweete sucklings blood
    that abounded
Beathlem's white with bones, babes bones all
    woefully scattred.
Childles mothers mourne, and howle with watry
    countnance,

All crye out for grief, and all crye out for a
    vengeance :
Vengeance light on a woolf, vengeance and plagues
    on a tyger,
Vengeance on this beast, vengeance on this bloody
    butcher.
  And when he thought his throane with firme
    fælicity grounded,
And his senseles soule with most security flattred,
Vengeance lights on a woolf, vengeance and
    plagues on a tyger,
Vengeance on that beast, vengeance on that bloody
    butcher.
Lyce did suck his blood, which first was cause of
    a bloodshed,
Vermyne tore his flesh, which babes flesh made to
    be mangled.
Soe let such men fare, that take a delight to be
    murdring,
Christs curse light on his head, that Christs flock
    loues to be spoyling.
  Now come back Joseph ; but come not nere
    bloody Jury,
Fly fro the butchers broode, let Nazzareth only
    receaue thee,
There shall thy deare Chylde in yeares and wit be
    a growing,

And with guifts of grace, with supream glory
    abounding.
Thence shall thy deare Chylde to the Church of
    God be repairing,
And doating Doctors and Priests diuinely reprouing:
Thincke not much therefore, if three dayes there
    hee abyded,
Father on Earth must yeelde, whylst Father in
    heu'n is obeyed.
  And now John that sprang in mothers wombe,
    was a preaching,
Teaching, baptizing, and Christs wayes duely
    preparing.
  When this John Christs head with water duly
    besprinckled,
And Christe from Jordan was now but newly
    remoued,
Sacred Ghost fro the skies flew downe all louely
    to Christes head,
And in forme of a Doue itself there sweetly reposed :
Then fro the heu'ns these woords with chereful
    glory resounded,
Thou art my deare chylde, in whome I doe meane
    to be pleased.
And forerunning John, John Baptist dayly reporteth,
Christe to be Lamb of God, that sins with mercy
    remoueth.

71

At these wondrous newes th'old Serpent deadly
    repyned,
And the renowned fame of Christe extreamely
    maligned,
Fearing this to be that great sou'raigne lordly
    Monarcha,
Sin-pard'ning Jesus, foretold long since by Sybilla :
And he remembred well, what plagues were duly
    denounced,
When greate grand-dame Eue with a bitter sweete
    he beguyled.
Therefore he now begins and takes occasion offred,
When fouretimes ten dayes from meate and drinck
    he refrained,
And in desert kept : he begins him thus to be
    tempting,
With colored friendship concealed treachery cloaking.
    Shall the coæternall and consubstantial offspring
Of God, soe many dayes, and soe many nights be a
    fasting ?
Shall those purpled cheekes, which earst so cheare-
    ful apeared,
Looke thus pale and wan, with too much penury
    pinched ?
Make these stones to be bread, for I know, if Sonne
    to the Thundrer

Speake but a woord, its doone : let cretures serue
     the Creator.

  But when he heard of Christe, that grace from
     mighty Iehoua

Strengthned more than bread, and fed man more
     than a Manna,

Then with a new stratageme to the Templs towre
     he repayred,

And Christe (soe Christe would) on a pynacle high
     he reposed,

Saying ; Leape to the ground, if thou be the Sonne
     of the Mighty,

Thy Fathers Angels are prest at an inch to receaue
     thee.

Yet when he heard Christe say, that God was not
     to be tempted,

And that hee alwayes had foolehardy presumption
     hated,

Sith both these proou'd naught, last cast hee
     began to be prouing,

And with spitefull rage, his latest part to be playing:

For when hee had brought Christe, by Christe's
     permission only,

Vnto a huge mountaine, which gaue full view to
     the glory

Of world and worlds wealth : World and worlds
     wealth wil I giue thee,

Sayd this damned fiend, if thou wilt learne to
  obey mee.
  Here Christe with iust zeale and indignation
    vrged,
That malapert rashnes with these woords boldly
  rebuked ;
Get thee away Sathan to the burning lake of
  Auernus,
Woorship alone is due to the sou'raigne Lord of
  Olympus.
  Then with dead despaire Christe too well
    knowne hee relinquisht,
Sith that hee saw himself and all his villany van-
  quisht.
  Lying Serpent thus confounded ; an Angel
    apeared,
And long-fasting Christe with chearefull foode he
  refreshed.
  Thenceforth Christe his life was nothing els
    but a teaching,
Preaching, and woorking of woonders woorthy the
  woondring.
Sicke are whole, lame goe, dumbe speake, blynde
  see the Redeemer,
Hearing's giu'n to the deafe, and clensed skynne
  to the leaper.

Netts eu'n burst with fish, and full boates gin to
    be sincking,
Water made to be wyne makes brydegroome
    greatly reioycing,
Wyndes are whist with a woord, and blustring
    storms be repressed,
And foaming seaes to a firme walk mightily changed.
Diu'ls roare out for feare, and haste their heauy
    departure,
Which tormented men with too too woeful a torture.
Fiue loaues, twooe fishes, fiue thousand fully re-
    freshed,
Yet twelue baskets full with broaken meate be
    reserued,
Seu'n loaues, feaw fishes, foure thousand fully
    refreshed,
Yet seu'n baskets fyld with broaken meate be
    reserued.
Elias came downe to behold life-giuer Jesus,
And Moses rose vp, to behold soule-sauer Jesus,
His face shyn de as sunne : himself transform'd
    in a moment,
Surpassing brightnes did stand in steede of a
    garment,
Mount Tabor glistred : sweete voyce came downe
    from Olympus,
Heare my beloued sonne, my dearely beloued Jesus.

Yea, dead men lyued: yet Jewes causd him to be
    dying,
Whoe raisd Lazarus vp, who dead Gyrle made to
    be lyuing.

THE PASSION, BURYALL, AND RESUR-
RECTION OF CHRISTE.

CHRISTE, whose blessed byrth causd
    Angells for to be singing :
    Christe, whose louing life forst diu'ls
themselues to be wondryng,
Christe, whose bitter death made templs vayle to
    be rentyng,
Grau's to be op'nyng, earth to be quaking, heu'ns
    to be lowring,
Geue mee the grace, sweete Christe, since euery
    thing is a mournyng,
For to recount these pangs, this crosse, this death
    by my mournyng.
    When that apoynted fight, that feareful combat
    aproached,
Fight with pangs of death, and hells vnsuffrable
    horrors,
Combat with mans syns, and Gods vnspeakable
    anger,

Then cursed capten Caiphas with his hellish ad-
    hærents
Contryued platforms, conspyred ioyntly togeather
For to betray that man which was mans only re-
    deemer.
    Yf that he hould on thus such wonders stil
      to be working,
Then farewell Pharisees, with Scribes, and onely
    renowmed
High Priests; and therefore its more than tyme to
    preuent hym.
Yet forbeare for a while, till solempne feasts be
    determyned,
Least this strange murder may chaunce to be
    cause of an vproare.
O dyuine doctors, devout Priests, woorthy protectors
Of Salomons temple, good graybeards; that for a
    feast day
Can vouchsaufe to delay this murder, this bloody
    outrage,
Not for loue of God, but for this feare of an vproare.
    But Christe foreknowing theyr treachery, came
      to the leper
Leper Symons house in Bethany: where when he
    supped,
Mary, (remembring how herself was lately released

77

From seu'n tormenters) kneeld downe to her only
    redeemer,
Washte his blessed feete with trickling teares that
    abounded,
Wypte hys blessed feete ; with her hayre that
    sweetly beseemed,
Kyst his blessed feete ; and heade, and feete then
    anoynted,
With precious sweete balme, with most odorifer-
    ous oyntment.
   But that most cursed captiue, that greedy
    deuouring
Murdrer, cut throate, thiefe, with his hellish
    treason abounding
Judas Iscariot, stil bent to the bag, to the budgett,
Gan to repyne and grudge, that this soe costly an
    oyntment
Was thus wasted away, which might haue beene
    by the purser,
Sould and geu'n to the poore : but alas this
    traiterus abiect
Meant t'enrich hymself, and not to be good to the
    needy,
As by his accursed stratagems it playnly apeared.
   For, when he lost this pray, his master he
    deadly maligned,

And balme box broaken brake Judas hart ful of
     enuy,
Damnable, infernall, outragius horrible enuy,
Soe that noe myschief, nor part of a thiefe, or a
     murdrer
Was by the vile reprobate, by the damned villen
     omytted,
Vntil hee had this losse, as hee tooke it, fully
     recou'red,
Vntil he had for gaine his master falsly betrayed.
  Christe fro the mount Olyuet with an asse coms
     seellyly ryding,
Poorely, without any pompe, to the pompous
     cytty repayring,
Some with flowring bowes his wayes had freshly
     adorned,
Some with fragrant flowers his passage sweetly
     prepared,
Some causd theyr garments by the highe way side
     to be scattred,
Euery man cry'de out with chearefull voyce to
     the heauens,
Hosanna sweete ympe of Dauid's gracius of-spring,
Hosanna to the King almighty of Israel holy,
Hosanna to the Lord of Lords, to the prince of
     Olympus,
Soe that on euery syde Hosanna sweetly resounded,

And sweete Hosanna from rocks with an eccho
    rebounded.

Yt was a plague to the Priests, to the fatbely
    Priests, to behould this,

Yt was a death to the Scribes, to the scraping
    Scribes to abyde this,

Yt was a hell to the prowd Pharisees for a truth
    to beleeue this ;

Yet, t'was a ioy to the yong and ould, for a truth
    to report this.

And for a truth, both yong and ould, went
    straight to the temple,

Straight to the temple went with Jesus seellyly
    ryding,

And yet on his poore asse with a princelyke glory
    triumphing.

Into the Church when hee came more lyke to a
    fayre or a market,

Then Salomons temple such chapmen hee quyckly
    remoued,

Ouerturned theyr seates, and tables iustly defaced,

His fathers orders, and seruice rightly reuyued :

But to the prowd Pharisees, to the Scribes, to the
    fatt Priests

It was more then a plague, then a death, then a
    hell to behould this,

Therefore once yet againe themselus they gyn
    to be styrring,
For t'entrappe Jesus : but loe, while this was a
    woorking,
In comes that cutthroate, that thiefe, yet freshly
    remembring,
How th'Alablaster box of balme his greedy deuowring
Clawes escaped afore : and then to the company
    hellish,
And Sathans synagogue, his murdring mynde he
    reuealed.
  Hayle sacred Cayphas, chiefe Priest, and mighty
    Protector
Of Jewish customes, and Hebriews laudable orders :
Hayle Scribes and Pharisees that teach and preach
    the renowmed
Doctrine of Moses : geue eare and mark what I
    tell you.
  This wandryng vpstart yprocrite, this Christus,
    Jesus,
Man, God, I know not what, doth abuse and dayly
    deceaue vs,
Vs fooles his folowers ; and mee vnworthyly hating,
Chiefly of all others with slaundrous taunts he
    reuyleth.
And yet I could forget this abuse and iniury
    priuate,

But that by these meanes he begins t'aspyre to the
    scepter,
For, what a sedition, what a styrr doth hee make,
    what an vproare ?
And what a sort be before, what a trayne comes
    dayly behynde him ?
His woonders woondring, his doctrine vaynely
    beleeuing,
His wayes with freshe flowres and branches
    dayntyly dressing,
His delicate fine feete with balmes most costly
    anoynting,
His royall person with tytles princely saluting,
His foaming palfray with rich roabes gayly
    bedecking,
Hosanna singing, and each where freely triumphing?
Yf that I bring hym bound, and soe cause all to
    be ended,
And people quyeted, say on, what shalbe my
    guerdon ?
What shall I haue, for I serue but a snudg, and
    am but a begger,
  Hereat Caiphas smylde, and Iewes all greatly
    reioyced;
And of theyr syluer, they peeces thyrty apoynted,
For this vile butcher, which causd this Lambe to
    slaughtred.

These things dispatched, those fathers ghostly
  departed,
Counsell's dissolued: Judas backe slyly returned.
  Christe with a curse by the way (most feareful
  syne to the faythles)
That fruyteles figgtree causd euermore to be
  fruytles.
  Christe rose from table (most perfect signe of a
  meeke hart)
And washt his fryends feete, teaching them for to
  be lowely.
  Christe foretould his death (most doubtles signe
  of a true God)
And did note to the rest, that shameles desperat
  outcast.
But woe woe to the wretch, but alas woe woe to
  the traytor,
Better he were not borne, then borne to a damnable
  horror.
  Christe tooke bread and wyne (most sacred
  signes to the faythful)
And gaue thancks to the Lord, and brake and gaue
  it among them,
Most cherefull sacrament, most loul' and lyuly
  remembrance
Of Christe his body crost, and blood shed freely
  for all men.

83

And now that Renegate that damned Apostata
    Judas

Coms to the Priest Caiphas, and there his brybe
    he receaueth,

Brybe for blood, Lambs blood, Gods Lambe : and
    bringeth a great rowte,

Of swearing cutters and souldiers duely prepared,

With lynckes and lanterns, with swerds and staues
    for an onsett,

Marching all in aray in due and martial order,

As though some fyeld were to be fought, or king
    to be conquer'd :

Whereas alas noeman was there with force to re-
    sist them,

But some feawe fishers, and theyr poore master
    Jesus.

  O valyant Judas, of a warlike company capten :

These be the synners plagues, these these be
    rewards to the wicked,

That not a mouse can creepe, not a leafe can
    shake, not a wynde blowe,

But theyr sowls with syn, theyr mynds with
    murder aboundyng,

Stil be a trembling, stil be a quiu'ring, stil be a
    quaking,

Quaking stil for dreede and feare of an hasty
    reuenging,

Afterclapp to be giu'n by the thundring Prince of
    Olympus.

  Christe after supper, gaue thancks, rose vp fro
    the table,

Came to the mount Olyuette ; then these woords
    gracius vttred ;

My faythfull folowers and fryends, my dearely
    beloued

And best companyons ; this night you shal be
    molested,

And sore offended, to behould some villanies offred :

For soe t'was written long since, and truely
    reuealed,

That your fryendly shepherd must needs at last be
    remoued,

And his sheepe scattred, wandring for want of a
    sheepsman.

But faythfull folowers and fryends, but dearly
    beloued

And best companyons, your mayster shall be
    reuyued,

And by death kill death, and ouer death be tri-
    umphing,

His faythful folowers visyting, he dearely beloued

And best companyons and fryends in Galyly seeing.

  Scarce had he sayd thus much : but Peeter
    stowtly repleyed ;

Not soe, sweete Master, though euery man be
    amased,
Euery man fly back, yet Peeter's fully resolued.
For noe loue of life, noe feare of death to be startyng :
Great woords, small woonders : But Jesus gaue
    hym a watch-woord,
His weaknes knowing, his rashnes meekly rebuking,
And sayd : Poore Peeter, pray, and leaue off thy
    protesting,
This night quickly, for all thy stowt and manly
    presuming,
Ere that a Cock crow twise, thou shalt thrice
    flatly deny mee.
  And now when that night, that dreadfull night
    was aproaching,
Christe did watch hymselfe, and wyld his friends
    to be watching,
Christe prayd thrice himselfe, and wyld his friends
    to be praying,
Christe with fearefull pangs, and dropps of blood
    was abounding,
Christe fell flat to the ground, and wisht that cup
    to be passing,
(Yet not his owne conceipt, but Fathers will stil
    obeying)
Christe at length came back, and found his friends
    to be sleeping,

Come, let's goe (quoth hee) now, its more than
    tyme to be styrring,
Loe here com's Judas, with a cursed kiss to betray
    mee.
  Eu'n as hee spake these woords, that martial
    army apeared,
Lynkes gaue light to the night, and causd their
    swoords to be glistring,
And fore-man Judas for a guyde went iollyly
    marching,
That vile vipers kisse, for a signe and token
    apoynting,
Then with a brazen face, past grace, Christe Jesus
    he kissed,
And sayd Hayle Mayster; to the which Christe
    mildly replyed,
Friend, Wherefore comst thou ? But Peeter rashly
    reuenging,
Christs disgrace, as he thought, who first came,
    first he requited,
And Malchus right eare from his head with a
    swoord was diuided.
  Whoso strikes with a swoord, with a swoord
    must looke to be stricken,
And blood seekes for blood: Stay Peeter, and
    learne to be lowly,

If that I meant to reuenge, sayd Christe, and
make a resistance,

Could not I ten thousand Angells haue quickly
procured,

Whose strength these forces might haue most
easily daunted ?

But then my Fathers edict should not be obeyed,

And scriptures verifyde : this spoken, he strangely
refixed

Malchus his eare to his head : O meeknes, charity,
mildnes,

Of true God, true man, longsuffring, infinit, endles :

This was enough t'haue caus1 brute beasts
themselues to be tamed,

Ragged rocks to relent, and harts of flynt to be
yeelding.

This done : Whom doe yee seeke, quoth Christe ?
To the which the renowmed

Craking swashbuklers, like meeke and humble
obeyssants,

Their mouth's scarce op'ning, sayd thus : Wee
seeke for Jesus.

Then, quoth Christe, He is heere : which words
diuinely proceeding,

From that sacred mouth, causd Judas sowle to be
trembling,

Theyr captens quaking, and euery man to be reeling,

And falling backward to the grownd, extreamely
    amased,
Like to a towre throwne downe by the roaring
    crash of a thunder,
Or to a man that's scorcht by the fearefull flash
    of a lightnyng.
  Christ for a while conceales that greate dyuynity
    dreadful,
Stayes that breath which makes heau'n, earth, and
    hell to be quaking,
Geu's them leaue to arise, and then more myldly
    demandeth,
Whom doe yee seeke ? Jesus, say they, of Nazareth
    only.
Haue not I sayd, he was here, quoth Christ ?
    What needs any further
Search ? What neede yee to bring swerds, staues,
    and armor abowt you ?
As though some famous thiefe, or notorius outlaw
Were to be suppressed ? did I not walk dayly
    among you ?
Did I not day by day teach, preach, and woork
    many woonders ?
Then might your Ealders and Scribes haue sought
    to represse mee.
But the prefixed tyme, the predestinat howre was
    apoynted,

And this is it : Therefore my Fathers Will be
    obeyed,
Noeman shall make any stand, noeman shall make
    any stryuing :
Loe here take Jesus : But these must not be
    arested,
Let them alone for a while, till greater things be
    reuealed.
  Christ then caught and bound ; his fryends with
    terror amased,
Euery man fled back, as Sheepe that wanted a
    sheepesman,
Or vanquisht souldyers disperst for want of a
    Capten,
  Whoe can alas that night, that cursedst night
    of a thowsand,
Those woorks of darcknes, that mockery, villany,
    treason,
Those byndings, beatings, spyttings, and fylthy
    reuylings
Counteruayle with woords, or thoughts, or streames
    of abounding
And still trickling teares? They brought hym
    bound to the high Priest,
Late high Priest Annas, sage Father, whoe for a
    pastyme,
Disdainefull pastime, not for deuotion, asked

Christ many ydle toyes and fond, not worthy the
   hearing,
Of fishmen folowers, and poore contemptible
   abiects,
Of new found doctrine on braine sick fantasy
   grownded.
   All that I spake, sayd Christe, was spoken
      abroade to the whole world,
All that I taught was taught in temple, among
   many thowsands,
In corners not a woord, in secreat place not a
   woonder,
They can tell what I taught, what I wrought, let
   them be reporters
Ask them. What Jack sawce, quoth a blewcoate
   knaue, be yee thus taught
With noe more reuerence and humble duty to
   awnswere
This reuerend Father? learne, and take this for a
   lesson :
Soe from a woord to a blow, with a sinfull fyste
   hee defyled
That synles sweete mouth, which these woords
   peaceably vttred;
Fryend, if I haue sayd yll, beare witnes, let mee
   be punisht,

91

Yff but well, why then doest thou vnworthyly
    stryke mee?

  Here any man might thinck, that Christ thus
    fowly abused,

Should haue beene pytyed, should haue bene
    fryendly releeued,

Of this sage Father : but alas, tis an Asse, not an
    Annas,

And sends Christ to the chiefe of theyr good com-
    pany Caiphas.

  Scarce was hee come to the howse, but anone
    they fall to reuyling,

Here's that princely Prophete, that towld vs soe
    many tydings

Here is Gods owne Sonne, that wrought us soe
    many wonders,

Famous carpet knight, and pardoner only renowmed,

Sorcerer, inchaunter, taleteller, noble abuser

Of fooles and matrones, that casts out diu'ls by the
    diu'ls help,

Plucks downe Gods temple with a trice, and buyld-
    eth a better

Only within three dayes : as twooe rogues falsly
    suborned,

Hyr'de by the owld hyrelings, had most vntruely
    deposed.

Then good Syr Caiphas, with great integryty
    asked,
What sayst thou feallow, to the crymes obiected
    against thee ?
Christ sayd iust noething, his damned iniquyty
    loathing,
    Caiaphas gan to be hoate, and tooke on lyke to
    a Prellate,
And coniuring Christe, charg'd hym by the mys-
    tery sacred
Of Gods dreedfull name, to declare it playnly
    among them,
Wheather he were that Christe, Gods Sonne, borne
    from the begynnyng ;
    Thou has sayd, quoth Christe, yet marck what
    further I tell you :
You shall see this Christ sitting on a mighty
    tribunall,
On God's owne right hand, in clowds with glory
    apearing.
    Then that puft-vp Priest from a bad man, turnd
    to a madman,
Rent his roabes in a rage, and, Blasphemy, blas-
    phemy roared,
What doe wee seeke for proofes hereof, what
    need any wytnes ?

Our selues haue heard all, hymself hath playnly
    reueald all.

What's to be herein doone? or what, doe ye
    thinck he deserueth?

Death, sayd euery man, Death, death with an
    eccho rebounded.

    Then those lewd rakehells with poysned rankor
       abounding,

His sweete face, ô griefe, with spyttle fylthy de-
    fyled,

His bloody cheeks, ô hell, with buffetts all to be
    bruysed,

Some stroake him blindfyeld, and then thus scorne-
    fuly taunted,

Now, good Christe arread, and gesse whoe gaue
    thee the buffet?

    Peeter saw all this, Peeter that manly protester,

Peeter styr'd not a foote; Peeter that mighty
    protector,

Peeter, stowt Peeter, by a gyrle, by a paltery
    damsell

Is dasht, is vanquisht, forsakes his Mayster Iesus,

Thrice forsakes, and twice fore-sweares his Mayster
    Iesus.

    And now Cock gan crow, and giu's him a
       friendly memento,

That mans flesh is frayle, that man's but a smoke,
	vapor,
His pride nought but dust, and all his glory, but
	ashes.
  Peeter in his cursing heard this Cock chearefully
	chaunting,
And saw Christe then a sharp soule-searching
	sight to be turning,
Yet with a louely regard, with a merciful eye to
	be looking.
Euery eye was a bowe, and euery looke was an
	arrow,
Eye and eye-arrow pierst Peeter's hart in a mo-
	ment,
Peeters hart and sowle: and there inflicted a
	deepe wound,
So deepe wound, that it had been no way possibly
	cured,
Were not his owne soules-wound with his owne
	teares all to be washed.
  Now he remembreth alas, his first foole-hardy
	presuming,
Now he detesteth alas, his last vnfriendly reuolt-
	ing :
Now that wan countnance, which feare of death
	had apaled,
All on a fire is set for shame of duty neglected,

Sith that blood, fro the face to the hart which
  lately retyred,
Back fro the hart to the face with speede is freshly
  repayred.
Now his maysters eyes in his eyes are euer apear-
  ing,
And therein doth he seeme his whole offence to be
  reading.
Now Cock crowes in his eares, and calls foorth day
  to be wytnes,
Wytness of euery woord that Peter spake to the
  darcknes.
Cock with an open mouth, and lowd voyce bowldly
  proclaymeth,
That bragging seruant his mayster cowldly re-
  nounceth.
Euery sight, each sound, iust accusation offreth,
And self - wounding sowle, self - condemnation
  vrgeth.
Noe rest, noe harts-ease : now loathed lyfe he
  detested
More, yea much more now, than death at first he
  abhorred.
  Lyfe, let Peeter dye; lyfe, leaue to be dayly
    prolonging
These my dolefull dayes, least lyfe soone drawn to
  an ending

Cause me to loose that lyfe, which neuer leaues to
    be lasting.

This frayle life, smale broyles and shortest iarres
    to be shunning,

Made me the greatest ioyes and endles peace to
    be leauing,

Made me deny my Lord, of lasting lyfe the begyn-
    nyng,

Made me renounce sweete life, for a foolish feare
    to be dying,

Lyfe, let Peeter dye ; many dayes heape on many
    mischiefs.

Blessed were those babes that dy'de, when merci-
    les Herode

Seeking one chyldes death, many Mothers made to
    be chyldeles :

Blessed, most blessed chyldren, whose tymely
    departure

Parted theyr sweete sowles from such, and soe
    many thowsand

Woes, who dyed afore they knew what t'was to
    be synnyng,

And fro the damnable earth to the highest heau'ns
    be remoued,

Lyke to a Lilly, before it chaunce by the frost to
    be nypped.

They, instead of mouths, theyre throates then
    sweetely did open.

And, for want of woords, powr'd forth theyr blood
    to the heauen.

O straunge thing, these babes are now with glory
    triumphing,

Which yet neuer afore did taste any part of a
    fighting :

Theyr yong heads with crownes of Martyrdome be
    adorned,

Ere any tender lockes had theyre heads sweetly
    bedecked:

Yea, theyr feete, that on earth were neuer seene
    to be treading,

Walk in Olympus now, and these in ioy be abiding.

But Peeters gray heares, draw graceles face to the
    graues-dore,

Peeters long lyuing, makes Peeters sowle to be
    doating,

Peeter lyu's, yea lyu's to deny his mayster Jësus,

Lyu's yea lyu's to renounce his lord and mayster
    Jësus,

Lyu's, and yet forsakes, forsweares lyfe-geauer
    Jësus.

Christe, who might commaund that glorious hoaste
    of Olympus,

Those spotles spirites, those euer-dutiful angels,

Sought, found, and tooke vs from soe many, soe
    many thowsands,
Vs ragged fishers, from soemany, soemany thow-
    sands,
Yet we alas his loue haue most vnlouely rewarded.
And this most kinde Christe haue most vnkindly
    requited,
Wee, most cursed crewe, of soemany, soemany
    thowsands,
Wee, woorst vipers broode, of soemany, soemany
    thowsands,
Wee, the detested twelue, of soemany, soemany
    thowsands
One with a cursed kisse his deare Lord falsly be-
    trayed,
Ten fled back for feare, when death and danger
    aproached,
And I the woorst of twelue, yea after soemany
    great woords,
Leaft, forsooke, forsware, Lord, Sou'raigne,
    Mayster Jësus.
  Whyl'st poore Peeter thus with mynde extrea-
    mely molested,
With deepe sobbs and sighs, with streames of
    teares that abounded,
Washed away those spotts, and most syncearely
    repented ;

Mornying came at last, and those damnable owt-
  casts

That condemned Christe, did bring hym bound to
  be slaughtred,

Bound, bruysd, and beaten to the Romayne
  Deputy Pilate,

Pilate, who for a Judg of lyfe and death was
  apoynted.

  In meane tyme, Judas possest with desperat
  horrors,

Clog'd with a sinfull sowle, with a dogged deadly
  repentance

Coms with his after clapps, when he see's his
  mayster Jësus

Thus condemned to the death, and runs in a rage
  to the high Priests,

Saying, Synned I haue, that guyltles blood to
  betray thus.

Yf thou haue synned, say they, looke thou to be
  plagued,

What care wee for that? w'haue kept tutch,
  giu'n thee thy wages.

  That woefull wages drew my destruction onward,

That graceles guerdon my death vntymely procured,

That brybe bred my bane : Take there your
    Mammon among you,

Take back your bloody brybe : soe threw theyr
    syluer among them :

And flinging headlong, enrag'de with an hellish
    Erynnis,

Hangd hymself on a tree : fit death for treachery
    faythles :

His loathed carkas was an ougly detestable obiect,

Spectacle infamous, most fearefull sighte to the
    people,

With gutts gushing foorth, with bowells broken
    asunder.

    Loe here, you Traytors, your treasons iustly re-
    warded,

Your Mayster Judas himself hath rightly requyted:

Your Mayster Judas dealt soe, that now to the
    worlds end

Of that name Judas, each traytor's named a Judas,

Euery faythles fryend from that tyme's called a
    Judas.

    Marck Peeters weakenes, marck Judas villany,
    fly from

Both dead dispayring and too much hasty presum-
    yng.

Peeter startled asyde for feare of death, with a
    faynt harte,

Judas slyded back for loue of a bride, with a false
　　harte :
Peeter neuer againe came home, but deadly re-
　　pyned.
　Judas thus bursting, highe Priests and Scribes
　　be amased.
And consulting long, at last they fulley resolued,
With that cursed coyne some peace of ground to
　　be buying,
For straungers buryall, with a fayned sanctyty
　　cloaking
That cursed bloodshed, that most vnnatural owt-
　　rage.
Soe this pryce of blood was payed for a fyeld of a
　　potter,
Called a fyeld of blood, for a signe of this bloody
　　murder.
　Christ is brought to the barr : Sir Pilate sits as
　　a bencher,
Priests be his accusers : many captall crymes,
　　many treasons,
And many seditions were there obiected against
　　him.
So much sayd, nought prou'd ; Christ standing
　　seellyly sylent,
By smoothing Pilates commaunde was sent to the
　　Tetrarche,

102

Herodes Tetrarche of Galyly, there to be judged,
Sith Christ seem'd to belong t'his jurisdiction only.
　Herode greatly reioyst, and looked for many
　　woonders
When Christe came : But Christe with sylence
　　wysely rebuked
This Tetrarchs tatling, and Priests vnruely revyl-
　　ings.
　Herode contemn'd Christe, when hee saw noe
　　hope of a wonder,
Sent hym back for a foole, to the first iudg deputy
　　Pilate,
All in a long whyte coate, for a scornefull mockery
　　cloathed.
Thus poore Christ, meeke lambe, was tost fro the
　　poast to the piller,
Wandring here and there, hence thence fro the
　　woolf to the slaughter.
　Pilate seeing Christ fro the Tetrarch saufly
　　retorned
Spake to the Priests and Scribes : This man
　　seem's stil to be guyltles,
Herode sends him back : its best hee be whipt for
　　a frantike
And soe loost at large : for I know you looke for
　　a prisner

At this feast, of course : say then, whoe shal be
    released ?
Barrabas, or Iesus ? What needest thou to be ask-
    ing
O pytyful Pilate ? thou know'st, theyr only desyr-
    ing
Is t'haue Christ murdred : thou giust this lambe
    to the woolus iawes.
Kill, kill Christ, say they, and geue vs Barrabas
    only.
—Barrabas, in theeiuing and murdring, barbarus
    owtlaw.—
    Then people pleasing Pilate, causd Christ to be
      scourged,
And in a scornefull sort to the Iews to be newly
    produced,
But kill, kill, they cry, and crucify, crucify Iesus.
    Pilate seeing Christe by the sowldyers all to be
      scourged,
Causd him then for a mock with a crowne of thorns
    to be crowned,
With royall garments and roabes of purple adorned,
And in a throane placed, with a recde in his hand
    for a scepter.
Some mockt, some spytted, some kneeld and fynely
    saluted,

Hayle ô king of Iews, for fame and glory renowmed.

Some with his owne scepter that sweete face all
  to be bruysed,

Euery one tooke paynes, that noe paynes might
  be omytted,

Noeman spar'd any cost, least Christ might
  chaunce to be spared :

Yet this was not enongh, t' appeare theyr villany
  monstrous,

But kill, kill, they cry, and crucify Iesus.

  Pilates wife in a dreame with Christ then
    greatly molested,

Perswades her good man for feare, that he might
  be released :

Yet noe dreames would serue t' appease theyr
  villany monstrous,

But kill, kill, they cry, and crucify, crucify Iesus.

  Then iust iudge Pilate in an open shew to the
    people,

His pure hands forsooth, with greate solempnyty
  washed,

Thincking so fro the guylt of guyltles blood to be
  quytted :

Noe wynde, noe water, could stay theyr villany
  monstrous,

But, kill, kill, they cry, and crucify, crucify
 Iesus.

Crucify coosnyng Christe, his death and blood be
 requyted

On Iewes that now lyue, and Iewish progeny
 after.

Cæsars faythfull fryend can abyde noe **Kyng** but a
 Cæsar,

Therefore looke Pilate, that this king soone be
 remoued.

  Christe in his owne coate now to the Iewes was
 lastly presented,

And by Pilate's doome—death's doome—giu'n vp
 to be crossed:

Whose Crosse, in Latyne, Greeke, Hebriew, had
 for a tytle

These woords, Here's Iesus, Iewes King, of Nazareth, added.

  Chiefe Iewes tooke Iesus prickt, whip't from the
 crowne to the anckles,

Faynt, weake, and feeble, scarce able for to be
 creeping:

Yet they layd on a Crosse, his shoulders heauyly
 loading,

Dryuing him foreward, til he fell downe vnder a
 burden,

Burden with deaths pangs, plagues, griefs, and
  horror abounding.
Christe and crosse falne downe, by chaunce one
  Symon aproached,
Whoe to be Crossecaryer, by the proud Priests
  then was apoynted,
Crossecaryer to a place, that in Hebriew's Golgatha
  called,
Place of dead mens sculls : where Christe they
  speedyly Crossed,
Feete and hands with nayles, with great nayles all
  to be mangled :
And, for a greater spyte, two theeues they causd
  to be hanged,
Hanged on eyther syde, and Christe almighty
  betweene them.
  Christe once nayled to the Crosse, now euery
    knaue is craking,
Prowd-harted Pharisees, fell Scribes, hypocritical
  Ealders,
Captens and souldyers, greate, smalle, fro the
  Priest to the Pyper,
Wagging theyre wise heads, laughing and scorne-
  fuly tauntyng,
Thou that sau'st others, now saue thyself from a
  mischif,

107

Thou that buyldst temples with a tryce, come
    downe fro the gallows,
Come Gods deare dearling, come king of Jews for
    the gybbett,
Leape from a crosse to a crowne, from a cursed
    tree to a kingdome.
    Christe, (ö louing Christe, long suffring Christe)
    thus abused,
Gaue not a check for a taunt, but alas very heart-
    yly prayed,
Father forgeue them, forget this villany Father.
    Hark and mark that thief, (that thief eu'n
    brought to the last gaspe)
How he reuyles his Lord: Peace thiefe, geue eare
    to thy fellow,
Wee for a synfull lyfe with death are iustly re-
    warded,
But Christs synles lyfe hath noe death duly de-
    serued,
Thou Christe, thou Jesus, thou Lord vouchesaufe
    to remember
Mee, mee, sinfull wretch, mee, when thou comest
    to thy kingdome.
    Christe heard and sayd thus, Thy prayers shall
    be regarded,
This day in Paradise with mee thou shalt bee
    receaued.

108

O blest thief, curst thief, Sheepe, Goate: Therefore
    let a synner
Not despaire, one thief is sau'd in an howre, in a
    moment :
But let a sinner feare, let a sinner not be presum-
    ing,
One thiefe only repents, and scapes in an howre,
    in a moment.
    Christs coate was seameles, for a syne of an
    absolut, endles,
And perfit kingdome : this coate soe fitly coharent
And all-wrought ouer, was nothing toucht by the
    souldyers,
Nor torne in peeces, nor cut, nor parted among
    them,
But lotts cast, that some one man might wholly
    receaue it,
That, what was foretold, might haue effectual
    ending.
    Christe now hangs on a tree, suffring vnsuffra-
    ble horrors,
Torments for mans sins, and God's vnspeakable
    anger :
Whylst Christe is suffring, whylst fearefull pangs
    be aproaching,
Sunne for Gods Sons griefe doth greeue, and gyns
    to be lowring:

Hydes his darckned face, lets golden rayes be
    eclipsed,
Seeing Light of light with pricking thorns to be
    crowned :
Heu'n and earth is darck fro the sixth howre vnto
    the nynth howre,
Heu'n and earth laments, and euery thing is a
    mourning :
Heu'n and earth laments, whylst Jesus Christe is
    a dying,
Heu'n and earth's comfort, heu'n and earth's only
    reuyuing.
    But now Christe gan faint, with an infinit
    agony troubled,
And Ely Ely, and Lamasabaethany cryed,
Father, deare Father, why should thy Son be
    refused ?
    Then bitter vinegar they raught, when he sayd,
    that he thirsted,
Which Christe once tasting, said, Father, now it
    is ended,
Thy will's fulfilled, thy lawes and heast be obeyed,
Take my sowle to thy hands ; Then his head he
    began to be bowing,
With those woords his life and endles passion en-
    ding.

Scarce did he yeeld his breath, but straight fro
the top to the bottom,
Temples vayle was rent, and torne, and broken
asunder,
Earth did quake, stones brake, graues op'ned,
dead men apeared.
Then captens, souldyers, men, matrones, all
the beholders
Smote theyr breasts, and said, this man was son
to the mighty,
Whose strange death eu'n makes lyue dead, and
dead to be lyuely.
Christe is dead indeede, his bones neede not to
be bruysed:
Yet for a further proofe, his side was speedily
pearced,
Pearc't with a speare, and thence pure blood, pure
water abounded.
Then noble Joseph, with faithfull frieud
Nicodemus
Did begg of Pilate, that blessed corps of Jësus,
Tooke it downe fro the crosse, fine lynnen duly
prepared,
With Myrrh and Aloes themselues it carefuly
wynded,
And in a late made tombe, wherein was no-body
chested,

That sweete corps (sweete corps of Christe al-
    mighty) reposed,

Rolled a stone to the graue, aod so all heauy
    departed.

    Yet the Priests left not, till they had watch-
    men apoynted,

And graues stone sealed, least Christe might
    chaunce to be stollen

By his wel-willers, as they then vainly pretended;

Sots, fooles, and mad-men, stil against this prick
    to be kicking,

And stil against this streame, this sacred streame
    to be striuing.

    For when third day came, there came with a
    terrible earth-quake

Gods Angel fro the skies, and rold that stone fro
    the graues-dore,

And there sate for a while : his face was like to a
    lightning,

His roabes white as snow, which made those
    watchmen amazed,

And halfe dead for feare : but th' Angel spake to
    the women,

—Twoo Maries, comming of purpose for to anoynt
    Christe

With precious spices, with sweete odoriferus
    oyntments—

You seeke here for Christe, here Christe is not to
    be sought for,
Christ is quicknd againe, and risn, as he truly
    reported,
And foretold his friends ; in Galyly there will hee
    meete them,
Loe, where lately hee lay : feare not, but boldly
    report it.
  As they ran to report, Christ Iesus plainly
    apeared,
And met them by the way, and bade them not be
    amazed,
But bring newes to the rest, that he would in
    Gaylyly see them.
  This doone, and they gone; poore watchmen
    ran to the Citty ;
And told all to the Priests ; who then with an
    obstinat error,
And wilfull blyndnes, these watchmen largely
    rewarded,
Willing them to report, and tell this abroade to
    the people,
That Christs disciples stole him by night fro the
    watchmen,
Whylst they lay sleeping. Which hæresy stoutly
    to this day

Stifneckt Iews mainteine: ô curst and damnable
    error,

O hard-harted Iews, that giue more eare to a
    hyreling

And brybed souldier, by the prowd Priests falsly
    suborned,

Than to the truth it self with soe great glory
    reuealed,

Than to the eyes which saw, to the eares which
    heard, to the fingers

And to the hands which felt that which was truly
    reported,

Hands which felt Chrysts hands and feete and
    sides to be wounded,

Eares which heard his woords and blessings
    sweetely delyu'red,

Eyes which saw and knew, that Christ in Galyly
    walked,

And foure times ten dayes in diuers places apear-
    ed :

Eyes which saw Christe eate, and then fro the
    earth to be lifted

Vp to the highest heau'ns, and there with glory
    receaued

On Gods owne right hand with iurisdiction endles:

Vntil he come to be Iudg of quick and dead, by
    the thundring

114

Sounde of a fearefull trumpe : and bring his sheepe
　　to the sheepefold
Immortall sheepefold,　and goates throw downe to
　　the darcknes
Æternall darcknes, fro the sacred face, fro the pre-
　　sence
Of God, there to abyde with Lucifer and his
　　adherents,
Plagued with a dying life, with a lyuing death,
　　with a roaring,
Weeping, and gnashing of teeth, and horrible
　　howling ;
Where's nought but woe, woe ; but a worme
　　stil greedily gryping,
Nought but a loathsome lake with fyre and sul-
　　phur abounding.

Finis.

Certaine Psalmes.

—

THE FIRST PSALME.

THRICE happy the man, that lends noe
  eare to the counsail
 Of soule-sicke sinners; nor frames his
feete to the foote stepps
Of backsliding guydes: nor sets him downe with
 a scorner
In the maligning chayre, that makes but a mock
 of Olympus.
 But to the living Lords edicts himself he re-
  ferreth,
And there in pleasures and treasures only reposeth:
Night and day by the same his footesteps duly
  directing,
Day and night by the same, hart, mynde, soule,
  purely preparing.
 This man's like to a tree, to a tree most happily
  planted
Hard by a brooke, by a brooke whose streames of
 siluer abounding

Make this tree her fruite, her pleasant fruite to
    be yeelding,
Yeelding fruite in tyme to the planters dayly re-
    ioycing.
    This tree's rooted deepe, her bowes are chere-
        fuly springing,
Her fruite neuer fades, her leaues looke liuely for
    euer :
This man's setted sure, his thoughts, woords,
    dayly proceedings.
Happy beginings haue, and haue as fortunat
    endings.
    Sinners are not soe : they and theyrs all in a
        moment,
All in a moment passe past hope, grace, mercy,
    recou'ry,
As weight-wanting chaffe that scattreth in euery
    corner,
Whyrled away fro the earth, hence, thence, by a
    blast, by a wynde puffe.
    Woe to the scorner then, whose soule wil
        quake to be iudged,
Quake when it heares that doome by the Judg
    almighty pronounced.
Woe to the sinner then, noe settled sinner ap-
    roacheth

Neare to the sinles Saincts, where ioy and glory
    aboundeth.

For, the triumphant God doth stil looke downe
    to the godly,

Their wayes well knowing, and them with mercy
    protecting :

But the reuenging Lord hath threatned a plague
    to the godles,

And theyr wayes shal away, and they themselues
    be a wayling.

THE SIXTH PSALME.

ORD forbeare to rebuke, forbeare, and
    stay thy reuenging
    Hand, in thy greate wrath and indigna-
tion endles.

Heale my wounds, my God, take some com-
    passion on mee;

My bones are bruysed, my strength is wholly de-
    cayed,

My sowle is troubled, my mynde extreamely
    molested,

How long shall thy wrath, and these my plagues
    be prolonged ?

Turne yet againe, good God, thy woonted mercy
    remember,

119

And this sowle, poore sowle, for thy greate mercy
  delyuer.
Saue my life from death, in death noe worthy
  remembrance
Of thy name is founde: and keepe my sowle fro
  the dungeon,
Infernall dungeon, where noe tonge yeelds any
  prayses.
  My hart with groanyng, my sowle is weary with
    anguish.
Euery night doe I wash my carefull couch with
  abounding
Streames of trickling teares : my flesh is myghtyly
  troubled,
My color all faded, my former bewty decayed,
For feare, all for feare of such as seeke to deuoure
  mee.
  But get away, get away all you that woork any
    myschief :
My sighes ascende vp, my prayers pierce to the
  heauens :
And such as my sowle with griefe vnworthyly
  vexed,
With shame and sorrow shall worthyly soone be
  requyted.

THE EYGHTH PSALME.

 PRINCE all-puysant, ô king al-mightyly
    ruling,
How wōdrous be thy works, and how
    strange are thy proceedings?
Thou hast thy greate name with most greate glory
    reposed
Ouer, aboue those Lamps, bright-burning Lamps
    of Olympus,
Eu'n very babes, yong babes, yong sucking babes
    thy triumphant
Might set foorth; to the shame of them which
    iniury offer,
Eu'n to the shame of them which damned blasph-
    emy vtter.
  When that I looke to the skies, and lyft myne
    eyes to the heauens,
Skies thyne owne hand-work, and heauens fram'd
    by thy fingers;
When that I see this Sunne, that makes my sight
    to be seeing,
And that Moone, her light, light half-darck, dayly
    renuing,
Sunne dayes-eye shynyng, Moone nights-light
    chereful apearing,

121

When that I see sweete Starres through christal
    skies to be sprinckled,
Some to the first spheare fixt, some here and there
    to be wandryng,
And yet a constant course with due reuolution
    endyng.
  Then doe I thinck, ô Lord, what a thing is man,
    what a wonder?
O what a thing is man, that thou soe greatly re-
    gardest?
Or what a thing's mankynde, which thou soe
    charyly tendrest?
  Thou hast man, this man, this blest man might-
    yly framed,
And with aboundant grace, with aboundant
    dygnyty crowned,
Not much inferior to thy sweete cælestial Angells
  Thou hast giu'n hym right and iurisdiction ouer
All thy wondrous woorkes, thou hast made hym
    to be mayster,
Hym chiefe mayster on earth, right Lord, and
    absolut owner
Of beast, fowle, and fishe on th' earth, ayre, water
    abyding.
  O prince all-puysant, ô King al-mightyly ruling,
How wondrous by thy woorks, and how strange
    are thy proceedings?

THE NINE AND TWENTETH PSALME.

OU Kings and rulers, you Lords and mighty Monarchaes,
  Whose hands with scepters, and heads with crownes be adorned,
Kneele to the King of Kings, and bring your dutifull offrings;
Lowt to the lyuing Lord; ascribe all might to the mighty
Alwayes-mighty Monarch: and learne to be rul'd by the ruler,
Which heu'n earth, and hell, rul's, overrules in a moment.
  For this is only that one, whose thundring voyce fro the clustred,
Clowds breaks foorth and roares, and horror brings to the whole world,
For this is only that one, whose fearefull voyce fro the heauens,
Cedars, tall cedars, teares, rents, and ryues fro the rooting,
Cedars of Libanus constrayns like calues to be leaping:
And Cedar-bearing Libanus, with frightened Hermon
Lyke to a yong Vnicorne makes here and there to be skipping.

123

For this is only that one, whose threatnyng
    voyce the deuouring
Lightnyngs flakes throwes downe, and terror
    brings to the deserts,
Teares downe trees and woods, makes hyndes for
    feare to be caluyng,
And that forelorne waste of Cadesh for to be
    tremblyng,
    Euery voyce his voyce, his prayse, and glory
      pronounceth,
His sacred temple with his honnor dayly resoundeth.
Ouer gulfs and deepes his royall throane he
    reposeth,
Ouerwhelmyng gulfes, and drownyng deepes he
    represseth,
And stil a lyuyng Lord, stil a king almighty
    remayneth,
And yet a Father stil : for he leaves not, stil to be
    sendyng
Strength to his owne elect, and inward peace for a
    blessing.

THE EYGHT AND THIRTITH PSALME.

SCOURGE mee not, my God, whylst thy
    wrath's kyndled against mee,
   Put mee not to rebuke, in thyne vnspeakable anger.

For, thy darts, ô God, dead darts, and dangerus
   arrowes

Stick fast, fast to my hart, ô Lord, stick fast to my
   hart-roote,

And thy hands, sore hands, presse and oppresse mee
   with anguish,

In my flesh noe health; in bones noe rest is abyding,

Thy wrath plagues my flesh, my syns to my bones
   be a poyson.

My syns, woefull wretch, my syns now growne
   to a fullnes

Ouergrow my head, curst head, and keepe mee
   stil vnder,

Lyke to a burden alas, my back too heauyly
   loading.

  My carefull carkas with sores lyes all to be
   wounded,

Festring sores with grosse corruption euer abounding,

Festring sores and wounds fro my synfull folly
   proceeding.

My pain's soe greeuous, my griefe soe greate, that
   it vrgeth,

Mee wyth a pale dead face, and crooked lyms to
    be creeping,
Myne inflamed loynes are filld with filthy diseases,
And noe part vntutcht, noe peece vnwounded
    apeareth.
Faynt and feeble I am ; sore bruysed, soe that I
    can not
But roare out for griefe of sowle, and horrible
    anguish.
   Lord, thou knowst my desyre, thou seest my
    dayly bewaylings ;
Hart hartles doth pant, and strengthles strength is
    abated,
Sightles sight is gone, and fryends vnfryendly
    departed,
And vnkynde kynsmen my wounded carkas ab-
    horring
Looke ; but a greate way of ; but come not neare
    to my comfort,
Thus forsaken I am, forlorne, contemptible abiect.
   They that sought my life, layd secrete snares to
    betray mee,
And, to deuoure my blood, conspyred dayly to-
    geather.
And I, for all this, alas, poore foole, stood seellyly
    sylent,

Lyke to a man that's deaf, and seems not a woord
 to be hearing,
Lyke to a man that's dumbe, and fear's his mouth
 to be op'nyng :
For, my fayth and trust in thee, my Lord, I
 reposed,
Thou must pleade my cause, and by thee I must
 be defended,
 Lord, I desyre that these my foes may not be
 triumphing
Ouer a contryte sowle : for when my foote was a
 slipping,
Then they laught and scornd, and seem'd to be
 greatly reioycing,
And in truth, my God, my plagues are day
 renued,
And my bleeding wounds lye always open afore
 mee,
Alwayes in my sight; for I must and will my
 destested,
Fylthy destested lyfe confesse, with an heauy re-
 membryng
Harty repentyng sowle. But, alas, my deadly
 malignyng
Foes are as much increaste, in might and number
 abounding.

These men alas, for that my sowle theyr fylthynes
    hated,
Life with death, ô Lord, and good with bad be
    requyting.
Helpe, ô Lord my God, make haste, draw neare to
    the needy,
Heɩp, ô God my Lord, and my saluation only.

THE FIFTITH PSALME.

OD, the triumphant God, th' æternall
    greate God of all gods
    Hath sent foorth Summons with a thū-
    dring voyce fro the heāues,
World-warnyng Summons, commaunding all in a
    moment,
All from th' east to the weast, to be prest, and
    make an aparance,
And performe theyr suyte to the court, to the
    greate, to the high court,
Greate high Syons court, sweete Syon : where hee
    apeareth
With surpassing grace, exceeding bewty abound-
    ing.
  God shal come, shall come with a voyce al-
    mightyly sounding ;

Greedy deuouring fyre shall goe with glory before
    hym,
And blustring tempests shall roare with terror
    about hym.
Heu'n from aboue shal hee call, and quaking earth
    to be wytnes,
Of this iust edict and sentence rightly pronounced.
   Bring my Saints, sayth God, goe bring my Saints
    to my presence,
Which haue vow'd theyre harts, and sworne theyr
    sowles to my seruyce,
And of this iudgement from iudg almighty pro-
    ceeding,
Those bright-burnyng gloabes of Christal-mantled
    Olympus,
Shalbe reporters true, and alwayes shalbe recorders.
   Heare mee, my deare flock, and thou, ô Israel
    heare mee,
Heare me thy God, thy Lord; and know that I
    am not agreeued,
Nor displeased a whytt, for want of customed
    offrings
Burnt offrings, sacrifice, and Honnors due to my
    altars.
What doe I care for a Goate? or what doe I care
    for a Bullock?

Sith Goates, and Bullocks, and beasts that range by
    the deserts,

Sith cattell feeding on a thousand hills be my owne
    goods ?

Myne owne proper goods be the fowles that fly to
    the mountaynes,

Myne be the beasts that run by the fyelds, and
    watery fountayns.

  If that I hunger, alas what neede I to tell thee,
    I hunger ?

Sith that th' earth is myne, and all on earth is
    abyding.

Thinck not, thinck not, alas, that I take any ioy
    to be eating

Bulls flesh : thinck not, alas, that I take a delight
    to be dryncking

Goates blood, guyltles blood: but make acceptable
    offring

Of thanks-geuying hart, and pay thy vowes to the
    highest.

Call me to help, when soe thou findst thyself to be
    helples,

Cry for grace, when soe thou thinckst thy sowle
    to be past grace :

And I wil heare, and help, giue grace, and strongly
    protect thee,

And thou lawde, and loue, sing, serue, and woor-
 thyly praise mee.
 But with a frownyng looke, this God spake
 thus to the godles;
With what face dar'st thou my sacred name be
 prophanyng
With those lying lipps, and mouth with murder
 abounding?
With what face dar'st thou with a fyled tong be
 professing,
And by defyled lyfe, and fowled sowle be denying?
With what face darst thou for an ostentation only
Seeke to reforme others, thyself soe fowly de-
 formed?
When thou meet'st with a thief, thou seek'st by
 theft to be thryuyng,
And walkst syde by syde as a copsemate fit for
 adulters.
Thy mouth's made to beguyle; and monstrous
 villany vttreth,
Thy lipps let foorth lyes: thy tongue vntruly
 defameth
Thyne owne mothers sonne: these, these be thy
 holy proceedings,
These be thy works; and sith that I seem'd for a
 while to be sylēt,

Thou thoughtst—wicked thought—my thoughts
    were lyke to thy owne thoughts,
And soe runnst headlong. But I come; but plagues
    be aproaching,
And when I come, then I stryke; whē I stryke,
    thē I beate thee to powder.
Thy bloody thoughts, lewde words, vile deeds wil
    I open in order,
And shew all to thy face : which thou shalt see
    to thy sorrow,
Know, and acknowledg to thy owne confusion
    endles.
  You that forget God, thinck on this : least hee
    remember
And forget not you; but roote you out in his
    anger,
Then shall noeman come, your damned sowles to
    delyuer.
  Prayse and thancksgiuing is a most acceptable
    offring;
And, if a man by my lawes his conuersation order,
Vnto the same I myself wil my saluation offer.

THE THREESCORE AND THIRTEENTH PSALME.

OD, th' æternall God, noe doubt, is good
to the godly,
Giuing grace to the pure, and mercy to
Israel holy :
And yet, alas, my feete, my faynt feete gan to be
slyding,
And I was almost gone, and fall'n to a dangerus
error.
For, my soule did grudg, my hart consumed in
anger,
And myne eyes disdayng'd, when I saw, that
such men abounded
With wealth, health, and ioy, whose myndes with
myschief abounded
Theyr body stowt and strong, theyr lyms stil
lyuely apearing
Neyther feare any panges of death, nor feele any
sicknes :
Some still mourne, they laughe; some lyue impor-
tunat ever,
They for ioy doe triumphe, and taste aduersyty
neuer,
Which makes them with pryde, with scorneful
pryde be chayned,

And with blood-thirsting disdaigne as a roabe to
    be cou'red.
Theyr fare is delicate, theyr flesh is dayntyly
    pampred,
Theyr eyes with fatnes start out, theyr greedy
    deuouring
Gutts, swell with swylling; and what fonde fancy
    descryeth,
Or lewd lust lyketh, that fortune fryendly afordeth,
Themselus most synfull cause others for to be
    synners
With theyr poysn'd breath, and vile contagius
    humors:
They check, scorne, controlle, looke, ouer looke,
    with a lordlyke
Imperious countnance; theyr mouth fowle blas-
    phemy vttreth,
And fro the forlorne earth, to the heau'ns dis-
    daingfuly mounteth.
    This surpassing pompe and pryde allureth a
    nomber
Eu'n of Gods owne flock—flock weake and weary
    with anguish—
Vnto the self same trade, which makes theyr glory
    the greater.
Tush, say they, can God, fro the highest heu'ns to
    the lowest

Earth, vouchsaulf, thinck you, those Princelike
    eyes to be bowing?
Tis but a vaine conceipt of fooles, to be fondly
    referring
Euery iesting trick, and trifling toy to the Thun-
    drer.
For loe, these be the men, whose soules are sear'd
    with an yron,
And yet these be the men, who rule and raigne
    with aboundance;
These, and whoe but these? Why then what
    meane I to lift vp
Cleane hands, and pure hart to the heau'ns? What
    meane I to offer
Praise and thanksgeuing to the Lord? What meane
    I to suffer
Such plagues with patience? Yea, and almost had
    I spoken
Eu'n as they did speake, which thought noe God
    to be guyding.
  But soe should I alas, haue iudgd thy folk to be
    luckles,
Thy sons forsaken, thy saincts vnworthily haples.
  Then did I thinck, and muse, and search what
    might be the matter,
But yet I could not, alas, conceaue so hidden a
    woonder:

Vntil I left myself, and all my thoughts did aban-
    don,
And to thy sacred place, to thy sanct'uary lastly
    repayred.
  Then did I see, ô Lord, these mens vnfortunat
    endings
Endings meete and fit for their vngodly begin-
    nings.
Then did I see how they did stand in their slippery
    places,
Lifted aloft, that their downefalling might be the
    greater.
Lyuing Lord, how soone is this theyr glory trium-
    phant
Dasht, confounded, gone, drownd in destruction
    endles ?
Their fame's soone outworne, theyr name's extinct
    in a moment,
Lyke to a dreame, that lyues by a sleepe, and dyes
    with a slumber.
  Thus my soule did greeue, my heart did languish
    in anguish,
Soe blynde were myne eyes, my minde soe plunged
    in error,
That noe more than a beast did I know this
    mystery sacred.

Yet thou heldst my hande, and keptst my soule
    fro the dungeon,
Thou didst guyde my feete, and mee with glory
    receauedst.
For what in heu'n or in earth shal I loue or
    woorthyly wonder
But my most good God, my Lord and mighty
    Jehoua ?
Though my flesh oft faint, my hart's oft drownèd
    in horror,
God neuer fayleth, but wilbe my mighty protector.
  Such as God forsake, and take to a slippery
    comfort,
Trust to a broken staffe, and taste of woorthy
    reuengement.
In my God therefore my trust is wholly reposed,
And his name will I praise, and sing his glory
    renowmed.

THE HUNDRED AND FOURTH PSALME.

YUING Lord, my soule shall praise thy
    glory triumphant,
    Sing thy matchles might, and shew thine
    infinit honnor.
Euerlasting light thou putst on like as a garment,

And purpled-mantled welkyn thou spreadst as a
    courtayne :
Thy parlor pillers on waters strangely be pitched,
Clowdes are thy charyots, and blustring wyndes
    be thy coursers,
Immortal Spyrits be thy euer-dutiful Harrolds,
And consuming fires, as seruants dayly be wayting.
    All-maintaining earths foundations euer abydeth
Layd by the Lords right-hand, with seas and
    deeps as a garment
Cou'red; seaes and deepes with threatning waues
    to the huge hills
Clyming; but with beck theyr billowes speedily
    backward
All doe recoyle; with a check their course is
    changd on a soddaine ;
At thy thundring voyce they quake: And soe doe
    the mountaines
Mount vpward with a woord; and soe alsoe doe
    the valleys.
Downe with a woord discend, and keepe their
    places apoynted :
Theyr meares are fixed, theyr bancks are mightily
    barred,
Theyr bounds knowne, least that, man-feeding
    earth by the rage of

Earth-ouerwhelming waters might chaunce to be
  drowned.
  Stil-springing fountaines distil fro the rocks to
  the ryuers,
And christall riuers flow ouer along by the
  mountaines:
There will wylde asses theyr scorched mouthes be
  refreshing,
And field-feeding beasts theyr thirst with water
  abating.
  Theyr by the wel-welling waters, by the syluer-
  abounding
Brookes, fayre-flying fowles on flowring bancks
  be abyding,
There shall sweete-backt byrds theyr bowres in
  bows be a building,
And to the waters fall theyr warbling voyce be a
  tuning.
  Yea those sun-burnt hills, and mountaines all to
  be scorched,
Cooling clouds doe refresh, and watery dewe fro
  the heauens.
Earth sets forth thy woorks, earth-dwellers all be
  thy wonders :
Earth earth-dwelling beasts with flowring grasse
  is a feeding;

Earth earth-dwelling men with pleasant hearbes
    is a seruing.
Earth brings harts-ioy wine, earth-dwelling men
    to be hartning,
Earth breedes chearing oyles, earth-dwelling man
    to be smoothing,
Earth beares lifes-foode bread, earth-dwelling men
    to be strengthning.
    Tall trees, vp-mounting Cedars are chearefuly
      springing,
Cedars of Libanus, where fowles theyr neasts be
    preparing ;
And Storkes in Firr-trees make their accustomed
    harbors.
    Wylde goats, doaes, and roaes dooe roue and
      range by the mountains,
And poore seely conyes to the ragged rocks be
    repayring.
    Night-enlightning Moone for certaine tymes is
      apoynted,
And all-seeing Sunne knowes his due tyme to be
    be sitting.
Sunne once soe sitting, darck night wraps all in a
    mantle
All in a black mantle : then beasts creepe out fro
    the dungeons,

Roaring hungry Lions theyr pray with greedy
    deuouring

Clawes and iawes attend, but by Gods only apoynt-
    ment :

When Sunne riseth againe, theyr dens they quick-
    ly recouer,

And there couch all day : that man may safely the
    day time

His dayes woorke apply, til day giue way to the
    darknes.

  O good God, wise Lord, good Lord, and only
    the wise God,

Earth sets foorth thy woorks, earth-dwellers all
    be thy wonders.

Soe be seaes alsoe, greate seaes, full fraught with
    aboundant

Swarms of creeping things, great, small : there
    shipps be a sayling,

And there lyes tumbling, that monsterus huge
    Leuiathan.

All these begge theyr food, and all these on thee
    be wayting;

If that thou stretch out thyne hand, they feede
    with aboundance,

If thou turne thy face, they all are mightily
    troubled ;

If that thou withdraw their breath they dye in a
    moment,
And turne quickly to dust, whence they were
    lately deriued,
If thy spirite breathe, their breath is newly cre-
    ated,
And the decayed face of th' earth is quickly re-
    uiued.
  O then, glory to God, to the Lord then, glory
    for euer ;
Whoe in his owne great works may worthily glory
    for euer.
This Lord lookes to the earth, and steedfast earth
    is a trembling,
This God touchteth mounts, and mountains huge
    be a smoaking.
All my life will I lawd this Lord ; whylst breath
    is abyding
In my breast, this breath his praise shall stil be
    a breathing.
  Heare my woords, my Lord, accept this dutiful
    offring,
That my soule in thee may euermore be reioyc-
    ing;
Roote the malignant race, race out their damnable
    ofspring ;

But my soule, ô Lord shall praise thy glory trium-
    phant,
Sing thy matchles might, and shew thyne infinit
    honnor.

Finis.

NOTES.

It may interest some to have these noticeable words and things in the 'Emanuell' and 'Psalms' of FRAUNCE recorded :

1. pp. 21-2 : Cf. our "Lord Bacon not the Author of the Paradoxes" and "Giles Fletcher".

2. p. 28, line 3 : 'Monarcha'.

3. p. 34, line 8 : 'bag, budgett'. Our modern use of 'budget' with application to the Chancellor of the Exchequer's annual statement, is quaintly illustrated herein.

4. p. 36, line 2 : 'fatbely' = fat belly or large paunched, the usual conception of a Monk contemporarily.

5. p. 40 : a very vivid description of the working of conscience.

6. p. 41. line 9 : 'sheepsman' : transition-form.

7. p. 41, line 12 : a favorite phrase of the Puritans, earlier and later. See also p. 46, line 6. SIR HENRY WOTTON works it in admirably in his famous hymn, "O Thou great Power!".

8. p. 43, line 4, 'Lynkes' = torches.

9. p. 44, line 11 : 'swashbucklers' = vain-glorious braggarts.

10. p. 45 : fine recognition of the silent out-flashing of the divinity of the Lord, and of the Lord's human sense of ignominy in being arrested as a 'thief' might be.

11. p. 47, line 8 : 'Jack-sawce'.

12. p. 38, line 4 : 'Anass' = an ass, not a bad pun in itself if it be somewhat misplaced. Line 12 fine.

13. p. 49, line 4, 'like a Prelate' : a memorable hit.

14. p. 50, line 4 : ' rake-hells ' : line 8, ' buffet' : line 11, ' dasht '.

15 p. 51, line 6 : a striking though perhaps conceitful delineation of the Saviour's eyes.

16, p. 52, line 3 : Christ's eyes omnipresen to Peter, very fine.

17. pp. 53-4 : The retrospective allusion to the Infant-slaying of Bethlehem, tender and beautiful.

18. p. 56, line 11 : ' tutch '.

19. p. 58, line 10 : ' Sir Pilate ' : line 14, ' seely ', and elsewhere.

20. p. 59, line 9, ' poast to the pillar ' : line 13, ' fran-tike '.

21. p. 61, line 3 : a Fullerian play on words.

22. p. 63, line 9, ' craking ' : line 11, ' pyper '.

23. p. 66, line 10, ' raught '.

24. p. 78, line 6 : · charyly '.

25. p. 79, line 4 : ' Lowt ' : *Scotice* ' loot ' or stoop : line 10, ' raynes '.

26. p. 81, line 11 : ' carefull ' : so elsewhere, = full of care.

27. p. 86, lines 6, 7, and elsewhere, a familiar use of ' alas '. See Glossary to our edition of DR. SIBBES.

28. p. 87, line 10 : copesmate = friend or associate.

29. p. 24, line 1 : ' purple-mantled *welkyn* ' : line 2, ' *parlor* pillers ' : line 14, ' meares '.

MISCELLANIES

OF

The Fuller Worthies' Library.

THE

POEMS

OF

JOHN NORRIS,

OF BEMERTON:

FOR THE

FIRST TIME COLLECTED AND EDITED

AFTER THE ORIGINAL TEXTS.

WITH

Memorial-Introduction and Notes.

BY THE

REV. ALEXANDER B. GROSART,

ST. GEORGE'S, BLACKBURN, LANCASHIRE.

PRINTED FOR PRIVATE CIRCULATION.

1871.

156 COPIES ONLY.

Contents.

150

Memorial-Introduction.

JOHN NORRIS.

BORN in 1657 at Collingbourne-Kingston, Wilts: his father clergyman of the parish. Historians of Wilts proud of the 'famous Mr. Norris.'

EDUCATED at Winchester School: Mr. Howard Staunton in his "Schools" of England has noted this.

'ENTERED' of Exeter College, Oxford, in 1676: 'sojourner' is Anthony-a-Wood's word in Athenæ.

PUBLISHED translation of "Effigies Amoris" in 1682: "Murnival of Knaves or Whiggism plainly display'd and burlesqu'd out of countenance" in 1683, and "Tractatus adversus Reprobationis absolutæ Decretum, novo Methodo et succentissimo compendio adornatus et in duos Libros digestus", 1683. On the last Wood wrote tartly, "Upon the first coming out of the said book, the author (a conceited youngster) was look'd upon as over pert, bold, and pragmatically daring to engage

in so profound a controversy, by publishing his
little and raw judgment concerning the said
decree." So written but suppressed by Bishop
Tanner. (See Bliss's edition of Athenæ, iv., 585.)

'COMMENCED' M.A. and elected 'Fellow' of
All Souls in 1680.

POEMS first published in 1684 with 'Idea of
Happiness' (originally issued in 1682-3) and
other of the after-'Miscellanies'.

RESIDENT in College in 'holy orders' five years.

'PRESENTED' to the Rectory of St. Loe in
Somersetshire, 1689.

TRANSFERRED in 1691 to the Rectory of BEMER-
TON, hallowed by saintly GEORGE HERBERT: a
tiny church that a hundred would crowd.

SOMEWHAT 'straitened' in circumstances: a
pathetic letter to Dr. Charlett reveals that £70
was the income of Bemerton, and also that the
Bishop of Salisbury (Burnet) was not 'friendly'
—on which more light is needed. (See Letters
written by eminent persons, 3 vols. 8vo, 1813,
and R. A. Wilmott's "Pictures of Christian
Life" (1841): c. vii., p. 119 et seqq.)

His religious and metaphysical writings composed and sent forth from Bemerton.

DIED 1711, 'aged 54', "having exhausted his
strength by intense application and long habits of

severe reasoning". So Wilmott, (as *supra*) and he adds, " On the south side of Bemerton Church a marble tablet commemorates his piety and his genius. The words of the epitaph are melancholy and appropriate—' *Bene latuit*. Here he lay, concealed from the pomp and vanity of life; here he sent up daily to the gate of heaven the music of a gentle and contented heart; here he wove those beautiful dreams of philosophy that seemed to recal not only the countenance, but the voice of Plato :

" The college boast, now turn'd the village guide."
(CRABBE's ' Borough '.)

That old and tranquil parsonage was to him a happy hiding-place."

Such were the (outward) facts in the life of the Recluse of Bemerton; and I have thus tabulated them summarily, because the purpose of our present little Introduction is literary rather than biographical, as being limited by what it introduces, to wit, his Verse. If his complete Works were collected and reproduced as the other Worthies of our Series have been, they would extend to more than the twenty volumes thus far issued. Hence his Poetry bears a very slender proportion to his entire Writings and still less to the object-matter of his most prolonged and deepest thought. The day will certainly come, and the man, that shall do long-deferred justice to the mystic-Platonists and Plotinists of the 17th century in England, including *the* JOHN SMITH of the vast family of John Smiths, RALPH CUDWORTH, BENJAMIN WHICHCOT, HENRY MORE, WIDRINGTON, WILKINS, and JOHN NORRIS ; and a foremost place must be assigned to the last as a penetrative and wise Thinker, who 'intermeddled' (a fine word from our English Bible) with intellectual and moral problems that are permanent as human, if I ought not to say divine, nature. An adequate Life and Exposition will there be in place and proportion as much as here they were out of place and proportion. It is humiliating that our English 'Histories of Philosophy' are serenely ignorant of one half of the richest and noblest thought clothed in the most charmingly coloured style, of our philosophic Literature. It is an opprobium that like the Alchemist 'searchers', the great, truly great and gracious Thinkers named—a few out of many—still await recognition and estimate worthy of them. With reference to NORRIS I do not say that his philosophy regarded broadly is sound. He drew too largely from MALEBRANCHE for that. I must admit too a certain haze (if it be golden

as a dawn among the mountains) lies over his
" Ideal World ". Nevertheless he did *think,* and
all genuine thinking deserves record. I suspect
also that his Sermons, by their very subtlety of
analysis as well as loveliness of wording and
tenderness of feeling, were lost on his rustic
auditory as ever were golden-mouthed JEREMY
TAYLOR's gorgeous eloquence on his Welsh hearers
Yet are they instinct with genius, fragrant with
the delicatest spice and ointment of the Temple,
and musical as is Apollo's lute. That his discourses on the " Beatitudes " of the " Sermon on
the Mount " had passed through fifteen *bond fide*
editions by 1728 is a noticeable thing in various
ways. These Sermons, and others, and his
" Essays " are radiant with beauty of fancy and
form. There are pages on pages that might be
set to music : or, it were more correct to say, set
themselves to music. His morality is deep and
pure. His ' Gospel ' rests on his Morality. No
more than the Master does he know ' *conversion* '
that is unevidenced by inward and outward
whiteness. If in the knowledge of his volumi-
nousness one can't help smiling at the close of
his Epistle to the Reader prefixed to the
" Miscellanies " of which the Poems formed a

part, one must also allow that he does ' *abound in sense* '.

But I must not allow myself to be tempted into further criticism of either his Life or other Writings in the present Introduction. I turn therefore now to the Poetry herein revived, in order to guide my Readers to look at it in itself and in relation to other Singers. I suspect very few are aware of the ' plunder' of our Poet by far inferior though more blazoned names : and it is due to him to establish this. Equally few, I fear, know the intrinsic worth and perfectness in almost every respect, of certain of these poems. Perchance our reprint may recal attention. I wish the Archbishop of Dublin had spared a page in his " Household Book of English Poetry " for the lines "On seeing a great person lying in state," which is worthy of Cowley in his happiest mood and incomparably beyond others that have found a place. I shall hope that a new edition of his Grace's book will accept our suggestion, and also insert the " Choice " and " My Estate."

I know not that I can better present the main notable thing about our Worthy's poetry than by transferring here our own paper in Notes and Queries (4th Series : IV. July 10th, 1869.) It is as follows :

158

"Every one knows how chagrined the poet of the "Pleasures of Hope" was on discovering that his striking simile in the couplet—

"What though my wingèd hours of bliss have been
Like angel visits, few and far between."

had been anticipated by his fellow-countryman in his well-known poem of "The Grave", in one of its *bits* that won't willingly be let die :—

"Alas! too well he sped! the good he scorn'd
Stalked off reluctant, like an ill-used ghost,
Not to return; or if it did, its *visits*
Like those of angels, short and far between."

It must be conceded, I think, that the earlier "short" is much preferable to the somewhat tautological "few", of the later poet. But has it been pointed out anywhere that JOHN NORRIS of Bemerton—well-nigh a quarter of a century before BLAIR was born—has given the felicitous simile with even nicer felicity? It occurs in his pathetic little "Parting", as follows :—

"How fading are the joys we dote upon,
Like apparitions seen and gone;
But those which soonest take their flight,
Are the most exquisite and strong.
Like angels' visits, short and bright;
Mortality's too weak to bear them long."

159

The idea, like another to be noticed immediately, seems to have been a favourite one ; for it is thus repeated in his " Lines to the memory of my dear Neece, M. C."

> " No wonder such a noble mind
> Her way again to Heaven so soon could find.
> *Angels, as 'tis but seldom they appear,*
> *So neither do they make long stay,*
> *They do but visit, and away.*
> *'Tis pain for them t' endure our too gross sphere.*
> We could not hope for a reprieve,
> She must dye soon, that made such haste to live."

I have a dim remembrance of having seen the former noted ; but Mr. Farrar, in his preface to a beautiful edition of " The Grave " (1858, 4o) is silent about both ; and as he specially singles out Blair's lines as " exquisite ", and in context, as supremely original, must have been unaware of NORRIS though referring to CAMPBELL.

That Norris was the source whence Blair fetched his simile, there can be no doubt. As I would now proceed to show, he has taken other of the *memorabilia* of " The Grave " from the same volume of " Miscellanies ". Few who have studied the poem forget the wistful inquiry of these Shakesperean lines :—

" Tell us, ye dead! will none of you in pity
To those you left behind, declare the secret ?
Oh! that some courteous ghost would blab it out!
What 'tis you are, and we must shortly be."

Norris has over and over, the same passionate
yearning and interrogation, while ' ghost' is a
very frequent word with him ; *e.g.* in his ' Meditation' you have this :

" *Some courteous ghost, tell this great secrecy*
  What 'tis you are, and we must be.
You warn us of approaching death, and why
May we not know from you what 'tis to dye ?
But you, having shot the gulph, delight to see
Succeeding souls plunge in with like uncertainty."

Here thinking and wording precede Blair.
Again :—

         " Act like a pious *courteous ghost,*
         And to mankind retrieve what's lost."

Then there are the remarkable, the very remarkable poems entitled "The Impatient" and
"Superstition "—than which there are few finer
things, in their immense longing and sorrow and
baffled speculation and appeal. But this is not
all. Here is another firm-lined and often-quoted
passage in " The Grave " :—

" Sure ! 'tis a serious thing to die ! my soul
What a strange moment must it be, when near
Thy journey's end, *thou hast the gulf in view !*
That awful gulf no mortal e'er re-passed,
To tell what's doing on the other side !
Nature runs back, and shudders at the sight ! "

Grander, because deeper and simpler, and not so
exclamatory, is Norris, twice-over, in " The Prospect ", and in the already cited " Meditation ": —

" *What a strange moment will that be,*
My soul, how full of curiosity,
When wing'd, and ready for thy eternal flight
On th' utmost edges of thy tottering clay,
    Hovering and wishing longer stay
Thou shalt advance and have eternity in sight !
When just about to try that unknown sea,
    What a strange moment will that be ! "

Now from " The Meditation ", which with " The
Impatient " I wish I could find space for in
full : —

" When Life's close knot by writ from destiny
    Disease shall cut or Age unty ;
When after some delays, some dying strife,
The soul stands shivering on the ridge of life :
With what a dreadful curiosity
Does she launch out into the sea of vast eternity."

So too in his " Wish " :—

162

" Death, that amazing curiosity ".

There are a number of lesser traces of Blair's reading of Norris; but these meantime may suffice. My copy of the *Miscellanies* is of the " fifth edition, carefully revised, corrected, and improved by the author ". The date is 1710, but that " to the Reader " is " June 1st, 1678 " [misprint for 1687]. " The Grave " was first published in 1743, I think. I would add that probably Campbell drew his simile of " angel-visits " from Norris rather than Blair, seeing that the opening of the " Pleasures of Hope " is only an echo of Norris in his " Infidel ". Here are both. First Campbell:—

" Why to yon mountain turns the musing eye,
Whose sunbright summit mingles with the sky ?
Why do those cliffs of shadowy tint appear
More sweet than all the landscape smiling near ?
'Tis distance lends enchantment to the view,
And robes the mountain in its azure hue."

Now Norris:—

" Thou mystery of fallacies !
  Distance presents the object fair,
With charming features and a graceful air.
But when we come to seize th' inviting prey,
Like a shy ghost, it vanishes away."

Without indulging in charges of plagiarism, where

the appropriations may have been tricks cozening the brain that the treasure was its own, not memory's, I feel sure that to all interested in our national poetry these details will be acceptable. It is a curious study to follow back the "familiar words" that are on all our lips. Much more frequently than is supposed, the consummate ultimate form has been the outcome of a long process and of many workers."[1]

Of the additional and equally unacknowledged indebtedness to Norris by BLAIR referred to in our preceding communication to "Notes and Queries" it may be as well to record three. Thus in "My Estate"—of which more anon—we read :

> " While you a spot of earth possess with care
> *Below the notice of the geographer......*"

This reappears in " The Grave " as,

> ...."The petty tyrant
> Whose scanty domains geographer ne'er noticed."

Again : in the finely-touched lines on " Seeing a great person lying in state " we have this :

> "I knew indeed before,
> That 'twas the great man's wretched fate,

---

[1] Pp. 28-29.

While with the living to endure
The vain impertinence of State ;
But sure, thought I, in death he'll be
From that and other troubles free :
What e'er his life, he then will bee
As free, as undisturb'd, as calm as I."

Compare in " The Grave " :

" Proud lineage now how little thou appearest
Below the envy of the private man.
Honour that meddlesome officious ill
Pursues thee even, nor there stops short.
Strange persecution when the grave itself
Is no protection from rude sufferance."

Once more, in " The Prospect " Norris has this :

" There with bright splendours must thou dwell,
And be—*what only those pure forms can tell.*"

Blair follows this almost literally in his Lines in
memory of LAW :

" *Now midst seraphic splendors shalt thou dwell
And be what only those pure forms can tell.*"

Even to our Worthy's eccentric use of words is
the later Poet a copyist, *e.g.* in " The Grave "
Friendship is called the "mysterious *cement* of the
soul" as music had been in the Verses " On a
Musician, supposed to be mad with music " :

165

> " Music, thou generous ferment of the soul,
> Thou universal *cement* of the whole."

So too Norris applies with quaint appropriateness
the adjective " sooty " to the wings of Night:
Blair to the ' Blackbird '.   Probably this will
suffice, and I fear that what with " The Grave's "
obligations to Norris and to HENRY MORE and
OLDHAM, and POPE, and QUARLES and others, his
supposed originality is no longer to be maintained.[1]
It is to be lamented that the Author did not in
some way indicate what he owed to others.
Larceny of this sort has an ugly look, all the more
that while there is all Milton's audacity of
' spoiling ', there is little or nothing of his splendid
transfiguration of whatever he takes.

Returning on " My Estate ", there occurs in
this poem a stanza that probably caught Wordsworth's eye.   Here it is :

> " Nay—what you'd think less likely to be true—
> I can enjoy what's your's much more than you.

---

[1] The Reader will do well to consult N. and Q. (4th S.
iv.; August 7th, 1869) for a paper in relation to mine from
Mr. W. B. Cook of Kelso, who draws further 'imitations'
from " Remarks " prefixed to an edition of Blair's Poems
published in 1805.   Dr. Charles Mackay in his short-lived
periodical " Robin Goodfellow " had also pointed out some
of the thefts from Norris.

Your meadow's beauty I survey,
Which you prize only for its hay.
There can I sit beneath a tree
And make an ode or elegy.
What to you care, does to me pleasure bring,
You own the cage, I in it sit and sing."

This recalls " Peter Bell " :

" A primrose by the river's brim
A yellow primrose was to him
And it was nothing more."[1]

Finer than Norris's ground-sentiment, however, is THOMAS RANDOLPH in his " Ode to Mr. ANTHONY STAFFORD to hasten him into the country " as follows :

. . . . " Where every word is thought and every thought
    is pure.
        Ours is the skie,
Whereat what fowl we please our hawk shall flye ;
        Nor will we spare
To hunt the crafty fox or timorous hare ;
        But let our hounds run loose
        In any ground they'l choose:
        The buck shall fall,
        The stag and all :
Our pleasures must from their own warrants be,

---

[1] I must cry *peccavi* for having dropped 'yellow' in my quotation of this in Essay on Henry Vaughan.

> For to my muse, if not to mee,
> I'me sure all game is free ;
> Heaven, Earth, are all but parts of her great royalty."[1]

THOMSON must have had this ringing through his memory when he wrote his famous apostrophe in the " Castle of Indolence " commencing " I care not Fortune what you me deny."

I have marked in its place one line from GRAY'S " Elegy " that might have been remembered from NORRIS. WILMOTT (as before) has pointed out another from one of his Sermons. Says he, " In the following passage we recognize the original of a very celebrated line in the Spleen, which Gray transferred into one of his own poems. " God " says Norris, " spake to man within, and he speaks to him without ; within, by the dictates of reason, by the light of inward truth, and by the secret whispers of his Spirit : without, by the visible frame and order of the creation ; wherein not only the heavens declare the glory of God, and the firmament shows his handy-work, but *even the meanest insect reads him a lecture of divinity, and preaches to him a sermon of adoration and devotion.*" Gray's line is :

> " *And insects from the threshold preach.*"

---

[1] Poems 1643, pp. 62-3.

We have in Norris also the idea of Gray's famous couplet :

> " Where ignorance is bliss,
> 'Tis folly to be wise."

in the lines " Against Knowledge " :

> " Since all's so false and vain below
> *There's nought so indiscreet as this, to know.*"

BURNS' renowned watchword,

> The rank is but the guinea's stamp,
> The man's the gowd for a' that."

was proclaimed faintlier in " My Estate " :

> " None of Fortune's blessings can
> Add any value to the man."

Even BYRON may have chanced on this in the "Irreconcilable" in his terrible demand of *"hate"* not love :

> " The way that's left you to befriend my fate
> *Is now to prove more constant in your hate.*"

Nor am I without a feeling that COLLINS earlier and SHELLEY and POE later kept the " Miscellanies " of our Recluse in recollection.

And now I cannot imagine one reading the poems that have come under our notice and

c 169

illustration, without being arrested : and there are others not inferior. The " Complaint of Adam turned out of Paradice " has things in it that are not unworthy of " Paradise Lost " itself, as the appeal to the angel :

> " Stay thou bright minister, one minute stay,
> Let me in Eden take one farewell round.
> *Let me go gather but one fragrant bough*
> Which as a relique I may keep and shew :
> Fear not the tree of life ; it were
> A curse to be immortal and not here. ''

The Hymns to " Sleep " and " Darkness " are curiously original and unforgetable. The " Infidel " repeatedly mentioned, in its second stanza has seed that has fructified in many later Poets and Preachers. Surely this is fine and finely put :

> " So to th' unthinking boy the distant sky
> Seems on some mountain's surface to rely ;
> He with ambitious haste climbs the ascent,
>   Curious to touch the firmament :
>   But when with an unweary'd pace
> Arriv'd he is at the long-wish'd for place,
> With sighs the sad defeat he does deplore,
> His Heaven is still as distant as before."

It may here be allowed me to record a child-story confirmatory, or at least illustrative of the last quotation. Three small boys of the respective ages of six, five, and four were overheard conversing about Heaven. How the little philosophers were led to it I know not, but certes they probed in their unconscious trueness some of the deepest things. At last the younger said to the elder (not the eldest) 'But Willie, how shall we get up to Heaven, when we die?' Quick as lightning replied the second with grave old-man face, ' Oh! I know how I shall get up—I will wait till the sun is low-low-low in the sky, and then I'll jump up and ride to heaven in the sun ': and so the problem was triumphantly solved, with the addition that papa and mama and all were also to jump up. The combined splendour and grotesqueness of the conception struck me, and may perchance my Readers.

Taken altogether it can't surely be held super-erogatory to revive Poems that are in themselves intrinsically noticeable, and that have quickened Singers such as have been named. The form, spurious-Pindaric, after Cowley—may not be all we would wish : but poetic thought and imagination are there and occasionally real bird-like notes.

The Poems of Norris as stated in the outset appeared originally in 1684 along with a second

171

edition of the " Idea of Happiness " and other Essays. This little volume contained only about a dozen of the after-collections, so much so that the Author did not reckon it an edition at all in his counting. It has two Latin pieces on the Duke of York and an " Atlas "—subsequently withdrawn and certainly neither deserving restoration. The volume has a daintily-worded Epistle to a lady-friend. A new and enlarged edition appeared in 1687 with a new epistle-dedicatory : another in 1692 : another in 1706 with the Preface mis-dated 1678 : another in 1710 : and so on to the 9th (really the 10th) in 1730—all having the Prose ' Miscellanies ' as the second and larger division of the volume. Our text is that of 1710 as having been the last issued during Norris's own life : but certain errors have been corrected by the preceding edition of 1706. We have reprinted the whole with our usual fidelity : but have greatly modified the capitals and italics, supposed, like feminine underlineations, to give emphasis, whereas they only confuse and deform. We have filled in references and slightly annotated with parallels from other poets probably known to Norris.

ALEXANDER B. GROSART.

Note.

Below is the title-page of the last edition published during his own life of the Volume whence we take Norris's Poetry, and which is our text. See our Intro-duction for details of the different editions. G.

A

COLLECTION

OF

Miscellanies:

Consisting of

POEMS, ESSAYS, DIS-
COURSES, & LETTERS,

Occasionally Written.

By *JOHN NORRIS*, Rector of *Bemerton*
near *Sarum*.

———*Diram qui contudit* Hydram.
Notaque Fatali *portenta labore subegit,*
Comperit Invidiam *supremo fine domari.*
Hor. Epist. Lib. 2. Epist. 1.

The Fifth Edition, carefully Revised, Corrected,
and Improved by the Authour.

LONDON:

Printed for *Samuel Manship*, at the *Ship* against the
Royal Exchange in *Cornhill*. 1710. [8vo.]

ADVERTISEMENT FROM THE AUTHOUR TO THE READER.

S it cannot be thought strange, that having by this edition an opportunity of revising this Book, I should comply with it: so neither can it, that when I did so, I should find many things in it—being a juvenile composition—which my now riper, and as I presume better judgment, cannot so well approve of. I have indeed found many things that were not as they should be ; some as to notion, some as to fact, and some as to manner of expression ; and accordingly what I have observ'd of this kind, at least in the most considerable instances, I have endeavour'd to rectifie, leaving out what was incorrigible, and making some improvements up and down as occasion offered. And tho' I cannot say it is now so correct as if it were the present production of my pen, yet I think it is indifferently[1] so. And accordingly, this edition is the edition which I would commend to Posterity, not owning

---

[1] = passably or tolerably.   G.

the former, any further than they agree with this.
In like manner as St. Austin says of his imperfect Book upon Genesis, written when he was
young, which he would have measured by what
he wrote afterwards upon the same subject, when
he was a bishop : *Breviter admoneo ut illi duodecem
libri legantur, quos longe postea Episcopus feci, et
ex ipsis de isto judicetur*.[1] The same with due
accommodation say I here, designing as I have
opportunity, to revise my other writings, and to
correct what is amiss in them. In the mean
while, all that I have further to say upon this
occasion is, that if there be any thing in the verse
part, that shall appear offensive in the strictness
of notion, as perhaps there may, this line in particular,

> But sure he coveted to have thee there.

I would not have it taken as offered for theological
or phylosophic truth, but only as a stroke of
poetry, which with equitable Readers, I hope will
find allowance,

---

[1] Augustini Retractationes, i. 18. G.

TO THE READER.

F all the tedious things in the world, I was ever the least friend to long Prefaces; and therefore I shall only commend to your hands this collection of Miscellanies, occasionally composed at several times, as my humour and leisure serv'd me, with a brief account of my design, as to both parts of the Collection.

Not to trouble you with a pompous discourse of the nature of Poetry, its measures of criticism, its variety, antiquity, its great use and excellence, and the like, which have been at large set forth by many curious pens, I have only leisure at present to observe that Poetry is of late mightily fall'n from the beauty of its idea, and from its ancient majesty and grandeur, as well as credit and reputation.

It may appear strange indeed, that in such a refining age as this, wherein all things seem ready to receive their last turn and finishing stroke, Poetry should be the only thing that remains

unimprov'd. And yet so it happens, that which
we generally have now a-days, is no more like
the thing it was formerly, than Modern Religion
is like Primitive Christianity.

'Tis with this as with our Musick. From grave,
majestic, solemn strains, where deep instructive
sense is sweetly convey'd in charming numbers,
where equal address is made to the judgment and
the imagination, and where beauty and strength
go hand in hand, 'tis now for the most part dwin-
dled down to light, frothy stuff, consisting either
of mad extravagant rants, or slight witticisms,
and little amorous conceits, fit only for a tavern
entertainment; and that too among Readers of a
Dutch palate.

The truth is, this most excellent and divine
art has of late been so cheapned and depretiated
by the bungling performance of some who
thought themselves inspired, and whose Readers
too have been more kind to them than their
planets, that Poetry is almost grown out of repute,
and men come strongly prejudiced against any
thing of this kind, as expecting nothing but froth
and emptiness : and to be a poet, goes for little
more than a country fidler.

But certainly he had once another character,

and that in as nice and wise an age as this.   If we may believe the great HORACE he was one,

> .... *Cui mens divinior atque os*
> *Magna sonaturum* .... [1]

He had then his temple surrounded with a divine glory, spoke like the oracle of the God of Wisdom, and could describe no hero greater than himself. Poetry was once the mistress of all the arts in the circle, that which held the reins of the world in her hand, and which gave the first, and—if we may judge by the effects—perhaps the best institutes for the moralizing and governing the passions of mankind.

The design therefore of the present undertaking is to restore the declining genius of Poetry to its primitive and genuine greatness, to wind up the strings of the Muses' lyre, and to shew that sense and gracefulness are as consistent in these as in any other compositions.   I design here all the masculine sense and argument of a dissertation, with the advantage of poetic fineness, beauty and spirit; and accordingly I have made choice for the most part of divine and moral subjects; and if

---

[1] Satires, i., 4, lines 43-4: for 'sonaturum' NORRIS misreads 'locuturum': corrected *supra*.   G.

I meddle with any other sort, I commonly turn the stream another way, as particularly in those two poems call'd Beauty and Love, which I have rescued from those sordid abuses they have hitherto suffer'd.

I confess 'tis a difficult province to make substantial massy sense yield to the softness of Poetry; and accordingly we find there are few poems after the divine and moral way, but what are stiff, flat, and insipid; but without this mixture, Poetry is nothing worth; and when it has it, it has all it can have, and is withal so divine a thing, that even PLATO I fancy, would give it entertainment in his Common-wealth.

I need not make any other apology for my conversing with the Muses; for I do not think it an employment beneath the character of a scholar; and though I have, in a manner, now set up my outmost pillar, yet I can't find in my heart to repent me of those few blank hours bestow'd in this exercise. For I have the example of some of the greatest and wisest in all ages to warrant me, and the greatness of SOLOMON is seen as much in his divine pastoral, the Canticles, as in his Proverbs or sermons; and the wise BEN-SIRACH, among other characters of his heroes, puts in this among the rest, that they were such as found out musical tunes, and recited verses in writing, *Eccl.* 44. 5.

And thus much for the verse part. Concerning the Essays and Discourses, I have only this to say, that I design'd in them as much brevity and clearness as are consistent with each other, and to abound in sense rather than in words : I wish all men would observe this in their writings more than they do. I'm sure the multitude of books and the shortness of life require it ; and sense will lye in a little compass, if men would be perswaded to vent no notions but what they are masters of ; and were angels to write, I fancy we should have but few folio's.

This is what I design'd and endeavour'd in the whole. Whether I have attain'd it or no, I submit to the judgment of the candid and indifferent[1] Reader.

J. NORRIS.

All Souls Coll.
    June 1, 1687.

---

[1] = impartial or unprejudiced. G.

THE PASSION OF OUR BLESSED SAVIOUR,
REPRESENTED IN A PINDARIQUE ODE.

....Quis talia fando
Temperet a lachrymis?[1] ....

AY bold licentious[2] Muse,
    What noble subject wilt thou chuse;
Of what great hero, of what mighty
      thing,
Wilt thou in boundless numbers sing ?
Sing the unfathom'd depths of Love,
—For who the wonders done by Love can tell,
By Love, which is it self all miracle ?—
Here in vast endless circles may'st thou rove ;
And like the travelling planet of the day
    In an orb unbounded stray.
Sing the great miracle of Love divine,
Great be thy genius, sparkling every line,
    Love's greatest mystery rehearse :
      Greater then[3] that,

---

[1] Virgil, Aeneid ii. 6, 8. G.   [2] = unrestrained. G.

[3] = than. G.

Which on the teeming chaos brooding sate,
And hatch'd with kindly heat the Universe.
How God in mercy chose to bleed, and dye,
    To rescue man from misery :
Man, not His creature only, but His enemy.

Lo, in Gethsemane, I see Him prostrate lye,
Press'd with the weight of His great agony.
    The common sluces of the eyes
To vent His mighty Passion won't suffice,
    His tortured body weeps all-o're,
        And out of every pore
Buds forth a precious gem of purple gore.[1]
How strange the power of Affliction's rod
When in the hand of an incensèd God !
    Like the commanding wand
        In Moses's hand,[2]
It works a miracle, and turns the flood
    Of tears into a sea of blood.
See with what pomp Sorrow does now appear !
How proud she is of being seated here !
    She never wore
    So rich a dye before.
    Long was He willing to decline

---

[1] So in the Passion of the Virgin Mother, " deck'd with
gems of purple gore." **G.**
[2] Exodus iv. 20. *et alibi.* **G.**

Th' encounter of the wrath divine.
   Thrice He sent for His release
  Pathetick embassies of peace :
At length, His courage overcame His doubt,
Resolv'd He was, and so the bloody flag hung
    out.[1]

And now the tragic scene's display'd,
Where drawn in full battalia are laid
    Before His eyes,
  That numerous host of miseries
  He must withstand, that map of woe
    Which He must undergo.
That heavy wine-press which must by Him be
    trod,
  The whole artillery of God.
  He saw that face, whose very sight
Chears angels with its beatific light,
Contracted now into a dreadful frown,
   All cloath'd with thunder, big with death
   And showers of hot burning wrath,
  Which shortly must be pourèd down.
  He saw a black and dismal scroll,
  Of sins past, present, and to come,
  With their intolerable doom

---

[1] St. Matthew xxvi. 39.   G.

Which would the more oppress His spotless soul;
  As th' elements are weighty proved,
When from their native station they'r removed.
He saw the foul ingratitude of those,
  Who would the labours of His love oppose;
And reap no benefit by all His agonies.
    He saw all this,
And as He saw, to waver He began,
And almost to repent of His great love for man.

When lo, a heavenly form all bright and fair,
Swifter than thought, shot through th' enlighten'd
    air.
    He who sat next th'imperial throne,
And read the counsels of the Great Three-One,
Who in eternity's mysterious glass,
Saw both what was, what is, and what must come
      to pass;
    He came with reverence profound,
And rais'd his prostrate Maker from the ground;
      Wiped off the bloody sweat
With which His face and garments too were wet:
And comforted His dark benighted mind,
With sovereign cordials of light refin'd.
This done, in soft addresses he began
To fortifie His kind designs for man:
Unseal'd to Him the Book of God's decree,

And shew'd Him what must be :
Alleg'd the truth of prophesies,
    Types, figures, and mysteries ;
How needful it was to supply,
With humane race, the ruins of the sky.
    How this would new accession bring
      To the celestial quire ;
And how withall, it would inspire
New matter for the praise of the great King.
How He should see the travail of His soul, and
    bless
Those sufferings, which had so good success.
How great the triumphs of His victory,
    How glorious His ascent would be,
What weighty bliss in Heaven He should obtain
    By a few hours of pain ;
Where to eternal ages He should reign.
He spake : confirm'd in mind the champion stood;
    A spirit divine
Through the thick veil of flesh did shine :
All-over powerful He was, all-over good.
    Pleas'd with his successful flight,
The officious[1] angel posts away
To the bright regions of eternal day ;
    Departing in a track of light.

---

[1] = doing kind offices. G

In haste for news, the heavenly people ran,
And joy'd to hear the hopeful state of man.

And now that strange prodigious hour,
When God must subject be to humane power ;
    That hour is come,
    Th' unerring clock of Fate has struck ;
'Twas heard below down to Hell's lowest room,
And straight th' infernal powers th' appointed
    signal took.
    Open the scene, my Muse, and see
Wonders of impudence and villany ;
    How wicked mercenary hands,
Dare to invade Him whom they should adore ;
With swords and staves, encompass'd round He
    stands,
Who knew no other guards but those of Heaven
    before.
Once with His powerful breath, He did repell
    The rude assaults of Hell.
    A ray of His divinity
Shot forth with that bold answer, ' *I am He* ' :
They reel and stagger, and fall to the ground ;[1]
    For God was in the sound.

---

[1] St. John xviii. 6 : cf. Fraunce's ' Emanuell ' in our
Miscellanies *in loco*. G.

The Voice of God was once again,
    Walking in the Garden, heard :[1]
And once again, was by the guilty hearers fear'd :
Trembling seiz'd every joint, and chilness every
    vein.
    This little Victory He won,
      Shew'd what He could have done.
But He to whom as chief was given,
The whole militia of Heaven,
      That mighty He,
Declines all guards for His defence,
But that of His inseparable innocence ;
And quietly gives up His liberty.
He's seiz'd on by the military bands,
    With cords they bind His sacred hands :
But ah! how weak, what nothings would they
    prove,
Were He not held by stronger ones of Love.

Once more, my weary d Muse, thy pinions try,
    And reach the top of Calvary.
A steep ascent : but most to Him Who bore
The burthen of a cross this way before.
—The cross ascends, there's something in it sure
    That moral is and mystical ;

---

[1] Genesis iii., 8.   G.

No heights of Fortune are from thee secure,
Afflictions sometimes climb as well as fall—
   Here breathe a while, and view
The dolefull'st picture Sorrow ever drew:
   The Lord of Life, Heaven's darling Son,
     The great, th' Almighty One,
With out-stretch'd arms, nail'd to a cursèd tree,
Crown'd with sharp thorns, cover'd with infamy:
     He Who before
   So many miracles had done,
   The lives of others to restore,
   Does with a greater, lose His Own.
Full three long hours His tender body did sustain,
   Most exquisite and poignant pain.
So long the sympathising sun his light withdrew,
And wonder'd how the stars their dying Lord
   could view.

   This strange defect of light,
Does all the sages in Astronomy affright,
   With fears of an eternal night.
Th' intelligences in their courses stray,
And travellers below mistake their way;
Wond'ring to be benighted in the midst of day.
Each mind is seiz'd with horror and despair,
And more o'respread with darkness than the air.
   Fear on, 'tis wondrous all, and new;

'Tis what past ages never knew,
Fear on, but yet you'll find,
The great eclipse is still behind.
The lustre of the Face divine,
Does on the mighty Sufferer no longer shine.
God hides His glories from His sight,
With a thick skreen made of Hell's grossest night.
Close-wrought it was, and solid, all
Compacted and substantial;
Impenetrable to the beatifick light.
Without complaint, He bore
The tortures He endur'd before;
But now, no longer able to contain,
Under the great hyperbole of pain,
He mourns, and with a strong pathetic cry,
Laments the sad desertion of the Deity.
Here stop, my Muse, stop and admire,
The breather of all life does now expire:
His milder Father summons Him away;
His breath obediently He does resign:
Angels to Paradise His soul convey;
And calm the relicts of His grief with hymns
divine.

ANNOTATIONS.

THIS ode is after the Pindarick way; which is the highest and most magnificent kind of writing in verse; and consequently fit only for great and noble subjects; such as are as boundless as its own numbers: the nature of which is to be loose and free; and not to keep one settled pace: but sometimes like a gentle stream, to glide along peaceably within its own channel; and sometimes, like an impetuous torrent, to roll on extravagantly, and carry all before it. Agreeable to that description of Horace:[1]

> Nunc pace delabentis Etruscum
> In mare, nunc lapides adesos,
> Stirpesque raptas et pecus et domos
> Volventis una non sine montium,
> Clamore vicinæque sylvæ.

And this may serve to explain the introduction of the poem:

> 'And hatch'd with kindly heat the Universe.'

Love in the Gentile theology, as a certain writer observes, is made the most antient of the Gods,

---

[1] Carm. iii. 29: lines 35-39: for 'nunc' read 'cum' and for 'Hetruscum' as printed by Norris, 'Etruscum' is substituted: the 'H' is noticeable. G.

and the sire of all things. Agreeably to what
Plutarch, as he says tells us, that for this reason
Hesiod made Love the most antient of the gods,
ἵνα πάντα δἰ ἐκεῖνον μετασχῇ γενέσεως.[1] And it is
described he says, by SIMMIAS RHODIUS,[2] in a pair of
wings, which suited well with the symbolical representation of the chaos by an egg, which was brooded
and hatch'd under these wings of Love. To which
also ARISTOPHANES,[3] as he notes, in some measure
alludes in his cosmogony. The plain and un-
disguised meaning of all which is this, That the
creation of the world was the effect of the divine
love. The end which God had in it being not the
acquisition of any good to Himself, but only the
communication of His own goodness and happiness. According to that of St. Austin, *Quæ non
ex indigentiâ fecisti, sed ex plenitudine bonitatis
tuæ.* [*Confess.* lib. 13. c. 4.]

> 'As th' elements are weighty proved,
> When from their native station they're removed.'

This is according to the Aristotelean hypothesis,
that the elements are not heavy in their own
places; which, whether it be true or no, I shall

---

[1] Plutarch (*Amator*. xiii. 12.) : Hesiod. Theog. 120. **G.**
[2] In a little poem called πτερύγιον· **G.**
[3] Aristophanes, *Aves*, 693-97. **G.**

not now dispute. However, it serves for an illustration, which is sufficient for my present purpose.

'He saw the foul ingratitude of those,' &c.

The bitter ingredients of our Lord's cup mention'd hitherto, were taken from things relating to His Own personal concern. But this last motive of His sorrow proceeds wholly on behalf of others; of whose final impenitence He is suppos'd to have a foresight. This I take to be a good and proper insinuation of the excellency of our blessed Lord's temper, His exceeding great love and philanthropy, when among the other ingredients of His passion this is supposed to be one, that there would be some, who, by their own default would receive no benefit from it.

'Unseal'd to Him the Book of God's decree, &c.

Whether the angel used these topicks of consolation or no, is a thing as indifferent to my purpose, as 'tis uncertain. In the Scripture it is only said in general, 'that there appear'd an angel from Heaven strengthning Him.'[1] However these arguments are such as are probable and pertinent; and that's sufficient.

---

[1] St. Luke xxii. 43.   G,

'In haste for news the heavenly people ran,
And joy'd to hear the hopeful state of man'.

It is highly reasonable to believe, that those blessed and excellent spirits, who out of their compassionate love and concern for mankind, usher'd in the news of our Saviour's nativity, with anthems of praise and thanksgiving; and are said likewise to rejoyce at the conversion of a sinner, were also mightily transported with joy, when they understood that our Saviour, notwithstanding the reluctancy of innocent nature, was at length fully resolv'd to undertake the price of our Redemption.

'Full three long hours his tender body did sustain,
Most exquisite and poignant pain.'

It is observed to have been the opinion of the antient Fathers, that the sufferings which our blessed Saviour underwent in His body, were more afflictive to Him than the same would have been to another man, upon the account of the excellency and quickness of His sense of feeling : and this opinion I take to be as reasonable, as 'tis pious. For since, according to the principles of Philosophy, the sense of feeling arises from the proportion of the first qualities, it follows that the better the complexion or temperament of any man is, the better his feeling must needs be. Now 'tis very reasonable to believe, that that man who was to be substantially united to the Godhead, and who was begotten by the miraculous over-shadowings of the Holy Spirit, should have a body endow'd with the best complexion, and most noble harmony of qualities that could be, that so it might be a suitable organ for His excellent soul. And if so, then it follows, that the flesh of our Lord's body was so soft and tender, and His feeling so exquisitely quick and sensible, as never any man's was before : and consequently, the severe usages which He underwent, not only at His Passion, but throughout His whole life, must needs be in a singular manner afflictive to Him. And hence appears the vanity of their opinion, who are little or nothing affected with the consideration of our Lord's Passion, because they think it was made light to Him, by reason of His union with the Godhead. 'Twas easie for Him—some inconsiderate persons are ready to say —to suffer this or this; for He was God, and not meer man, as we are. True, He was so; but His being God, did no way lessen the punishment He underwent as man, but only supported Him in His existence under it, in the same manner as God is supposed, by an act of His Almighty power, to preserve the bodies of the damn'd, incorruptible among the everlasting burnings. But this I think is no kindness to them. Neither did the society of the divine Nature any more diminish the sufferings of our dearest Lord ; nay, in one respect, it prov'd an accidental aggravation to them, because upon the account of this noble union, He had given Him a body of a most admirable complexion and harmonious temperature, and consequently of a flesh exceeding tender, and most exquisitely perceptive of the least impressions.

' So long the sympathizing sun his light withdrew,
And wonder'd how the stars their dying Lord could view.

The eclipse which accompany'd the Passion of our Saviour was so remarkable and miraculous, that 'twas taken notice of by the Gentile historians. There are three things which made this eclipse so very remarkable ; the time of its appearance, the time of its duration, and the degree of it. 1. For the time of its appearance, it was at full moon, when the moon was not in conjunction with, but in opposition to the sun. And this appears not only from the testimony of Dionysius, who is observ'd to affirm that he saw it at that time, but also from the time of our Lord's Passion, which, according to the relation of the Evangelist, was

197

at the celebration of the Passover. Now the Jews
were bound to celebrate the Paschal solemnity
always at full moon ; as is to be seen in the
twelfth of Exodus. This was no time therefore
for a natural eclipse, because 'twas impossible
that the moon should then interpose betwixt us
and the sun. 2. For the time of its duration, it
was full three hours : which is another evidence
that this was no natural eclipse : For the natural
eclipse of the sun can never last so long, both
because of the great disproportion between the
sun's magnitude, and that of the moon, and because of the swift motion of the latter. 3. For
the degree of it, it was a total eclipse. The sun
was so darkened, that—as an eminent Historian
is said to report, writing of the eclipse—the stars
appear'd. And that is another argument that it
was no natural phœnomenon, it being impossible
that the body of the moon, which is so infinitely
less than that of the sun, should totally eclipse it.
Now all these three remarkables are comprised in
the compass of these two verses. For in that it
is said that the ' sun withdrew his light ' it is
intimated that the light of the sun was not inter-
cepted by the ordinary conjunction of the moon,
but that by an extraordinary commission from the

God of Nature, the sun reign'd[1] in his light, and suspended the emission of his beams. And this denotes the time of its appearance, viz. when the moon was not in conjunction. The time of its duration is implied by the words, ' So long.' And lastly, the degree of it is implied in the last verse, where the appearance of the stars is not directly expressed, but only insinuated and couch'd, for the more elegancy of the thought.

' And calm the relicts of His grief with hymns divine.'

It is here supposed, that the passion of our Saviour was now over, and His Father's wrath fully appeased. For whatever becomes of the doctrine of Christ's local descent into Hell, concerning which I am not minded at present to move any dispute, I cannot think that He went thither, there to suffer any torment or punishment. His own words upon the cross ' *It is finish'd* ', do apparently contradict it. But yet, though the bitter cup was wholly drunk off upon the cross, 'tis natural to imagine some little relish[1] of it to remain behind for a time. Though all His sufferings and penal inflictions were ended before His death, yet, I suppose—and I think very naturally—some

---

[1] = reined. G.   [2] = taste. G.

little discomposures of mind, remaining like the
after-droppings of a shower, which His soul could
not immediately shake off, upon her release from
the body. In allusion to that of VIRGIL :

> Inter quas Phœnissa recens a vulnere Dido
> Errabat sylva in magna.... [1]

Where the poet fancies the ghost of Dido being
newly releas'd from the pains of love, could not
presently forget her shady walks and melancholy
retirements : Now these remains of sorrow and
after-disturbances of mind which cleav'd to the
soul of the holy Jesus, I suppose here to be allay'd
by the music of angels in His passage to Paradice.

---

[1] Aeneid, vi. 250.   G.

Note.

The Reader will please turn to page 46, where he will find the
original source probably of Gray's and of Thomson's verse-delineation
of Poetry, as follows :
> "Now the rich stream of music winds along,
> Deep, majestic, smooth and strong,
> Thro' verdant vales, and Ceres' golden reign :
> Now rolling down the steep amain,
> Headlong, impetuous, see it pur ;
> The rocks and nodding groves rebellow to the roar."
> (Progress of Poesy, I. 1.)
> "In thy full language speaking mighty things,
> Like a clear torrent close, or else diffus'd
> A broad majestic stream, and rolling on
> Thro' all the winding harmony of sound."
> (Liberty ii. 257.) G.

A HYMN UPON THE TRANSFIGURATION.

HAIL King of Glory, clad in robes of light,
    Out-shining all we here call bright:
    Hail Light's divinest galaxy,
Hail express image[1] of the Deity.
Could now thy amorous Spouse Thy beauties view,
    How would her wounds all bleed anew!
    Lovely Thou art all o're and bright,
Thou Israel's glory, and Thou Gentile's light.

But whence this brightness, whence this suddain
    day?
    Who did Thee thus with light array?
    Did Thy divinity dispence
T' its consort a more liberal influence?
Or did some curious angel's chymick art
    The spirits of purest light impart,
    Drawn from the native spring of Day,
And wrought into an organizèd ray?

How e're 'twas done, 'tis glorious and divine,
    Thou dost with radiant wonders shine,
    The sun with his bright company,
Are all gross meteors if compar'd to Thee.
Thou art the fountain whence their light does
    flow,

---

[1] Hebrews i., 3.   G.

But to Thy will Thine own dost owe.
For—as at first—Thou didst but say,
' Let there be light,' and straight sprang forth
 this wondrous day.

Let now the Eastern princes come and bring
 Their tributary offering.
There needs no star to guide their flight,
They'll find Thee now, great King, by Thine Own
 light.[1]
And thou, my soul, adore, love, and admire,
 And follow this bright guide of fire.
 Do thou thy hymns and praises bring
Whil'st angels with veil'd faces, anthems sing.

THE PARTING.

EPART! The sentence of the damn'd I
 hear;
 Compendious grief, and black despair.
I now believe the Schools with ease,
—Tho once an happy infidel—
That should the sense no torment seize,
Yet pain of loss alone would make a Hell.

---

[1] So CRASHAW in his Hymn on the Nativity:
 " We saw Thee and we blessed the sight,
 We saw Thee by Thine Own sweet light." G.

Take all, since me of this, you Gods, deprive,
 'Tis hardly worth while to live.
  Nought in exchange can grateful prove,
  No second friendship can be found
  To match my mourning widow'd love ;
Eden is lost, the rest's but common ground.

Why are the greatest blessings sent in vain,
 Which must be lost with greater pain ?
  Or why do we fondly admire
  The greatest good which life can boast ?
  When Fate will have the bliss expire :
Like life, with painful agonies 'tis lost.

How fading are the joyes we dote upon,
 Like apparitions seen and gone :
  But those which soonest take their flight,
  Are the most exquisite and strong.
  Like angels' visits, short and bright ;
Mortality's too weak to bear them long.

No pleasure certainly is so divine
 As when two souls in love combine:
  He has the substance of all bliss,
  To whom a vertuous friend is given :
  So sweet harmonious friendship is
Add but eternity, you'll make it Heaven.

The minutes in your conversation spent
    Were festivals of true content.
    Here, here, an ark of pleasing rest,
    My soul had found that restless dove,
    My present state methought was best,
I envy'd none below, scarce those above.

But now the better part of me is gone,
    My sun is set,[1] my turtle flown.
    Tho here and there of lesser bliss
    Some twinkling stars give feeble light,
    Still there a mournful darkness is,
They shine but just enough to shew 'tis night.

Fatal divorce! What have I done amiss,
    To bear such misery as this?
    The world yields now no real good,
    All happiness is now become
    But painted and deluding food:
As meer a fiction as Elysium.

Well then, since nothing else can please my taste,
    I'll ruminate on pleasures past.
    So then[2] with glorious visions blest,

---

[1] "*Thy sun is set*, thy Spring is gone": (GRAY, Ode
on the Spring,) So earlier Herrick and Rowley, as in
Mitford's Gray. G.

[2] Query = when? G.

The waking hermit finds no theme
That's grateful to his thoughtful breast,
He sweetly recollects his pleasing dream.

TO A LADY, SUPPOSED TO ASK, WHAT LIFE WAS?

'TIS not because I breathe and eat,
　　'Tis not because a vigorous heat
　　Drives round my blood, and does
　　　　impart
Motion to my pulse and heart :
'Tis not such proofs as these can give
Any assurance that I live :
No, no, to live is to enjoy ;
What marrs our bliss does life destroy :
The days which pass without content,
Are not liv'd properly, but spent.
Who says the damn'd in Hell do live ?
That word we to the blessèd give :
The sum of all whose happiness
We by the name of life express.
Well then, if this account be true,
To live is still to live with you.

205

THE THIRD CHAPTER OF JOB
PARAPHRASED.

URS'D, ever curs'd be that unhappy day,
    When first the sun's unwelcom ray
    I saw with trembling eyes, being newly
        come
From the dark prison of the womb.
When first to me my vital breath was lent,
That breath which now must all in sighs be spent.

Let not the sun his chearing beams display
    Upon that wretched, wretched day ;
But mourn in sables, and all over shroud
    His glories in a sullen cloud.
Let light to upper regions be confin'd,
And all below as black as is my mind.

Curs'd be the night which first began to lay
    The ground-work of this house of clay :
Let it not have the honour to appear
    In the retinue of the year.
Let all the days shun its society,
Hate, curse, abandon it as much as I.

Let Melancholy call that night her own,[1]
    Then let her sigh, then let her groan :

---

[1] " And Melancholy marked him for her own."
    GRAY: '*Elegy written in a country Churchyard.*'   G.

A general grief throughout all Nature spread,
 With folded arms, and drooping head.
All harps be still, or tun'd to such a strain
As fiends might hear, and yet not ease their
 pain.

Let neither moon nor stars, with borrow'd light,
 Checquer the blackness of that night :
But let a pure unquestion'd darkness rear
 Her sooty wings all o're the air;
Such as once on th' abyss of chaos lay,
Not to be pierc'd by stars, scarce by the edge of
 Day.

Why was there then, ah, why a passage free
 At once for life and misery ?
Why did I not uncloister'd from the womb
 Take my next lodging in a tomb ?
Why with such cruel tenderness and care
 Was I nurs'd up to sorrow and despair ?

For now in sweet repose might I have lain
 Secure from any grief or pain :
Untouch'd with care, my bed I should have
 made
 In Death's cool and refreshing shade.
I should have slept now in a happy place,
All calm and silent as the empty space.

207

There where great emperours their heads lay
    down,
  Tir'd with the burthen of a crown.
There where the mighty, popular, and great,
    Are happy in a dear retreat;
Enjoy that solid peacs which here in vain,
In grotts and shady walks they sought t' obtain.

None of Hell's agents can or dare molest
    This awful sanctuary of rest.
No prisoner's sighs, no groanings of the slave,
    Disturb the quiet of the grave.
From toil and labour here they ever cease,
And keep a sabbath of sweet rest and peace.[1]

Why then does Heaven on mortals life bestow
    When 'tis thus overtax'd with woe?
Why am I forc'd to live against my will,
    When all the good is lost in ill?
My sighs flow thick, my groans sound from afar,
Like falling waters to the traveller.

---

[1] So Pope,
    " Peaceful sleep out the *Sabbath* of the tomb"
(" To Mrs. M. B. on her birth-day".) G.

SERAPHICK LOVE.

'TIS true, frail Beauty, I did once resign
    To thy imperious charms this heart of
       mine.
There didst thou undisturb'd thy scepter sway,
    And I methought was pleas'd t'obey.
    Thou seem'st so lovely, so divine,
    With such sweet graces didst thou shine,
    Thou entertain'st my amorous sense
    With such harmonious evcellence,
    That, credulous and silly I,
With vain, with impious idolatry,
Ador'd that star which was to lead me to the
    Deity.

But now, thou soft enchantress of the mind,
Farewel! a change, a mighty change I find;
The empire of my heart thou must resign,
    For I can be no longer thine.
    A nobler, a diviner guest,
    Has took possession of my breast;
    He has, and must engross it all,
    And yet the room is still too small.
    In vain you tempt my heart to rove,
A fairer object now my soul does move,
It must be all devotion, what before was love.

209

Through Contemplation's optics I have seen
Him who is ' fairer than the sons of men ':[1]
The source of good, the light archetypall,
    Beauty in the original.
    ' The fairest of ten thousand ' He
    Proportion all and harmony.
    All mortal beauty's but a ray
    Of His bright ever-shining day ;
    A little feeble twinkling star,
Which now the sun's in place must disappear ;
There is but One that's good, there is but One
    that's fair.

To thee, Thou only fair, my soul aspires
With holy breathings, languishing desires.
To Thee m' inamoured, panting heart does move,
    By efforts of ecstatic love.
    How do Thy glorious streams of light
    Refresh my intellectual sight !
    Tho broken, and strain'd through a skreen
    Of envious flesh that stands between !
    When shall m' imprison'd soul be free,
That she Thy native uncorrected light may see,
And gaze upon Thy beatifick face to all eternity ?

---

[1] Psalm xlv. 2. G.

THE RETIREMENT.

ELL, I have thought on't, and I find
This busie world is nonsense all ;
I here despair to please my mind,
Her sweetest honey is so mixt with gall.
Come then, I'll try how 'tis to be alone,
Live to my self a while, and be my own.

Iv'e try'd, and bless the happy change ;
So happy, I could almost vow
Never from this retreat to range,
For sure I ne'r can be so blest as now.
From all th' allays[1] of bliss I here am free,
I pity others, and none envy me.

Here in this shady lonely grove,
I sweetly think my hours away,
Neither with business vex'd, nor love,
Which in the world bear such tyrannick sway :
No tumults can my close apartment find,
Calm as those seats above, which know no storm
     nor wind.

Let plots and news embroil the State,
Pray what's that to my books and me ?

---

[1] = alloys. G.

Whatever be the kingdom's fate,
Here I am sure t' enjoy a monarchy.
Lord of my self, accountable to none,
Like the first man in Paradise, alone.

While the ambitious vainly sue,
And of the partial stars complain,
I stand upon the shore aud view
The mighty labours of the distant main,
I'm flush'd with silent joy, and smile to see
The shafts of Fortune still drop short of me.

Th' uneasie pageantry of State,
And all the plagues of thought and sense
Are far remov'd ; I'm plac'd by Fate
Out of the road of all impertinence.
Thus, tho my fleeting life runs swiftly on,
'Twill not be short, because 'tis all my own.

THE INFIDEL.

AREWEL fruition, thou grand cruel cheat
    Which first our hopes does raise and then
       defeat.
Farewel thou midwife to abortive bliss,
   Thou mystery of fallacies.
    Distance presents the object fair,
With charming features and a graceful air,

But when we come to seize th' inviting prey,
Like a shy ghost, it vanishes away.

So to th' unthinking boy the distant sky
Seems on some mountain's surface to rely ;
He with ambitious haste climbs the ascent,
 Curious to touch the firmament :
 But when with an unweary'd pace
Arriv'd he is at the long-wish'd-for place,
With sighs the sad defeat he does deplore,
His heaven is still as distant as before.

And yet 'twas long e're I could throughly see
This grand impostor's frequent treachery.
Tho often fool'd, yet I should still dream on
 Of pleasure in reversion.
 Tho still he did my hopes deceive,
His fair pretensions I would still believe.
Such was my charity, that tho I knew
And found him false, yet I would think him true.

But now he shall no more with shews deceive,
I will no more enjoy, no more believe.
Th' unwary jugler has so often shewn
 His fallacies, that now they'r known,
 Shall I trust on ? the cheat is plain,
I will not be impos'd upon again.
 I'll view the bright appearance from afar,
 But never try to catch the falling star.

ON A MUSICIAN SUPPOSED TO BE MAD
WITH MUSICK.

OOR dull mistake of low mortality,
　　To call that madness which is ecstacy.
　　　　'Tis no disorder of the brain,
His soul is only set t' an higher strain.
Out-soar he does the sphere of common sense,
　　Rais'd to diviner excellence ;
But when at highest pitch, his soul out-flies,
Not reason's bounds, but those of vulgar eyes.

So when the mystick Sibyl's sacred breast
Was with divine infusions possest,
　　'Twas rage and madness thought to be,
Which was all oracle and mystery.
And so the soul that's shortly to commence
　　A spirit free from dregs of sense,
Is thought to rave, when she discourses high,
And breathes the lofty strains of immortality.

Musick, thou generous ferment of the soul,
Thou universal cement of the whole ;
　　Thou spring of passion, that dost inspire
Religious ardours, and poetick fire,
Who'd think that madness should b' ascrib'd to
　　　thee,
　　That mighty discord to thy harmony ?

214

But 'twas such ignorance that call'd the gift
    divine
Of various tongues, rage, and th' effects of wine.[1]

But thou, seraphick soul, do thou advance
In thy sweet ecstacy, thy pleasing trance :
    Let thy brisk passions mount still higher,
Till they join to the element of fire.
Soar higher yet, till thou shalt calmly hear
    The musick of a well-tun'd sphere :
Then on the lumpish mass look down, and thou
    shalt know
The madness of the world, for groveling still
    below.

THE CONSOLATION.

 GRANT 'tis bad, but there is some relief
    In the society of Grief.
    'Tis sweet to him that mourns, to see
A whole house clad in Sorrow's livery.
Grief in communion does remiss appear,
Like harsher sounds in consort,[1] which less grate
    the ear.

---

[1] Acts of the Apostles, ii.,15.   G.
[1] So in MILTON's Hymn of the Nativity :
    ...." with your ninefold harmony,
Make up full *consort* to the angelic symphony.'

Men would not curse the stars did they dis-
        pense
    In common their ill influence.
    Let none be rich, and poverty
Would not be thought so great a misery.
Our discontent is from comparison ;
Were better states unseen, each man would like
    his own.

Should partial seas wreck my poor ship alone,
    I might with cause my fate bemoan.
    But since before I sink, I see
A numerous fleet of ships descend with me,
Why don't I with content my breath resign ?
I will, and in the greater ruine bury mine.

Dr. George Macdonald thus remarks on the word in
Antiphon (p 205) " *Consort* is the right word scientifically.
It means the *fitting together* of sounds according to their
nature.   *Concert*, however, is not wrong.   It is even
more poetic than *consort*, for it means a *striving together*
which is the idea of all peace: the strife is *together*, and
not of one against the other.   All harmony is an ordered,
a divine strife.   In the contest of music, every tone re-
strains its foot, and bows its head to the rest in holy
dance."   G.

THE CHOICE.

Stet quicunque volet potens
Aulæ culmine lubrico, &c.[1]

O, I shan't envy him, who'er he be,
  That stands upon the battlements of
    state ;
   Stand there who will for me,
  I'd rather be secure than great.
Of being so high the pleasure is but small,
But long the ruin, if I chance to fall.

Let me in some sweet shade serenely lye,
Happy in leisure and obscurity ;
    Whilst others place their joys
   In popularity and noise.
Let my soft minutes glide obscurely on,
Like subterraneous streams, unheard, unknown.

Thus when my days are all in silence past
A good plain country-man I'll dye at last.
    Death cannot chuse but be
   To him a mighty misery,
Who to the world was popularly known,
And dies a stranger to himself alone.

---

[1] Seneca, *Thyestes*, 1 391. G.

THE MEDITATION.

T must be done—my soul—but 'tis a strange,
　　A dismal and mysterious change,
When thou shalt leave this tenement of clay,
And to an unknown somewhere wing away;
When Time shall be Eternity, and thou
Shalt be thou know'st not what, and live thou
　　know'st not how.

Amazing state!　No wonder that we dread
　　To think of Death, or view the dead.
Thou'rt all wrapt up in clouds, as if to thee
Our very knowledge had antipathy.
Death could not a more sad retinue find,
Sickness and Pain before, and Darkness all behind.

Some courteous ghost, tell this great secrecy,
　　What 'tis you are, and we must be.
You warn us of approaching death, and why
May we not know from you what 'tis to dye?
But you, having shot the gulph, delight to see
Succeeding souls plunge in with like uncertainty.

When life's close knot by writ from Destiny,
　　Disease shall cut, or age unty;
When after some delays, some dying strife,

The soul stands shivering on the ridge of life ;
With what a dreadful curiosity
Does she launch out into the sea of vast Eternity !

So when the spacious globe was delug'd o'er,
   And lower holds could save no more,
On th' utmost bough th' astonished sinners stood,
And view'd th' advances of th' encroaching flood.
O'er topp'd at length by th' element's encrease,
With horrour they resign'd to the untry'd abyss.

THE IRRECONCILABLE.

 LITTLE thought — my Damon — once, that you
   Could prove, and what is more, to me, untrue.
Can I forget such treachery and live ?
Mercy it self would not this crime forgive.
Heaven's gates refuse to let apostates in,
No, that's the great unpardonable sin.

Did you not vow by all the powers above,
That you could none but dear Orinda love ?
Did you not swear by all that is divine,
That you would only be and ever mine ?
You did, and yet you live securely too,
And think that Heaven's false as well as you.

Believe me, love's a thing much too divine
Thus to be ap'd, and made a mere design.
'Tis no less crime than treason here to feign,
'Tis counterfeiting of a royal coin.
But ah! Hypocrisy's no where so common grown
As in most sacred things, Love and Religion.

Go seek new conquests, go, you have my leave,
You shall not grieve her whom you could deceive.
I don't lament, but pity what you do,
Nor take that love as lost, which ne'r was true.
The way that's left you to befriend my fate,
Is now to prove more constant in your hate.

THE ADVICE.

Prudens futuri temporis exitum
Caliginosa nocte premit Deus. Hor[ace].[1]

HAT'S forming in the womb of Fate
Why art thou so concern'd to know?
Dost think 'twou'd be advantage to thy
state?
But wiser Heaven does not think it so.
With thy content thou wouldst this knowledge
buy,

Carm. Lib iii. 29, lines 29-30. G.

No part of life thou'dst pleasant find
For dread of what thou see'st behind,
Thou would'st but tast of the inlightning fruit
    and dye.

Well then, has Heaven events to come
Hid with the blackest veil of Night ;
But still in vain if we forestall our doom,
And with prophetick fears our selves affright :
Grand folly ! whether thus 'twill be or no
    We know not, and yet silly man
    Secures his evils what he can,
And stabs himself with grief, lest Fate should miss
    the blow.

Be wise, and let it be thy care
    To manage well the present hour;
Call home thy ranging thoughts and fix them here,
This only mind, this only's in thy power.
The rest no setled, steddy course maintain,
    Like rivers, which now gently slide
    Within their bounds, now with full tide
O'erflow, whom houses, cattle, trees resist in vain.

'Tis he that's happy, he alone
    Lives free and pleasant that can say
With every period of the setting sun,
I've lived, and run my race, like him to day.

To morrow let the angry heavens frown,
　　Or smile with influence more kind,
　　On chance depends what's yet behind,
But sure what I have seiz'd already's all my own.

　　Fortune who no diversion knows
　　Like Disappointment, laughs to see
How variously she can her gifts transpose,
Sometimes to one, sometimes t'another free.
Be sure to enjoy her while she's pleas'd to stay.
　　But if for flight she does prepare,
　　Don't you at parting drop a tear,
But hold your virtue fast, for that alone you may.

TO HIMSELF.

OT yet convinc'd ? why wilt thou still
　　　pursue
　　　Through nature's field delusive bliss ?
'Tis false, or else too fugitive if true ;
Thou may'st assoon thy shadow overtake as this.
The gaudy light still dances in thy eye ;
　　Thou hot and eager in the chase
Art drawn through many a thorny rugged place,
Still labouring and sighing, but can'st ne'er come
　　nigh.

Give o'r my soul, give o'er, nor strive again
 This treacherous chymic gold to find.
Tell me, why shouldst thou fancy there remain
Days yet to come more sweet, than those thou'st
  left behind.
A wiser chymist far than thou, t'obtain
 This jewel all his treasures spent,
But yet he fail'd in's grand experiment,
And all he gain'd was this, to know that all was
  vain.[1]

Forbear, and at another's cost be wise,
 Nor longer this coy mistress woo.
He's mad that runs where none can win the prize,
Why should'st thou lose thy mistress, and thy
  labour too?
Heaven does but sport with our simplicity
 By laying jewels in our way,
For when we stoop to seize the glittering prey,
They'r snatcht away again, and baulk our greedy
  eye.

'Tis so, the choicest good this world can give
 Will never stand fruition's test.
This all by experience find, yet few believe,

---

[1] Solomon in his wail *Vanitas Vanitatum* of Ecclesiastes.
G.

And in the midst of cheats hope they shall once
　　be blest.
Strange magick this.　So witches tho they find
　　No comfort from their airy meat,
Forget at next cabal their slender treat,
And greedily again fall to their feast of wind.

But thou my soul thy strong conviction shew,
　　And never reach at bliss again.
Our best good here is Nature's bounds to know,
And those attempts to spare, which else would be
　　in vain.
Here then contain thy self, nor higher good
　　In this inchanted place pursue.
And pity those short-sighted souls that do ;
The world is best enjoy'd, when 'tis best under-
　　stood.

THE REFUSAL.

THINK not to court me from my dear
　　retreat,
　　No I protest 'tis all in vain.
My stars did never mean I should be great,
　　And I the very thought disdain.
Or if they did, their will I'll disobey,
And in my little orb remain as fix'd as they.

Honour, that idol which the most adore,
    Receives no homage from my knee.
Content in privacy, I value more
    Than all uneasie dignity.
How should that empty thing deserve my care,
Which Virtue does not need, and Vice can never
      bear?

Shall I change solid and unenvy'd joys
    Of a serene, tho humble state,
For splendid trouble, pomp and senseless noise?
    This I despise as well as hate.
Poor gain of that condition, which will be
Envy'd by others, and as much dislik'd by me.

HYMN TO DARKNESS.

HAIL thou most sacred venerable thing!
    What Muse is worthy thee to sing?
    Thee, from whose pregnant universal
      womb
All things, even Light thy rival, first did come.
What dares he not attempt that sings of thee
    Thou first and greatest mystery?
Who can the secrets of thy essence tell?
Thou like the light of God art inaccessible.

225

Before great Love this monument did raise,
    This ample theatre of praise.
Before the folding circles of the sky
Were tun'd by Him who is all harmony.
Before the morning stars their hymn began,
    Before the councel held for man.
Before the birth of either Time or Place,
Thou reign'st unquestion'd monarch in the empty
      space.

Thy native lot thou didst to Light resign,
    But still half of the globe is thine.
Here with a quiet, and yet aweful hand,
Like the best emperours thou dost command.
To thee the stars above their brightness owe,
    And mortals their repose below.
To thy protection Fear and Sorrow flee,
And those that weary are of light, find rest in thee.

Tho light and glory be th' Almighty's throne,
    Darkness is His pavilion.
From that His radiant beauty, but from thee
He has His terror and His majesty.
Thus when He first proclaim'd His sacred Law,
    And would His rebel subjects awe.
Like princes on some great solemnity,
H' appear'd in's robes of State, and clad Himself
      with thee.

The blest above do thy sweet umbrage[1] prize,
    When cloy'd with light, they veil their eyes.
The vision of the Deity is made
More sweet and beatifick by thy shade.
But we poor tenants of this orb below
    Don't here thy excellencies know,
Till Death our understandings does improve,
And then our wiser ghosts thy silent night-walks
        love.

But thee I now admire, thee would I chuse
    For my religion, or my Muse.
'Tis hard to tell whether thy reverend shade
Has more good votaries or poets made,
From thy dark caves were inspirations given,
    And from thick groves went vows to Heaven.
Hail then thou Muse's and Devotion's spring,
'Tis just we should adore, 'tis just we should thee
        sing.

THE INVITATION.

Come my beloved let us go forth into the field, let us
lodge in the villages. Cantic. vii., 11.

OME thou divinest object of my love,
        This noisy region don't with us agree ;
        Come let us hence remove,

= shadow. G.

I cannot here enjoy my self or thee.
　　Here Vice and Folly keep their court,
Hither their chiefest favourites resort,
Debauchery has here her royal chair,
　　This is her great metropolis,
What e'er we see or hear contagion is;
Their manners are polluted like the air.
　　From both unwholsom vapours rise
And blacken with ungrateful steams the neigh-
　　　bouring skies.

Come we'll e'n to our country-seat repair,
The native home of Innocence and Love.
　　There we'll draw purer air,
And pity monarchs, sitting in our grove.
　　Here Virtue has her safe retreat,
Abandon'd by the many and the great.
Content does here her peaceful scepter sway;
　　Here Faithfulness and Friendship dwell,
And Modesty has here her humble cell:
Come my Beloved, come, and let's away.
　　Be thou my angel good and kind,
And I'll n'er look at Sodom which we leave behind.

In fields and flow'ry meadows, woods and groves,
The first and best delights of humane kind,
　　There we'll enjoy our loves

All free, and only to ourselves confin'd.
　　Here shall my eyes be fixt on thee,
Till every passion be an extasie.
Each hour to thee shall be canonical ;
　　The sweets of Nature shall not stay
My soul, but only shew to thee the way ;
To thee ! Thou beauty's great original.
　　　Come my Beloved, let's go prove
These sweet advantages of peace, content, and
　　love.

SITTING IN AN ARBOUR.

HUS ye good powers, thus let me ever be
　　　Serene, retir'd,. from love and business
　　　free ;
The rest of your great world I here resign
　　To the contentions of the great ;
　　I only ask that this retreat,
　　This little tenement be mine.
All my ambition's to this point confin'd ;
Others inlarge their fortunes, I my mind.

How calm, how happy, how serene am I !
How satisfy'd with my own company !
To few things foreign my content I owe ;
　　But in myself have almost all

Which I dare good or pleasing call,
  Or—what's as well—I fancy so.
Thus I affect an independent state,
And—as a creature can—in self I terminate.

Pleas'd with a various scene of thought I lie,
Whil'st an obliging stream slides gently by
Silent and deep as is the bliss I chuse ;
    All round the little wingèd quire,
    Pathetic, tender thoughts inspire,
    And with their strains provoke my Muse.
With ease the inspiration I obey,
And sing as unconcern'd, and as well pleas'd as
    they.

If ought below deserve the name of bliss,
It must—whate'er the great ones think—be this.
So once the travelling patriarch doubly blest
    With dreams divine from Heaven sent,
    And his own heaven of content,
    On's rocky pillow took his rest,
Angels stood smiling by and said, were we our
    bliss
To change, it should be for a state like his.

'Tis strange so cheap, and yet so great a good
Should by so very few be understood.
That bliss which others seek with toil and sweat

For which they prodigally wast
Their treasures, and yet miss at last,
Here I have at an easie rate.
So those that costly physick use in vain,
Sometimes by cheap receipts their health obtain.

THE COMPLAINT.

ELL 'tis a dull perpetual round
    Which here we silly mortals tread;
    Here's nought I'll swear worth living
      to be found,
I wonder how 'tis with the dead.
Better I hope, or else ye powers divine
Unmake me, I my immortality resign.

    Still to be vex'd by joys delay'd
    Or by fruition to be cloy'd?
Still to be wearied in a fruitless chase,
    Yet still to run, and lose the race?
Still our departed pleasures to lament
Which yet when present give us no content?

    Is this the thing we so extol,
    For which we would prolong our breath?
Do we for this, long life a blessing call
    And tremble at the name of Death?

Sots that we are to think by that we gain
Which is as well retain'd as lost with pain.

Is it for this that we adore
    Physicians, and their art implore?
Do we bless Nature's liberal supply
    Of helps against mortality?
Sure 'tis but vain the tree of life to boast,
When Paradise, wherein it grew, is lost.

Ye powers, why did you man create
    With such insatiable desire?
If you'd endow him with no more estate
    You should have made him less aspire.
But now our appetites you vex and cheat
With real hunger, and phantastic meat.

A PASTORAL UPON THE BLESSED VIRGIN, GONE FROM NAZARETH TO VISIT ELISABETH. WHEREIN THE SADNESS OF THE COUNTRY NAZARETH IS DESCRIBED DURING THE ABSENCE OF THE VIRGIN.

Translated out of RAPIN.[1]

The Speakers are *Asor*, *Alphæus*, and *Zebede*.

Asor.

AND why Alphæus, in this sweet shade dost thou
Make songs, which are not seasonable now,
Since we of fair Parthenia are bereft !
Parthenia has our fields and mountains left.

Alph.   Ay something 'twas my pipe was t'other day
So strangely out of tune, and in so hoarse a key.

Zeb.   And I too this misfortune might have known
By some late signs, had my thoughts been my own.
My little goats as I to pasture led
When the grass rises from its dewy bed.
I wonder'd why the new born flowers hung down
Their languid heads, as if scorch'd by the sun.

---

[1] Renati Rapini *Carmina* : Vol. i. p. 24,   Paris 1681 :
Eclogæ Sacræ viii.   G.

The lilly and the rose to droop were seen,
And so did the immortal evergreen,
Parthenia—alas—was gone————
For hee sweet maid, lilly and rose did grieve,
The evergreen thy absence did perceive.

    Asor.   There grows a shady elm in our yon[1]
    grove
Where philomel wou'd constantly repair,
Sweet philomel, of all the joy and love
And with melodious accents fill the air.
When Parthenis was here, this shady tree,
Was never, never from her music free.
But now divine Parthenia is gone,
Silent and sad she wanders up and down,
And among thorns and lonely hedges makes her
    moan

    Alph.   Whil'st thou fair nymph didst bless us
    with thy stay,
Each grove was sprightly, every wood was gay.
The boughs with birds, the caves with swains did
    ring,
And the shrill grasshopper about the field did sing.
But now each wood is silent as the grave,
Nor does the shepherd whistle in his cave,

---

    [1] Query—misprint for ' yonder '? But cf. 'that
yonder' in this poem, page 90, line 17. G.

Nor does the bird sit chirping on the bough,
Nor is the grasshopper to be heard now.

Zeb. The fields with living springs were fruit-
ful made,
And every spring had his refreshing shade,.
Sweet flowers to the bees were ne'er deny'd,
The fold with grass was constantly supplied.
Now Parthenis is gone, the industrious bee
Can't flowers procure with all his industry :
The folds want grass, the fields their living springs,
Nor have the fountains now their shady coverings :
Divine Parthenia ! with thee we've lost
All the delights our rural life could boast.

Asor. My little goats were boldly wont to go
And climb the desert hills, my sheep would do so
too :
Then happy sheep, the wolf the fold did spare,
The heat the infant trees, the rain the ripen'd ear.

Alph. Thou now perhaps sweet nymph art
trave'ling o'er
Some craggy hills, unknown to thee before,
Whilst we sit here among the shady trees,
And swallow down each cool refreshing breese.

Zeb. Say you sweet western blasts that gently
blow
And you fair rivers that as swiftly flow,
You who so often have been vocal made

By swains that pipe and sing under the shade ;
Say, now when Phœbus holds the middle sky
Under what rock does sweet Parthenia lye ?
Or through what coasts may I her wandrings trace ?
Or in what fountain sees she now her lovely face ?
Ah ! Tho our way of life be plain and course[1]
Yet don't thou like thy country e'er the worse
Since 't'as thy happy parent been and nurse.

    Asor.   Ah ! where's that sweet retreat can
      thee detain,
If thou thy native country do'st disdain ?
Here are pure springs, and o'er the springs are
      bowers,
Fine woods and fruit trees, and a world of flowers.

    Alph.   But why, fair nymph, would'st thou be
      absent now,
When the sweet strawberry raises up his head,
Like morning sun all delicately red,
And odorous blossoms spring from every bough ?

    Zeb.   Don't you my sheep that yonder bank
      come near
'Tis to Parthenia sacred all that's there,
Nor wou'd the grass be touch'd by any but by her.

    Asor.   Before fierce Boreas blow with's bois-
      terous mouth.

---

[1] = coarse.   G.

Or rainy weather come on from the South,
Be sure Parthenia to return again,
Lest by the cold thou suffer, or the rain.

Alph. In a choice garden is reser'vd for thee,
Sweet marjoram, and a large myrtle tree ;
Myrtles thou always lov'st, come then if now
Thou still lov'st flow'rs as thou wert wont to do.

Zeb. Ripe apples now hang dangling on the
tree
Ready to drop, and only stay for thee.
The fig of thy delay too dost complain,
The tender fig, but let them both remain
'Till thou to thy dear Nazareth return again.

Asor. Return sweet nymph, and with thee
thou shalt bring
All the delights and beauties of the Spring.
Fresh grass again shall on the mountain grow,
The rivers shall with milk and nectar flow,
The woods shall put on their green livery,
And Nature in her pomp shall wait on thee.
The country swains shall flowers and presents
bring,
And I a violet garland for my offering.
With me shall Azarias come along
Who with a smooth-wrought pipe shall play the
song ;
The song that Israel's Shepherd as he stood

By Jordan's bank, play'd to the listning flood.

 Alph. But if thou longer should'st our hopes
  deceive.

With rushes I'll a basket for thee weave;

Here thy own Nazareth I'll represent,

How all things here thy absence do lament;

The little goats thou wandring here shalt see

Mournful and sad, and all for want of thee.

The rivers which before flow'd swift and clear

As glad the image of thy face to bear,

Shall move benum'd and slow, whilest on each hand

Appears the thirsty and forsaken sand.

The corn shall droop and languish in the field,

The meadows no fresh grass or herb shall yield,

The fir-tree which with stately pride before,

Her curious shady locks towards heaven spread,

Shall now with down-cast boughs and pensive head,

Thy absence mourn, and thy return implore.

Thou round about shalt all things weeping see,

If tears in rush-work may decipher'd be.

 Zeb. Preserve ye powers, if you don't us disdain,

The nymph, whilest she runs panting o'er the plain.

And while she's absent since she once had love

For these our fields, take care, ye powers above

That neither rivers do their banks o'erflow,

Nor storms the pastures spoil, or ripen'd corn o'er-
  throw.

Asor.   From night-fires let our stalls—sweet
    nymph—be free,
Defend from heat the rose, from cold the myrtle-
    tree,
While rose and myrtle are belov'd by thee,
That if you chance to cast a longing eye
Back on these fields, now naked and forlorn,
We may have still some flowers left to supply
Garlands t' express our joy, and dresses you t'
    adorn.

    Alph. Haste not, if through rough ways thy
    journey lye,
Haste not, the heat will prove an injury.
Let not the sun thy brighter beauties spoil :
Ah! why wilt thou undo thy self with too much
    toil ?
Take pleasing shelter in some gentle shade
'Till the day slacken, and the heat be allay'd.

    Zeb. Parthenia, why dost thou our hopes pro-
    long ?
Perhaps too some ill pipe, and worser song
Now grate thy ears, whil'st thy poor country swain
On the deaf winds bestows sweet lays in vain.
Hang there my pipe till she return, and be
A silent monument of my misery.
For what are songs or mirth without her com-
    pany ?

Azor. Our hills shall mourn while distant
    coasts you bless,
Anamis shall not dance nor Sabaris.
The fields, the naked fields no songs shall know,
And brooks their discontent by murmuring streams
    shall shew.
Thus did the swains the absent nymph lament,
The neighbouring woods to Heav'n the doleful
    accents sent.

THE TENTH ODE OF THE SECOND BOOK
OF HORACE TRANSLATED.

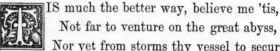

'TIS much the better way, believe me 'tis,
    Not far to venture on the great abyss,
    Nor yet from storms thy vessel to secure;
To touch too nigh upon the dangerous shore.

The golden mean, as she's too nice to dwell
Among the ruins of a filthy cell,
So is her modesty withall as great
To baulk the envy of a princely seat.

Th' ambitious winds with greater spite combine
To shock the grandeur of the stately pine.
The height of structures makes the ruin large,
And clouds against high hills their hottest bolts
    discharge.

An even well-pois'd mind, an evil state
With hope, a good with fear does moderate.
The Summer's pride, by Winter is brought down,
And flowers again the conquering season crown.

Take heart, nor of the laws of Fate complain,
Tho now 'tis cloudy, 'twill clear up again.
The bow Apollo does not always use
But with his milder lyre sometimes awakes the
        Muse.

Be life and spirit, when Fortune proves unkind,
And summon up the the vigour of thy mind.
But when thou'rt driven by too officious gales,
Be wise, and gather in the swelling sails.

THE DISCOURAGEMENT.

HAT wou'd the wise mens censure be,
        I wonder, should they hear me say
        I was resolv'd to throw my books
            away;
How wou'd some scorn, and others pity me!
Sure he's in love, 'tis for some charming Eve
That he like Adam paradise does leave.
    This only difference would be
    Between my great grandsire, and me,

That I my paradise forego
For want of appetite to know.

'Tis not that knowledge I despise ;
  No, you misconstrue my design ;
Or that t' enthusiasm I incline,
And hope by inspiration to be wise.
'Tis not for this I bid my books adieu,
No, I love learning full as well as you,
    And have the arts' great circle run
    With as much vigour as the sun
    His Zodiac treads, till t'other day
    A thought surpris'd me in my way.

Thought I, for anything I know,
  What we have stamp'd for science[1] here,
Does only the appearance of it wear,
And will not pass above, tho current here below ;
Perhaps they've other rules to reason by,
And what's truth here, with them's absurdity.
    We truth by a refracted ray
    View, like the sun at ebb of day :
    Whom the gross, treacherous atmosphere,
    Makes where it is not, to appear.

Why then shall I with sweat and pain

---

[1] = knowledge of our English Bible in I Timothy vi.,
20. G.

Dig mines of disputable oar ?[1]
My labour's certain, so is not my store,
I may hereafter unlearn all again.
Why then for truth do I my spirits waste,
When after all I may be gull'd at last ?
    So when the honest patriarch thought
    With seven years labour he had bought
    His Rachel's love, by morning light
    He found the errour of the night.

Or grant some knowledge dwells below,
    'Tis but for some few years to stay
Till I'm set loose from this dark house of clay,
And in an instant I shall all things know.
Then shall I learn t' accumulate degrees,
And be at once made master of all sciences.
    What need I then great sums lay out,
    And that estate with care forestall,
    Which when few years are come about,
    Into my hands of course will fall ?

---

[1] = ore. G.

THE LXIII. CHAPTER OF ISAIAH PARA-PHRASED TO THE SIXTH VERSE.

A PINDARIQUE ODE.

STRANGE scene of glory! am I well
  awake?
  Or is't my Fancy's wild mistake?
It cannot be a dream, bright beams of light
Flow from the vision's face, and pierce my tender
  sight.
 No common vision this, I see
Some marks of more than common majesty.
 Who is this mighty hero, who?
With glories round His head, and terrour in His
  brow?
From Bozrah lo He comes, a scarlet die
 O'respreads His cloaths, and does outvy
 The blushes of the morning sky.
Triumphant and victorious He appears,
And honour in His looks and habit wears:
How strong He treads, how stately does He go!
 Pompous and solemn is His pace,
And full of majesty, as is His face.
 Who is this mighty hero, Who?
'Tis I Who to my promise faithful stand,
I Who the powers of Death, Hell, and the Grave,
 Have foil'd with this all-conquering hand,
I Who most ready am, and mighty too to save.

Why wear'st Thou then this scarlet die ?[1]
　　Say mighty hero, why ?
Why do Thy garments look all red
Like them that in the wine-fat tread ?
The wine-press I alone have trod,
The vast unweildy frame, which long did stand
Unmov'd, and which no mortal force could e'er
　　command,
　　The ponderous mass I ply'd alone
　　And with Me to assist were none ;
A mighty task it was, worthy the Son of God.
Angels stood trembling at the dreadful sight,
Concern'd with what success I should go through
　　The work I undertook to do ;
　　Inrag'd I put forth all My might
And down the engine press'd, the violent force
Disturb'd the universe, put Nature out of course.
The blood gush'd out in streams, and chequer'd
　　o're
　　My garments with its deepest gore ;
With ornamental drops bedeck'd I stood,
And writ My victory with My enemy's blood.

　　The day, the signal day is come
When of My enemies I must vengeance take ;

---

[1] = dye, as before.　G.

The day when Death shall have its doom,
And the dark kingdom with its powers shall shake.
Fate in her kalendar mark'd out this day with red,
She folded down the iron leaf, and thus she said,
This day, if ought I can divine be true,
 Shall for a signal victory
Be celebrated to posterity :
Then shall the Prince of Light descend
And rescue mortals from th' infernal fiend,
Break through his strongest forts, and all his host
 subdue.
This said, she shut the adamantin volume close
And wish'd she might the crouding years trans-
 pose ;
So much she long'd to have the scene display,
And see the vast event of this important day.

And now in midst of the revolving years,
 This great, this mighty one appears :
 The faithful traveller the sun
Has number'd out the days, and the set period
 run.
 I lookt, and to assist was none,
 My angelick guards stood trembling by,
  But durst not venture nigh :
In vain too from My Father did I look
 For help, My Father Me forsook.

246

Amaz'd I was to see
How all deserted Me.
I took My fury for My sole support
And with My single arm the conquest won,
Loud acclamations fill'd all Heaven's court,
The hymning guards above
Strain'd to an higher pitch of joy and love,
The great Jehovah prais'd, and His victorious Son.

THE ELEVATION.

TAKE wing—my soul—and upwards bend
thy flight,
To thy originary[1] fields of light.
Here's nothing, nothing here below
That can deserve thy longer stay;
A secret whisper bids thee go
To purer air, and beams of native day.
Th' ambition of the towring lark out-vy,
And like him sing as thou dost upward fly.[2]

How all things lessen which my soul before

---

[1] = primitive: a good example of a rarely used word,
preferable to the technically-used examples of the Dic-
tionaries. G.

[2] " And singing ever soarest, and soaring ever singest."
Shelley : Ode to a Skylark. G.

Did with the groveling multitude adore!
  Those pageant glories disappear,
  Which charm and dazzle mortals eyes :
  How do I in this higher sphere,
How do I mortals, with their joys despise!
Pure, uncorrupted element I breath,
And pity their gross atmosphere beneath.

How vile, how sordid here those trifles shew
That please the tenants of that ball below!
  But ah! I've lost the little sight,
  The scene's remov'd, and all I see
  Is one confus'd dark mass of night.
What nothing was, what nothing seems to be :
How calm this region, how serene, how clear!
Sure I some strains of heavenly musick hear.

On, on, the task is easie now and light,
No steams of earth can here retard thy flight.
  Thou needst not now thy strokes renew,
  'Tis but to spread thy pinions wide,
  And thou with ease my seat wilt view,
Drawn by the bent of the ethereal tide.
'Tis so I find; How sweetly on I move,
Nor let[1] by things below, nor help'd by those
  above!

---

[1] = obstructed. So in Collect for the First Sunday

But see, to what new region am I come?
I know it well, it is my native home.

    Here led I once a life divine,
    Which did all good, no evil know:
    Ah! who wou'd such sweet bliss resign
For those vain shews which fools admire below?
'Tis true, but don't of folly past complain,
But joy to see these blest abodes again.

A good retrieve: but lo, while thus I speak,
With piercing rays, th' eternal day does break,
    The beauties of the face divine,
    Strike strongly on my feeble sight:
    With what bright glories does it shine!
'Tis one immense and ever-flowing light.
Stop here my soul; thou canst not bear more bliss,
Nor can thy now rais'd palate ever relish less.

ANNOTATIONS.

THE general design of the precedent poem is to represent the gradual ascent of the soul by contemplation to the supreme good, together with its firm adherency to it, and its full acquiesence in it. All which is done

in Advent, sore " *let* and hindred in running the race that is set before us." **G.**

figuratively, under the allegory of a local eleva-
tion from the feculent regions of this lower world.

> ' Pure uncorrupted element I breath,
> And pity their gross atmosphere beneath.'

By 'pure uncorrupted element' is meant the
refined intellectual entertainments of the divine
life, which are abstracted from all corporeal
allays.[1] 'Hδονας τας ἑαυτον as PLATO is I think
observ'd to call them, those pleasures which are
proper to man as such. By 'gross atmosphere' is
meant the most drossy gratifications of the animal
life, which comes as short in purity of the divine,
as the thick atmosphere does of the pure æther.

> 'No steams of earth can here retard thy flight,' &c.

The thing intended in the whole stanza is to in-
sinuate the great facility and pleasure of the divine
life to one that is arrived to an habit of it. For
as the magnetick influence of the earth can have no
force upon him that is placed in the upper regions,
beyond the sphere of its activity, so—which is the
counterpart of the allegory—the inclinations of
the animal nature have little or no power over
him, who has advanc'd to the heights of habitual

---

[1] = allays, as before.   G.

contemplation. He looks down upon, and observes the tumults of his sensitive appetite, but no way sympathizes with it; he views the troubled sea, but with the unconcernedness of a stander by, not as one that sails in it. His soul tho in conjunction with his body is yet above the reach of its gusts and relishes, and from her serene station at once sees and smiles at its little complacencies. As LUCAN says of the soul of POMPEY, when advanced to the etherial regions.

> .... Illic postquam se lumine vero
> Implevit, stellasque vagas miratur, et astra
> Fixa polis, vidit quanta sub nocte jaceret
> Nostra dies, risitque sui ludibria trunci.[1]

And here I cannot chuse but take notice of a difficulty which is very incident to the business in hand, and wherewith I my self was once very much perplex'd when I first applied my thoughts to moral contemplations. 'Tis in short this, we have a receiv'd axiom that the difficulty of the performance commends the merit of a good action. Now if so, it seems to follow that he who by a long habitual course of piety and virtue has made his duty easy and natural to himself, will be less

---

[1] Lucan, *Phars.* ix. 11, 12. G.

perfect than another who does hardly abstain from
vice, or than himself before the aquisition of that
habit, and then that Εγκράτεια which ARISTOTLE
in his Ethics makes only a semi-virtue, because of
the difficulty of its performance, will for that
very reason become *virtus heroica*, and if so, to make
a progress in virtue will involve a contradiction.
This I confess appear'd to me no inconsiderable
intricacy when it first occur'd to my thoughts,
and I could not presently unwind my self from
it.

But in answer to it I consider, 1st. That when
the difficulty of the performance is said to commend the action, 'tis not so to be understood as if
difficulty did in itself, as an ingredient, add any
moment to the excellency of a man's virtue, but
only that 'tis a sign of it *a posteriori*. Because
were not a man endow'd with such a degree of
virtue, he would not be able to conquer the suppos'd difficulty. So that if a man has a stock of
resolution sufficient to conquer such a difficulty,
his virtue is the same, tho he never be ingaged
in it. For all the virtue is absolv'd in the .degree
of resolution, the difficulty is only a sign or indi-
cation of it. And upon this consideration 'tis that
those whom nature has befriended with such an
'Ευφυία or happy constitution, as carries with it

252

little or no temptation to vice, may yet be account-
ed virtuous, because their resolution to virtue may
be so firm and peremptory, that they would ad-
here to it notwithstanding any opposition.

2ly. I consider that we are to distinguish of a
twofold difficulty. 1st. There is a difficulty
which arises from the nature of the work itself.
And 2ly. There is a difficulty which arises from
the disposition of the agent. Now 'tis not this
later difficulty that commends the excellency of
virtue, but only the former, which is no ways
diminish'd by the habit. For after the induction
of the habit, the work remains the same in its
own nature, which it was before; the only change
is in the agent, who by his habit is render'd ex-
pedite and ready for the performance of what is
good. But as for the later difficulty which proceeds frrm the agent himself, that is so far from
commending the worth of any good action, that
it derogates much from its commendation. 'Tis
easiness of performance that here gives the value.
He that abstains from sensual pleasures with
great abhorrency, and has set himself at a wide
distance from it, discovers more and has more of
a virtuous resolution, than he whose mind stands
almost in an equipoise, and does but just abstain.
For since we become virtuous by a right applica-

tion of our wills, the excellency of our virtues must be measured by the greater or less strength of our resolutions. And consequently, he who by habit has made his virtue most natural and easie to him, is arrived at the greatest perfection.

'Drawn by the bent of the æthereal tide'.

This is in allusion to the Cartesian hypothesis of vortices or whirl-pools of subtile matter The mystic sense is this, that the higher a seraphic soul advances in the contemplation of the supreme Good, the stronger he will find its attractions.

'I know it well, it is my native home.'

This verse with the whole stanza proceeds upon the Platonic hypothesis of præ-existence. I shall not here dispute the problem. Those that desire to be satisfied concerning it, I refer to the works of that oracle of profound wisdom and learning, the excellent Dr. [HENRY] MORE, to an ingenious treatise called *Lux Orientalis*,[1] and to the account of ORIGEN. In the mean while I hope the most rigid maintainer of orthodoxy will allow me the liberty of alluding to it as an hypothesis;

---

[1] This is one of "Two choice and useful treatises", viz, *Lux Orientalis*, or an Enquiry into the opinion of the Eastern Sages concerning the Præexistence of Souls' by Joseph Glanvil: originally published in 1662. G.

If not, I'm sure the laws of Poetry will. My business here was to imitate Nature, and to represent how a soul would be affected in such a case, supposing it true : which I think I have not done amiss. For so the ingenious Platonist, BOETHIUS,

> Huc te si reducem referat via,
> Quam nunc requiris immemor,
> Hæc dices, memini, patria est mihi,
> Hinc ortus hic sistam gradum.

' 'Tis one immense and ever-flowing light.'

My business was here to give a compendious description of God. Now among all the representations we have of Him, I thought none so agreeable to the genius of poetry as a sensible one, and of all those I could not find a better in all the inventory of the Creation, than that of light. I shall not here endeavour a parallel. It may suffice to say, that the representation is warranted by authority, both humane and divine. The School of PLATO represents God under the similitude of light, or lucid fountain; for that I suppose, BOETHIUS may be presumed to mean by his *Fons Boni Lucidus*. And Holy Scripture goes further, and says in express terms, that ' God is light, and in Him is no darkness at all ': John i. 5.

THE CURIOSITY.

UNHAPPY state of mortals here below,
    Whom unkind Heaven does inspire,
    With such a constant, strong desire,
When they've such slender faculties, to know !
And yet we not content to bear the pain,
    Of thirst unquencht and fruitless love,
    With one more curse our ills improve,
And toil and drudge for what we ne're can gain.

With what strange frenzy are we all possest,
    Contented ignorance to refuse,
    And by laborious search to lose,
Not the enjoyment only, but our rest !
Something like oar[1] does on the surface shine ;
    We taken with the specious shew,
    With pains dig in the flattering mine
But all alass in vain, Truth lies more low.

The greatest knowledge we can ever gain
    From studying Nature, Books, or Men,
    Serves just t' employ dull hours ; but then
It yields less pleasure than it costs us pain.
Besides, so short and treacherous is our age,
    No sooner we are counted wise,

---

[1] = oar. G.

But envious Death shuts up our eyes ;
Just as our part is learnt, we quit the stage.

Could I among the nobler spirits find
　　One that would lay aside his state,
　　And be my kind confederate,
That suddainly I might inrich my mind ;
'Twould be some pleasure this, if happy I
　　Could once at ease sit and survey
　　And my great victory enjoy,
And—not as now—still labour on and dye.

THE 114TH PSALM PARAPHRASED.

HEN conquer'd by the plagues of Moses'
　　　　　rod
　　Th' Egyptian tyrant gave command
　　That Israel should depart his Land,
Israel the chosen family of God.
　　Among them dwelt the Holy One,
Juda His sanctuary, and Israel was His throne.

The sea beheld this scene, and did admire,
　　Each wave stood silently to see
　　The power of the Divinity ;
They saw, and fled the dreadful guide of fire.

257

And Jordan too divided stood,
The priests the sacred ark bore through the yielding flood.

Mount Sinai with great horrour struck and dread,
  Forgot her weight, and in a trance
  Like a light ram, did skip and dance;
She fear'd, and fain would hide her palsy head.
  The hills their mother mountain saw,
The little hills, and like young sheep they stood
  in awe.

What made thee to retreat, thou mighty sea?
  Tell me, for never any shore
  Knew such a wondrous tide before,
And thou great Jordan; say, what ailèd thee?
  Say sacred mount, what meant thy trance,
And you small under-hills, why did you skip and
  dance?

You need not think it shame to own your fear;
  What you dismaid, the same would make
  The universal fabrick shake;
The cause was great, for Jacob's God was there,
  That God who did the rock subdue,
And made it melt in tears, tho' harder far than
  you.

THE 148TH PSALM PARAPHRASED.

 COME let all created force conspire
A generall hymn of praise to sing ;
Join all ye creatures in one solemn
    quire,
And let your theme be Heaven's almighty King.

Begin ye blest attendants of His seat,
    Begin your high seraphic lays,
'Tis just you should, your happiness is great,
And all you are to give again, is praise.

Ye glorious lamps that rule both night and day,
    Bring your Allelujahs too ;
To Him that tribute of devotion pay
Which once blind Superstition gave to you.

Thou first and fairest of material kind,
    By whom His other works we see,
Subtile and active as pure thought and mind,
Praise Him that's elder, and more fair than thee.

Ye regions of the air His praises sing,
    And all ye virgin waters there,
Do ye advantage to the consort bring,
And down to us the Allelujah bear,

In chaunting forth the great Jehovah's praise
    Let these the upper consort fill ;

He spake, and did you all from nothing raise ;
As you did then, so now obey His will.

His will, that fix'd you in a constant state
    And cut a track for Nature's wheel,
Here let it run said He, and make it Fate,
And where's that power which can this law repeal ?

Ye powers that to th' inferiour world retain,
    Join you now with the quire above.
And first ye dragons try an higher strain,
And turn your angry hissings into praise and
        love.

Let fire, hail, snow and vapours that ascend
    Unlock'd by Phœbus' searching rays,
Let stormy winds ambitiously contend,
And all their wonted force imploy in praise,

Ye sacred tops which seem to brave the skies,
    Rise higher, and when men on you
Religious rites perform and sacrifice,
With their oblations send your praises too.

Ye trees whose fruits both men and beasts consume
    Be you in praises fruitful too ;
Ye cedars, why have you such choice perfume
But that sweet incense should be made of you ?

260

Ye beasts with all the humble creeping train
    Praise Him that made your lot so high ;
Ye birds who in a nobler province reign
Send up your praises higher than you fly.

Ye sacred heads, that wear imperial gold,
    Praise Him that you with power arrays,
And you whose hands the scale of Justice hold,
Be just in this, and pay your debt of praise.

Let sprightly youth give vigour to the quire,
    Each sex with another vye ;
Let feeble Age dissolv'd in praise expire,
And infants too in hymns their tender voices try.

Praise Him ye saints who piety profess
    And at His altar spend your days ;
Ye seed of Israel your great patron bless,
'Tis manna this, for angels food is praise.

A PASTORAL ON THE DEATH OF HIS SACRED MAJESTY KING CHARLES THE SECOND.[1]

Menalcas, Thrysis and Daphnis.

Thyr. HAT, sad MENALCAS? Sure this pleasant shade
Was ne'er for such a mournful tenant made.
All things smile round thee, and throughout the grove
Nature displays a scene of joy and love.
But shepherd where's thy flock?————
Sure they in some forbidden pastures stray
Whilst here in sighs thou numbrest out the day.

Men. Ah Thyrsis, thou could'st witness heretofore
What strange affection to my flock I bore.
Thou know'st my Thyrsis, the Arcadian plain

---

[1] Born 1630 : died 1685. It is somewhat trying to lovers of NORRIS to find him glorifying ' his *sacred* majesty' Charles the Second. Dying among his harlots as the wretched man did, it is truly deplorable to have his memory so extolled. If such a bestial life might be thus canonized to the verge of blasphemy who ought to be reprobated? Alas! for the influence of ultra-royalism.   G.

Could not afford a more industrious swain,
But I no longer now that mind retain.

    Thyr. What change so great but what Love's
        power can make?
Menalcas does his kids, and tender lambs forsake.
So I, when slave to Galetia's eyes,
Did neither city nor the country prize,
But all their sports, and my flock too despise.
Hang thou my pipe—said I, on yonder tree,
For then—alas—I had no taste for melody.
Obscurely in thick woods I sate alone,
And sigh'd in consort to the turtle's moan.

    Men. 'Tis not fond Love that causes my dis-
        tress;
No Thyrsis, you'r mistaken in your guess.
The glorious prize I have in triumph born,
I am no longer now Alexis scorn.
Or if I were, I now could be unmoved
At every scornful glance, nor care where e'er he
    loved.
A nearer grief preys on my spirits now,
And I beneath a heavier burthen bow.
The gentle god of the Arcadian plains
Pan that regards the sheep, Pan that regards the
    swains,
Great Pan is dead————
Throughout the fields the doleful tidings ran,

A swoon seiz'd all the shepherds at the death of
 Pan.
Of Pan—But see the rest that tree will shew
Which bears the sad inscription of my woe,
Where, with the bark my sorrows too will grow.
 Thyr. How shepherd, is it by Fame's trumpet
  said
That Pan the best of all the gods is dead?
Whom oft w' adored, and whom because we knew
As good as they, we thought him as immortal too?
'Tis strange; but omens now I find are true,
In yonder copse a shady oak there stood,
Stately, well rooted, and it self a wood;
Her branches o'er the inferiour trees were spread,
Who all ador'd her as their soveraign head:
Hither, when heated by the guide of Day,
While their young wanton goats did skip and
  play.
Hither the swains would constantly repair,
Here sing, and in the ample shade drink fresher
  air.
This tree when I my goats to pasture drove,
While all was clear above, and still, throughout
  the grove,
Struck by some secret force fall down I saw,
The wood-nymphs all were seiz'd with wonder,
  grief, and awe.

Nor had I left this ruin far behind,
When lo—strange sight—a nightingal I find,
Which from brisk airs, enlivening all the grove
Coo'd on a suddain like a mournful dove.
Amaz'd I stand, and on my pipe essay
With some brisk song her sorrows to allay;
But all in vain. She from the lofty tree
Kept on her sad complaint, and mourn'd and
     droop'd like thee.

   Men. And why these slighter things dost thou
     relate?

Nature herself perceiv'd Pan's mighty fate.
She fainted when he drew his latest breath,
And almost sympathiz'd with him to death.
Each field put on a languid dying face
The sheep not minding food, with tears bedew'd
     the grass.
The lyons too in tears their grief confest,
And savage bears, Pan's enemies profest.
The nymphs all wept, and all the noble train
Of deitys that frequent the court of Pan.
Eccho, that long by nought but voice was known,
In sounds repeated others woes, but wept her own.
Th' Arcadians mourn'd, and press'd beneath the
     weighty care
With cruelty they charg'd the gods and every
     star.

Thyr. And well they might; Heaven could
    not shew a deity
More mild, more good to his votaries than he.
He was all love, all peace, all clemency;
H' allur'd the love, and melted down the hate
Of all : he had no enemy but Fate.
Pan kept the fields, from wolves secur'd the stall,
He guarded both the humble shrubs and cedars
    tall.
The Summer's heat obey'd Pan's gentle hand,
And Winter winds blew soft at his command,
He blest the swains with sheep, and fruitful made
    their land.
Weep shepherds, and in pomp your grief express,
The ground with flowers, yourselves with cypress
    dress.
Let the Arcadians in a solemn train
March slowly on, let mournful accents fill the
    plain, ·
Do this at least in memory of Pan.
    Daph. But why this vain expence of tears and
    breath ?
D' ye think Pan lost and swallowed up in death ?
He lives, and with a pleas'd and wondering eye
Contemplates the new beauties of the sky.
Whence on these fields he casts propitious rays,

Now greater than our sorrow, greater than our
    praise.
I saw—for why mayn't I rehearse the sight—
Just as the stars were kindled by the queen of
    Night
Another new-made milky way appear,
I saw, and wonder'd what event it might prepare.
When lo great Pan amaz'd my trembling sight,
As through th' æthereal plains he took his flight
Deck'd round with rays, and darting streams of
    light.
Triumphant was his march, a sacred throng
Of gods inclos'd him, Pan was all their song,
The sky still brighten'd as they went along.
    Men. Thy vision be all truth————
But who shall now the royal sheep-crook hold,
Who patronize the fields, who now secure the
    fold?
    Daph. Discharge that care, the royal stock does
    yield
Another Pan to patronize the field,
An heir of equal conduct does the scepter sway,
One who long nurtured in the pastoral way,
In peace will govern the Arcadian plains,
Defend the slender flocks, and cheer the drooping
    swains.

Thyr. Come then, let's tune the pipe t' a brisker
    key,
Let's with a dance our sorrows chase away,
And to new Pan in sports devote the day,

SATIETY.

HASTE on dull Time, thy wingèd minutes
    haste,
    I care not now how soon thou bring'st
  my last.
    But what I've liv'd I plainly know,
    The total sum of all below.
The days to come, altho they promise more,
I know will be as false as those that went before.

The best of life tho once, enjoy'd, is vain,
And why ye Powers the self-same o'er again ?
    The comedy's so dull, I fear,
    'Twill not a second acting bear.
No, I've enough; I cannot like the sun,
Each day the self-same stage, and still unwearied,
    run.[1]

---

[1] The " unwearied sun " occurs earlier in FLATMAN's
Morning Hymn. G.

What cruel laws are these that me confine,
Thus still to dig in a deceitful mine ?
    Be just ye Powers, my soul set free,
    Give her her native liberty,
'Tis 'gainst the stage's law to force my stay,
Iv'e seen an act or two and do not like the Play.

THE REPLY.

INCE you desire of me to know
    Who's the wise man, I'll tell you who.
    Not he whose rich and fertile mind
Is by the culture of the arts refin'd ;
Who has the chaos of disorder'd thought
By Reason's light, to form and method brought.
    Who with a clear and piercing sight
Can see through niceties as dark as night,
    You err, if you think this is he,
Though seated on the top of the Porphyrian tree.[1]

---

[1] Doubtless by the '*Porphyrian tree*' the olive is meant, the allusion being to its growing on the cave of the Nymphs (Homer, *Od.* xiii. 102-12.) '*Porphyry*' (De Antro Nympharum § 32) interprets it as a symbol of the wisdom of God and intellectual nature, the cave itself being an image of the world. **G.**

Nor is it he to whom kind Heaven
A secret cabala has given
T' unriddle the mysterious text
Of Nature, with dark comments more perplext.
Or to decypher her clean writ and fair,
But most confounding puzling character.
    That can through all her windings trace
This slippery wanderer, and unveil her face.
    Her inmost mechanism view,
Anatomize each part, and see her through and
    through.

Nor he that does the science know
Our only certainty below,
That can from problems dark and nice
Deduce truths worthy of a sacrifice.
Nor he that can confess the stars, and see
What's writ in the black leaves of Destiny.
    That knows their laws, and how the sun,
His daily and his annual stage does run;
    As if he did to them dispence,
Their motions, and there sate supream intelligence.

Nor is it he—although he boast
Of wisdom, and seem wise to most—
Yet 'tis not he, whose busy pate
Can dive into the deep intrigues of State.

That can the great Leviathan controul,[1]
Manage and rule't, as if he were its soul.

    The wisest king thus gifted was,
And yet did not in these true wisdom place.

    Who then is by the wise man meant ?
He that can want all this, and yet can be content.

MY ESTATE.

OW do I pity that proud wealthy clown,
    That does with scorn on my low state
        look down !

    Thy vain contempt dull earth-worm cease,
    I won't for refuge fly to this,
    That none of Fortune's blessings can,
      Add any value to the man.

This all the wise acknowledge to be true ;
But know I am as rich, more rich than you.

While you a spot of Earth possess with care,
Below the notice of the Geographer,
    I by the freedom of my soul,
    Possess, nay more, enjoy the whole ;
    To th' Universe a claim I lay ;

---

[1] Probably there is an intended *hit* here at HOBBES'
'*Leviathan*'. G.

Your writings shew perhaps you'll say,
That's your dull way, my title runs more high,
'Tis by the charter of Philosophy.

From that a firmer title I derive
Than all your courts of Law doth ever give.
    A title that more firm doth stand
      Than does even your very land,
      And yet so generous and free,
      That none will e'er bethink it me,
Since my possessions tend to no man's loss,
I all enjoy, yet nothing I ingross.

Throughout the works divine I cast my eye,
Admire their beauty, and their harmony,
    I view the glorious host above,
      And Him that made them, praise and love,
      The flowery meads and fields beneath,
      Delight me with their odorous breath.
Thus is my joy by you not understood
Like that of God, when He said all was good.

Nay—what you'd think less likely to be true—
I can enjoy what's yours much more than you.
    Your meadow's beauty I survey,
      Which you prize only for its hay.
    There can I sit beneath a tree,

And write an ode or elegy.
What to you care, does to me pleasure bring,
You own the cage, I in it sit and sing.[1]

THE CONQUEST.

N power or wisdom to contend with thee
Great God, who but a Lucifer would dare?
  Our strength is but infirmity,
And when we this perceive our sight's most clear:
But yet I will not be excell'd thought I,
In love, in love I'll with my Maker vy.
I view'd the glories of Thy seat above,
And thought of every grace and charm divine,
  And further to increase my love
I measured all the heights and depths of Thine.
Thus there broke forth a strong and vigorous
  flame,
And almost melted down my mortal frame.

But when Thy bloody sweat and death I view,
I own—dear Lord—the conquest of thy love.
  Thou dost my highest flights outdo,
I in a lower orb, and slower move.
Thus in this strife's a double weakness shewn,
Thy love I cannot equal, nor yet bear my own.

---

[1] See our Memorial-Introduction on this poem and
appropriations of it and resemblances.   G.

THE IMPATIENT.

HAT envious laws are those of Fate,
 Which fix a gulph—blest souls—'twixt
  us and you!
How 'twou'd refresh and chear our mortal state,
 When our dejected looks confess
 The emptiness of earthly bliss,
Could we in this black night your brighter glories
  view!

 Vain comfort when I thus complain,
To hear the wise and solemn gravely say,
Your grief and curiosity restrain,
 Death will e'er long this bar remove,
 And bring you to the blest above,
Till then with this great prospect all your longings
  stay.

 But ah the joy peculiar here
Does from the greater excellence arise,
'Twill be worth nothing in an equal sphere.
 Let me your noble converse have
 Blest spirits, on this side the grave,
I shall hereafter be as great as you, as wise.

 Besides, when plung'd in bliss divine
I shall not taste, nor need this lesser joy.

What comfort then does from this prospect shine.
'Tis just as if in depth of night,
You rob a traveller of his light ;
And promise to restor't when 'tis clear day.[1]

CONTENT.

BLESS my stars I envy none,
Not great, not wealthy, no nor yet the
wise ;
I've learn't the art to like my own,
And what I can't attain to, not to prize.
Vast tracts of learning I descry
Beyond the sphere perhaps of my activity,
And yet I'm ne'er the more concern'd at this,
Than for the gems that lye in the profound abyss.

Should I my proper lot disdain,
As long as further good eclipses mine,
I may t' Eternity complain,

---

[1] The close reminds of a story assigned (as usual) to a son
of Erin, who when asked whether he preferred the light
of the moon ' to the light of the sun, replied promptly
" Yes: for bedad the sun shines through the day when
we can do without him, but the moon at night, when we
can't get on at all, at all without her."   Poor wise and
foolish Pat ! G.

And in the mansions of the blest repine.

    There shall I numbers vast espy

Of forms more excellent, more wise, more blest
    than I.

I shall not then lament my unequal fate,

And why should larger prospects now molest my
    state ?

    Where all in equal stations move

What place for harmony can there be found ?

    The lower spheres with those above

Agree, and dance as free and briskly round.

      Degrees of essences conspire

As well as various notes t' accomplish Heaven's
    quire.

Thus will I have't below, nor will I care

So the result be harmony, what part I bear.

AGAINST KNOWLEDGE.

WELL let it be the censure[1] of the wise,
    That wisdom none but fools despise :
    I like not what they gravely preach

    And must another doctrin teach,

Since all's so false and vain below,

There's nought so indiscreet as this, to know.

---

[1] Judgment or verdict. G.

The thoughtless, dull and less discerning mind
   No flaws in earthly joys can find,
    He closes with what courts his sight,
    All coin will pass by his dim light.
   Though often baulk't, he hopes for rest,
Sleeps on and dreams, and is in error blest.

But he that has refin'd and high-rais'd sense,
   Can nothing taste but excellence.
    Nor can he Nature's faults supply,
    By Fancy's happy imag'ry.
   He sees that all fruition's vain,
Can't taste the present, nor yet trust again.

Our joys, like tricks, do all on cheats depend,
   And when once known, are at an end.
    Happy and wise, two blessings are
    Which meet not in this mortal sphere;
   Let me be ignorant below,
And when I've solid good, then let me know.

SEEING A GREAT PERSON LYING IN STATE.

ELL now I needs must own
   That I hate greatness more and more;
'Tis now a just abhorence grown
   What was antipathy before:

What other ills I could dispence,
And acquiesce in providence.
But let not Heaven my patience try
With this one plague, lest I repine and dye.

I knew indeed before.
That 'twas the great man's wretched fate,
While with the living to endure
The vain impertinence of State ;
But sure thought I, in death he'll be
From that and other troubles free :
What e'er his life, he then will lye
As free, as undisturb'd, as calm as I.

But 'twas a gross mistake ;
Honour, that too officious ill,
Wont even his breathless corps forsake,
But haunts and waits about him still.
Strange persecution, when the grave
Can't the distressèd martyr save !
What remedy can there avail,
Where Death the great catholicon does fail ?

Thanks to my stars that I
Am with so low a fortune blest,
That what e're blessings Fate deny,
I'm sure of privacy and rest.
'Tis well ; thus lone I am content,
278

And rest as in my element.
Then Fate, if you'll appear my friend,
Force me not 'gainst my nature to ascend.

No, I would still be low,
Or else I would be very high,
Beyond the state which mortals know,
A kind of semi-deity.
So of the regions of the air
The highest and lowest quiet are,
But 'tis this middle height I fear,
For storms and thunder are ingendred there.

SECOND CHAPTER OF THE CANT[ICLES]
FROM VERSE 10 TO 13.

'WAS my Beloved spoke,
I know His charming voice, I heard
Him say,
Rise up, My love, My fairest one awake,
Awake, and come away.

The Winter all is past
And stormy winds that with such rudeness blew;
The heavens are no longer overcast,
But try to look like you.

The flowers their sweets display,
The birds in short preludiums tune their throat,

279

The turtle in low murmurs does essay
  Her melancholy note.

  The fruitful vineyards make
An odorous smell; the fig looks fresh and gay;
Arise my love, my fairest one awake,
  Awake and come away.

TO A FRIEND IN HONOUR.

SOME thoughtless heads perhaps admire[1]
  to see
  That I so little to your titles bow;
But wonder not my friend, I swear to me
  You were as great before as now.
  Honour to you does nothing give,
  Tho' from your worth much lustre she receive.

Your native glory does so far out-do
  That of the sphere wherein you move,
That I can nothing but your self in you
  Observe, admire, esteem or love.
  You are a diamond set in gold,
The curious, the rich stone, not this behold.

All that to your late honour you can owe
  Is only that you're brought in view;

---

[1] = wonder. G.

You don't begin to have, but men to know,
　　Your votaries are increas'd, not you.
　　So the sun's height adds not t' his light,
But only does expose him more to sight.

To some whose native worth more dimly shin'd
　　Honour might some improvement give,
As metals which the sun has less refin'd
　　A value from their stamp receive.
　　But you like gold pass, for no more
Tho stamp'd, than for your weight you wou'd
　　before.

A DIVINE HYMN ON THE CREATION.

WAKE my lyre, and thy sweet forces
　　joyn
　　With me to sing an hymn divine;
Let both our strains in pleasing nnmbers flow,
But see, thy strings with tediousness and pain
　　Arise into a tuneful strain :
　　　　How canst thou silent lye?
　　The Universe is harmony,
　　Awake, and move by sympathy,
My heart's already tun'd, O why art thou so slow?

Jehovah is our theme, th' Eternal King,
　　Whose praise admiring angels sing,

They see with steddy and attentive eyes,
His naked beauties, and from vision raise
   To wondrous heights their love and praise.
     We mortals only view
   His back-parts, and that darkly too ;
   We must fall short, what shall we do ?
But neither too can they up to His grandeur rise.

No power can justly praise Him but must be
   As great, as infinite as He ;
He comprehends His boundless Self alone,
Created minds too shallow are and dim,
   His works to fathom, much more Him.
     Our praise at height will be
   Short by a whole infinity,
   Of His all glorious Deity,
He cannot have the full, and stands in need of
   none.

He can't be less, nor can He more receive,
   But stands one fix'd superlative.
He's in Himself compendiously blest ;
We, acted by the weights of strong desire
   To good without ourselves aspire,
     We're always moving hence
   Like lines from the circumference,
   To some more inlodg'd excellence,
But He is one unmov'd self-center'd point of rest.

Why then, if full of bliss that ne're could cloy,
  Would He do ought but still enjoy ?
Why not indulge His self-sufficing state,
Live to Himself at large, calm and secure,
   A wise eternal epicure ?
    Why six days work, to frame
    A monument of praise and fame
   To Him whose bliss is still the same ?
What need the wealthy coin, or He that's blest
  create ?

Almighty love the fairest gem that shone
  All round, and half made up His throne.
His favourite and darling excellence,
Whom oft He would His royal virtue stile,
   And view with a peculiar smile,
    Love movèd Him to create
    Beings that might participate
   Of their Creator's happy state,
And that good which He could not heighten, to
  dispence.

How large thy empire, Love, how great thy sway !
  Omnipotence does thee obey.
What complicated wonders in thee shine !
He that t' infinity it self is great
   Has one way to be greater yet ;
    Love will the method shew,

'Tis to impart; what is't that thou
O sovereign passion can'st not do ?
Thou mak'st divinity it self much more divine.

With pregnant love full-fraught, the great Three-
One,
Would now no longer be alone.
Love, gentle love, unlockt His fruitful breast,
And 'woke the ideas that there dormant lay,
Awak'd their beauties they display :
Th' Almighty smil'd to see
The comely form and harmony
Of His eternal imag'ry ;
He saw 'twas good and fair, and th' infant plat-
form blest.

Ye seeds of being, in whose fair bosoms dwell
The forms of all things possible ;
Arise, and your prolific force display ;
Let a fair issue in your moulds be cast
To fill in part this empty waste.
He spake.   The empty space
In mediately in travel[1] was
And soon brought forth a formless mass :
First matter came undress'd, she made such haste
t' obey.

---

[1] Travail.   G.

But soon a plastick spirit did ferment
    The liquid dusky element.
The mass harmoniously begins to move,
' Let there be light ' said God! 'twas said and
    done,
    The mass dipt through with brightness,
    shone.
      Nature was pleas'd to see
    This feature of divinity,
    Th' Almighty smil'd as well as she,
He own'd His likeness there, and did His first-born
    love.

But lo, I see a goodly frame arise
    Vast folding orbs, and azure skies,
With lucid whirl-pools the vast arch does shine,
The sun by day shews to each world his light,
    The stars stand sentinel by night.
      In midst of all is spread
    That pondrous bulk whereon we tread,
    But where is its foundation laid ?
'Tis pompous all and great, and worthy hands
    divine.

Thy temple's built great God but where is he,
    That must admire both it and Thee ?
Ope one scene more, my Muse, bless and adore,
See there in solemn councel and debate

The great divine triumvirate.
    The rest one word obey'd
  'Twas done almost before 'twas said ;
  But man was not so cheaply made,
To make the world was great, but t' epitomise it more.

Th' accomplish'd work stands His severe review
    Whose judgment's most exactly true.
All things are good, said God, they answer well
    Th' ideas which within Me dwell ;
      Th' angelick voices, joyn
    Their praise to the applause divine,
    The morning stars in hymns combine,
And as they sung and play'd, the jocant[1] orbs
    danc't round.

With this Thy quire divine, great God I bring
    My eucharistick offering.
I cannot here sing more exalted layes,
But what's defective now I will supply
    When I enjoy Thy deity.
      Then may'st thou sleep my lyre,
    I shall not then thy help require,
    Diviner thoughts will then me fire
Than thou, tho' play'd on by an angel's hand,
    canst raise.

---

[1] =jocund. G.

PLATO'S TWO CUPID'S.[1]

HE heart of man's a living butt,[2]
   At which two different archers shoot,
   Their shafts are pointed both with fire,
Both wound our hearts with hot desire.

In this they differ, he that lyes
A sacrifice t' his mistress eyes,
In pain does live, in pain expire,
And melts and drops before the fire.

But he that flames with love divine,
Does not in th' heat consume, but shine.
H' enjoys the fire that round him lies,
Serenely lives, serenely dyes.

So devils and damnèd souls in Hell
Fry in the fire with which they dwell;
But angels suffer not the same,
Altho their vehicles be flame.

The heart whose fire's divine and chaste,
Is like the bush that did not waste.
Moses beheld the flame with fear,
That wasted not, for God was there.

---

[1] See Plato's *Symph.* iii., p. 180 D. G.
[2] The 'mark' at which arrows are aimed. G.

A WISH.

HATEVER blessing you my life deny,
    Grant me kind Heaven this one thing
      when I dye.
I charge thee guardian spirit hear,
And as thou lov'st me, further this my prayer.

When I'm to leave this grosser sphere, and try
Death, that amazing curiosity,
    When just about to breath my last,
Then when no mortal joy can strike my taste.

Let me soft melting strains of musick hear,
Whose dying sounds may strike death to my ear;
    Gently the bands of life unty,
Till in sweet raptures I dissolve and dye.

How soft and easie my new birth will be,
Help'd on by Musick's gentle midwifery!
    And I who 'midst these charms expire,
Shall bring a soul well tun'd to heav'ns quire.

TO DR. [HENRY] MORE. AN ODE.

O Muse, go hasten to the cell of Fame,
    —Thou know'st her reverend aweful
      seat—
It stands hard by your blest retreat,

Go, with a brisk alarm assault her ear,
　　Bid her her loudest trump prepare,
　　To sound a more than human name ;
　　A name more excellent and great
　　Than she could ever publish yet ;
Tell her she need not stay till Fate shall give
A license to his works, and bid them live.
His worth now shines through Envy's base alloy,
'Twill fill her loudest trump and all her breath
　　　employ.

Learning, which long like an inchanted land,
　　Did human force and art defie,
And stood the virtuoso's best artillery,
　　Which nothing mortal could subdue,
Has yielded to this hero's fatal hand,
By him is conquer'd, held, and peopled too.
　　Like seas that border on the shore
The Muses' suburbs some possession knew,
But like the deep abyss their inner store
Lay unpossess'd, till seiz'd and own'd by you :
　　Truth's outer courts were trod before,
Sacred was her recess, that Fate reserv'd　for
　　More.

Others in Learning's chorus bear their part
　　And the great work distinctly share :
Thou our great catholick professor art,

All science is annex'd to thy unerring chair.
   Some lesser Synods of the wise
The Muses kept in Universities ;
   But never yet till in thy soul
Had they a councel oecumenical,
   An abstract they'd a mind to see
Of all their scatter'd gifts, and summ'd them up
    in thee.
   Thou hast the arts' whole Zodiack run,
   And fathom'st all that here is known.
   Strange restless curiosity,
   Adam himself came short of thee,
He tasted of the fruit, thou bear'st away the tree.

   Whilst to be great the most aspire,
Or with low souls to raise their fortunes higher.
Knowledge the chiefest treasure of the blest,
   Knowledge the wise man's best request,
Was made thy choice; for this thou hast declin'd
A life of noise, impertinence, and state,
   And what e're else the Muses hate,
And mad'st it thy own business to inrich thy
    mind.
How calm thy life, how easie, how secure,
   Thou intellectual epicure.
Thou as another Solomon hast try'd
All Nature through, and nothing to thy soul deny'd.

Who can two such examples shew ?
He all things try'd t' enjoy, and you all things to
    know.

By Babel's curse and our contracted span,
Heaven thought to check the swift career of man.
    And so it prov'd till now, our age
Is much too short to run so long a stage.
And to learn words is such a vast delay,
That we're benighted e'r we come half way.
    Thou with unusual haste driv'st on,
    And dost even Time itself out-run.
    No hindrance can retard thy course,
    Thou rid'st the Muses' wingèd horse ;
Thy stage of Learning ends e'r that of life be done.
There's now no work left for thy accomplish'd mind,
But to survey thy conquests, and inform mankind.

THE PASSION OF THE VIRGIN MOTHER, BEHOLDING THE CRUCIFIXION OF HER DIVINE SON.

IGH to the fatal and yet sovereign wood,[1]
    Which crouds of wondring angels did
        surround,
Devoutly sad the holy mother stood,

---

[1] An echo of the opening of the 'Stabat Mater'.   G.

And view'd her Son, and sympathiz'd with every
    wound.

Angelick piety in her mournful face,
Like rays of light, through a watry cloud did
    shine;
Two mighty passions in her breast took place,
And like her Son, sh' appear-d half human, half
    divine.

 She saw a blacker and more tragic scene,
Than e'r the sun before, or then would see;
In vain did Nature draw her dusky screen,
She saw, and wept, and felt the dreadful agony.

Grief in the abstract sure can rise no higher
Than that which this deep tragedy did move;
She saw in tortures and in shame, expire
Her Son, her God, her Worship and her Love.

That sacred head, which all divine and bright,
Struck with deep awe, the votaries of the East,
To which a star paid tributary light,
Which the—then joyful—mother kiss'd, ador'd
    and blest.

That head which angels with pure light had
    crown'd,
Where wisdom's seat and oracle was plac'd;

Whose air divine threw's[1] traitors to the ground,
She saw with pointed circles of rude thorns em-
    brac'd.

Those hands whose sovereign touch were wont to
    heal
All wounds and hurts that others did endure,
Did now the piercings of rough iron feel,
Nor could the wounded heart of his sad mother cure.

No, no, it bled to see His body torn,
With nails, and deck'd with gems of purple gore ;
On four great wounds to see Him rudely born,
Whom oft her arms a happy burthen found before.

It bled to hear that voice of grief and dread,
Which the Earth's pillars and foundations shook ;
Which rent the rocks, and woke the sleeping dead,
My God, my God, O why, why hast Thou me
    forsook ?

And can the tide of sorrow rise more high ?
Her melting face stood thick with tears to view,
Like those of heaven His setting glories dye,
As flowers left by the sun are charg'd with even-
    ing dew.

---

[1] In a contemporary-marked copy ' his ' is deleted as
a superfluous syllable : perhaps ' threw's as = threw his,
is what the Author meant. G.

But see Grief spreads her empire still more wide,
Another spring of tears begins to flow,
A barbarous hand wounds His now sensless side :
And death that ends the Son's,   renews   the
       mother's woe.

She sees now by the rude inhuman stroke,
The mystic river flow, and in her breast
Wonders, by what strange figure th' angel spoke,
When among'st all the daughters he pronounc'd
       her blest,

Thus far did Nature, Pity, Fear and Love,
And all the passions their strong efforts try,
But still tho dark below, 'twas clear above,
She had—as once her son—her strengthning angel
       by.

Gabriel the chiefest of th' Almighty's train
That first with happy tidings blest her ear,
Th' archangel Gabriel, was sent again,
To stem the tide of grief, and qualifie her fear.

A large prospective wrought by hands divine
He set before her first enlightned eye,
'Twas hewn out of the heaven christalline,
One of whose ends did lessen, th' other magnifie.

With that His sufferings he expos'd to sight,

With that His glories he did represent;
The weight of this made th' other seem but light,
She saw the mighty odds, ador'd and was content.

DAMON AND PYTHIAS : OR, FRIENDSHIP IN PERFECTION.

Pyth.' 'TIS true—my Damon—we as yet have been
Patterns of constant love, I know;
We have stuck so close no third could come between,
But will it—Damon—will it still be so?

Da. Keep your love true, I dare engage that mine
Shall like my soul immortal prove.
In friendship's orb how brightly shall we shine
Where all shall envy, none divide our love!

Pyth, Death will; when once—as 'tis by Fate design'd—
T' Elisium you shall be remov'd,
Such sweet companions there no doubt you'll find,
That you'll forget that Pythias e'r you lov'd.

Da. No, banish all such fears; I then will be
Your friend and guardian angel too.

295

And tho with more refin'd society
I'll leave Elysium to converse with you.

   Pyth. But grant that after Fate you still are
      kind,
     You cannot long continue so ;
When I, like you, become all thought and mind,
By what mark then shall we each other know ?

  Da. With care on your last hour I will attend,
     And lest like souls should me deceive,
I closely will embrace my new-born friend,
And never after my dear Pythias leave.

THE INDIFFERENCY.

HETHER 'tis from stupidity or no,
    I know not; but I ne're could find
    Why I one thought or passion should
      bestow
On fame, that gaudy idol of mankind.
Call me not Stoick ; no, I can pursue
Things excellent with as much zeal as you :
    But here I own my self to be
    A very luke-warm votary.

Should thousand excellencies in me meet,
    And one bright constellation in me frame,

'Tis still as mens phantastick humours hit
Whether I'm written in the book of Fame.
So tho the sun be ne're so fair and bright,
And shine with free uninterrupted light,
 'Tis as the clouds disposèd are,
 E're he can paint his image there.

The world is seldom to true merit just,
 Through envy or through ignorance,
True worth, like valour, oft lies hid in dust,
While some false hero's grac'd with a romance.
The true God's altar oft neglected lies,
When idols have perfumes and sacrifice.
 And though the true One some adore,
 Yet those that do blaspheme are more.

Yet grant that merit were of fame secure,
 What's reputation, what is praise?
Who'd one day's toil, or sleepless night endure,
Such a vain Babel of esteem to raise?
Pleas'd with his hidden worth, the great and wise
Can, like his God, this foreign good despise;
 Whose happiness would n'er be less.
 Tho none were made to praise or bless.

Even I who dare not rank myself with those
 Who pleas'd into themselves retire,
Find yet in great applauses less repose,

And do fame less, less than my self admire.
Let her loud trumpet sound me far and near,
Th' Antipodes will never of me hear.
    Or were I known throughout this ball,
    I've but a point, when I have all.

Then as for glory which comes after Fate,
    All that can then of me be said,
I value least of all, it comes too late :
'Tis like th' embalming of the sensless dead.
Others with pleasure, what me labour cost,
May read, and praise ; but to me all is lost.
    Just as the sun no joy does find
    In that his light, which chears mankind.

Or should I after Fate has closed my eyes,
    Should I my living glories know,
My wiser, improv'd soul will then despise
All that poor mortals say or think below.
Even they who of men's ignorance before
Complain'd, because few did their works adore,
    Will then the self same censure raise,
    Not from their silence, but their praise.

Or grant 'twou'd pleasure bring to know that
    After my death live still in fame ;
Those that admire me too must shortly dye,
And then where's my memorial, where my name?

My fame, tho longer liv'd, yet once shall have
Like me, its death, its funeral, its grave.
   This only difference will remain,
    I shall, that never rise again.

Death and destruction shall e're long deface
   The world, the work of hands divine,
What pillars then, or monuments of brass
Shall from the general ruin rescue mine ?
All then shall equal be; I care not then
To be a while the talk and boast of men.
   This only grant, that I may be
   Prais'd by Thy angels; Lord, and Thee.

THE INFIRMITY.

N other things I ne're admir'd to see
   Men injured by extremity.
   But little thought in happiness
There might be danger of excess :
At least I thought there was no fear
Of ever meeting with too much on't here.

But now these melting sounds strike on my sense
   With such a powerful excellence ;
   I find that happiness may be
   Screw'd up to such extremity,

That our too feeble faculties
May not be said t' enjoy, but suffer bliss.

So frail's our mortal state, we can sustain,
　　A mighty bliss no more than pain.
　　We lose our weak precarious breath,
　　Tortur'd or tickled unto death.
　　As sprights and angels alike fright,
With too much horror, or with too much light.

Alass! I'm over-pleas'd, what shall I do
　　The painful joy to undergo?
　　Temper your too melodious song,
　　Your dose of bliss is much too strong;
　　Like those that too rich cordials have,
It don't so much revive, as make me rave.

What cruelty 'twou'd be still to confine
　　A mortal ear to airs divine?
　　The curse of Cain you have on me,
　　Inverted by your harmony,
　　For since with that you charm'd my ear,
My bliss is much too great for me to bear.

Relieve this paroxysm of delight,
　　And let it be less exquisite.
　　Let down my soul; 'tis too high set;

I am not ripe for Heaven yet.

Give me a region more beneath,

The element's too fine for me to breath.

THE ARREST.

WHITHER so fast fond Passion dost thou rove,

    Licentious and unconfin'd ?

Sure this is not the proper sphere of love,

Obey, and be not deaf, as thou art blind.

    All is so false and treacherous here,

That I must love with caution, and enjoy with fear

Contract thy sails, lest a too gusty blast

    Make thee from shoar launch out too far ;

Weigh well this ocean, e're thou make such haste,

It has a nature very singular.

    Men of the treacherous shoar complain

In other seas, but here most danger's in the main.

Should'st thou, my soul, indulge thy forward love,

    And not controul its headlong course,

The object in th' enjoyment vain will prove,

And thou on nothing fall with all thy force.

So th' eager hawk makes sure of 's prize,
Strikes with full might, but overshoots himself
    and dyes.

Or should'st thou with long search on something
    light
  That might content and stay thy hand,
All good's here wing'd, and stands prepar'd for
    flight,
'Twill leave thee reaching out in vain, behind.
  Then when inconstant Fate thou'st proved,
Thou'lt sigh, and say with tears, I wish I ne're
    had loved.

Well then ye softer Powers, that love command
  And wound our breasts with pleasing smart,
Gage well your launce, and bear a steddy hand,
Lest it run in too deep into my heart.
  Or if you're fixed in your design
Deeply to wound my heart, wound it with love
    divine.

TO THE MEMORY OF MY DEAR NEECE,
M. C.

Y tears to ease my grief I've try'd,
    And philosophick med'cins have applied;
    From books and company I've sought
      relief,

I've used all spells and charms of art,
  To lay this troubler of my heart;[1]
I have, yet I'm still haunted by my grief.
  These give some ease, but yet I find
'Tis poetry at last must cure my mind.

  Come then, t'asswage my pain I'll try,
By the sweet magick of thy harmony.
Begin my Muse, but 'twill be hard I know
  For thee my genius to screw
  To heights that to my theme are due,
The weight of grief has set my soul so low.
  To grace her death my strains should be
As far above mortality as she.

  Is she then dead, and can it be
That I can live to write her elegy?
I hoped, since 'twas not to my soul deny'd
  To sympathise in all the pain
  Which she, tho long, did well sustain,
T' have carried on the sympathy and dy'd.
  But Death was so o're pleas'd I see
At this rich spoil, that she neglected me.

---

[1] " Vainly I had sought to borrow
    From my books surcease of sorrow,
      Sorrow for the lost Lenore ". Poe.   G.

Yet has she, of all things made me bare,
But life, nor was it kindness here to spare
So when th' Almighty would t' inform mankind
    His Eastern hero's patience try
    With the extreams of misery ;
He gave this charge to the malicious fiend ;
    Of all life's blessings him deprive,
Vex him with all thy plagues, but let him live.[1]

Yet I will live—sweet soul—to save
Thy name, since thee I cannot from the grave.
I will not of this burthen life, complain
    Tho tears than verses faster flow,
    Tho I am plung'd in grief and woe,
And like th' inspirèd Sybils write in pain.
    To dye for friends is thought to be
Heroick, but I'll life endure for thee.

    'Tis just, since I in thee did live
That thou shouldst life and fame from me receive.
But how shall I this debt of justice pay ?
    The colours of my poetry
    Are all too dead to copy thee,
'Twill be abuse the best that I can say.
    Nature that wrought thy curious frame
Will find it hard to draw again the same.

---

[1] Job ii., 6.   G.

In council the Almighty sate
When He did man his master-piece create,
His agent Nature did the same for thee ;
    In making thee she wrought for fame,
    And with slow progress drew thy frame,
As he that painted for Eternity.
    In her best mould she did thee cast,
But thou wast over-wrought, and made too fine to
        last.

    Thy soul the saint of this fair shrine,
Was pure without alloy, and all divine.
Active and nimble as æthereal light,
    Kind as the angels are above
    Who live on harmony and love,
The rays thou shott'st were warm, as well as
        bright :
    So mild, so pleasing was thy fire,
That none could envy, and all must admire.

    Sickness, to whose strong siege resign
The best of natures, did but set forth thine.
Wisely thou didst thy passions all controul,
    And like a martyr in the fire
    Devout and patient did'st expire,
Pains could expel, but none untune thy soul.

Thou bore'st them all so moderately
As if thou mean'st to teach how I should mourn
   for thee.

   No wonder such a noble mind
Her way again to Heaven so soon could find.
Angels, as 'tis but seldom they appear,
   So neither do they make long stay ;
   They do but visit, and away,
'Tis pain for them t' endure our too gross sphere.
   We could not hope for a reprieve.
She must dye soon, that made such haste to live.

   Heaven did thy lovely presence want,
And therefore did so early thee transplant.
Not 'cause He dar'd not trust thee longer here,
   No, such sweet innocence as thine
   To take a stain was too divine,
But sure He coveted to have thee there ;
   For meaner souls He could delay,
Impatient for thine, He would not stay.

   The angels too did covet thee
T' advance their love, their bliss, their harmony.
They'd lately made an anthem to their King,
   An anthem which contain'd a part
   All sweet, and full of heavenly art,
Which none but thy harmonious soul could sing.

'Twas all heaven's vote thou should'st be gone
To fill th' Almighty's quire, and to adorn His
 throne.

Others when gone t' eternal rest
Are said t' augment the number of the blest.
Thou dost their very happiness improve ;
 Out of the croud they single thee,
 Fond of thy sweet society.
Thou wast our darling, and art so above.
 Why should we of thy loss complain
Which is not only thine, but Heaven's gain ?

There dost thou sit in bliss and light,
Whilst I thy praise in mournful numbers write.
There dost thou drink at Pleasure's virgin spring,
 And find'st no leisure in thy bliss
 Ought to admire below, but this.
How can I mourn, when thou dost anthems sing ?
 Thy pardon my sweet saint I implore,
My soul ne're disconform'd from thine before.

Now will I now : My tears shall flow
No more, I will be blest 'cause thou art so.
I'll borrow comfort from thy happy state,
 In bliss I'll sympathize with thee
As once I did in misery,

And by reflection will be fortunate.

I'll practice now, what's done above,
And by thy happy state my own improve.

THE RESIGNATION.

ONG have I view'd, long have I thought,
    And held with trembling hand this bitter
      draught?
'Twas now just to my lips applied,
Nature shrank in, and all my courage dy'd.
    But now resolv'd, and firm I'll be,
Since Lord, 'tis mingled, and reach'd out by Thee.

    I'll trust my great Physician's skill,
I know what He prescribes can ne'er be ill;
    To each disease He know's what's fit,
I own Him wise and good, and do submit,
    I'll now no longer grieve or pine,
Since 'tis Thy pleasure Lord, it shall be mine.

    Thy med'cine puts me to great smart,
Thou'st wounded me in my most tender part;
    But 'tis with a design to cure,
I must and will Thy sovereign touch endure.
    All that I priz'd below is gone,
But yet I still will pray, ' Thy will be done '.

Since 'tis Thy sentence I should part
With the most precious treasure of my heart,
    I freely that and more resign,
My heart it self, as its delight is Thine,
    My little all I give to Thee,
Thou gav'st a greater cost, Thy Son, to me,

    He left true bliss and joy above,
Himself He emptied of all good, but love :
    For me He freely did forsake
More good, than He from me can ever take.
    A mortal life for a divine
He took, and did at last even that resign.

    Take all great God, I will not grieve,
But still will wish, that I had still to give.
    I hear thy voice, Thou bid'st me quit
My paradice, I bless and do submit.
    I will not murmur at Thy word,
Nor beg Thy angel to sheath up his sword.

TO MY GUARDIAN ANGEL.

TOWN—my gentle guide—that much I
        owe
    For all thy tutelary care and love,
Through life's wild maze thou'st led me hitherto,

Nor ever wilt—I hope—thy tent remove ;
　　But yet t'have been compleatly true,
　　Thou should'st have guarded her life too.
Thou know'st my soul did most inhabit there,
I could have sparèd thee, t' have guarded her.

But since by thy neglect, or Heaven's decree,
She's gone t' encrease the pleasures of the blest,
Since in this sphere my sun I ne're shall see,
Grant me—kind spirit—grant me this request.
　　When I shall ease my charge and dye,
　　—For sure I think thou wilt be by—
Lead me through all the numerous host above,
And bring my new-flown soul to her I love.

With what high passion shall we then embrace !
What pleasure will she make t' impart to me
The rites and methods of that sacred place,
And what a Heaven 'twill be to learn from thee !
　　That pleasure I shall then I fear
　　As ill as now my sorrow bear ;
And could then any chance my life destroy,
I should I fear then dye again with joy.

THE DEFIANCE.

ELL Fortune, now—if e're—you have
    shewn
    What you had in your power to do,
My wandring love at length had fix'd on one,
One who might please even unconstant you.
    Me of this one you have deprived
On whom I stay'd my soul, in whom I liv'd,
    You've shewn your power and I resign,
But now I'll shew thee Fortune, what's in mine.

    I will not, no I will not grieve,
    My tears within their banks shall stand;
Do what thou wilt, I am resolved to live,
Since thee I can't, I will my self command.
    I will my passions so controul
That neither they, nor thou shalt hurt my soul;
    I'll run so counter to thy will,
Thy good I'll relish, but not feel thy ill.

    I felt the shaft that last was sent,
    But now thy quiver I defy.
I fear no pain from thee or discontent,
Clad in the armour of philosophy.
    Thy last seiz'd on me out of guard,
Unarm'd, too far within thy reach I dar'd,
    But now the field I'll dearly sell,
I'm now—at least by thee—impassable.

311

My soul now soars high and sublime
Beyond the spring of thy best bow,
Like those who so long on high mountains climb
Till they see rain and thunder here below.
In vain thou'lt spend thy darts on me,
My fort's too strong for thy artillery,
    Thy closest aim won't touch my mind,
Here's all thy gain, still to be thought more blind.

SUPERSTITION.

CARE not tho it be
    By the preciser sort thought Popery;
      We poets can a license shew
    For every thing we do,
Hear then my little saint, I'll pray to thee.[1]

    If now thy happy mind
Amidst its various joys can leasure find
      T' attend to anything so low
      As what I say or do,
Regard, and be what thou wast ever, kind.

    Let not the blest above
Engross thee quite, but sometimes hither rove;
      Fain would I thy sweet image see

---

[1] Cf. COWLEY on the death of CRASHAW. G.

And sit and talk with thee,
Nor is it curiosity but love.

Ah what delight 'twou'd be
Would'st thou sometimes by stealth converse with
me!
How should I thy sweet commerce prize
And other joys despise!
Come then, I ne're was yet deny'd by thee.

I would not long detain
Thy soul from bliss, nor keep thee here in pain.
Nor should thy fellow-saints e're know
Of thy escape below,
Before thou'rt miss'd thou should'st return again.

Sure Heaven must needs thy love
As well as other qualities improve.
Come then and recreate my sight
With rays of thy pure light,
'Twill chear my eyes more than the lamps above.

But if fate's so severe,
As to confine thee to thy blissful sphere,
—And by thy absence I shall know
Whether thy state be so—
Live happy, but be mindful of me there.

THE COMPLAINT OF ADAM TURN'D OUT
OF PARADISE.

ND must I go, and must I be no more
The tenant of this happy ground ?
Can no reserves of pity me restore,
Can no atonement for my stay compound?
All the rich odours that here grow I'd give
To Heaven in incense, might I here but live.
   Or if it be a grace too high
To live in Eden, let me there but dye.

Fair place, thy sweets I just began to know,
   And must I leave thee now again ?
Ah why does Heaven such short-liv'd bliss bestow?
A taste of pleasure, but full draught of pain.
I ask not to be chief in this blest state,
Let Heaven some other for that place create.
   So 'tis in Eden, let me but have
An under-gardiner's place, 'tis all I crave.

But 'twill not do I see, I must away,
   My feet prophane this sacred ground ;
Stay then bright minister, one minute stay,
Let me in Eden take one farewell round.
Let me go gather but one fragrant bough
Which as a relique, I may keep and shew ;
   Fear not the tree of life ; it were
A curse to be immortal, and not here.

'Tis done ; now farewel thou most happy place,
  Farewel ye streams that softly creep,
I ne're again in you shall view my face.
Farewel ye bowers, in you I ne're shall sleep,
Farewel ye trees, ye flowery beds farewel,
You ne're will bless my state, nor you my smell.
    Farewel thou guardian divine,
To thee my happy rival I resign.

O whither now, whither shall I repair
  Exil'd from this angelic coast ?
There's nothing left that's pleasant, good or fair,
The world can't recompence for Eden lost.
'Tis true, I've here a universal sway,
The creatures me as their chief lord obey ;
    Yet the world tho all my seat,
Can't make me happy, tho it make me great.

Had I lost lesser and but seeming bliss,
  Reason my sorrows might relieve.
But when the loss great and substantial is,
To think is but to see good cause to grieve.
'Tis well I'm mortal, 'tis well I shortly must
Lose all the thoughts of Eden in the dust.
    Senseless and thoughtless now I'd be,
I'd lose even my self, since I've lost Thee.

TO SLEEP.

REAK off thy slumber gentle god
  And hither bring thy charming rod ;
  The rod that weeping eyes does close
And gives to melancholy hearts repose ;
With that my temples stroke, and let me be
  Held by thy soft captivity.
  But do not all my senses bind,
  Nor fetter up too close my mind :
Let mimic Fancy wake, and freely rove,
And bring th' idea of the saint I love.[1]

  Her lovely image has been brought
  So often to my waking thought,
  That 'tis at length worn out and dead,
And with its fair original is fled.
Or else my working over-thoughtful mind
  With much intention[2] is made blind,
  Like those who look on objects bright
  So long till they quite lose their sight.
Ah cruel Fates, is't not enough for you
To take my saint, but I must lose her image too ?

  Thee gentle charmer I implore

---

[1] Cf. this and the following, with MILTON's wonderful
sonnet on a vision of his dead wife. G.

[2] = introspection. G.

This my lost treasure to restore ;
    Thy magic vertues all apply,
Set up again my bankrupt memory.
Search every cell and corner of my brain,
    And bring my fugitive again. .
    To thy dark cave thy self betake
    And 'mong thy dreams enquiry make ;
Summon the best ideas to appear
And bring that form which most resembles her.

    But if in all thy store there be
    None—as I fear—so fair as she,
    Then let thy painter Phancy, limn
Her form anew, and send it by a Dream.
Thou can'st him all her lively features tell
    For sure I think thou knew'st her well.
    But if description wont suffice
    For him to draw a piece so nice,
Then let him to my breast and heart repair,
For sure her image is not worn out there.

THE GRANT.

'TWAS when the tide of the returning day
    Began to chase ill forms away,
    When pious dreams the sense employ,
And all within is innocence and joy,

My melancholy, thoughtful mind
O'recome, at length to sleep resign'd ;
Not common sleep, for I was blest
With something more divine, more sweet than
    rest.

She who her fine-wrought clay had lately left,
    Of whose sweet form I was bereft,
    Was by kind Fancy to me brought,
And made the object of my happy thought.
    Clad she was all in virgin white.
    And shone with empyrean light ;
    A radiant glory crown'd her head,
She stream'd with light and love, and thus she
    said.

And why this grief and passion for the blest ?
    Let all your sorrows with me rest.
    My state is bliss, but I should live
Yet much more happy, would you cease to grieve.
    Dry up your tears—dear friend—and be
    Happy in my felicity.
    By this your wisdom you'll approve,
Nay—what you'd most of all commend—your
    love.

She spake, dissolv'd I lay and overcome,
    And was with exstasie struck dumb ;

But ah the fierce tumultuous joy
Its own weak being, hasten'd to destroy.
   To see that lovely form appear
   My spirits in such commotion were,
   Sleep could no more their force controul,
They shook their fetters off, and free'd my unwill-
     ing soul.

What bliss do we oft to delusion owe !
   Who would not still be cheated so !
   Opinion's an ingredient
That goes so far to make up true content,
   That even a dream of happiness
   With real joy the soul does bless;
   Let me but always dream of this,
And I will envy none their waking bliss.

THE ASPIRATION.

OW long great God, how long must I
Immur'd in this dark prison lye !
Where at the grates and avenues of
   sense
My soul must watch to have intelligence.
Where but faint gleams of thee salute my sight.
Like doubtful moon-shine in a cloudy night.[1]

---

[1] "Like cloudy moonshine in some shadowy grove."
GILES Fletcher's *Cave of Despair* in Christ's Victorie. G.

When shall I leave this magic sphere,
And be all mind, all eye, all ear!

How cold this clime! and yet my sense
Perceives even here thy influence.
Even here thy strong magnetic charms I feel,
And pant and tremble like the amorous steel.
To lower good, and beauties less divine
Sometimes my erroneous needle does decline;
But yet—so strong the sympathy—
It turns, and points again to thee.[1]

I long to see this excellence
Which at such distance strikes my sense.
My impatient soul struggles to disengage
Her wings from the confinement of her cage.
Would'st thou great Love this prisoner once set
free,
How would she hasten to be link'd with Thee.
She'd for no angel's conduct stay,
But fly, and love on all the way.

---

[1] Norris echoes Vaughan the Silurist here.   Cf. his
" To Amoret Walking in a starry evening " (Vol. II. pp.
15—16, and his numerous uses of the 'magnet' as a
simile.   G.

THE DEFENCE.

HAT I am colder in my friendship grown,
 My faith and constancy you blame,
 But sure th' inconstancy is all your own,
I am, but you are not the same.
 The flame of love must needs expire
If you subtract what should maintain the fire,

While to the laws of Vertue you were true,
 You had, and might retain my heart;
Now give me leave to turn apostate too,
 Since you do from your self depart.
 Thus the reform'd are counted free
From schism, tho they desert the Roman See.

The strictest union to be found below
 Is that which soul and body ties,
They all the mysteries of friendship know,
 And with each other sympathise.
 And yet the soul will bid adieu
T' her much distemper'd mate, as I leave you.

THE RETRACTATION.

'VE often charg'd all sublunary bliss,
 With vanity and emptiness:
 You woods and streams have heard me oft
  complain

321

How all things, how even your delights were vain.
Methought I could with one short simple view
Glance o're all humane joys and see them through.
      But now great Preacher pardon me.
I cannot wholly to thy charge agree,
For Musick sure and Friendship have no vanity.

No, each of these is a firm massy joy,
    Which tho eternal, will not cloy.
Here may the venturous soul live on, and find,
Grasp what she can, that more remains behind.
Such depths of joy these living springs contain,
As man t' Eternity can never drain.
    These sweets the truth of Heaven prove,
Only there's greater bliss with saints above,
Because they've better musick there, and firmer
      love.

THE PROSPECT.

HAT a strange moment will that be,
    My soul, how full of curiosity,
    When wing'd, and ready for thy eternal
      flight
On th' utmost edges of thy tottering clay,
    Hovering and wishing longer stay,

Thou shalt advance, and have Eternity in sight!
When just about to try that unknown sea,
  What a strange moment will that be!

  But yet how much more strange that state
When loosen'd from th' embrace of this close
      mate
Thou shalt at once be plung'd in liberty,
And move as free and active as a ray
  Shot from the lucid spring of day!
Thou who just now was clogg'd with dull mor-
      tality,
How wilt thou bear the mighty change, how know
  Whether thou'rt then the same or no!

  Then to strange mansions of the air
And stranger company must thou repair!
What a new scene of things will then appear!
The world thou by degrees wast taught to know
  Which lessen'd thy surprise below,
But knowledge all at once will overflow thee
      there.
That world as the first man did this, thou'lt see,
  Ripe-grown, in full maturity.

  There with bright splendours must thou dwell,
And be what—only those pure forms can tell.

There must thou live a while, gaze and admire,
Till the great angel's trump this fabrick shake,
    And all the slumbring dead awake,
Then to thy old, forgotten state thou must retire.
This union then will seem as strange, or more,
    Than thy new liberty before.

    Now for the greatest change prepare,
To see the only great, the only fair.
Vail now thy feeble eyes, gaze and be blest ;
Here all thy turns and revolutions cease,
    Here's all serenity and peace :
Thou'rt to the centre come, the native seat of
    rest.
There's now no further change nor need there be ;
    When one shall be variety.

THE RETURN.

DEAR Contemplation, my divinest joy,
    When I thy sacred mount ascend
    What heavenly sweets my soul employ !
Why can't I there my days for ever spend ?
When I have conquer'd thy steep heights with
    pain
What pity 'tis that I must down again !

And yet I must; my passions would rebel
　　Should I too long continue here:
　　No, here I must not think to dwell,
But mind the duties of my proper sphere.
So angels, tho they heaven's glories know,
Forget not to attend their charge below.

THE 137TH PSALM PARAPHRASED TO THE 7TH VERSE.

ENEATH a reverend gloomy shade,
　　Where Tigris and Euphrates cut their
　　　　way,
With folded arms and heads supinely laid
We sate, and wept out all the tedious day,
　　Within its banks grief could not be
Contain'd, when Sion, we remember'd thee.

　　Our harps with which we oft have sung
In solemn strains the great Jehovah's praise,
Our warbling harps upon the trees we hung,
Too deep our grief to hear their pleasing lays.
　　Our harps were sad, as well as we,
And tho by angels touch'd, would yield no har-
　　mony.

　　But they who forc'd us from our seat,
The happy Land, and sweet abode of rest,

325

Had one way left to be more cruel yet,
And ask'd a song from hearts with grief opprest.
    Let's hear, say they, upon the lyre
One of the anthems of your Hebrew quire.

    How can we frame our voice to sing
The hymns of joy, festivity, and praise,
To those who're aliens to our heavenly King,
And want a taste for such exalted layes?
    Our harps will here refuse no sound;
An holy song is due to holy ground.

    No, dearest Sion, if we can
So far forget thy melancholy state
As now thou mourn'st, to sing one chearful strain,
This ill be added to our ebb of fate;
    Let neither harp nor voice e're try
One hallelujah more, but ever silent lye.

THE 139TH PSALM PARAPHRSED TO THE 14TH VERSE.

N vain, great God, in vain I try
    T' escape Thy quick all-searching
      eye.
Thou with one undivided view
Dost look the whole creation through.
The unshap'd embryo's of my mind

Not yet to form our likeness wrought,
The tender rudiments of thought
Thou see'st, before she can her own conception
    find.

My private walks to Thee are known,
In solitude I'm not alone ;
Thou round my bed a guard dost keep,
Thy eyes are open, while mine sleep.
My softest whispers reach Thy ear :
'Tis vain to fancy secrecy;
Which way so e're I turn Thou'rt there,
I am all round beset with Thy immensity.

I can't wade through this depth, I find,
It drowns and swallows up my mind.
'Tis like Thy immense Deity,
I cannot fathom that, or Thee.
Where then shall I a refuge find
From Thy bright comprehensive eye?
Whither, O whither shall I fly,
What place is not possest by Thy all-filling mind !

If to the heavenly orbs I fly,
There is Thy seat of majesty.
If down to Hell's abyss I go
There I am sure to meet Thee too.
Should I with the swift wings of Light

327

Seek some remote and unknown Land,
Thou soon would'st overtake my flight,
And all my motions rule with Thy long-reaching
　　hand.

Should I t' avoid Thy piercing sight,
Retire behind the skreen of Night,
Thou canst with one celestial ray
Dispel the shades, and make it day.
Nor need'st Thou by such mediums see ;
The force of Thy clear radiant sight,
Depends not on our grosser light ;
On light Thou sitt'st enthron'd, 'tis ever day with
　　Thee.

The springs which life and motion give
Are Thine, by Thee I move and live.
My frame has nothing hid from Thee,
Thou know'st my whole anatomy.
T' an hymn of praise I'le tune my lyre ;
How amazing is this work of Thine !
With dread I into my self retire,
For tho the metal's base, the stamp is all divine.

TO DR. PLOT, ON HIS NATURAL HISTORY
OF STAFFORDSHIRE.[1]

WHAT strange perversity is this of man!
　　When 'twas a crime to taste th' inlightn-
　　　　ing tree
　He could not then his hand refrain,
None then so inquisitive, so curious as he.
But now he has liberty to try and know
　　God's whole plantation below ;
　　Now the angelic fruit may be
Tasted by all whose arms can reach the tree :
　　H' is now by licence careless made,
The tree neglects to climb, and sleeps beneath the
　　shade.

Such drowsie sedentary souls have they
Who could patriarchal years live on,
　　Fixed to hereditary clay,
　　And know no climate but their own.
　　Contracted to their narrow sphere,
　　Rest before knowledge they prefer,
　　And of this globe wherein they dwell
No more than of the heavenly orbs can tell.

---

[1] Robert Plot, LL.D. a celebrated Antiquary, born
1641 : died April 30th, 1696. His " Natural History "
supra, was published in 1686. G.

As if by Nature plac'd below
Not on this earth to dwell, but to take root and
    grow.

Dull souls, why did great Nature take such care
To write in such a splendid character;
    If man the only thing below
    That can pretend her hand to know,
    Her fair-writ volume does despise,
    And tho design'd for wisdom won't be wise ?
Th' Almighty gets no praise from this dull kind,
The sun was never worship'd by the blind.
Such ignorance can ne're devotion raise,
They will want wisdom and their Maker praise.

They only can this tribute duely yield
    Whose active spirits range abroad,
    Who traverse o're all Nature's field
And view the great magnificence of God.
They see the hidden wealth of Nature's store
Fall down and learnedly adore ;
But they most justly yet this tribute pay
Who don't contemplate only, but display,
Comment on Nature's text, and to the sense
    Expose her latent excellence ;
Who like the sun, not only travel o're
The world, but give it light that others may adore.

In th' head of these heroic few
Our learnèd author here appears in view,
Whose searching genius like lamp of day
    Does the Earth's furniture display,
Nor suffers to lye bury'd and unknown
    Nature's rich talent or his own.
Drake and Columbus do in thee revive,
And we from thy research as much receive.
Thou art as great as they, for 'tis all one
New worlds to find, or nicely to describe the
    known.

On mighty hero, our whole isle survey,
Advance thy standard, conquer all the way.
    Let nothing but the sea controul
    The progress of thy active soul.
    Act like a pious courteous ghost,
    And to mankind retrieve what's lost.
With thy victorious charitable hand
Point out the hidden treasures of our Land.
Envy or Ignorance do what they will,
Thou hast a blessing from the Muses hill.
Great be thy spirit as thy works divine,
Show thou thy Maker's praise, we poets will sing
    thine.

THE EXCHANGE.

WHEN Corydon had lost his liberty
 And felt the tyrant's heavy chain;
  He swore, could he but once get free,
He'd never, no, he'd never love again.

But stay dull shepherd, if you quench your fire,
 Too dear will you buy your liberty:
  Let not such vigorous heats expire,
I'll teach thee how to love, and yet be free.

Take bright Urania to thy amorous breast.
 To her thy flaming heart resign;
  Void not the room, but change the guest,
And let thy sensual love commençe divine.

The swain obey'd, and when he once had known
 This foretaste of the joys above,
  He vow'd, though he might be his own,
Yet he would ever, yes he'd ever love.

THE REFINEMENT.

WELL 'twas a hard decree of Fate,
 My soul, to clip thy pinions so,
  To make thee leave thy pure ethereal
   state,
And breath the vapours of this stream below,

Where he that can pretend to have
Most freedom, 's still his body's slave.

Was e're a substance so divine
With such an unlike consort joyn'd?
Did ever things so wide, so close combine
As massy clods and sun-beams, earth and mind ?
When yet two souls can ne're agree
In friendship, but by parity.

Unequal match! what wilt thou do,
My soul, to raise thy plumes again ?
How wilt thou this gross vehicle subdue,
And thy first bliss, first purity obtain ?
Thy consort how wilt thou refine,
And be again all o're divine?

Fix on the sovereign thy fair eye,
And kindle in thy breast a flame ;
Wind up thy passions to a pitch so high
Till they melt down, and rarify thy frame.
Like the great prophet then aspire,
Thy chariot will like his, be fire.[1]

---

[1] Elijah : 2 Kings ii. 11 *et alibi*.   G.

TO MELANCHOLY.

YSTERIOUS passion, dearest pain,
    Tell me, what wondrous charms are
      these
  With which thou dost torment or please,
I grieve to be thy slave, yet would not freedom
    gain.
    No tyranny like thine we know,
    That half so cruel e're appear'd,
    And yet thou'rt lov'd as well as fear'd,
Perhaps the only tyrant that is so.

    Long have I been thy votary,
    Thou'st led me out to woods and groves,
    Made'st me despise all other loves,
And give up all my passions, all my soul to thee.
Thee for my first companion did I chuse,
    First, even before my darling Muse ;
    And yet I know of thee no more
Than those who never did thy shrine adore.

    Thou'rt mystery and riddle all,
    Like those thou inspirest, thou lov'st to be
    In darkness and obscurity.
Even learnèd Athens thee an unknown God might
    call[1]

---

[1] Acts of Apostles, xvii. 23.   G.

Strange contraries in thee combine,
Both Hell and Heaven in thee meet,
Thou greatest bitter, greatest sweet,
No pain is like thy pain, no pleasure too like thine.

'Tis the grave doctrin of the Schools
That contraries can never be
Consistent in th' high'st degree,
But thou must stand exempt from these dull narrow rules.
And yet 'tis said the brightest mind
Is that which is by thee refin'd.
See here a greater mystery,
Thou mak'st us wise, yet ruin'st our philosophy.

THE DISCONTENT.

NOT that it is not my fate,
To stand upon the dangerous heights of State,
Nor that I cannot be possest
Of th' hidden treasures of the East,
Nor that I cannot bathe in Pleasure's spring,
And rifle all the sweets which Nature's gardens bring
Do I repine, my destiny,
I can all these despise, as well as you deny.

It shall not discompose my mind
Though not one star above to me prove kind.
     Their influence may sway the sea,
     But make not the least change in me.
They neither can afflict my state, nor bless,
Their greatest gifts are small, and my desires are
       less.
     My vessel bears but little sail,
What need I then a full and swelling gale ?

     And yet I'm discontented too,
Perhaps y' aspiring souls as much as you ;
      We both in equal trouble live,
      But for much different causes grieve,
You, that these guilded joys you can't obtain ;
And I, because I know they're empty all and vain.
      You still pursue in hopes to find,
I stand and dare not flatter on my mind.

      This tree of knowledge is, I see,
Still fatal to poor man's felicity.
      That which yields others great repast,
      Can't please my now enlighten'd taste.
Before, tho I could nothing solid find,
Yet still with specious prospects I could please
       my mind.
      Now all the farthest I can see
      Is one perpetual round of vanity.

BEAUTY.

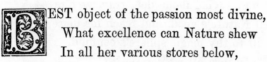EST object of the passion most divine,
    What excellence can Nature shew
    In all her various stores below,
  Whose charms may be compar'd to thine?
  Even light it self is therefore fair
Only because it makes thy sweets appear.

Thou streaming splendour of the Face divine
    What in the regions above,
    Do saints like thee adore or love,
  What excellence is there like thine?
  I except not the Divinity,
That great and sovereign good, for thou art He.

He's Beautie's vast abyss and boundless sea,
    The primitive and greatest Fair;
    All His perfections beauties are,
  Beauty is all the Deity.
  Some streams from this vast ocean flow,
And that is all that pleases, all that's fair below.

Divine perfection who alone art all
    That various scene of excellence
    Which pleases either man or sense,
  Tho thee by different names we call!
  Search Nature through, thou still wilt be
The sum of all that's good in her variety.

337

Love, that most active passion of the mind,
 Whose roving flame does traverse o're
 All Nature's good, and reach for more,
 Still to thy magic sphere's confin'd.
 'Tis beauty all we can desire,
Beauty's the native mansion of Love's fire.

Those finer spirits who from the croud retire
 To study Nature's artful scheme,
 Or speculate a theorem,
 What is't but beauty they admire?
 And they too who enamour'd are
Of Virtue's face, love her because she's fair.

No empire, sovereign Beauty, is like thine,
 Thou reign'st unrivall'd and alone,
 And universal is thy throne,
 Stoicks themselves to thee resign.
 From passions He they ne'er so free
Something they needs must love, and that is thee.

He whom we all adore, that mighty He,
 Owns thy supream dominion,
 And happy lives in thee alone,
 We'er blest in Him, and He in thee:
 In thee He's infinitely blest,
Thou art the inmost center of His rest.

Pleas'd with thy form which in His essence shin'd,
　　Th' Almighty chose to multiply
　　This flower of His Divinity
　　And lesser beauties soon design'd.
　　The unform'd chaos He remov'd,
Tinctur'd[1] the mass with thee, and then it lov'd.

But do not thou my soul, fixt here remain,
　　All streams of beauty here below
　　Do from that immense ocean flow,
　　And thither they should lead again.
　　Trace then these streams, till thou shalt be
At length o'rewhelm'd in Beauty's boundless sea.

LOVE.

MPERIAL passion! Sacred fire!
　　When we of meaner subjects sing,
　　Thou tun'st our harps, thou dost our
　　　souls inspire,
'Tis love directs the quill, 'tis love strikes every
　　string.
　　But where's another Deity
　　T' inspire the man that sings of thee?

---

[1] Cf. our Vaughan *s.v.* in Index of Words, on 'tincture'. G.

W' are by mistaken chymists told,
That the most active part of all
The various compound cast in Nature's mould,
Is that which they mercurial spirit call.
But sure 'tis love they should have said,
Without this even their spirit is dead.

Love's the great spring of Nature's wheel,
Love does the mass pervade and move,
What 'scapes the sun's, does thy warm influence
feel,
The Universe is kept in tune by love.
Thou Nature giv'st her sympathy,
The center has its charm from thee.

Love did great Nothing's barren womb
Impregnate with his genial fire;
From this first parent did all creatures come,
Th' Almighty will'd, and made all by desire.
Nay more, among the sacred Three,
The third subsistence is from thee.

The happiest order of the blest
Are those whose tide of love's most high,
The bright seraphick host; who're more possest
Of good, because more like the Deity.
T' him they advance as they inprove
That noble heat, for God is love.

Shall then a passion so divine
Stoop down and mortal beauties know ?
Nature's great statute law did ne're design
That heavenly fire should kindle here below ;
Let it ascend and dwell above,
The proper element of love.

THE CONSUMMATION : A PINDARICK ODE.

THE rise of monarchies, and their long, weighty fall
My Muse out-soars ; she proudly leaves behind
The pomps of Courts, she leaves our little all,
To be the humble song of a less reaching mind.
In vain I curb her tow'ring flight ;
All I can here present's too small.
She presses on, and now has lost their sight,
She flyes, and hastens to relate
The last and dreadful scene of Fate,
Nature's great solemn funeral.
I see the mighty angel stand
Cloath'd with a cloud, and rain-bow round his head,
His right foot on the sea, his other on the land,
He lifted up his dreadful arm, and thus he said ;
By the mysterious great Three-One

341

Whose power we fear, and truth adore
I swear the fatal thred is spun,
Nature shall breath her last, and Time shall be no
    more.
The antient stager of the day
Has run his minutes out, and numb'rd all his way.
The parting isthmus is thrown down
And all shall now be overflown.
Time shall no more her under-current know
But one with great Eternity shall grow,
Their streams shall mix, and in one circling channel
    flow.
He spake, Fate writ the sentence with her iron
    pen,
And mighty thundrings said, Amen!
What dreadful sound's this strikes my ear?
'Tis sure th' archangels trump I hear,
Nature's great passing bell, the only call
Of God's, that will be heard by all.
The Universe takes the alarm, the sea
    Trembles at the great angel's sound,
    And roars almost as loud as he,
Seeks a new channel, and would fain run under
    ground.
The Earth it self does no less quake,
And all throughout, down to the center shake,

The graves unclose, and the deep sleepers there
    awake.
    The sun arrested in his way,
      He dares not forward go,
But wondring stands at the great hurry here
    below;
The stars forget their laws, and like loose planets
    stray.
    See how the elements resign
Their numerous charge, the scatter'd atoms home
    repair,
Some from the Earth, some from the sea, some
    from the air :
    They know the great alarm,
    And in confus'd mixt numbers swarm,
Till rang'd and sever'd by the chymistry divine.
The Father of mankind amaz'd to see
The globe too narrow for his progeny.
    But 'tis the closing of the age,
And all the actors now at once must grace the
    stage.

Now Muse exalt thy wing, be bold and dare,
    Fate does a wondrous scene prepare;
The central fire which hitherto did burn
Dull like a lamp in a most clammy urn,
Fann'd by the breath divine begins to glow,

343

The fiends are all amaz'd below.

But that will no confinement know,

Breaks through its sacred fence, and plays more free

Than thou with all thy vast Pindaric liberty.

Nature does sick of a strong fever lye :

The fire the subterraneous vaults does spoil ;

 The mountains sweat, the sun does boil ;

 The sea, her mighty pulse, beats high ;

 The waves of fire more proudly rowl ;

 The fiends in their deep caverns howl,

And with the frightful trumpet mix their hideous cry.

 Now is the tragic scene begun ;

 The fire in triumph marches on ;

The Earth's girt round with flames, and seems another sun.

But whither does this lawless judgement roam ?

 Must all promiscuously expire

 A sacrifice in Sodom's fire ?

Read thy commission, Fate ; sure all are not thy due,

 No, thou must save the virtuous few

But where's the angel guardian to avert the doom ?

Lo, with a mighty host he's come :
I see the parted clouds give way ;
I see the banner of the cross display.
Death's conqueror in pomp appears,
In His right hand a palm He bears,
And in His looks redemption wears :
Th' illustrious glory of this scene
Does the dispairing saints inspire
With joy, with rapture, and desire ;
Kindles the brighter life that dormant lay within,
Th' awaken'd virtue does its strength display
Melts and refines their drossy clay ;
New-cast into a pure ætherial frame,
They fly and mount aloft in vehicles of flame.
Slack here my Muse thy roving wing,
And now the world's untun'd, let down thy high-
set string.

FREEDOM.

I DO not ask thee Fate, to give
This little span a long reprieve.
The pleasures here are all so poor
and vain,
I care not hence how soon I'm gone.
Date as thou wilt my time, I shan't complain ;
May I but still live free, and call it all my own.

Let my sand slide away apace;
　　I care not, so I hold the glass,
Let me my time, my books, my self enjoy,
Give me from cares a sure retreat;
Let no impertinence my hours imploy,
That's in one word, kind Heaven, let me ne'er be
　　　　great.

　　In vain from chains and fetters free
　　　　The great man boasts of liberty.
He's pinnion'd up by formal[1] rules of State;
　　Can ne'er from noise and dust retire;
He's haunted still by clouds that round him wait,
His lot's to be in pain, as that of fools t' admire.

　　Mean while the swain has[2] calm repose,
　　　　Freely he comes and freely goes.
Thus the bright stars whose station is most high,
　　Are fix'd, and by strict measures move,
While lower planets wanton in the sky,
Are bound to no set laws, but humoursomly[3] rove.

---

[1] Misprinted in 1710 and subsequent editions ' former ':
we restore ' formal ' from the 4th edition (1706).　G

[2] Misprinted ' his ' in 1710 edition: corrected from 4th
edition (1706).　G.

[3] = changeably.　G.

TO HIS MUSE.

OME Muse, let's cast up our accounts,
and see
How much you are in debt to me:
You've reign'd thus long the mistress of my heart,
You've been the ruling planet of my days,
In my spare-hours you've had your part,
Ev'n now my servile mind your sovereign will
obeys.
Too great such service to be free,
Tell me what I'm to have for being thy votary.

You have preferments in your gift, you say,
You can with gold my service pay ;
I fear thy boast, your sacred hill I'm told
In a poor, curs'd and barren country lies ;
Besides what's state to me, or gold,
These you long since have taught me to despise.
To put me off with this, would be
Not to reward, but tax my ill proficiency.

But fame you say will make amends for all,
This you your sovereign blessing call,
The only lasting good that never dies,
A good which never can be bought too dear,
Which all the wise and virtuous prize,
The gods too with delight their praises hear.

This shall my portion be, you say,
You'll crown my head with an immortal bay.

Give me a place less high, and more secure,
 This dangerous good I can't endure.
The peaceful banks which profound silence keep
The little boat securely passes by,
 But where with noise the waters creep
Turn off with care, for treacherous rocks are nigh.
 Then Muse farewell, I see your store
Can't pay for what is past, and I can trust no
 more.

Finis.

MISCELLANIES

OF

The Fuller Worthies' Library.

THE

POEMS

OF

LUCIUS CAREY,

VISCOUNT FALKLAND:

FOR THE

FIRST TIME COLLECTED AND EDITED

AFTER THE ORIGINAL TEXTS.

WITH

Memorial-Introduction and Notes.

BY THE

REV. ALEXANDER B. GROSART,

ST. GEORGE'S, BLACKBURN, LANCASHIRE.

PRINTED FOR PRIVATE CIRCULATION.

1871.

Contents.

Contents

Memorial-Introduction.

"See Falkland dies the virtuous and the just."
> ALEXANDER POPE : Essay on Man, Epistle iv.

"Unqualified and unsuspected praise may also be given to some others who followed in his [Lord Falkland's] course : high-minded and steady friends of liberty, who yet, to use the metaphor of one of them, 'had they seen the crown of England on a hedge-stake', would have remained with it to the death to defend it."
> LORD NUGENT : Memorials of Hampden, Vol. ii., p. 188.

ADY THERESA LEWIS in her "Lives of the Friends and Contemporaries of Lord Chancellor Clarendon: illustrative of Portraits in his Gallery" (3 vols. 8vo. 1852), has given the first place to our present Worthy ; and if it is only just to the matterful folios of the old "Biographia Britannica", to state that neither in relation to FALKLAND nor others, has she added much to facts previously known, it must equally be conceded that she has put these facts with a charm and brilliance and insight such as the earlier

Biographers never thought of. Moreover Lady Lewis has interwoven "Speeches" and "Letters" and extracts from other writings, that are simply referred to in the "Biographia". To these authorities the Reader will turn who would know as fully as seems possible thus far, the Life of our FALKLAND : but one, in this as in so many cases, must hope for publication some day of the treasures of family-papers too long left to gather dust and grime. Not until the noble examples of the houses of LINDSAY and EGLINTON and others have been followed, shall the world adequately KNOW our great historic names.

It is simply as a Poet or Writer of characteristic Verse that I have at present to do with LUCIUS CAREY, VISCOUNT FALKLAND : and that bears a very slight proportion to his utterances and actions otherwise. So that it were out-of-place to give in this Introduction anything like a Life. I have had occasion to make the same remark concerning JOHN NORRIS : and as with him I limit myself to a tabular statement of main facts, and shall add DR. TRIPLET's humbler and CLARENDON's splendid eulogium, and the obverse of the medal (so-to-say) in HORACE WALPOLE's criticism, with answer thereto, and the judicial estimate of SANFORD.

BORN at Burford, Oxfordshire, in or about the

year 1610 : eldest son of SIR HENRY CAREY of
Berkhampstead and Aldenham, Herts, and of
Elizabeth, daughter and sole heir of Lawrence
Tanfield, chief Baron of the Exchequer.   Sir
Henry raised to the peerage of Scotland, Novem-
ber 19th, 1620, by the title of VISCOUNT FALKLAND,
after the palace of Scotland's kings.   Appointed
Lord Deputy of Ireland in 1622, whither his
family removed.

EDUCATED in the outset at Trinity College,
Dublin : but all contemporary registers have disappeared.

RETURNED to England in his eighteenth year,
thoroughly accomplished.

ENTERED at St. John's College, Oxford : no
record of his attendance but a (published) letter
to Dr. Beale reveals that he was held to be, and
held himself as, a ' son ' of St. John's (B. B. as
before and Lady Lewis).

CHALLENGED SIR. F. WILLOUGHBY : put into
" Fleet Prison " 1629-30.   A quaint Letter of
his Father to the King (Charles I.) printed in the
" Cabala " : an earlier and better text than Lady
Lewis's in Chetham MS. (8012).   ANTHONY
A-WOOD calls him " a wild youth " : so only as SIR
PHILIP SIDNEY was, proud and sensitive and
swiftly passionate, never licentious or riotous.

355

In 19TH YEAR found himself, through his grand-father, in possession of "two very good houses very well furnished (worth about £2000 per annum) in a most pleasant country, and the two most pleasant places in that country" (Clarendon).

STUDIOUS and retired at inheritance of GREAT TEW: a ' prodigious ' reader.

FATHER died in September, 1633 : and name and estate inherited.

RETIRED rigidly to Great Tew for ' *study* ' : his house a kind of free College for his most eminent contemporaries, *e.g.* SHELDON, HENRY HAMMOND, MORLEY, CHILLINGWORTH, EARLE, CRESSY, TRIPLET, SANDYS, and greatest of all, BEN JONSON. At Great Tew chiefly was the "Religion of Protest-ants" composed, and Bishop Barlow in his "Remains" would seem to intimate obligations on the part of CHILLINGWORTH to FALKLAND, but doubtful beyond exchange of thoughts in the long-nighted conversations. The obligations would be mutual: for Falkland's "Discourse" of the "Infallibilitie of the Church of Rome" unques-tionably was talked out with the great Answerer of Jesuit KNOTT.

REBELLION (so-called) in Scotland 1638-9 : Viscount Falkland joined the king : verse-addresses to by COWLEY and WALLER on his ' safe ' return,

interesting biographically rather than poetically,
as is Sir Francis Wortley's later Elegy, albeit
Cowley turns his praise felicitously *e. g.*—

> " This great prince of knowledge is by Fate
> Thrust into th' noise and business of a State.
> All virtues, and some customs of the Court,
> Other men's labours, are at least his sport;
> While we......................
> Pace dully on, oft tire and often stay,
> Yet see his nimble Pegasus fly away.
> 'Tis Nature's fault, who did thus partial grow,
> And her estate of wit on one bestow,
> Whilst we, like younger brothers, got at best
> But a small stock, and must work out the rest.
> How could *he* answer't, should the State think fit
> To question a monopoly of wit.
> Such is the man whom we require, the same
> We lent the North ; untouch'd as is his fame :
> He is too good for war, and ought to be
> As far from danger as from fear he's free.
> Those men alone (and those are useful too),
> Whose valour is the only art they know,
> Were for sad war and bloody battle born ;
> Let them the State defend, and *he* adorn ".—

ELECTED Member of Parliament for Newport,
in 1640 : first speech on proposed impeachment
of STRAFFORD : others on Ship money—impeachment of Lord Finch, and Speech to House of Lords
in support of it.

DEBATE on ' Episcopecy' : vehement Speech against the ' Bishops ' : associated with Pym, Hampden, &c., &c,

OVERTURES from the King: 'accepts' office as Secretary of State and Chancellor of the Exchequer.

'REMONSTRANCES' of House of Commons: 'breach.'

' CIVIL WAR' : writes the royal State-papers.

BATTLE of Newbury : courts ' danger,' despondent.

DEAD: ' slain at Newbury, September 20th, 1643 in ' 34th year '.

A very short, quick-consumed Life, 1610 and 1643 rounding commencement and close : yet as JONSON sang finely in his " Pindarick Ode to the immortal memory and friendship of that noble pair, Sir Lucius Carey and Sir Henry Morison " of the latter, who was FALKLAND's brother-in-law (or rather would have been, but he died shortly before the marriage) :

> It is not growing like a tree,
> In bulk, doth make man better be ;
> Or standing long an oak, three hundred year,
> To sell a log at last, dry, bald, and sear :
> > A lily of a day
> > Is fairer far in May,
> Although it fall and die that night :
> It was the plant and flower of light.

In small proportions we just beauties see :
And in short measures life may perfect be.''[1]

Even our brief enumeration of outward FACTS
prepares us for literary likings and culture, and
independent of Clarendon's imperishable portraiture, it is satisfying to have DR. TRIPLET's simpler
and not less reverential, though overlooked words,
in his Epistle to our Worthy's son, prefixed to
the "Discourse of Infallibity" with additions
(1651.) We may cull a few sentences : " While
others studied the heraldry of horses, of doggs, or
at the best their owne, he though not inferior
to his neighbours in descent or honour, knowing
how much more glorious it is to be the first then
the last of a noble family (blood without vertue
making vice more conspicuous) was so far from
relying upon that empty title, that he seemed
ipse suos genuisse parentes, to have begotten his
ancestors, and to have given them a more illustrious life then he received from them. Though
there were so much true worth treasured up in
him, as well divided had been able to set up a
hundred pretenders, yet so much modesty withall
that the hearing of anything was more pleasing to

---

[1] In the " Underwoods ": Falkland repaid the Ode
with interest afterwards.

him than one tittle of his owne praise." Again :
" I may not forget his vast natural parts : *Dixit
ex tempore* saith PLINY of Isæus, *sed tanquam diu
scripserit*, and I may truly apply it to him; his
answers were quick and suddain, but such as
might very well seem to have been meditated.
In short his abilities were such as though he
needed no supplies of industry, yet his industry
such as though he had no parts at all. How
often have I heard him pitty those hawking gentlemen, who if unseasonable weather for their
sports had betrayed them to keep house, without
a worse exercise within doores, could not have
told how to have spent their time, and all because
they were such strangers to such good companions, with whom he was so familiar, such as
neither clog nor weary any with whom they converse, such company as Erasmus so much ex-
tolleth."   Once more, and deeper and invaluable
in relation to his theological-controversial books.
" His religion (for that I should begin with) was
the more eminent, because the more early, at
that age when yong gallants thin'k least of it ;
when they yong candidates of Atheisme begin
to dispute themselves out of a beleefe in a deity,
urging hard against that which indeed is best for
them that it should never be, a iudgment to come ;

then, I say, that salvation which these mention
with a scoff and a jeere, he began to work out
with fear and trembling, and effectually to remember, that is to honour and serve his Creator
in the daies of his youth." Finally : " Though
his courage were as great as his wit and learning
(and that is expression high enough) his valour
so undaunted and dreadlesse, as his great fall
witnest, in that fatal haile that made more or-
phans then his children ; yet to do an ill or
an uncivill thing, he was an arrant coward."

Turning now to CLARENDON, it is infinitely
touching to mark how broad and unlifted to the
close, was the shadow that fell across his stormy
and chequered Life, from the death of FALKLAND.
Their friendship was as deep and tender as
woman's for man in the best of both, and if the
yearning and wistfulness that break pathetically
out alike in the " History " and " Diary " and
" Letters ", be somewhat feminine, it is not dis-
honouring, contrariwise is very noble. With every
abatement the ' Life ' of his friend by CLARENDON
carries truth on the face of it. The lines are
identical with those of TRIPLET, only flooded with
a transfiguring glory. We have too few such
portraits in history to be willing to turn this
magnificent one to the wall as untrue, and " all

time" shall cherish it. I glean such portions
as are fitting for this Introduction. Every one
who has books at all has the "History" and the
full portrait can readily be studied there. "I
must here take leave", begins CLARENDON, "a
little longer to discontinue this narration : and if
the celebrating the memory of eminent and extraordinary persons, and transmitting their great
virtues, for the imitation of posterity, be one of
the principal ends and duties of history, it will
not be impertinent in this place to remember a
loss which no time will suffer to be forgotten, and
no success or good fortune could repair. In this
unhappy battle was slain the Lord Viscount
Falkland : a person of such prodigious parts of
learning and knowledge, of that inimitable sweetness and delight in conversation, of so flowing
and obliging a humanity and goodness to mankind, and of that primitive simplicity and integrity
of life, that if there were no other brand upon
this odious and accursed Civil War, than that
single loss, it must be most infamous and ex-
ecrable to all posterity.

Turpe mori, post te, solo non posse dolore.

Before this Parliament, his condition of life was
so happy that it was hardly capable of improve-

362

ment.   Before he came to be twenty years of
age, he was master of a noble fortune, which descended to him by the gift of a grandfather, without passing through his father or mother, who
were then both alive, and not well enough contented to find themselves passed by in the descent.
His education for some time had been in Ireland,
where his father had been Lord Deputy ; so that
when he returned to England, to the possession of
his fortune, he was unentangled with any acquaintance or friends, which usually grow up by the
custom of conversation ; and therefore was to
make a pure election of his company ; which he
chose by other rules than were prescribed to the
young nobility of that time.   And it cannot be
denied, though he admitted some few to his
friendship for the agreeableness of their natures,
and their undoubted affection to him, that his
familiarity and friendship, for the most part, was
with men of the most eminent and sublime parts
and of untouched reputation in point of integrity ;
and such men had a title to his bosom.   He was
a great cherisher of wit, and fancy, and good
parts in any man ; and, if he found them clouded
with poverty or want, a most liberal and bounti-
ful patron towards them, even above his fortune ;
of which, in those administrations he was such

a dispenser, as, if he had been trusted with it to such uses, and if there had been the least of vice in his expence, he might have been thought too prodigal. He was constant and pertinacious in whatsoever he resolved to do, and not to be wearied by any pains that were necessary to that end. And therefore having once resolved not to see London, which he loved above all places, till he had perfectly learned the Greek tongue, he went to his own house in the country, and pursued it with that indefatigable industry, that it will not be believed in how short a time he was master of it, and accurately read all the Greek histories. In this time, his house being little more than ten miles from Oxford, he contracted familiarity and friendship with the most polite and accurate men of that University; who found such an immenseness of wit, and such a solidity of judgement in him, so infinite a fancy, bound in by a most logical ratiocination, such a vast knowledge, that he was not ignorant in any thing, yet such an excessive humility, as if he had known nothing, that they frequently resorted and dwelt with him, as in a college situated in a purer air, so that his house was a university in a less volume, whither they came not so much for repose as study, and to examine and refine those grosser proportions, which laziness and consent made current in vulgar conversation." Again : " He was superior to all those passions and affections which attend vulgar minds, and was guilty of no other ambition than of knowledge, and to be reputed a lover of all good men ; and that made him too much a contemner of those arts, which must be 'indulged in the transactions of human affairs." Finally : " Thus fell that incomparable young man in the four and thirtieth year of his age, having so much dispatched the true business of life, that the eldest rarely attain to that immense knowledge, and the youngest enter not into the world with more innocency : whosoever leads such a life, needs to be the less anxious upon how short warning it is taken from him."[1]

Every lover of his country in her great names, must rejoice in so splendid a ' digression ' as gave to universal Literature a historic portraiture like that and its context : and he has a narrow soul who will refuse to do it kindred honour with that paid to MILTON's of PRESIDENT BRADSHAW, with which alone may it be mated.

It falls to us now to furnish HORACE WALPOLE's

---

[1] History of the Rebellion, book vii. pp. 444-55, (edn. 4o. 1816).

somewhat cynical and ultra-shrewd and shrewish
commentary on CLARENDON's estimate of FALK-
LAND in his " Royal and Noble Authors ". Here
it is: " There never was a stronger instance of
what the magic of words and the wit of an historian can effect, than in the character of this lord,
who seems to have been a virtuous, well-meaning
man with a moderate understanding (see his
Speeches which by no means shew great parts)
who got knocked on the head early in the civil
wars because it boded ill; and yet by the happy
solemnity of my lord Clarendon's diction, lord
Falkland is the favorite personage of that noble
work. We admire the pious Aeneas who, with all
the unjust and usurping pretensions, we are
taught to believe was the sent of heaven; but it
is the miserable Pallas we regret, though he was
killed before he had performed any action of consequence. That lord Falkland was a weak man,
to me appears indubitable. We are told he acted
with Hampden and the patriots, till he grew better
informed what was law. (It is evident from his
speech against the judges that this could not be
entirely the case; for he there asserts that those
men had not only acted contrary to ancient laws and
customs, but even to some made in that reign.)
It is certain that the ingenious Mr. Hume has

shewn that both king James and king Charles
acted upon precedents of prerogative which they
found established. Yet will this neither justify
them nor Lord Falkland. If it would, wherever
tyranny is established by law, it ought to be sacred
and perpetual. Those patriots did not attack king
Charles so much for the violation of the law, as to
oblige him to submit to the amendment of it ; and
I must repeat, that it was great weakness to
oppose a prince for breaking the law, and yet
scruple to oppose him when he obstructed the
correction of it. My lord Falkland was a sincere
Protestant; would he have taken up arms against
Henry the eight for adding new nonsense to
established Popery, and would he not have fought
to obtain the Reformation ? Again : When he
abandoned Hampden and that party, because he
mistrusted the extent of their designs, did it
justify his going over to the king ? With what—
I will not say conscience—but with what reason
could he who had been so sensible of grievances,
lend his hand to restore the authority from whence
these grievances flowed ? (See his speech against
the Bishops). Did the usurpation of Cromwell
prove that Laud had been a meek pastor ? If
Hampden and Pym were bad men and ambitious,
could not Lord Falkland have done more service

to the State by remaining with them and checking
their attempts and moderating their counsels, than
by offering his sword and abilities to the king ?
His lordship had felt the tyranny, did not he know
that if authorized by victory, that neither the king's
temper nor government were likely to become
more gentle ?   Did he think that loss of liberty or
loss of property are not such but when the laws of
the Land allow them to be so ? Not to descant too
long : it is evident to me that this lord shewed much
debility of mind and a kind of superstitious scruples,
that might flow from an excellent heart, but by
no means from a solid understanding. His refus-
ing to entertain spies or to open letters when
Secretary of State, were the punctilios of the
former, not of the latter ; and the putting on of a
clean shirt to be killed in, is no proof of sense
either in his lordship or in the historian (White-
locke) who thought it worth relating. Falkland's
signing the declaration that he did not believe
the king intended to make war on Parliament and
at the same time subscribing to buy twenty horse
for his majesty's service, comes under a description, which for the sake of the rest of his character
I am willing to call great infatuation ''.

   This is cold-blooded and incisive—the pen
turned into a dissecting knife—and it must be

sorrowfully admitted that WALPOLE does put his
finger on blots that it won't do with Mr. Mitford
to describe in his criticism of it, as "flippant and
paradoxical censures and capricious imagination."
(Gentleman's Magazine, as onward p. 42.)

Nevertheless he fastens on the ' mole ' and fails
to see the bulged forehead. With the political
points I am not called to intermeddle further than
to claim for so high-souled and genuine a man as
FALKLAND, INTEGRITY of motive in his resiling
from the larger issues declared for by HAMPDEN
and PYM, and CROMWELL, as well as an UPRIGHT
adherence to monarchy, spite of the falsities and
treacheries of the (then) king (and none saw through
him more penetratively than his Secretary of State).
But it is simply grotesque to have a man of the
calibre of HORACE WALPOLE pronouncing against
the intellectual character of such as Falkland.
He superciliously refers to the speeches, and de-
preciates them. We differ *toto cælo.* The
" Speeches " are extant, and others : and every
capable and impartial reader of them will recog-
nise them to be ' solid ', well-reasoned, well-put,
alternately eloquent and playfully homely, just
such Speeches (bating scriptural allusions of the
age) that would ' wield ' the House of Commons to-
day and fire the country. His tone is lofty his

invective keen; his wit, vivid and mordant; his 'resemblances', ready; his *ana*, pat; his wealth of resource, self-evident. Lady THERESA LEWIS's estimate is fully warranted when she says: "for clearness of statement, force of argument, correct antithesis, pointed satire, and high moral feeling, they may claim a distinguished place in the ranks of Parliamentary eloquence" (p. 178). Even more emphatically does all this hold of the State-Papers prepared for the King by him. They are grave, weighty, wise, noble utterances, and touched with a sweet sadness and hope against hope. I do not know but these Papers did more than even Vandyck's pathetic portrait to 'establish' Charles in the affections of the Royalists, and those not Royalists, afterwards. Some bear his signature: others only the King's: but the Falkland family would only be rendering justice to an ancestor who deserves well of them, were they to bring together worthily his Speeches and State-Papers, and all his Writings. His "Discourses" of Infallibility and the Episcopacy, and the sequels to them, reveal other sides of his intellect and scholarly attainment. There is through and through these treatises a unique POWER, and in manner you have a true Christian gentleman. I do not wonder that CLARENDON should have written of them before publication : " he writ two large discourses against the principal position of that Religion, with that sharpness of style, and full weight of reason, that the Church is deprived of great jewels in the concealment of them, and that they are not published to the world." WALPOLE's word ' weak ' is specially inappropriate. One can't read his slightest Letter (as that to Dr. Beale) without being impressed with ' *strength* ' as his characteristic in every way.

I close these personal matters with SANFORD's summary in his " Studies and Illustrations of the Great Rebellion " (1858) : " Lucius Carey, Viscount Falkland, who must be considered as representing the most conscientious among these seceders, was a man of varied attainments and deep learning, and at the same time of a morbidly sensitive disposition. He was not one of those calculating politicians who weigh every action of their lives in the balance of their own interests : but was open to the impression of violent prejudices and dislikes, which, as each gained the ascendant, carried him into the very opposite extremes. His hatred to episcopacy at the beginning of the Long Parliament was so strong, that under its influence he would seem at times to be beyond Pym in his hostility to the Court : but when a morbid dread of anarchy and the overthrow of constitutional monarchy took possession of his mind, he saw only the danger which existed, as he thought, from the progress of the popular party, and threw himself into the arms of the king. That he should find in that sphere feelings congenial to his own was not to be expected ; but the most melancholy fact of his history is that, after having abandoned the popular party through dread of anticipated excesses, he sanctioned by his presence, if not by his actual connivance, projects on the part of Charles which were wholly inconsistent with the preservation for the future of any constitutional rights. Want of balance of judgment was the defect in Falkland's character : it was not that he did not reflect; but that he suffered himself to be scared by possible evils on one side of the question without balancing them against the certain evils attendant on the other." (pp 383-4.)

It had been more correct to have said ' the King threw himself into Falkland's arms' as similarly Walpole is wrong in stating he ' *offered* ' his sword and abilities to the king. The truth is here as so often, the nearer we get to Charles I., the more ' crooked' and contemptible he proves to be : and the very noblest partook of shame by mere association with him. The 'Answers' returned for the King by Falkland shew how greatly his Secretary strove to ennoble the sorry and treacherous creature he served : and one can't help feeling that the peril of Newbury as earlier at Edgehill was courted because of the fading away of the lustre of his ideal. There lay probably his human ' weakness' : but it is to be softly, tearfully whispered of not maligned.

The Poems of our Worthy, now for the first time collected, have the extrinsic undying interest that they are his, and that in various ways they have unmistakeably, his impress, and so are valuable autobiographically. Intrinsically perhaps, Bishop EARLE's verdict is not far from accurate : "Dr. Earle, says AUBREY, "would not allow Lord Falkland to be a good poet, though a great wit; he writ not a smooth verse, but a good deal of sense". Granted that the verse is not altogether 'smooth' : but then Sternhold and Hopkins were 'smooth', and without the 'sense'. The sense is something, even when as Mr. MITFORD puts it, it is thrown out on casual hints, being as it were, only the off-flowering of his deeper studies " (as onward p. 42). There are occasional lovely 'similes' and the subjects of the Elegies make us doubly thankful for them.

That FALKLAND was regarded as a true Poet if only he had cultivated his faculty is pleasantly confirmed by SUCKLING in his "Session of the Poets" :

> "A Session was held the other day,
> And Apollo was at it himself, they say,
> The laurel that had been so long reserved,
> Was now to be given to him best deserved.
>
> Hales sat by himself, most gravely did smile
> To see them about nothing keep such a coil ;
> Apollo had spied him, but knowing his mind,
> Pass'd by, and *call'd Falkland who sate just behind.*
>
> *But he was of late so gone with divinity,*
> *That he had almost forgot his poetry;*
> *Though to say the truth and Apollo did know it,*
> *He might have been both his priest and his poet."*

Very touching are the allusions anticipative of an early death in the closing poem to Sandys of our little collection, which also seems really to have been his last.   How solemn are words like these therein :

> " How e're I finish here, my Muse her daies
> Ends in expressing thy deserved praise,
> Whose fate in this seemes fortunately cast,
> To have so just an action for her last.
> And since there are, who have been taught that death

Inspireth prophecies, expelling breath,
I hope when these foretell what happie gaines
Posteritie shall reape from these thy paines
. . . . . belief will not refuse
To the last accents of a dying Muse."

LADY THERESA LEWIS knew only the ' Eclogue'
on BEN JONSON, Lines on the death of Dr. Donne
and Verses to Grotius. She has reprinted the two
former. The late accomplished Rev. JOHN MITFORD
was the first to call attention to the Poetry
of Falkland. This he did in the " Gentleman's
Magazine " (as below[1]) and through our late and
lamented friend JOHN BRUCE, Esq., was the first
to publish the long Elegy on the Lady-Marquesse
of Hamilton. He erroneously gave the 3rd Lord
Falkland's wretched (few) lines on Lord Hastings
from the *Lachrymæ Musarum* (1649) as our
Falkland's and forgot altogether the notable
tribute to Dr. Donne. The whole have been
collated carefully with the original texts and
MSS. : and we have been startled with the
number of misprints and misreadings of Mr.
Mitford, besides departure from the Author's own
orthography. We commenced marking in foot-notes

---

[1] For 1835 : Vol 158 pp. 42-3. See also 43-8 : 268-
272 : 389-92. For 1838 : pp. 154 *et seqq* and 272 *et seqq*.

these *errata* : but they proved so flagrant and frequent that we desisted, as unwilling to deform our
pages as well as reluctant to shew short-comings in
one who in so many ways did noble service to our
poetical Literature.   The following may be accepted as specimens :   'direct' for 'divert',
' wayes' for 'bayes ', ' rash ' for ' vast', ' incite '
for ' recite ', 'ragged too ' for ' be so ', ' though '
for ' through ', ' colde ' for ' colder ', ' new ' for
' more', ' animate ' for ' imitate ', ' bend ' for
' bent ', ' woefull ' for 'usefull ', ' chymists' for
'chymicks', ' supplies ' for ' supples '.   A few
we have felt obliged to notice in their places.

It affords us no little gratification to execute
the task of love assigned to Mr. Bruce by Mr.
Mitford.   Such notes as are taken from the
" Gentleman's Magazine " are marked with the
initials of Mr. Mitford and Mr. Bruce respectively.   The Author's own have F and mine G—
the whole (not very numerous) intended to help
the Reader to a knowledge of facts and circumstances belonging to the several pieces.   And so
I end our little Introduction with an adapted
snatch from *Paradisus Animæ :*

> " O Falkland ! spirit free from gall,
> Thy words like drops of honey fall,
> 　　　　Distilled in sweetest charity :

May we, like thee, grow meek and still ;
The Christ our hearts with sweetness fill,
  Beyond all Earth's felicity ".

ALEXANDER B. GROSART.

*** The following books and tractates of Lord Falkland I found in the Library of Trinity College, Dublin. No. 1 seems to have been deposited in the Library by its noble Author. Throughout he has corrected misprints and other things with the nicest carefulness :

1. A Speech made to the House of Commons concerning Episcopacy. By the Lord Viscount Faulkland. London, Printed for Thomas Walkely, 1641 (4to). Title-page and pp. 3—6. (Trinity College, as above, R. R. pp. 8.)

2. The Speech or Declaration of the Lord Favlkland to the Lords of the Vpper House, upon the delivery of the Articles of the Commons Assembly in Parliament against the Lord Finch. London, Printed for John Bartlett, and are to be sold at Austin's Gate. 1641. (4to) Title-page and pp. 9.

3. A Letter Sent from the Lord Falkland, Principal Secretarie to his Majestie. To the Right Honourable Henry, Earle of Cumberland, at York. Sept. 30, 1642. Concerning the late Conflict before Worcester, with the state of his Majestie's Armie now at Shrewsbury. To-gether with his Majesties Speech to the Gentry and

Freeholders of the County of Salop, Septemb. 28, 1642. Printed at York, Octob. 1, and now reprinted at London for J. T. October 7, 1642.(4o). Title-page and pp, 6 [unpaged].

4. The Humble Petition of the Inhabitants of the County of Essex to his Majesty. With his Majesties Gratious Answer thereunto. Also the Petition presented by the inhabitants of the afore said County to both Houses of Parliament. Printed, by his Majesties Command at Oxford, January 11. By Leonard Lichfield, Printer to the University. 1642. Title-page and pp. 6. *₊* The Answer signed Falkland.

5. A Dravght of a Speech concerning Episcopacy, By the Lord Viscount Falkland. Found since his " Death amongst his Papers, written with his own hand. Oxford. Printed by Leonard Lichfield, Printer to the Vniversity, 1644. (4to). Title and pp. 9.

6. Of the Infallibilitie of the Church of Rome. A Discourse written by the Lord Viscount Falkland. Now first published from a Copy in his owne hand. Oxford, Printed by H. Hall, Printer to the University. 1645. (4to). Title and pp. 18. [Very imperfect aud inaccurate.]

7. Sir Lucius Cary, late Lord Viscount of Falkland, His Discourse of Infallibility, with an Answer to it : And his Lordship's Reply. Never before published. Together with Mr. Walter Mountague's Letter concerning the changing his Religion, Answered by my Lord of Falklrnd. London, Printed by Gartrude Dawson, for Iohn Hardesty, and are to be sold at the Signe of the Black Spread Eagle, in Duck Lane, 1651. (4to.) Title-page— 10 pages signed Triplet., Ep.-Dedicatory—Preface pp. 8,

signed I. P.—Treatise, &c. pp. 25 [all unpaged] Answer,
&c., pp. 1—49 : Lord Falkland's Answer pp. 51-298.

Besides these there are enumerated (8) Speech
on Ill Councellors about the King. 1640. (9)
Speech against the Bishops, Feb. 9, 1640. (10)
A Letter to Mr. F. M. at end of Charles
Gataker's answer to Five Captious Questions.
1673. The Letter to Dr. Beale, usually enumerated among his Works, is a short Note
merely, given in Biog. Brit. (*s.n.* Carey) and by
Lady Lewis (pp. 8-9). I suspect No. 9 is the
same with No. 1.

Poems of Viscount Falkland.

I. AN ELEGY ON DR. DONNE: BY SIR LUCIUS CARY.[1]

POETS attend, the elegie I sing
Both of a doubly-naméd priest and king :
Instead of coates and pennons bring
    your verse,
For you must be chiefe mourners at his hearse :
A tombe your Muse must to his fame supply,
No other monuments can never die ;
And as he was a two-fold priest; in youth
Apollo's ; afterwards the voyce of Truth,
God's conduit pipe for grace, Who chose him for
His extraordinary embassador :
So let His liegiers[2] with the poets joyne ;
Both having shares, both must in grief combine :

---

[1] Dr. Donne: born 1573 : died March 31st 1631. Our text is from the 1639 edition of the Poems : but collation of after-editions shews no various readings. G.

[2] = ambassadors or ministers of the Gospel, usually spelled 'lieger'. G.

Whil'st Johnson[1] forceth with his elegie
Teares from a griefe-unknowing Scythian's eye,
(Like Moses, at whose stroke the waters gusht
From forth the rock and like a torrent rusht)
Let Lawd[2] his funerall sermon preach, and show
Those vertues, dull eyes were not apt to know,
Nor leave that piercing theme, till it appeares,
To be Goodfriday, by the Churche's teares.
Yet make not grief too long oppresse our powers,
Lest that his funerall sermon should prove ours.
Nor yet[3] forget that heavenly eloquence,
With which he did the bread of life dispense ;
Preacher and orator discharg'd both parts,
With pleasure for our sense, health for our hearts,
And the first such, (though a long studied Art,
Tell us our soule is all in every part)
None was so marble, but whil'st him he heares
His soul so long, dwelt onely in his eares,
And from thence (with the fiercenesse of a flood
Bearing downe vice) victual'd with that blest
          food

---

[1] Throughout Ben Jonson's name is spelled Johnson
by Falkland. G.

[2] *Sic* : Laud no doubt meant, a very noticeable point as
one remembers the Author's attitude towards him subsequently. He died in 1645. G.

[3] Lady Theresa Lewis, as before, misprints 'let'. G.

Their hearts ; His seed in none could faile to grow,
Fertile he found them all, or made them so :
No druggist of the soul, bestow'd on all
So catholikely a curing cordiall.
Nor onely in the pulpit dwelt his store ;
His works work'd much, but his example more :
It selfe was oftentimes Divinitie :
That preach'd on worky[1] dayes, his Poetry
Those Anthems (almost second Psalmes) he writ
To make us know the Crosse, and value it,
(Although we owe that reverence to that name
We should not need warmth from an under flame)
Creates a fire in us so neare extreame
That we would die for, and upon this theame.
Next his so pious Litanie, which none can
But count divine, except a Puritan ;
And that but for the name, nor this, nor those
Want anything of sermons, but the prose.
Experience makes us see, that many a one
Owes to his countrey his religion ;
And in another, would as strongly grow,
Had but his nurse and mother taught him so :
Not he, the ballast on his judgement hung :
Nor did his preconceit do either wrong :
He labour'd to exclude what ever sinne

---

[1] = work-day or week-day. G.

By time or carelesnesse had entred in ;
Winnow'd the chaffe from wheat, but yet was
    loath
A too hot zeale should force him burne them both;
Nor would allow of that so ignorant gall,
Which to save blotting often would blot all ;
Nor did those barbarous opinions owne,
To think the organs sinne, and faction, none.
Nor was there expectation to gaine grace
From forth his sermons onely, but his face ;
So primitive a looke, such gravitie
With humblenesse, and both with pietie ;
So mild was Moses' countenance, when he pray'd
For them whose Satanisme his power gainsaid ;
And such his gravitie, when all God's band
Receiv'd his word (through him) at second hand,
Which joyn'd, did flames of more devotion move
Then ever Argive Hellen's could of love.
Now to conclude, I must my reason bring,
Wherefore I call'd him in his title, king :
That kingdome the philosophers believ'd
To excell Alexander's, nor were griev'd
By feare of losse (that being such a prey
No stronger then one's selfe can force away) :
The kingdome of one's selfe, thus he enjoy'd,
And his authoritie so well imploy'd,
That never any could before become

So great a monarch in so small a roome ;
He conquer'd rebell passions, rul'd them so,
As under-spheares by the first Mover goe ;
Banisht so farre their working, that we can
But know he had some, for we knew him man.
Then let his last excuse his first extreames :
His age saw visions, though his youth dream'd
    dreams.

II. AN EGLOGUE ON THE DEATH OF BEN JOHNSON, BETWEEN MELYBÆUS AND HYLAS.[1]

Melybœus.

HYLAS, the cleare day boasts a glorious
    sunne,
    Our troope is ready, and our time is
    come ;
That fox who hath so long our lambs destroi'd,

---

[1] From " Jonsonus Virbius, or the Memorie of Ben Johnson revived by the friends of the Muses. 1638 (4o). In our edition of Sir John Beaumont's Poems we have given his son's Lines from this volume. **G.** [See a Letter from Sir Kenelm Digby to Dr. Duppa, relative to the publication of Jonsonus Virbius " (from Harl. **MS.** 4153. f. 21) in Private Memoirs of Sir K. Digby. p. liii. **M.**] [Ben Jonson born 1574 : died August 16. 1637. **G.**]

And daily in his prosperous rapine joy'd,
Is earthed not farre from hence; old Aegon's sonne,
Rough Corilas, aud lusty Coɪydon,
In part the sport, in part revenge desire,
And both thy tarrier[1] and thy aid require.
Haste, for by this, but that for thee wee staid
The prey-devourer had our prey bin made.

   Hylas. Oh! Melybæus now I list not hunt,
Nor have that vigor as before I wont;
My presence will afford them no reliefe,
That beast I strive to chase, is only griefe.

   Mil. What meane thy folded armes, thy downe-
      cast eyes,
Teares which so fast descend, and sighs which rise?
What meane thy words which so distracted fall,
As all thy ioyes had now one funerall?
Cause for such griefe, can our retirements yeeld?
That followes Courts, but stoopes not to the field.
Hath thy stern step-dame to thy sire reveal'd
Some youthful act, which thou couldst wish con-
      cealed?
Part of thy herd hath some close thiefe convey'd
From open pastures to a darker shade?
Part of thy flock hath some fierce torrent drown'd?
Thy harvest failed? or Amarillis frown'd?

---

   [1] = terrier, *i. e.* a dog. G.

Hyl. Nor love, nor anger, accident, nor thiefe
Hath raised the waves of my unbounded griefe!
To cure this cause, I would provoke the ire
Of my fierce step-dame or severer sire ;
Give all my heards, fields, flocks, and all the
    grace
That ever shone in Amarillis' face.
Alas! that bard, that glorious bard is dead,
Who, when I whilome cities visited,
Hath made them seeme but houres which were
    full dayes,
Whilst he vouchsaft me his harmonious layes,
And when he lived, I thought the countrey then
A torture, and no mansion but a den.
    Mel. Johnson you meane, unlesse I much doe
    erre,
I know the person by the character.
    Hyl. You guesse aright, it is too truely so,
From no lesse spring could all these rivers flow.
    Mel. Ah, Hylas! then thy griefe I cannot call
A passion, when the ground is rationall ;
I now excuse thy teares and sighes, though those
To deluges, and these to tempests rose.
The great instructor gone, I know the age
No lesse laments, than doth the widdow'd stage,
And only Vice and Folly now are glad—
Our gods are troubled, and our prince is sad.

He chiefly who bestowes light, health, and art,
Feeles this sharpe griefe pierce his immortall
      heart,
He his neglected lire away hath throwne,
And wept a larger, nobler Helicon,
To finde his hearbs, which to his wish prevaile
For the lesse loved, should his owne favorite faile ;
So moan'd himself, when Daphne he ador'd.
That arts relieving al, should faile their lord.
    Hyl. But say, from whence in thee this know-
      ledge springs,
Of what his favour was with gods and kings?
    Mel. Dorus, who long had known men, books,
      and townes,
At last the honour of our woods and downes,
Had often heard his songs, was often fir'd
With their inchanting power, ere he retired,
And ere himselfe to our still groves he brought
To meditate on what his Muse had taught ;
Here all his joy was to revolve alone,
All that her musicke to his soule had showne,
Or in all meetings to divert the streame
Of our discourse, and make his friend his theame,
And praising works which that rare loome had
      weaved,
Impart that pleasure which he had receaved.
So in sweet notes (which did all tunes excell,

But what he prais'd) I oft have heard him tell
Of his rare pen, what was the use and price,
The bayes of vertue, and the scourge of vice;
How the rich ignorant he valued least,
Nor for the trappings would esteeme the beast;
But did our youth to noble actions raise,
Hoping the meed of his immortal praise.
How bright and soone his Muse's morning shone,
Her noone how lasting and her evening none!
How speech exceeds not dumbenesse nor verse
     prose,
More than his verse the low rough rimes of those
(For such his seene, they seem'd,) who highest
     rear'd,
Possest Parnassus ere his power appear'd;
Nor shall another pen his fame dissolve,
Till we this doubtfull probleme can resolve :—
Which in his workes we most transcendent see,
Wit, judgment, learning, art, or industry:
Which ' *till* ' is never, so all jointly flow,
And each doth to an equall torrent grow.
His learning such, no author, old or new
Except his reading, that deserved his view;
And such his judgement, so exact his test
As what was best in bookes, as what bookes best,
That had he join'd those notes his labours tooke

From each most praised and praise-deserving
      booke,
And could the world of that choise treasure boast,
It need not care though all the rest were lost:
And such his wit, he writ past what he quotes,
And his productions farre exceed his notes,
So in his workes where ought inserted growes,
The noblest of the plants ingrafted showes,
That his adopted children equall not
The generous issue his own braine begot;
So great his art, that much which he did write.
Gave the wise wonder, and the crowd delight.
Each sort as well as sex admir'd his wit,
The hees and shees, the boxes and the pit ;
And who lesse lik't within, did rather chuse
To taxe their judgements, than suspect his Muse.
How no spectator his chaste stage could call
The cause of any crime of his ; but all
With thoughts and wils purg'd and amended rise,
From th' ethicke lectures of his comedies,
Where the spectators act, and the sham'd age
Blusheth to meet her follies on the stage:
Where each man finds some light he never sought,
And leaves behind some vanitie he brought ;
Whose politicks no lesse the minds direct,
Then these the manners ; nor with less effect.
When his majesticke tragedies relate,

All the disorders of a tottering State,
All the distempers which on kingdomes fall
When ease, and wealth, and vice are generall—,
And yet the minds against all feare assure,
And telling the disease, prescribe the cure:
Where, as he tels what subtle wayes, what friends
(Seeking their wicked and their wisht-for ends)
Ambitious and luxurious persons prove,
Whom vast desires or mighty wants doth move
The generall frame to sap and undermine,
In proud SEJANUS and bold CATALENE;
So in his vigilant PRINCE and consul's part,
He showes the wiser and the nobler arts,
By which a State may be unhurt upheld,
And all those workes destroy'd which hell would
        build
Who (not like those who with small praise had writ,
Had they not cal'd in judgment to their wit).
Us'd not a tutoring hand his to direct,
But was sole workeman and sole architect.
And sure by what my friend did daily tell
If he but acted his own part as well
As he writ those of others, he may boast
The happy fields hold not a happier ghost.
    Hyl. Strangers will think this strange, yet he,
        deare youth
Where most he past beleefe, fell short of truth;

Say on, what more he said—this gives reliefe,
And though it raise my cause, it bates my griefe.
Since Fate's decreed him now no longer liv'd,
I joy to hear him by thy friend reviv'd.

Mel. More he would say and better (but I spoile
His smoother words with my unpolisht stile)
And having told what pitch his worth attain'd,
He then would tell us what reward it gain'd;
How in an ignorant and learn'd age he swaid
(Of which the first he found, the second made);
How he, when he could know it, reapt his fame,
And long outliv'd the envy of his name;
To him how daily flockt, what reverence gave
All that had wit, or would be thought to have,
Or hope to gaine, and in so large a store
That to his ashes they can pay no more;
Except those few, who censuring, thought not so,
But aim'd at glory from so great a foe:
How the wise, too, did with meere wits agree
As Pembroke,[1] Portland,[2] and grave Aubigny;[3]

---

[1] The 'renowned' William Herbert Earl of Pembroke whose poems were most unworthily edited and published, by Dr. Donne's son in 1630. G.

[2] Query—Jerome Weston, second earl of Portland: died 16th May, 1662. His father was a favorite ambassador of James I. G.

[3] Lord d' Aubigny, the 'Aulbanie' of Jonson's Conversations, &c., p. 19. (1842). G.

Nor thought the rigid'st senator a shame
To contribute to so deserv'd a fame :
How great Eliza,[1] the retreate of those
Who weake and injured, her protection chose,
Her subjects' joy, the strength of her allies,
The fear and wonder of her enemies,
With her judicious favours did infuse
Courage and strength into his younger muse ;
How learnèd James,[2] whose praise no end shall
     finde,
(But still enjoy a fame pure like his mind),
Who favoured quiet and the arts of peace
(Which in his halcion days found large increase) ;
Friend to the humblest if deserving swaine,
Who was himself a part of Phoebus' traine ;
Declared great Johnson worthiest to receive
The garland which the Muses' hands did weave,
And though his bounty did sustain his dayes
Gave a more welcome pension in his praise ;
How mighty Charles,[3] amidst that weighty
     care,
In which three kingdomes as their blessing
     share,
Whom as it tends with ever watchfull eyes

---

[1] Queen Elizabeth. G.   2 James I. G.
[3] Charles I. G.

That neither power may force, nor art surprise
So bounded by no shore, graspes all the maine,
And farre as Neptune claimes, extends his reigne;
Found still some time to heare and to admire
The happy sounds of his harmonious lire,
And oft hath left his bright exalted throne,
And to his Muse's feet combined his own :
As did his Queen,[1] whose person so disclosed,
A brighter nimph than any part imposed,[2]
When she did joine by an harmonious choise
Her gracefull motions to his powrfull voice ;
How above all the rest was Phoebus fir'd
With love of arts, which he himselfe inspir'd,
Nor oftner by his light our sence was cheer'd
Than he in person to his sight appeard ;[2]
Nor did he write a line but to supply
With sacred flame the radiant God was by.

> *Hyl.* Though none I ever heard this last re-
> hearse

I saw as much when I did see his verse.

> *Mel.* Since he when living did such honors
> have,

---

[1] In his Maskes. F.

[2] Mr. Mitford makes sad havoc of this couplet
by misprinting ' disclosed ' (twice) as the final word of
each line. G.

What now will piety pay to his grave?
Shall of the rich (whose lives were low and vile,
And scarce deserve a grave, much less a pile)
The monuments possesse an ample roome,
And such a wonder lye without a tombe ?
Raise thou him one in verse, and there relate
His worth, thy griefe, and our deplorèd state ;
His great perfections our great losse recite,
And let them meerely weepe who cannot write.

  Hyl. I like thy saying, but oppose thy
    choise ;
So great a taske as this requires a voice
Which must be heard and listned to by all,
And Fame's owne trumpet but appears too small :
Then for my slender reede to sound his name,
Would more my folly than his praise proclaime ;
And when you wish my weaknesse sing his
    worth,
You charge a mouse to bring a mountaine forth.
I am by nature formed, by woes made dull,
My head is emptier than my heart is full ;
Griefe doth my braine impaire, as tears supply,
Which makes my face so moist, my pen so dry.
Nor should this work proceed from woods and
    downes,
But from th' academies, courts, and townes ;

Let Digby,[1] Carew,[2] Killigrew,[3] and Maine,[5]
Godolphin,[5] Waller,[6] that inspirèd traine,
Or whose rare pen beside deserves the grace
Or of an equall or a neighbouring place,
Answer thy wish, for none so fit appeares
To raise his tombe as who are left his heires;
Yet for this cause no labour need be spent,
Writing his workes he built his monument.

Mel. If to obey in this thy pen be loth
It will not seem thy weaknesse but thy sloth.
Our townes prest by our foes' invading might,
Our ancient Druids and young virgins fight,
Employing feeble limbes to the best use;

---

[1] Sir Kenlem Digby : born 1603 : died 1665. G.

[2] Thomas Carew the Poet : born 1589 : died 1638. See
Carew's Poems, ed. Hazlitt, p. xxxvii. G.

[3] Thomas Killigrew, known as King Charles' Jester.
Died 1682. G.

[4] Dr. Jasper Mayne : died 1672 : a Dramatist and Versifier as well as Preacher. Curiously enough Falkland
himself is associated with these same names in George
Daniel's MS. poems :

  " The noble *Falkland, Digbie, Carew, Maine,*
    Beaumond, Sands," &c.

                    See Hazlitt's Carew, as supra, p. xlv.

[5] Sidney Godolphin : occasional Versifier. Died 1643.
G.

[6] Edmund Waller the Poet. Died 1687. G.

So Johnson dead, no pen should plead excuse :
For elegies, howle all who cannot sing,
For tombes, bring turfe who cannot marble bring.
Let all their forces mix, joyne verse to rime,
To save his fame from that invader, Time ;
Whose power, though his alone may well restraine
Yet to so wisht an end no care is vaine ;
And Time, like what our brookes act in our sight,
Oft sinkes the weightie and upholds the light ;
Besides, to this, thy paines I strive to move,
Less to expresse his glory than thy love.
Not long before his death, our woods he meant
To visit, and descend from Thames to Trent.
Meet with thy elegy his pastorall,
  And rise as much as he vouchsaft to fall.
Suppose it chance no other pen doe joine
In this attempt, and the whole worke be thine,
When the fierce fire the rash boy kindled, raign'd,
The whole world suffered—earth alone complain'd :
Suppose that many more intend the same,
More taught by art and better known to fame ;
To that great deluge, which so farre destroid,
The earth her springs, as Heaven his showers
        emploid,
So may, who highest markes of honours weares,
Admit meane partners in this flood of teares ;
So oft the humblest joine with loftiest things,

Nor onely princes weep the fate of kings.

    Hyl. I yeild, I yeild! Thy words my thoughts
      have fir'd,
And I am less perswaded than inspir'd;
Speech shall give sorrow vent, and that releefe,
The woods shall echo all the cittie's griefe.
I oft have verse on meaner subjects made:
Should I give presents and leave debts unpaid?
Want of invention here is no excuse,
My matter I shall find, and not produce,
And (as it fares in crowds) I onely doubt
So much would passe, that nothing will get out;
Else in this worke which now my thoughts intend,
I shall find nothing hard but how to end.
I then but aske for time to smooth my layes,
(And imitate in this the pen I praise)
Which by the subject's power embalm'd, may last
Whilst the sun light, the earth doth shadows cast;
And feather'd by those winges, fly among men,
Farre as the fame of Poetry and Ben.

                             F<small>ALKLAND</small>.

III. AN ECLOGUE UPPON THE DEATH OF THE LADIE MARQUESSE HAMIL·TON, BETWEENE AMARILLIS AND CLORIS.

[The following poem was discovered by the late JOHN BRUCE, Esq., afterwards so successful a Worker and literary Antiquary, among the Harleian MSS. 6947, article 31. It was communicated by him to the Gentleman's Magazine (Vol. 163 : pp. 153-160) as ' never before printed ' and Mr. Mitford gave it welcome, urging later that his modest Correspondent would collect and edit Falkland's Verse (Vol. 163 : p 172). Mr. Bruce furnishes these notes on the ' fair ladie' : " The lady whom the Eclogue commemorates was Mary, the first wife of James, Marquis and afterwards Duke, of Hamilton. Endowed with that fatal beauty which distinguished the race of Villiers, from which, on her mother's side, she was descended, she was, at the same time, eminent for other and higher qualities. Bishop Burnet speaks of her in terms which almost seem borrowed from the poem before us. " She was Lady," he says, " of the Queen's Bed-chamber, and admitted by her Majesty into an entire confidence and friendship ; and not only was her

399

honour unstained, but even her fame continued
untouched with calumny, she being so strict to
the severest rules as never to admit to those
follies which pass in that style for gallantry. She
was a most affectionate and dutiful wife, and
used to say, ' She had every reason to bless God
for having given her such a husband, whom as
she loved perfectly, she was not ashamed to obey.'
But that which crowned all her other perfections
was the deep sense she had of religion ; she lived,
and died in the communion of the Church of
England, and was a very devout person. Many
years before her death, she was so exact in observ-
ing her retirements to her closet, that, notwithstanding all her avocations, and the divertisements
of Court, (as the writer was informed by one that
had lived with her,) no day passed without her
bestowing large portions of her time on them,
besides her constant attendance on the chappel ".
(Memoirs of the Dukes of Hamilton, p 407, edit.
1667.) This worthy subject for the muse of Lord
Falkland, died on the 10th. of May, 1638." Of the
Eclogue itself, Mr. Bruce observes : "The merits of
the poem are equal to those of the best of the poems
you [Mr. Mitford in Gentleman's Magazine] have
published, and, making allowance for blemishes
attributable to the false taste of the time, it may

be pronounced a fanciful and elegant composition.
It contains similes of great beauty, and lines
which are singularly harmonious." The MS. is
signed ' Fauckland ' and Mr. Bruce thought the
signature autograph. This seems a mistake : but
the spelling even of names of the same person, on
the same page, was at the period, extremely
arbitrary and uncertain. We have collated the
text of the Gentleman's Magazine with the
Harleian MS. with advantage. G.]

Am.

LORIS, alas ! what could soe long divide
Thy soe lov'd selfe from soe belov'd a
side ?
Thou wert not wont to have the power to stay
From thy deare Amarillis a wholle day :
For my firme love soe long, spent all on thee,
A love almost of the same age with mee,
Thou ow'st mee soe thyselfe, when I am left
Att all by thee, that absence is a theft ;
Nor can thy wordes excuse soe blacke a crime ;
How great soe'r the cause, how short the tyme :
Could I but how I bore your absence showe,
(Or rather could I not beare it,) could you knowe
My thoughts, and my distracted passions see
You to accuse yourselfe would ioyne with mee :

What dire mishap was ever tould by fame,
Or loveing fancies have the heart to frame ;
All accidents which our fraile lives pursue,
What man can suffer, or what fate can doe,
Did then, as yours, to my sad thoughts arise,
And shew you soe to my affrighted eyes :
Divided thoughts my doubtfull minde did teare,
Which fear'd the more not knowing what to feare :
Sometymes I fear'd in your intended way
Some fatall beast had met soe faire a pray :
Sometymes I fear'd some pitfall, or some gynne,
Made with intent to cast destroyers in,
By want of care mishapt uppon by you,
Had harm'd us more then those could ever doe ;
I fear'd some satyr, by your beauty fir'd
Had to the ruyn of your fame aspir'd
Or river God (mov'd both with love and shame
That all his streames could not allay the flame)
Had you or forc'd or by some wile betrai'd,
And to his wat'ry pallaces convay'de :
I fear'd all dangers any life can prove,
But, above all, I fear'd your want of love :
Were not my parents' care my hardest fate,
Which cloth'd in love works the effects of hate,
Then not by them restrain'd, I, like the winde,
Had run to seeke that which I fear'd to finde,

And search't each nooke, made hollowe by the
    waves,
Clim'd highest rocks, and entred darkest caves,
Had left noe place unransack't by my care,
As now noe God was left unsought by prayer;
I scarce am yet reviv'd, but still I feare
That I am not awake and you not heare.
   Clo. How can I pardon grant, how can you
    move,
For your least doubt of my immortall love?
Not young Amintas, glory of our plaines,
Hope of our nimphes, and envy of our swaines,
Although his love his loveliness transcend,
Although his words, thoughts, and deedes make
    mee their end,
Though he proclaimes mee all his wishe and care,
And only askes mee of the Godes in prayer:
His best of wheat and creame before mee poures,
Bringes mee his fairest fruite, his freshest floures.
What birds his twigs, what fish his nets can take
All that his silkewormes or his bees, can make,
The friskingst calves and kids his pastures hold,
And purest lambes the honour of his fould;
Courts mee with verse which gains the generall
    praise,
To which even Ægon grants away the bayes,
Which, whilst he tunes, to hearken after him,

The bird to fly, the fish forget to swym ;
Could make mee misse thee one appointed houre,
Or any secret in his bosom poure
Withheld from thine, nor by all actions prove
Freindshipp may rule with greater power than love :
Affection made that fault which now made thee
Unjust, to charge a want of it in mee :
Shee lov'd herselfe, to you her love were light
Would bring you danger to obtain your sight;
Nor should I hope your freindshipp, were I knowne
With perill of your health to buy my owne :
Soe rather chose my sicknes to endure,
Than your infeccon[1] should beget my cure.

   Am. What pestilence doth this our realme
      affright,
For some neglected sacrifice or rite ?
How ere the cause were just could Phebus please,
This plague should one so like his Daphne cease ?[2]
To mee, soe struck, how could you faile to send ?
Your greatest danger askt your greatest friend :
My skill in hearbes, though small, had serv'd to
      prove
Noe mercenary hand can tend like love.

   Clo. If such a sicknes had opprest my powers
Soe soone my eyes had not been joyd by yours :

---

    [1] = infection. G.   [2] = seize. G.

Not all the lives a plague could beare away
Doubled, to us would our great losse repay.
Whose griefe retain'd mee, fearing to impart
Sorrow to yours from my infected hearte ;
Before your sight, like the bright torch of day
My clowdy mistes of grieffe could chase away.

   Am. I and Amintas well, what cause could
     raise
So deep a griefe, and aske so high a praise ?
And hee is well and now by yonder grove,
His fayrest sheep the fayrer sheapard drove.

   Clo. My flockes I guided and did guiding sing,
Neere the chief mansion of the greatest king :
Whose providence with greater care doth keepe
His royal fold, than wee preserve our sheepe.
There saw a troope, of which each glorious dame,
With forme and state did love and service clayme :
Soe shew her nymphes when chast Diana crownes
Eurotas' banks in Cynthus loftie downes ;
So faire a traine to Paphos welcome home
Returnèd Venus, joyes to see her come
After long stay, and to expresse it poures
On all her altars frankincense and flowers :
But these, alas ! though not in graces lesse,
Wanted that ioy which their full heartes possesse :
These eyes, though shining store of teares did
     yeald

The grief with beautie did dispute the field !
So lookes the day when, though the sunne extends
His goulden beames, yet raine withall descends;
Soe when offended Jove a tempest poures
On our ripe corne shewes lightning mixt with
    shoures.
I knew them soone, which I before had seene,
Grac'd by attendance on our matchles queene,
Nor wondred longer how they shone so bright,
Since guilded dayly by soe faire a light;
But this (though seene) exceeded my beliefe,
That plac't neere her they could have cause for
    griefe :
Yet still they griev'd, and after made it knowne,
They griev'd her griefe more than they wept their
    owne.
    Am. I fear'd her death had beine their sorrow's
    cause,
Say bouldly on, now needes no longer pause :
What in this story can be worth my feare,
Since she is safe, and seeing you are heare ?
    Clo. Now wearied with their sorrowes, and
    their way
Neere the fresh bankes of silver Thames they lay,
And wept soe fast as if they meant to try
To weepe a floud like that they wept it by,

Whose faces bow'd, and bright, and moist, did
    shew
Like lillies looded[1] with the morning dew :
Now upp they lept and with such rage they flung,
As doe the heifers by a hornet stung :
Long sighes sometimes and silent sobs they sent,
Which above wordes expresse their discontent ;
Soe sadly humm our bees when, from their seate
Disturb'd, they fly to seeke a new retreate ;
Or haveing labour'd long with art to stive[2]
Their welmade hony in their welform'd hive,
They finde, return'd but from some neighboring
    coast,
Their fellowes dead, and all their nectar lost :
Sometymes in lowder cries their griefes resound,
Which ease not them and (all) their hearers
    wound ;
Soe have I heard that lyonesses, reft
Of their lov'd younge by the bould hunter's theft,
With open throat and streacht out voyces, teare
The nighbouring eares and the more nighbouring
    ayre ;
All other wayes tried to assuage their griefe
They try if wordes can yeald them more reliefe ;
All in complaints their scalding passion vent,

---

    [1] = loaded. G.   [2] = store. G.

In the same thoughts and almost wordes consent :—
" Ah! heavenly Gods, who will believe your eares
Or marke our actions, or regard our prayers?
Since death durst such a pietie invade
For whose deer safetie all our vowes were made?
Why shut you upp what you did hardly showe?
Whie knew we her we might not always knowe?
How crosse it workes against (y)our main designe
To give to such a life soe short a line,
If virtue bee your wish, for whoe could more
Advance that worke and banisht truth restore?
How shall wee now in seas of vice bee tost,
That have our pilot and our compasse lost!
Howe blest an age had her example made!
How, without mixture, puritie had swaid!
Had shee but liv'd to overlooke our state,
And prune and water what she set so late;
And staid to forme us by her virtuous view,
As like to her as shee was like to you!
Ah! how their very sight her soule did grieve,
Whoe would your powers (dis)serve or not beleve?
What priest more frequent orison would pay?
What prince more offeringes on your altars lay?
How sharpe a judge of all her homebread thoughts!
How weake a censurer of all fforaigne faults!
Whoe could such balmè for different woundes
    prepare?

Soe temper insolence and calme despaire?
Whoe taught the simple like her, or whoe drew
Like her, the learn'd to practise what they knew?
Whoe else could ill, drest in noe shape entice?
Whoe else fear'd nothing for herselfe but vice?
Whoe else ioy'd more in finding whome to make
Share of her bountie, than they could to take?
Whoe hath with bountie such compassion showne
As all the griefs she met had beene her owne?
What was to[o] hard to act or low to doe
But her soft pittie soon could prompt her to?
Who more restrain'd her freindship? yet did shew
Such care of all, that it was hard to knowe
(Soe did her tender soule her ayde extend)
The greatest stranger from her greatest freind?
And no lesse favour to her foes had showne,
But that a life so lovely, could have none:
Nor was that onely lovely, nor the case
Did shame the jewell, for, had Nature's grace,
Created all immortall whoe for faire
Might with immortall goddesses compare,
Now on her herse wee had not cipresse spread
Had not lov'd her livinge, and not mourn'd her
        dead;
Nor had or griev'd, or fear'd, to see disioyn'd
Soe rare a bodie from soe pure a minde:
Great God of shades, and greater then before,

Now this our treasure hath increast thy store,
When Orpheus' harpe pleaded his suite to thee,
Charming, or asking his Euridice.
Eyther his love or grief, or art prevail'd
To gaine the lesse belov'd and lesse bewail'd.
Now all the pearles dropt from the fairest eyes
(A ransom might the greediest wish suffice),
Move not thy most inexorable spight
To let the day againe behould her light;
Although the voyce that doth this boone require
Hath charms to shame the once-prevayling lire.
In iust revenge I hope her form divine
Will give a jelousie to Proserpine,
And in the veines a feircer fire will breede
Than those which thy tormented subiects feede."—
Much more they said, and floods of teares they
      wept,
Whilst mine with theirs an equall measure kept;
Not onely, with compassion toucht, to see
Them mourn for her as I should mourn for thee;
But wonder to[o] that such exalted powers
Had soules as soft and pittiful as ours.
Then I perceav'd that, as feirce earthquakes make
Noe less the pallace than the cottage quake,
Soe highest states and lowest fortune prove
Like motions from the equall power of love;
Or, if in either quarter passions flowe,

They most can love and grieve who most can knowe.
Since I left them these thoughts have been
    the theefe
With which I labour'd to divert my griefe;
Since I left you, thus have I spent my tyme;
This caus'd that absence which you count a crime.

    Am. Yet all their greife did not the subiect
    showe;
Knowe you the nimphe for whome they sorrow'd
    so?

    Clo. By fairest Grenewich, whose well seated
    towres,
In sweetness strive with Flora's freshest bowres,
There where att once our greedy eyes survay
Hills, plaines, and groves, the citie and the sea,
Wee oft have seene her move, and heard her talke
Blessing the banks where she vouchsaft to walke;
Shee often in the sunn's declyning heate,
(Risinge to us when hee began to sett),
Would view the downes where wee our flocks did
    keepe,
And stay to mark the bleating of our sheepe;
And often from her heigth hath stoopt to praise
Our countrey sportes, and heare our countrey
    layes,
Sharing with us, after her ended walke,
Our homely cates, and our more homely talke.

Am. I knowe her nowe ! O foole ! that could
    not see
By that discription that it must bee shee,
Meethinks I heare her as shee us'd rehearse
Some choyser part of thy Amintas' verse :
Or see her tast, in some remoter shade,
The sillibubs which thy faire hands had made.

  Clo. What beauty did in that faire forme
    reside !
What any greatness hath, excepting pride !
Eyes of soe modest, yet soe bright a flame,
To see her and to love her was the same :
And if by chance, when shee did neere us stand,
Her bright smoth[1] palme but touch't my ruder
    hand
That did both sences soe at once delight,
The purest swans seem'd neether soft nor white.

  Am. Lesse grace a well-form'd face the spark-
    ling eyes.
Lesse grace the spangled starres the azure skies,
Lesse grace our flowers the stalkes to which they
    ioyne,
The vines the garden, and the grapes the vine,
Lesse graces wool the sheepe, and grass the plaines

---

[1] = smooth.   G.

Then she grac't all whose bloud supplied her
    veines.
   Clo. Think how shee grieves to whome the
    world did owe
This noble nymphe for whome it sorrowes soe !
Gods, give her comfort in soe sad a dearth,
Her death will paine her more then did her birth.
   Am. Think how hee suffers whose sad share
    is most,
Wee only grieve for that which he hath lost,
Whose heart with hers was ioynd in mutuall fire,
And whoe possest alone what all admire.
   Clo. Wee weried with our sorrow, seeke reliefe ;
They, court their passion and embrace their griefe,
And feare to drie their teares or plaint refraine,
As in her sorrowes death shee died againe ;
Or to loose that, at least, were to be reft,
Of some dire legacy which she had left.
   Am. Nor would I loose my griefe, nor ever must,
If that be lasting as the cause is just :
And could you soone from such a griefe bee free,
I halfe would feare you scarce would grieve for
    mee.
   Clo. Willowes and waves be witnesses how all
The nimphes, the gods did too, too cruel call !
Harke ! how the wilder beastes howl out their
    moanes !

How answear'd by the woods and rockie stones!
Marke how the heardes and flockes doe daylie passe
The slighted waters and neglected grasse.

 Am. How great a change wrought in so small
  a tyme!
How brambles grow in place of eglantine!
Where with most hope wee sow'd our best of
  graine
See darnell, cockle, and could poppie raigne:
There rankest weedes, burrs, thornes and thistles
  viewe
Where banks of violetts and roses grew.

 Clo. Lesse ioy in feaste and games the young
  and gladd;
Lesse comfort take the pensive and the sadd
In thicker groves where bowes exclude the sunn,
And streames with purling on the peebles run;
Lesse ioy our wearied and our thirstie swaines
(Their haycocks pil'd uppon our scorchèd plaines)
In June, or when the dog-starre, raignes to finde
Some fresher shade or softer breath of winde,
And tast the springs, whose purer waters drill.[1]
From the high topp of some exalted hill,
And by that water (while that winde did sweepe

---

[1] See our Index of Words, *s.v.*, to Henry Vaughan,
Silurist, for use of this word and annotations. G.

The moveing bowes) to steal a gentle sleepe ;
Lesse ioy the hearers of Amintas layes,
Lesse ioys Amintas in the hearers praise ;
Lesse ioy our pipes on frisking flockes conferr,
Then thou, and I, and all, did ioy in her.

   Am. Whilst bees love flow'rs, whilst fishes ioy
      in floodes,
Whilst kids love fearne, and hunters love the
      woods,
Whilst sheep on fragrant meades delight to move,
Whilst conies rockes, and wee each other love,
Wee will this nimphe before all nimphes preferre,
And they no praise shall gaine whoe praise not
      her.

   Clo. For (could she of no other graces boast,
The rest of Fortune's guiftes and Nature's lost,
Whoe her soe long, soe neere had leve to serve,
Whoe this attendant could alone deserve
Must gaine a lasting and a glorious name,
        Gloriana's ⎫
                ⎬ fame.
Shot from a ray of Henrietta's[2] ⎭

   Am. Soone as her coarse[3] with best of gums
      preserv'd

---

  [1] = Elizabeth, from Spenser. Henrietta is written on
the line and Gloriana right above. G.

  [2] Queen of Charles I. G.

  [3] = corse or body. G.

Honours a tombe, on that let this be carv'd :
The greatest sorrow that the age hath knowne :
The greatest wonder any age hath showne :
Though highest matcht, and born of noblest blood,
More faire then great, and yet lesse faire then
        good.[1]
    Clo. What heat my heart invades ? my feeble
        brest
Some mightie God hath by his power possest ;
My voice is but the organ to his will ;
His wordes beleve, and his commands fulfill.
" Then was your griefe, now let your ioy be more ,
And now invoke whom you did late deplore.
Shee, plac't in light to mortall eyes unus'd,
With a celestiall glory circumfus'd,[2]
No mist from knowledge her cleere soule debarres,
Lookes downe on cloudes and treades uppon the
        starres,
Hates warre and strife, and favours peace and rest
Noe wolves your flockes, nor shall you wolves
        infest.

---

[1] The foregoing four lines introduced from the margin. G.

[2] ' Circumfus'd ' is written in a different hand and ink
in a space that had been left blank, and at the end of
which was ' infus'd ' erased. G.

On her particular protestation bould
Pales[1] the field, and Pan may leave the fould,
All ioyntly shew how her new power doth please
The humblest virgins with the Driades.
You hills, for joy to heavens your voyces raise
Shrubbs sound her name, and nimphs resound her
          praise.
Oh! shine propitious still! four altars bee;
Two to Diana sacred, two to thee,
Which, when our solemne sacrifices crowne,
Our voice directed to our God's renowne,
When for ourselves we ask content and peace,
When for our heardes, fields, flockes, we aske
          encrease,
When severall bowles of milke you offer'd see,
When equall jarres of oyle are power'd to thee,
When young Amintas' pipe resoundes thy praise,
And Aegon answeares in alternate layes,
When change of mirth is by Iacchius[2] made
By winter's fire, and in the summer's shade;
When such whose antick postures most content,

---

[1] Oddly misread by Mr. Bruce 'Ilas' : = the tutelar
divinity of shepherds, in whose honour the festival *Palilia*
was celebrated. Cf. our edn. of Lord Brooke, Vol. I. p
154 : "Here Pales, there Pomona fruitful be." G.

[2] Query = Iacchus = the religious name of the mystic
Bacchus at Athens and Eleusis? G.

The satyr's frisking gambols represent;
May then our wordes to thy blest hearing peirce,
With whome, on earth, thy favour did converse;
Our humble praise and prayers benignely take,
That we may pay the vowes which then we make.[1]

FAUCKLAND.

IV. AN EPITAPH VPON THE EXCELLENT COVNTESSE OF HVNTINGDON.[2]

HE cheife perfections of both sexes joyn'd,
With neither's vice nor vanity combind.
Of this our age the wonder, loue, and
care,
The example of the following, and dispaire.

---

[1]   The last two lines are from the margin.   G.

[2]   From " A Sermon preached at Ashby de-la-zouch in
the Covntie of Leicester: at the Funerall of the truely
noble and vertuous Lady Elizabeth Stanley, one of the
daughters and coheires of the right honourable Ferdinand,
late Earle of Derby, and late wife to Henrie, earle of
Huntingdon, the fifth earle of the Familie.   The 9. of
February,   Anno. Dom. 1633.   By I. F.   London 1635,
(4o).   The Epitaph immediately follows the title-page on
separate leaf.   Archbishop Trench has admitted above
Epitaph, into his select poems of the " Household Book of
English Poetry " (1868 : p. 133) and his Grace adds this

Such beauty, that from all hearts loue must flow
Such maiesty, that none durst tell her so.
A wisdome of so large and potent sway,
Rome's Senate might have wisht, her Conclaue
    may.
Which did to earthly thoughts so seldome bow,
Aliue she scarce was lesse in heaven, then now.
So voyd of the least pride, to her alone
These radiant excellencies seem'd vnknowne.
Such once there was: but let thy greife appeare,
Reader, there is not: Huntingdon lies here.
    By him who saies what he saw.

FALKLAND.

---

note, "Elizabeth, wife of Henry Hastings, fifth Earl of
Huntingdon, is the lady commemortaed in this fine epitaph
' by him who says what he saw '—for this is the attestation
to the truth of all that it asserts, which Lord Falkland,
mindful of the ordinary untruthfulness of epitaphs, thinks
it good to subscribe ". (p. 403). G.

V. TO HUGO GROTIUS.

TO THE AUTHOR.[1]

UR Age's wonder, by thy birth the fame
    Of Belgia, by thy banishment the shame :
    Who to more knowledge younger didst
        arrive
Than forward Glaucias ; yet art still alive.
Whose masters oft (for suddenly you grew
To equall, and passe those, and need no new)
To see how soon, how farre, thy wit could reach
Sat down to wonder when they came to teach.
Oft then would Scaliger[2] contented be
To leave to mend all times,[3] to polish thee,
And of that paines[4] effect did highlier boast,
Than had he gain'd all that his fathers lost.[5]
When thy Capella[6] read (which till thy hand

---

[1] Prefixed to George Sandys' translation of ' Christ's Passion : a Tragedy by Grotius. 1640.' 12o : Grotius, born 1583, died August 28th, 1645.   G.

[2] Joseph Justus Scaliger : born 1540 : died January 21, 1609.   G.

[3] The reference is to the younger Scaliger's great work *De Emendatione Temporum.*   G.

[4] = painstaking.   G.

[5] Verona.   F.

[6] Grotius, while a youth, published an editton of **M. M.** F. Capella, the Roman Polygrapher.   G.

Had clear'd, few grave and learnd did understand;
Though well thou might'st at such a tender age
Have made ten lessons of the plainest page.)
That king of criticks stood amaz'd to see
A worke so like his own, set forth by thee:
Nor with lesse wonder on that worke did look
Than if the Bridegroom[1] had begot the book.
To whom thy age and art seem'd to unite,
At once the youth of Phœbus, and the light.
Thence lov'd thee with a never-dying flame
As the adopted heire to all his fame;
For which care, wonder, love, thy riper dayes,
Paid him with just, and with eternal praise.
Who gaind more honour from one verse of thine,
Than all the Canës[2] of his princely line:
In that he joy'd, and that oppos'd to all,
To Titius[3] spight, to hungrie Schoppius[4] gall.

---

[1] Mercurie in it marries Philosophy. F.

[2] Canis was the family name of the Scaligers: and the arms, two dogs climbing a ladder. M. [We were sorry to find the great tomb in Verona of the Scaligers sadly neglected and desolate. Pity so quaint a specimen of the architecture of the century (to say no more) should be left to perish. G.]

[3] Rob. Titius was the critic against whom Scaliger wrote his Vvo Villiomarus. M.

[4] Scaliger frequently defended himself against Schoppius. M.

To what (with cause disguis'd) Bonarcius writes[1]
To Delrio's rage, and all his Loyolties.[2]
But though to thee, each tongue, each art be
     known
As all thy time that had imploi'd alone;
Though Truth doe naked to thy sight appeare,
And scarce can we doubt more then thou can'st
     cleare;
Though thou at once dost diferent glories joyne,
A loftie Poet, and a deep Divine;
Canst in the purest phrase cloath solid sence,
Scaevola's law in Tullie's eloquence;
Though thy employments have exceld thy pen,
Shew'd thee much skil'd in books, but more in
     men,
And prov'd thou can'st at the same easie rate,
Correct an author, as uphold a State;
Though this rare praise doe a full truth appeare
To Spaine, and Germany, who more doe feare
(Since thou thy aid didst to that State afford)

---

[1] Scribanius, justly ashamed of his right name. F.
[*i.e.* Scribonius wrote under the name of Bonaracius. G.]

[2] Martin Anthony Delrio, the Jesuit Commentator on
Holy Scripture: born 1551: died 1608. Mr. Mitford by
printing 'loyalties' for Loyolties [=disciples of Loyola,
or Jesuit] has unfortunately rendered the line nonsensi-
cal. G.

The Swedish councils then the Swedish sword :
All this yet of thy worth makes but a part
And we admire thy head lesse then thy heart ;
Which (when in want) was yet too brave to close
(Though woo'd) with thy ungratefull countrie's
    foes,
When their chiefe ministers strove to entice,
And would have bought thee at what ever price.
Since all our praise and wonder is too small,
For each of these, what shall we give for all ?
All that we can, we doe—a pen divine,
And differing onely in the tongue from thine,[1]
Doth thy choice labours with successe rehearse,
And to another world transplants thy verse ;
At the same height to which before they rose,
When they forc'd wonder from unwilling foes :
Now Thames with Ganges may thy labours praise'
Which there breed faith, and here devotion raise.[2]
Though your acquaintance all of worth pursue,
And count it honour to be known of you ;
I dare affirme your catalogue does grace
No one, who better does deserve a place :
None hath a larger heart, a fuller head,

---

[1] That is, GEORGE SANDYS. G.
[2] His *De Veritate Religionis Christianæ* intended to
convert the Indians. F.

For he hath seen as much as you have read :
The neerer countries past, his steps have prest
The new found world, and trod the sacred East ;
Where, his brows due, the loftier palmes doe
    rise,
Where the proud Pyramids invade the skies ;
And, as all think who his rare freindship own,
Deserves no lesse a journey to be known.
Vllyses, if we trust the Grecian song,
Travell'd not farre, but was a prisoner long ;
To that by tempest forc'd : nor did his voice
Relate his fate : his travels were his choice,
And all those numerous realmes, returnd agen,
Anew he travel'd over with his pen.
And, Homer to himselfe, doth entertaine,
With truths more usefull then his Muse could
    faine.
Next Ovid's Transformations he translates
With so rare art, that those which he relates
Yeeld to this transmutation, and the change
Of men to birds and trees, appeares not strange :
Next the poetick parts of Scripture, on
His loome he weaves, and Job and Solomon
His pen restores with all that heavenly quire,
And shakes the dust from David's solemn lyre .
From which, from all with just consent he wan

The title of the English Buchanan,[1]—
Now to you both, great paire, indebted thus,
And like to be, be pleas'd to succour us
With some instructions, that it may be said
Though nothing crost,[2] we would that all were
    paid.
Let us at least be honest bankrouts[3] thought,
For now we are so far from offering ought,
 Which from our mighty debt some part might
    take,
Alas! we cannot tell what wish to make,
For though you boast not of the wealth of Inde,
And though no diadems your temples binde,
No power, or riches equals your renown ;
And they which weare such wreaths, need not a
    crown.
Soules, which your high and sacred raptures know,
Nor by sinne humbled to our thoughts below,
Who whil'st of heaven the glories they recite
Finde it within, and feele the joyes they write.
Above the reach or stroke of fortune live,

---

[1] GEORGE BUCHANAN *the* Historian, but greater still as
Poet and translator of the Psalms into Latin verse. G.

[2] = crossed out, as when a debt is paid. G.

[3] = bankrupts. G.

Not valuing what she can inflict or give ;
For low desires depresse the loftiest state,
But who lookes down on vice, looks down on Fate.

FALKLAND.

VI. TO MY NOBLE FRIEND, MR. GEORGE SANDYS, UPON HIS EXCELLENT PARAPHRASE ON THE PSALMS.[1]

HAD I no blushes left, but were of those
    Who praise in verse what they despise
      in prose,
Had I this vice from vanity or youth,
Yet such a subject would have taught me truth :
Hence it were banish'd, where of flattery
There is no use, nor possibility.
Else thou hadst cause to feare, lest some might
    raise
An argument against thee from my praise.
I therefore know thou canst expect from me
But what I give, Historicke Poetry.
Freindship for more could not a pardon win,
Nor think I numbers make a lie no sinne,
And need I say more than my thoughts indite,

---

[1] From edition of 1638.   G.

Nothing were easier than not to write,
Which now were hard : for wheresoere I raise
My thoughts, thy severall paines extort my praise.
First, that which doth the pyramids display :
And in a work much lastinger than they,
And more a wonder, scornes at large to shew
What were indifferent if true or no :
Or from its lofty flight stoope to declare
What all men might have known, had all bin
　　　　there.
But by thy learnèd industry and art,
To those who never from their studies part
Does each Land's laws, beliefe, beginning shew
Which of the natives, but the curious know.
Teaching the frailty of humane things
How soon great kingdoms fall,—much sooner
　　　　kings.
Prepares our soules, that chance cannot direct
A machin at us more than we expect.
We know that toune is but with fishers fraught,
Where Theseus govern'd, and where Plato taught :
That spring of knowledge, to which Italy
Owes all her arts and her civility,
In vice and barbarisme supinely rowles ;
Their fortunes not more slavish than their soules.
Those churches, which from the first heriticks wan
All the first fields, or led (at least) the van,

In whom these notes, so much requirèd, be,
Agreement, miracles, antiquity.
Which can a never-broke succession show
From the Apostles down; (here bragg'd of so)
So but confute her most immodest claime
Who scorn a part, yet to be all doth aime.
Lie now distrest between two enemy-powers,
Whom the West damns, and whom the East
    devoures.
What state than theirs can more unhappy be,
Threatned with hell, and sure of poverty.
The small beginning of the Turkish kings,
And their large growth, shew us that different
    things
May meet in one third; what most disagree
May have some likenesse; for in this we see
A mustard-seed may be resembled well
To the two kingdoms, both of heaven and hell,
Their strength, and wants, this work hath both
    unwound,
To teach how these t' increase, and that con-
    found,
Relates their tenets, scorning to dispute;
With error, which to tell is to confute;
Showes how even there where Christ vouchsaft to
    teach

Their Dervices[1] dare an imposter preach.
For whilst with private quarrels we decaid,
We way for them and their religion made ;
And can but wishes now to heaven preferre
May they gaine Christ, or we His sepulchre.
Next Ovid cals me ; which though I admire
For equalling the author's quickening fire,
And his pure phrase ; yet more, remembering it
Was by a mind so much distracted writ.
Bus'nesse and warre, ill midwives to produce
The happy offspring of so sweet a muse,
Whilst every unknowne face did danger[2] threat,
For every native there was twice a Gete.
More ; when (return'd) thy worke review'd, ex-
    posed
What pith before the hiding bark inclosed,
And with it that essay, which lets us see[3]
Well by the foot what Hercules would be.
All fitly offer'd to his princely hands
By whose protection learning chiefly stands ;
Whose vertue moves more pens,[4] than his power
    swords

---

1 Mr. Mitford misprints ' services ' : = dervishes or (in
a sense) priests. G.

2 Mr. Mitford misprints ' anger '. G.

3 Virg. Aen. lib. 1. F.

4 Mr. Mitford drops inadvertently ' moves '. G.

And theme to those, and edge to these affords.
Who could not be displeased, that his great fame
So pure a muse, so loudly should proclaim
With his Queene's praise in the same model cast,
Which should not lesse then all their annalls last.
Yet though we wonder at thy charming voice,
Perfection still was wanting in thy choice ;
And of a soule which[2] so much power possest,
That choice is hardly good which is not best.
But though thy muse were ethnically chast
When most fault could be found, yet now thou hast
Diverted to a purer path thy quill,
And chang'd Parnassus Mount to Sion's Hill ;
So that blest David might almost desire
To heare his harp thus echo'd by thy lyre.
Such eloquence, that though it were abused
Could not but be (though not allow'd) excused,
Join'd to a worke so choice, that though ill done,
So pious an attempt praise could not shun.
How strangely doth it darkest texts disclose,
In verses of such sweetnesse, that even those
From whom the unknown tongue conceales the
        sense,
Even in the sound must finde an eloquence.

---

[1] The same misprints 'sharply'. G.
[2] The same drops 'which'. G.

For though the most bewitching musicke could
Move men no more than rocks, thy language
     would :
Those who make wit their curse, who spend their
     brain,
Their time, and art in looser verse, to gain
Damnation and a mistres, till they see
How constant that is, how inconstant she :
May from this great example learne to sway
The parts th' are blest with, some more blessed
     way.
Fate can against thee but two foes advance,
Sharpe-sighted, Envy, and blinde Ignorance.
The first (by nature like a shadow neare
To all great acts) I rather hate than feare.
For them (since whatsoever most they raise
In private, that they most in throngs dispraise,
And know the ill they act, condemn'd within)
Who envies thee, may no man envy him.
The last I feare not much, but pity more,
For though they cannot the least fault explore,
Yet if they might the high tribunall clime,
To them thy excellence[1] would be a crime,
For eloquence with things prophane they joine,

---

[1] Mr. Mitford misprints ' eloquence ', his eye catching
it from next line.   G.

Nor count it fit to mixe with things divine,
Like art and paintings laid upon a face
Of itselfe sweet; which more deforme than
　　　grace.
Yet as the church with ornament is fraught
Why may not that be too, which there is taught.
And sure that vessel of election, Paul,
Who Judaised with Jews, was all to all,
So to gaine some, would be, at least, content
Some for the curious, should be eloquent.
For since the way to heaven is rugged, who
Would have the way to that way, be so
Or thinks it fit we should not leave obtaine
To learne with pleasure what we act with paine.
Since then some stay unless their path be even,
Nor will be led by solecisms to heaven,
And though a habit scarce to be controll'd,
Refuse a cordial when not brought in gold,
Much like to them to that disease inur'd[1]
Which can be no way but by music cur'd.
I joy in hope, that no small piety
Will in their colder hearts be warmed by thee ;
For as none could more harmony dispense
So neither could thy flowing eloquence

---

[1] In margin ' Tarantula '.　G.

So well in any task be used as this,
To sound His praises forth, Whose gift it is.

——————— Cui non certaverit ulla
Aut tantum fluere, aut totidem durare per annos.[1]

FALKLAND.

VII.   TO MY NOBLE FRIEND MR. SANDYS,
UPON HIS JOB, ECCLESIASTES, AND
THE LAMENTATIONS, CLEARLY, LEARN-
EDLY, AND ELOQUENTLY PARA-
PHRASED.[2]

WHO would inform his soul, or feast his
sense,
And seekes or piety, or eloquence;
What might with knowledge vertue joyn'd inspire
And imitate the heat and light of fire—
He those in these by thee may find embrac't
Or as a poet or a paraphast.
Such raies of the Divinitie are shed
Throughout these works, and every line o'respread,
That by the streames the spring is clearely showne,
And the translation makes the authour knowne.

---

[1] Virgil : Georg. ii. 99, 100. G.
[2] From the edition of 1638. G.

Nor, he being knowne, remaines his sence conceal'd;
But so by thy illustrious pen reveal'd,
We see not plainer that which gives us sight,
Than we see that, assisted by thy light,
All seemes transparent now, which seem'd per-
 plext,
The inmost meaning of the darkest text.
So that the simplest may their soules assure,
What places meane, whose comments are obscure.
Thy pen next, having clear'd thy Maker's will,
Supples our hearts to love, and to fulfill ;
And moves such pittie, that her power layes
That envie, which thy eloquence doth raise
Even I (no yeelding matter) who till then
Am chiefe of sinners, and the worst of men ;
(Though it be hard a soule's health to procure
Vnlesse the patient doe assist the cure),
Suffer a rape by Vertue, whilst thy lines
Destroy my old, and build my new designes,
Shee by a power, which conquers all controule
Doth without my consent possesse my soule.
Those mists are scatter'd which my passions bred,
And for that short time all my voice is dead.
Those looser poets whose lacivious pen
Ascribing crimes to Gods, taught them to men :
Who bent their most ingenious industrie,
To honour vice and guild impietie :

Whose labors have not onely not imployed
Their talents, but with them their soules destroy'd
Though of the much remov'd and distant time,
Whose lesse enlightened age takes from their
　　crime,
With no defence with all their arts devise,
When thou against them shalt in iudgment rise ;
When thou, a servant, such whose like are rare,
Fill'd with a usefull and a watchfull care,
How to provide against thy Lord doe come,
With great advantage the entrusted summe ;
And thy large stocke even to His wish imploy
Shalt be invited to thy Master's joy.
The wise, the good applaud, exult to see
The Apollinarii[1] surpas'd by thee.
No doubt their workes had found in every time
An equall glory, had they equal'd thine.
How they expect thy art should health assure,
To the sicke world by a delicious cure ;
Granting like thee no leech their hope deserves.
Who purgest not with rhewbarb, but preserves.
What numerous legions of infernall sprights
Thy splendor dazles, and thy musicke frights ;
For what to us is blame, to them is wounds,

---

[1] Socrates Scholasticus.　M.

Whom griefe strikes, feare distracts, and shame
    confounds,
To finde at once their magicke counter-charm'd
Their arts discovered, and their strength disarm'd :
To see thy writings tempt to vertue more
Than they by their's assisted, could before
To vice or vanitie : to see delight
Become their foe, which was their satellite ;
And that the chief confounder of their state
Which had been long their most prevailing bait ;
To see their empire such a losse endure,
As the revolt even of the epicure.
Those polite-pagan-Christians[1] who doe feare
Truth in her voyce, God in His Word to heare ;
(For such, alas ! there are) doubting the while
To harme their phrase, and to corrupt their stile,
Considering th' eloquence which flowes from hence,
Had no excuse, but now have no pretence.
These both to pens and minds direction give,
And teach to write, as well as teach to live.
Those famous herbes which did pretend to man
To give new youth ; chymicks who brag they can
A flower to ashes turn'd, by their art's power
Returne those ashes back into a flower ;
May gain beliefe, when now thy Job we see

---

[1] The cause of Castalios' translation.   G.

So soil'd by some, so purifi'd by thee.
Such was his change, when from his sordid fate
He reascended to his wonted state ;
To see wee yearly a fresh Spring restore
Those beauties, Winter had deflour'd before ;
Soe are we taught the resurrection must
Render us flesh and blood from dirt and dust.
To Job's dejected first, and then rais'd minde
Is Solomon in all his glory ioyn'd.
Lesse specious seem'd his person when he shone
In purple garments, on his golden throne.
His eloquence call'd from the farthest south
To learne deepe knowledge from his sacred mouth,
One weake and great—a woman and a queene :
Which (his conceptions in the language seene)
So likely seemes, that this no wonder drawes,
When with the great effect we match the cause.
Nor had we wondred had the storie told
His fame drew more then all his realmes could
      hold :
For no lesse multitudes doe I expect
To heare (whilst on these lines their thoughts
      reflect)
To have in this cleare glasse[1] their follies knowne ;

---

[1] Ecclesiastes. F.

Nor will there fewer prove, who in their owne,
From these thy tears[1] shal learne to wash their
    crimes,
And owe salvation to thy heavenly rimes.

VIII. ANOTHER TO SANDYS.

SUCH is the verse thou writ'st, that who
    reads thine
    Can never be content to suffer mine ;
Such is the verse I write, that reading mine
I hardly can beleeve I have read thine ;
And wonder that, their excellence once knowne,
I nor correct, nor yet conceale, mine owne.
Yet though I danger feare then censure lesse,
Nor apprehend a breach like to a presse,
Thy merits now the second time inflame,
To sacrifice the remnant of my shame.
Nor yet (as first) alone, but joyn'd with those
Who make the loftiest verse seeme humblest
    prose,
Thus did our Master, to His praise, desire
That babes should with philosophers conspire
And infants their hosannas should unite
With the so famous Areopagite.

---

[1] Lamentations.   F.

Perhaps my stile, too, is for praise most fit,
Those shew their judgement least, who shew their
　　wit,
And are suspected, least their subtiller aime
Be rather to attaine than to give fame.
Perhaps whilst I my earth doe interpose,
Betwixt thy sunne and them, I may aid those,
Who have but feebler eyes, and weaker sight,
To beare thy beames and to support thy light.
So thy eclipse by neighbouring darkness made,
Were no injurious, but a usefull shade ;
How e're, I finish here ; my Muse her daies
Ends in expressing thy deservèd praise,
Whose fate in this seemes fortunately cast,
To have so just an action for her last.
And since there are, who have been taught, that
　　death
Inspireth prophecie, expelling breath,
I hope when these foretell what happie gaines
Posteritie shall reape from these thy paines,
Nor yet from these alone, but how thy pen
Earthlike, shall yearely give new gifts to men;
And thou fresh praise and wee fresh good receive.
(For he who thus can write, can never leave),
How Time in them shall never force a breach,
But they shall alwayes live and alwaies teach,
That the sole likelihood which these present,

Will from the more-raised soules command assent.
And the so taught will not beliefe refuse,
To the last accents of a dying Muse.

FALKLAND.

finis.

MISCELLANIES

OF

The Fuller Worthies' Library.

LICIA AND OTHER LOVE-POEMS

AND

RISING TO THE CROWNE OF RICHARD THE THIRD

BY

GILES FLETCHER, LL.D.

Edited, with Memorial-Introduction and Notes

AND

NEW FACTS, &c.,

IN THE

LIVES OF PHINEAS FLETCHER AND GILES FLETCHER.

BY THE

REV. ALEXANDER B. GROSART,

St. GEORGE'S, BLACKBURN, LANCASHIRE.

PRINTED FOR PRIVATE CIRCULATION.
1871.

156 COPIES ONLY.

Note.

OF 'Licia' only two exemplars and a proof-sheet fragment, are known : one complete and the fragment, in the Bodleian, the other, which was also complete, in the renowned Library of my admirable friend, the Rev. THOMAS CORSER, M.A., Stand Rectory, at whose Sale it fetched upwards of £20. In our Memorial-Introduction to PHINEAS FLETCHER we incidentally established the authorship of "Licia" : but in the Introduction to the present reprint the evidence is re-stated, with additions. My friend Rev. J. H. Clark, M.A., West Dereham, Norfolk, has taken the pains to translate (for the first time) the short Latin pieces *Ad Amorem* and *Ad Lectorem* prefixed to Licia. They will be found in their places. To him also I owe thanks for genealogical researches in all directions. I take this opportunity of acknowledging my debt to the MSS. of the late JOSEPH HUNTER, so happily preserved for the Nation in the British Museum. I have rarely gone to the *Chorus Vatum* without finding something useful. I wish the more earnestly to pay this tribute to an accomplished and laborious Antiquary in the present instance, because it has been thoroughly satisfactory to find my own independently worked-out conclusions verified by his.

I would call attention to the Will of PHINEAS FLETCHER recovered by me since issuing my edition of his Poetry. It is added, with other interesting things on both the brothers, as an Appendix to the Memoir of their father.

As with all our reprints we have studiously adhered to the Author's own text and orthography, save in the usual

B   443

(slight) reduction of capitals and italics.   The Memoir will be found, as in all the others, very much more substantive and adequate than any previously written, and certain long-standing errors corrected.   G.

₊ See additional Notes on the elder Fletcher at close of the present Poems.

Memorial-Introduction.

GILES FLETCHER LL.D.

FROM a living descendant of the FLETCHERS —the REV. JOHN R. FLETCHER D.D., of Quethiock, Cornwall—I have received a most interesting family-paper, by which it appears that the FLETCHERS came from the NETHERLANDS, whence a well-authenticated tradition makes them to immigrate in the reign of Edward the IVth., and where they had been ennobled for many generations. Curiously enough only very recently, a gentleman in HOLLAND forwarded to DR. FLETCHER an antique seal of the FLETCHERS that had been handed down in his family for centuries; and by an impression of it sent me, the supporters (in heraldic phrase) confirm the alleged nobility. *In passing* it may be recorded that the armorial bearings of the seal correspond precisely with those in an early edition of Beaumont and *Fletcher's* Works, now in Exeter

445

College, Oxford. By the genealogical details of
the Paper (*supra*) the FLETCHERS are traced in
considerable numbers in Yorkshire and in Norfolk
and Suffolk and Cumberland.

Since our Memoirs of PHINEAS and GILES
FLETCHER were issued, we have sought far and
wide and through many fellow-workers, to
recover more on the Father and Mother of our
present Worthy, and so their grandfather and
grandmother ; nor altogether without success as
regards the former. I am now able to localize more
definitely the fact of the tablet-epitaph at Cranbrook, that the good Vicar of Cranbrook, RICHARD
FLETCHER, was of " the province of York " :[1] for
in a copy of FULLER belonging to my friend
Joshua Wilson, Esq., of Tunbridge Wells, that
renowned Antiquary, RALPH THORESBY has annotated in the margin that RICHARD FLETCHER,
Bishop of London, was born at Great Liversedge,
Yorkshire. He gives no authority, but was
himself so thorough and trustworthy, that there

---

[1] 'Province ' is the word in the epitaph, *as supra*, what
ever it may have been intended for. If used in the
ecclesiastical sense it might embrace all the northern
dioceses comprised in the 'province' of the Archbishop
of York.

can be no question he had good reason for correcting FULLER's doubtful and doubtfully put statement that he was " of Kent ". I suspect however that THORESBY has confounded the son with the father, and that not the Bishop, but his father was born at Great Liversedge or as it is now styled Liversedge simply. I find that in the diocese of York and around if not at LIVERSEDGE, there were FLESSHERS, FLESHERS and FLETCHERS, as far back as 1500 or thereby, and ecclesiastically related. Thus in the accounts of one of Archbishop Savage's executors (Abp. of York) a " Dominus Robertus Flessher " occurs thus : " Domino ROBERTO FLESHER et quinque presbyteris celebrantibus quinque Missas de quinque Vulneribus, XXd : Domino ROBERTO FLESHER in pecunia, xls : Puero domini Roberti Flessher, meanti ad scolas Cant. XIId."[1] It is difficult to make out whether these payments concerned the Archbishop or his executor MARTIN COLYNS, treasurer of the cathedral of York and one of the leading clergy of the diocese. But it seems evident that

---

[1] Testamenta Eboracensia, Vol. IV. Surtees Society No. 53 p 307. Sir John Neville of Liversedge in his Will dated 20th. December, 1501 (*ibid* p 199) appoints Apb. Savage supervisor.

at that time an ecclesiastic of some importance,
named FLESHER, was connected with the cathedral dignataries.   The item concerning the ' boy '
going to Cambridge is very interesting.   Probably
the FLETCHERS were in some of their branches a
clerical family before the Reformation: for turning
to the *Kal. Ecclesiasticus*, Temp. Henry VIII.,
(1534) various FLETCHERS appear in the LIVER-
SEDGE region of Yorkshire *e. g.* a THOMAS FLETCHER
was rector of the church of Kyrkbramwyth, rural
deanery of Doncaster, also a ROBERTUS FLESSHER
incumbent of the Vicarage of Wemersley, deanery
of Pontefract, and a THOMAS FLESSHER, incumbent
of the Chantry of the Blessed Mary in the Church
of Sandall, near Wakefield, in the same Deanery,
and again an EDWARDUS FLETCHER, rector of
Wydenerpole, Deanery of Byngham.   Then a
RICHARDUS FLETCHER appoints a payment for
Masses ('Missas'), as Robert Fletcher before.
Some day some Yorkshire Antiquary may be able
to trace our RICHARD FLETCHER to one or other of
these branches.   The occurence of so many
FLETCHERS in and around LIVERSEDGE or in South
and West Yorkshire, becomes the more memorable to us in that the later FLETCHERS cherished
life-long gratitude towards the NEVILLES, who
were *the* Family of Liversedge.   Thus in dedica-

ting " Christ's Victorie " to "the Right Wor-
shipvull and Reverend Mr. Doctour Nevile,
Deane of Canterburie and the Master of Trinitie
Colledge in Cambridge " Giles Fletcher (*filius*)
thus gratefully states his obligation to him: "As I
haue alwaies thought the place wherein I liue,
after heauen, principally to bee desired, both
because I most want and it most abounds in
wisdome, which is fled by some with as much
delight, as it is obtained by others, and ought to be
followed by all : so I cannot but next unto God
for euer acknowledge myselfe most bound vnto
the hand of God (*I meane yourselfe*) *that reacht
downe as it were out of heaven, unto me, a benefit
of that nature and price,* then which, I could wish
none, (onely heauen itselfe excepted) either more
fruitful and contenting for the time that is now
present, or more comfortable and encouraging for
the time that is alreadie past, or more hopefull
and promising for the time that is yet to come ",
—all which refers to the '*magnificent*' Dean's
patronage and sending of him to the University.
It would appear therefore that relationships begun
at Liversedge between the Fletchers and the
Nevilles were continued and sustained long
afterwards. If only we were nearer the facts,
it should emerge in all liklihood that an elder

449

FLETCHER had some place of trust in the service of the lordly house of the Nevilles. The bearing of all this on the authorship of "Licia" &c. will appear in the sequel.

From whichever of the Yorkshire FLETCHERS generally, or Liversedge Fletchers specifically, RICHARD FLETCHER, father of the Bishop and of our DR. GILES FLETCHER, sprang—if indeed he were not himself the 'boy' sent to Cambridge, though probably he was a generation later (*supra*) —our earliest explicit glimpse of him is, that in his admission to the University our DR. GILES FLETCHER describes himself as of WATFORD, Herts, " ætat 17 ", thus informing us that in 1548 his parents were resident there and also that WATFORD not Kent (as so long mis-stated) was his birth-place. From lack of documents I have failed to verify the incumbency or residence of the paternal Fletcher at Watford: but I am imformed that the fact is certain from the University entry.[1]   Richard Fletcher is found next at BISHOP STORTFORD from

---

1 It is just possible that young Giles might describe himself as of Watford and mean simply to designate that he was then resident there, and that still Liversedge must be regarded as his birth-place in common with his elder brother Richard, according to Thoresby, as *supra*.

1551 to 1555. There too alas! the early documents are sadly imperfect: but again the fact is
certain. I have been fruitlessly aided by willing
friends in trying to get at data relative to Watford and Bishop Stortford. I had hoped to recover
the name of the mother of our Worthy and her
death—for she does not seem to have been at
Cranbrook. To Cranbrook RICHARD FLETCHER
was 'presented' by the patron, ARCHBISHOP PARKER,
in July, 1559. Where he was from 1555-6 to
1558-9 has not explicitly come down, but in Foxe
it comes out that in 1555 he was a witness of the
martyrdom of Wade, at Dartford in Kent, and
in 1557 he was at Frittenden in same county. It
was not until 1566 he was 'presented' to
SMARDEN in Kent—held with Cranbrook. Perhaps we shall not greatly err if in these years we
find the period of his sufferings as told in his
Cranbrook epitaph, where we read that "tem-
poribus Marianis......adversa multa et *vincula
pertulit*". This would seem to indicate imprisonment and 'fetters.' It is affirmed of Bishop Bonner
that he made use of a prison formerly attached
to the castle at Bishop Stortford, for the confinement of convicted Protestants, of whom one at
least was burned on Goose Green adjoining. We
can scarcely suppose that the worthy Vicar would

escape the tender mercies of the new diocesan : the marvel is that he was not actually put to death.

One place in the poems now re-printed gives scope for a world of imaginative romance as well earlier as later, the simple prose being that DR. GILES FLETCHER inherited his love of 'Travell' from his father, who if we aright interpret the allusions, must at some time have visited Persia and the East. Here are the lines (Sonnet xxii) :

> " I might have dyed, before my lyfe begunne,
> When as *my father for his countrie's good*
> *The Persian's favour and the Sophy wonne* :
> But yet with daunger of his dearest blood
> Thy father (sweet) whome daunger did beset,
> Escapèd all, and for no other end,
> But onely this, that you he might beget, &c."

We ask wistfully if by ' *dearest blood* ' Mrs. Fletcher could be meant? A shadow lies over the elder FLETCHER's part prior to and in the times of the Reformation, save his ' bondage and imprisonment' in Marian days. The tablet-epitaph tells us that he was the first Reformation 'pastor' of Cranbrook, and that he was among the earliest ' ordained' by Bishop Ridley ' *martyr*.'

The little that has been transmitted to us concerning FLETCHER (pater) shews him to have been a ' parish *priest* ' (albeit he had shunned the

name in loyalty to the ONE PRIEST) after GEORGE
HERBERT'S own heart : and it is inevitable that
the boys, Master RICHARD and GILES—there were
a John and a PRISCILLA also[1]—laid in the Vicarage
and Grammar School of Cranbrook, the founda-
tion of their after-scholarship and culture.   Our
GILES went from Cranbrook to Eton, probably in
1560 or thereby : for WILMOTT, BOND, and all the
authorities, are mistaken in giving 1565 as the
date of his admission as ' scholar ' there, seeing
that he was so admitted by election from Eton
27th August, and ' matriculated ' at King's College, Cambridge, 12th November, 1565, aged
seventeen, as already noted.   He successively and
successfully went through his degrees and honours,
being Fellow 28th August, 1568 : proceeded A.B.,
1569, and commenced A.M. 1573 : deputy-Orator
of the University 1577, in which year (28th October)
the Provost of his College enjoined him to divert

---

[1] See our Memoir of PHINEAS FLETCHER, Vol. I., pp.
xxvii-viii.   I take this opportunity of correcting a singular oversight of my own in this place   The ' *soror* ' to
whom the Poet dedicated his Locustæ must have been
another daughter of Dr Giles Fletcher, not *his* sister : or
she may have been a *sister*-in-law.

to the study of Civil Law: LL D. 1581.[1] It is
pleasant to know that both sons were full of all
tenderest love and reverence for their Father;
and that so long as he lived they are found visiting him. Better still, it is peculiarly satisfying to
know from a hitherto unpublished and unused MS.
preserved among the treasures of the WILLIAMS'
LIBRARY (London), that in a time of trial
to the ' old Vicar ' in his parish, from the working
of the Papal ' leaven ' left, his son RICHARD spoke

---

1 For these entries I owe thanks to Mr. Luard and Mr.
Wright of Cambridge, as before. I myself accepted 1565
as the Eton date, formerly, misled by all the authorities.
The Eton Registers are imperfect. See Mr. Bond's erudite reprint of Dr. Fletcher's " Russe Commonwealth "
for the Hakluyt Society (1856), p. cxx. Since above was
written I have been favoured with the fragment of the
Athenæ Cantabrigienses, Vol. III. left by the late lamented
Mr. C. H. Cooper : and I am glad to find therein my dates
and other entries confirmed. To the notice of our Worthy
herein, I am indebted for his birth-place and date, and
other references, the first verified for me by Mr. Bradshaw
of the University Library, as before. With reference to
the Goad quarrels, it may be stated that in this fragment
of Athenæ is an interesting Memoir of him, the *data* of
which make it the more strange that Giles Fletcher should
have been found opposing him. Dr. Goad died a few
weeks later than our Fletcher, viz. 24th April, 1610.

out very nobly and truly. The Vicar had a like-minded man in JOHN STROUD—as a little later another in DUDLEY FENNER—and when he preached the simple Gospel there were those who took offence after the world-old fashion.[1] The Vicar of RYE, (to which he had been presented by Lord BUCK-HURST,) RICHARD FLETCHER *(filius)* came over on 27th July, 1575, and preached in his father's Church at Cranbrook from the story of the 'healing' of the 'lame man' at the temple-gate 'Beautiful', as told in the third chapter of the Acts of the Apostles. The sermon is a powerful and manly one : and I like and I am sure my readers will like, to come on these words in it : "My father and Mr. Stroud have been very successful in healing your spiritual lameness, the glory of which belongs to your Saviour and Redeemer, nevertheless I call upon you to highly esteem both my father and Mr. Stroud, as instruments in the hands of God ", and he then burningly calls upon them to remember the superstition and bondage to which they were subject

---

1 I have, as before, to acknowledge right heartily the kind helpfulness of Mr. W. Tarbutt of Cranbrook, a local Historian in his own homely unpretending way, worth half-a dozen of your stately County-Historians who overlook the very things wanted.

under their former teachers. So it continued :
and at last the two sons united in placing the
quaint mural monument that remains, over the
honoured 'gray head'.[1]

Returning on the University career of our
Worthy, GILES FLETCHER became involved in
College quarrels and complaints against DR. ROGER
GOAD, Provost of King's, that brought him into
unenviable notoriety as well as drew on him the
displeasure of the all-potent " Lord Treasurer "
Burleigh. A series of characteristic Letters from
FLETCHER to Burleigh and the Provost, is preserved in the Lansdowne MSS. of the British
Museum : and it so chances that we are the first
to utilise them—others (as Mr. Bond) having
contented themselves with mere references and
the very slightest quotation. We reproduce the
whole, because (a) These Letters give us a glimpse
of academic life and furnish unused materials for
the Cambridge Athenæ, and (b) In that we are

---

[1] The inscription is given *in extenso* in our PHINEAS
FLETCHER, Vol. I. pp. xxvi-vii. Mr. Tarbutt, as before,
favoured me with a capital photograph of the mural
tablet—white marble and a brass with a black border.
There is at bottom the conventional skull, and above is
a Bible with a leaf turned down, and other quaintly carven
' storied ' symbols.

enabled by them to correct a somewhat important mistake made by the Rev. GEORGE WILLIAMS, B.D. in his " Memoir and Correspondence of William Millington, D.D., First Provost of King's College, Cambridge," in relation to our Author's ' *Querela*'.

GOAD succeeded a PHILIP BAKER, as Provost of King's, and seems to have inherited rather than deserved "hatred and opposition ".[1] Personally he stood high (avowedly) with the 'complainants': and the " Lord Treasurer" stood resolutely by him. A " Querela " that took the form of an Eclogue after Theocritus—of which more anon—written by our impetuous young ' Fellow ' with a refrain of " Solvite conjugii nova vincula, solvite Daphnin," probably reached the alert ears of BURLEIGH : and so drew down on its Author his mordant interrogations. Be this as it may, account was rendered, apologies made, submissions exacted. Turning to the Letters, it will suffice our end, to leave the student to consult the original

---

[1] In the " Memoir ", &c., mentioned *supra*, it is placed beyond question that Dr. Dillingham in accepting an old tradition libelled Dr. Millington in his heading of the " Querela ". To Baker, not Millington, belongs the odium of that libel. But as we shew onward, the erudite Writer of the Memoir falls into a kindred blunder in assigning the " Querela " to Baker instead of Goad, *i.e.* in its subject.

Latin, and give our rendering (for the first time).
The three opening letters bear the same date, viz.
22nd May, 1576 (so endorsed). We take the
Latin one to begin with, as having more of the
defensive than the others. It commences solemnly
enough "Testor deum opt. max teq. simul (illus-
trissime domine, &c.) Thus, in full: " I call the
supreme God to witness, and thee also, illustrious
Sir, whose judgment I exceedingly revere, that
in this matter I have no other end in view but
domestic peace [domesticam pacem] and the public
good. But if there be any one to whom domestic
disputes and these academic strifes are very dis-
pleasing, I myself am one, honoured Sir, whom
both my own temperament has disposed to peace,
and whom those studies in which if I be not
equally proficient I yet am wont to delight in
greater measure, have always withdrawn from
contentions. Touching our Provost, who is doubtless a most excellent and (if he had made the best
of himself) a most moderate man, I could say
at greater length what and how high my opinion
has ever been; if my judgment could confer any
distinction upon him, and had not my own con-
tinual report previously declared it. Wherefore
if anything unfair [inique], anything impertinent
[petulanter] or insulting [contumeliose] have been

spoken (for I confess there has been too much), I declare [profiteor] that it has been done not only without my consent, but even against my will and in opposition to my effort. Yet since I have received no private injury from him, I seem to have acted foolishly, in thoughtlessly and imprudently casting away the good opinion of him formed from many good offices in a suit, relying honoured Sir, on thy prudence and equity.[1]

Our fraternity [= College] has the very flower of the best youth. I have seen this fraternity depraved by the worst examples, the studies of many kindled by no rewards and their industry weakened and interfered with by unduly heavy punishments: and on the other hand impunity granted to others who are thus recommended neither by learning, industry nor character. Pardon me, honoured and worthy Sir, if I in my concern for our domestic reputation [*i. e.* of the

---

[1] I am not altogether sure that I see my way through this portion, and therefore add here the original: A quo tamen cum nulla priuatim iniuria lacessitus sim, inepte fecisse videor, qui illius gratiam collectam plurimis officiis, temere ac imprudenter effuderim dica (honoratissime domine) fretus tua prudentia, et æquitate.

College] proceeded further in my zeal than either
my own disposition or the judgment of a thinking
man, demanded. If I had been permitted to
follow my own design I would have accused no
one ; I would have implored thy help, which is not
wont to be refused to any one; which even now
I beseech very urgently. Thy fortune has nothing
greater than to be able, nor thy nature anything
better than to be willing to give help, to very
many.   It is for thy wisdom and equity to decide
how much and what kind.   The humble suppliant
of thy dignity, Aegedius Fletcher ".[1]

The preceding Letter is endorsed "Aegedius
Fletcher, excusing himself for siding against their
Provost ".   Either a message or written answer
must have intimated that more of apology and less
of ' excusing ', would be acceptable : for under
same date are the English papers of ' submission '.
The one is signed by other two ' offenders ' and
on the back after their names is written "Their
first submission ".   Here it is *verbatim* :

"Wee moste humblie beseach yor Lordshipp, to bee or
good Lord and to heare our humble submission. Wee
acknowledge our vndiscrete, and vnreverente dealinge
vnto your Lordship, and howe our dutie to the Colledge

---

[1] Lansdowne MSS. xxiii. No. 24.

ought not to have made vs so farr forgett our dutie to the Provoste; But wee proteste before God, that verie conscience moved vs to complaine and to him wee referr the truth. And doe moste humblie submitt vs to your Authoritie for the faulte in manner. Wee have but two thinges in this poincte, our Lyvinge and our honestie : to confesse grallie, were to resiste or owne Consciences. To lease [sic] our Colledg, is to vndoe our selves. wee are poore and simple, yor Lordship is noble, and wise to considre the truth, and to respecte our Calamitie, And if it shall please your Lordship to deale m'cifullie wth vs and our Colledge, wee truste it shall not repente your Lordship to have sett up Mr Provostes credit wth out our vtter shame and vndoinge ; if yowe shall deale otherwise, our onlie comforte is that wee hope God wch knowith our hartes and seeth our Calamitie in his good tyme will reveale our innocencye to your Lordshipp.

                    Your honors moste
                        humble Orators
                            Giles Fletcher
                            Robert Liles
                            Robert Johnson ".[1]

(Endorsed) " 22 Maij.
            Fletcher
            Lilesse
            Johnson
        Their first Submissiō ".
[In pencil " 22 May, 1576 ".]

---

[1] Lansdowne MSS. Vol. xxiii. No, 19.

The second, which no doubt accompanied the other, is from our Fletcher himself, being endorsed " 22 May, 1576. Giles Fletcher." It is as follows :

" In most humble wise submitting my self before your Honour, I acknowledg and confesse that I have verye vndiscreatlye and contrary to my dutye and that good perswasion whiche I had of Mr. Provost whome I iudge to be the servaunt of God, accompanied those whiche have exhibited Articles against him tending to his discreadit and have my self very vnadvisely healped forward that matter: In the which I see and confesse after due examining the most part to be verye false tempered with vnseemlye and odious woords (others light and frivolous) for the most part not toutching him but to be referred to others whome they cōcern, whiche notwithstanding I had never assented vnto if certaine abuses wherewith I found my self grieved had not moved me therevnto. In this also confessing and acknowledging my fault that being grieved therewith I deferred [sic] not those abuses unto him who I am perswaded would have punished them as the qualitie of the fault deserved : ffor the which as well as for the rest in most humble wise I crave pardon, referring the reformation thereof wholy to yowr most honourable consideration whiche can far better iudg of thes matters thē our selves.

Giles ffletcher."[1]

Endorsed
    " 22 May, 1576,
    Giles Fletchar."

---

[1] Lansdowne MSS. Vol. XXIII. No. 20.

A "proud spirit" was evidently chafed in writing these Letters to one prouder still : a feeling of justification such as was inevitable on an issue based in part at least on the legal axiom " The more 'tis a truth Sir, the more 'tis a libel ", underlies acknowledgment of over ' zeal ' and fervour. One might have expected the ' Submission '— collective and individual—to end the matter : but it did'nt. A fourth Letter to the Provost and a fifth letter to Burleigh on the same day—23rd May, 1576, or the day succeeding the ' Submission" papers—remain to attest our Offender's eagerness to put himself right. Again we translate. First of all to Dr. GOAD : this Letter being headed "To the most cultured Master Goad, Provost of King's College [" Ornatissimo viro Mro Goado Præposito Collegii Regalis"] and endorsed "Mr. Fletcher his submission to yᵉ Provost."

" I would call thee to witness, learned Sir, at greater length, what and how high my opinion of thee has ever been, if in these times it were not suspected by thee; and had not my long-continued respect and my conversations with many concerning thee, previously declared it. I am led to it both by thy private kindness and by thy domestic example, which has always been of

such a kind as became a good man, and one furnished with the remaining virtues [et cum reliquis
virtutibus instructi], and especially adorned with
those distinctions by which learned men are recommended to honours; and I exceedingly rejoiced
that thou camest amongst us for our domestic
advantage and public adornment. We also had
the advantage of thy reputation for piety and
integrity, which wonderfully kindled the love of
others. Although these things tended to the
advantage of the entire community, yet also they
seemed to me to furnish private and special reason for honouring thee. For it is an unworthy
thing that to him to whom all are much indebted,
each individual should be unwilling to be very
much indebted, and to shew that indebtedness
in the best methods, if they can; or if they
are unequal to that, by inferior means. Since
I judged all this most certain, I seem to have
acted inconsistently in now aspersing or per-
mitting others to injure the reputation of him
of whom I myself formerly thought so favour-
ably and honourably, and in thoughtlessly and
imprudently abandoning this good opinion of a
most worthy man, which I had formed from very
many kindnesses. But of thy charity [humani-
tatem = kindness] pardon me, who have erred

not so much intentionally as by mistake. Suffer
me in this cause even to add a defence, though I
most freely acknowledge blame in it. Since I
desire that in all things thou shouldst be most
illustrious, I have never thought that thy merit
should be called in question; but rather the im-
portunity of those who disturbed the common
peace, who, if they had followed their own
authorities (to whom all duty both public and
private is due) would never have destroyed our
affairs by such great and frequent conflagrations.
It is incredible, thou sayest: yet on my conscience
I most solemnly affirm it. And indeed it seemed
to me to have happened by the divine kindness,
that this affair which has been handled by us
rather odiously against thy worth, at length reached the ears of the most honourable BURLEIGH,
whom all acknowledge to be the ornament of this
State. For nothing could have happened more
desirably for thy reputation, than that this affair
should be understood by so great a man, who
should be able to prove thy innocence by his own
judgment; which all know to be most equitable:
or more useful to us for the remainder of our lives
than to be restrained by the wisdom of him who
should be able by his own judgment and authority to rebuke our rashness. For it ought not to

appear to us so onerous [*grave*] a matter to be
censured by wise men and those who excel the
rest in dignity (though that is very painful to a
sensitive mind) as to be invigorated by their
advice, wisdom and kindness. But what I do
was my own suggestion, in briefly acknowledging
to thee that in which I have now heavily offended.
Yet I do it most willingly. But as to commit this
was the part of our folly, so to remit it is the part
of thy wisdom and kindness. We acknowledge that
the whole affair has been undertaken by us rashly
and foolishly, that there is much that is unfair,
severe, odious and ought not to be endured. In
this, our youth scarcely furnishes an excuse. To
undertake this was imprudent and to defend it,
rash; but to acknowledge that you rashly begin
and stubbornly defend, is the part of a better
judgment and will Aegidius Fletcher ".[1]

Following up the Letter to the Provost—surely
a very manly and gentlemanly one, even as read in
our necessarily somewhat bald rendering—as
already stated, another was addressed on same day
to Burleigh. Once more we translate : " To the
illustrious Lord Burleigh, Lord High Treasurer
of England, and the most honoured Chancellor of

---

[1] Landsdowne MSS. Vol. xxiii. No. 26.

the University of Cambridge. Most honoured
Lord, he who ventures to deal with thee in many
words, knows not thy wisdom; he who does not
venture, thy equity. Wherefore since your Lordship kindly received our petition, in which we
have explained the state of our College; we have
thought it the part of our study, to offer to your
Lordship, our most humble thanks. And that
your Lordship may understand how anxiously we
are awaiting what you may think fit to determine
in this business, we have undertaken to expound
briefly the reason of our error in this cause and
of our petition; with this reservation that whatever shall seem good to your Lordship should be
approved of by us. Since it was free for us—
permission having been obtained—to appeal to
your Lordship, we have committed our cause to
the just and most humane hands of your Lordship.
To this end we have brought forward on paper
and roughly arranged individual quarrels of our
Fellows, so that if your Lordship should require
arguments, it may be seen from them that we
sought what was suitable and opportune for us.
These writings one of us, contrary to our wish,
displayed as the heads of our quarrel. Wherefore we were so astonished and confounded when
we first appeared in the presence of your Lordship,

that we could think of no excuse whatever in the matter. Accordingly we acknowledge our rashness and stupidity, and give the praise to God and thanks to your Lordship, that by the judgment of your wisdom and the honour of your example, we now first understand what is the fruit of our letter; and we beseech you in greater measure, that your Lordship, though you might do it justly, would not overpower and destroy our broken-down cause, with this weight of imprudence. As to what pertains to the injury of our College, we beg from your Lordship and the University, and I individually, that you would hear and understand this :—that rewards are not conferred for learning but for partizanship, that there is no one who has taken a degree in any branch of knowledge; that there are some so unlearned and of so little diligence that they have no interest in the affairs of the College ; that these persons are so unskilled and unprovided in all parts of our government that they propose for themselves no object beyond their own private ease; that they keep out honourable and proved young men who would succeed to their posts with a better hope ; that all openings to the advantage of the College are kept shut, though before this time, we never made any opposition to the utility of these men ; that there are some of us who have been continually vexed and harrassed with punishments, while those who took their part, notwithstanding their complaints and our opposition, are dissolute and abandoned persons. We bring forward to your Lordship's notice, the quarrel touching these injuries to our College, under the influence of a sense of duty and right; not as accusers but as suppliants ; not that we desire that those injuries should be avenged, but that they should be corrected; and therefore we most humbly pray that your Lordship will not neglect this opportunity, by which you will earn the name of the second Founder of our College. As regards ourselves, as we seek nothing else save the restitution of concord amongst the different orders, and of the study of letters in our College ; so we are prepared humbly to accept the decrees of your Lordship, and we doubt not that God, moved by our misfortunes, has permitted the episcopal authority to be thus abrogated, that at length our calamities may be relieved and checked by your singular wisdom and authority."[1] There is no signature to the preceding : but it is endorsed " 23 Maij 1576. Mr Fletcher to my L.

---

[1] Lansdowne MSS. Vol. XXIII. No. 27.

Complaints, how all things went into disorder in
yᵉ College by reason of a *Studium* faction" and
another endorsement " Mr. Fletcher's Apologie".

These careful endorsations and alterations in
Burleigh's own hand and the preservation of every
scrap, incidentally prove the marvellous minute-
ness of the High-Treasurer's surveillance and the
high estimate of Fletcher formed by him.
A final letter after the 'judgment' of the noble
Chancellor, closes these singular documents. As
before addressed, and as before translated by us :
" We have received at thy hand, most illustrious
Burleigh, a benefit great and most excellent, which
demands not simply the thanks of a single letter,
but the honour of perpetual remembrance.   But
my duty and the desire of the College required
that I should intimate to your Lordship by letter,
how gratefully we bear in mind this favour towards us and our College.   For when we were
pressed on every side by our own imprudence, the
authority of our adversaries and your just displeasure ; your singular and incredible clemency
raised us from our fall, endured our faults and
corrected our errors.   Indeed our unhappy College, distracted with perpetual discords, and
deprived of the light of learning, has so revived
by this your judgment, as to be conscious that it

owes all its health to your Lordship : which we
consider will be not only a great advantage to us
but also an example to the rest. For both
our youth, when the thing is known, and
your severity, understood by them, will be careful
and circumspect; and their seniors, beholding your
equity and reverencing your wisdom, will give
much more thought to their own conduct and
duties. Concerning ourselves, though it is necessary that we live in College as carefully as
possible so as not to give any confirmation to
those numerous and certain rumours which are
disseminated through the University touching our
disgrace ; yet it is most pleasing to us that the
Provosts put a much more favourable interpreta-
tion on our disgrace, and that many kinds of
duties are left to us, by which we may earn the
fruits of your judgment and the favour of your
kindness. We therefore pray, most illustrious
Lord, that since it is you alone who can settle our
College, you would listen only to the voice of
your own wisdom, and adjudge a decree most honourable to the Provost, if he shall obey your
decisions ; we pray, I say, by the living God,
that you would cause this benefit, which is in
itself most famous, to be firmly established by
your authority. We, as becomes grateful men,

eagerly accept your incredible munificence, and
shall govern ourselves in moderation, and shall
leave the thanks to be offered to the God in
whom the benefit originated. We acknowledge
our highest gratitude to be ungrateful. Aegedius
Fletcher." The foregoing Letter is endorsed
" 28 May, 1576, Aegedius Fletcher. Thanks
for a judgment ye Treasurer had past in ye
College case." And so the matter ended, and
infirm-willed (apparently), if amiable and worthy
DR. GOAD, retained his Provost-ship spite of the
bitter " Solvite " of the " Querela " of our
Worthy. It may be as well to explain here that
the " Querela " now and before alluded to, form s
one of three Latin Eclogues published for the first
time by Dr. WILLIAM DILLINGHAM in a small
volume of Poemata (1678). Its heading is
" Querela Collegii Regalis " and the burden of its
complaint the editor conjectures to have been the
preference of DR. MILLINGTON, Provost, for Yorkshire men, on account of which he adds, " ab
Rege Fundatore ad Aulam de Clare relegatus est."
DR. DILLINGHAM was ignorant of the authorship
of these three Eclogues, having published them as
" incerti Authoris ", otherwise the fact that our
Fletcher was himself of the ' province' of York,
might have started a suspicion of misapplication

of the "Querela" to DR. MILLINGTON. Mr. WILLIAMS, (as before) has disproved the MILLINGTON reference : but the preceding Correspondence shews that he is himself equally astray in substituting PHILIP BAKER. By internal evidence here and elsewhere, (always uncertain) Mr. WILLIAMS is positive that it was at BAKER the " Querela " was aimed. Two things suffice to shew this to have been impossible (*a*) BAKER who succeeded BRASSIE in 1558 was "ejected on complaint of the Fellows in 1569 " : (*b*) FLETCHER's own ' Apology ' is addressed to DR. GOAD and the date of the complaints and strife against him is 1576 to whom and to which year or shortly before accordingly, the " Querela " belongs.

The College and University career of our Worthy, while indisputably studious and laborious —as even the letters to Burleigh reveal— must have been somewhat stormy toward the closing terms. But the GOAD " rebellion " does not appear materially to have hindered his advance, although I suspect the dragon-teeth were sown during it, out of which came the burning accusations later of PHINEAS FLETCHER, as touched on in our Memoir of him. Be this as it may, the son of the Vicar of Cranbrook (the sons indeed) was not of the ' stuff' to be put down or allow himself

473

to be a cipher in the ongoings of a stirring time. Doubtless the years 1576-80 were well filled-up by 'studies' and the usual College employments of a man of mark.

Early in 1580 (O. S. 1581) a centrally influential event in every man's life, and to Literature took place, viz. the marriage of our FLETCHER on 16th January, to JOAN SHEAFE of Cranbrook, while in April, 1582 "Phineas", and in a year or two later "Giles," was born—sons destined to eclipse their father's renown, albeit none would have more passionately resented such a possibility than they.[1]   Pleasant to know that the "good Vicar", (almost) certainly united his two sons in the bonds of marriage in his own Church.   Pleasant too that the poet-grand-children played around his knees.   Tears, soft and white, would brim the young eyes as the 'old grey head' was laid beneath the chancel-floor, and perchance their earliest lesson in Latin was the finely-touched mural-tablet epitaph placed on the wall of the venerable Church.   It would seem that the newly-married pair took up house (as the

[1] See our Phineas Fletcher, Vol, I. pp. xxviii-xxxvi for full notice of the Sheafes, and of the Poets' birth-places, &c., &c.

phrase runs) at Cranbrook : for PHINEAS the
eldest was born there. But as GILES was born in
London, there had been doubtless temporary
removal at least to the metropolis. There he was
at the seat of empire : and *his* was a sovran nature.
So early as 3rd July, 1580, he had been Commiss-
ary to DR. BRIDGEWATER, chancellor of the Diocese
of Ely. Then, under 1581 in STRYPE's Life of
Archbishop GRINDAL (Oxford 1821, pp. 396-7)
we have this entry : " The metropolitical Visitation went forward. In prosecution whereof
the commission issued out, dated at London, July
the 5th, from Aubrey and Clark, for the visiting
the Church at Chichester ", of which diocese he
was Chancellor in 1582. It was directed to
Richard, Bishop of the Diocese ; and also to GILES
FLETCHER, LL.D., Henry Blaxton, Daniel Gardiner, and William Cole, Masters of Art, and John
Drury, Bachelor of Laws ". More noticeable still,
from *Notitia Parliamentaria* it appears that he
sat in Parliament in 1585 with HERBERT PELHAM,
Esq., for Winchelsea.[1] Either preceding or succeeding his entrance into the House of Commons—
probably both—he was in the service of the great

---

[1] Willmott's Lives of the Sacred Poets (1834) p. 28, was
the first to observe this in N. P.

Queen as a "Commissioner" in SCOTLAND, with
THOMAS RANDOLPH (the Amyntas of the Eclogues):
a Letter by our Fletcher from Edinburgh to
Walsingham is dated 17th May, 1586: and he
is found at Hamburg with SALSTONHALL in
1587,[1] and in HOLLAND, and in GERMANY. Fuller
earlier ("Worthies" I. p. 502) and BIRCH later
(Memoirs of Queen Elizabeth Vol. II. p. 78)
records these facts: and afterwards his Bishop-
brother referred to them. Exact dates, save at
Edinburgh and Hamburg, are lacking: but the
commissions are certain. He was probably
Secretary to the Ambassadors. We have in
PHINEAS FLETCHER's poems repeated allusions to his
father's manifold State-journeyings, including *the*
embassy by which most of all he is remembered, to
wit, to RUSSIA in the Armada year, 1588. Under
the name of "Thelgon" he thus recounts his
travels, in the 1st Piscatory Eclogue:

From thence [Cambridge] a shepherd great, pleas d with
    my song,
Drew me to Basilissa's [Elizabeth] courtly place:
Fair Basilissa, fairest maid among
The nymphs that white-cliffe Albion's forests grace.

---

[1] Hunter MSS. 24, 487: and see Wheler on Commerce
p. 64.

Her errand drove my slender bark along
  The seas which wash the fruitful German's land
And swelling Rhene [Rhine] whose wines run swiftly
    o're the sand.

But after-bold'ned with my first sucesse,
I durst assay the new-found paths, that led
To slavish Mosco's dullard sluggishnesse :
Whose slothfull sunne all Winter keeps his bed,
But never sleeps in Summer's wakefulnesse :
  Yet all for nought : another took the gain :
Faitours, that reapt the pleasures of another's pain !

And travelling along the Northern plains,
At her command, I past the bounding Tweed,
And liv'd awhile with Caledonian swains."[1]

Similarly in the second Eclogue :

"From thence he furrow'd many a churlish sea :
The viny Rhene, and Volgha's self did passe,
Who sleds doth suffer on his watry lea,
And horses trampling on his ycie face."[2]

So elsewhere : and unhappily never without an under-tone of plaint and even complaint. It will be noticed that the " travelling along the northern plain " past " the bounding Tweed " in the Eclogue, follows the Russian embassy : so that it

---

[1] Our Phineas Fletcher Vol. II. pp. 243-5.
[2] *Ibid* pp. 254-5.

might seem that the Scottish commission came after the return from " Mosco ; " but it is not so. His mission to Scotland preceded it by two years. I have been so fortunate as to recover from the Public Record Office the Letter to WALSINGHAM already referred to : and I am pleased to be the first to print it.   Here it is :

" My humble duetie remembred, Right Honourable, knowing yr good care for the Church of god at home, I thought you couldbee content to hear how thinges sta..d with it hear.   A..d thearfore ..ave noted to your H. what hath passed hithertoe in their generall Assemblie begoon hear the Xth of this present, if peradventure yr H. may find leysure to peruse it.[1]   It pleased my L. Ambassadour at his last writing to conferre with mee about my abode in this countrey after his retourn for suche service as shouldbee thought meet. Hee wished mee to advise well vpon it.   Which my self have doon pro & contra accord-ing to my reason. And bycause I kniew it to coom from his very good affection (whearof I have had good experience both in this iourney and before) I referred my self to him again so far foorth as that (if hee so pleased) hee might make mention hearof to yr H. who can far best iudge whither I bee meet for that service or that for mee. ffor my self I am not desirous to follow any ambitious course, yett having strove with the world now soom good time to attain to soomwhat whearwith to sett my self

---

[1] This enclosure has unfortunately disappeared.   G.

forward in the course of my profession & yet destitute of
means, I wouldbee very glad to bee employed (specially
by y$_r$ H. to whom I have vowed my service and my self)
in soom honest service that exceedeth not the measure
and proportion of my mean qualitie. Whearof y$_r$ H. can
far better iudge than I of my self. To whome wholy I
referre my self both in this and what so ells to bee com̄-
aunded & disposed of after y^r good pleasure.

The Lord allmightie increase y^r H. with all his good
blessinges.

ffrom Edenborough the 17th of May. 1586.

Y$_r$ H. most humble
G. Fletcher.

(Endorsed) **17 May. 1586.**

ffrom Dr. ffletcher.[1]

13

I suspect the "Faitour" who reaped "the gain"
of the Russe journey must have been JEROME,
afterwards SIR JEROME HORSEY, whose accounts of
his 'Travells' Mr. BOND has associated with our
FLETCHER's still quick book of the "Russe Common wealth"—than which there are few quainter,
keener, more memorable. He set out in 1588 to
and returned from Russia in 1589. His Book
which had been put into rough form on the way
home, was published in 1591 : but notwithstanding

---

[1] State Papers, Scottish Series, Vol. xxxix. No. 84. It
is inadvertently calendared as from Dr. *George* Fletcher.

its fine Epistle-Dedicatory to Elizabeth, the
" Russian Merchants " of England secured its
suppression, in dread of angering the Czar.   To
Mr. BOND's admirable Introduction to his reprint
I refer the Reader anxious to know more, for
interesting details and documentary evidence.[1]
According to one of FULLER's many anecdotes our
Worthy felt on his return home, much as DANIEL
may be supposed to have done when he escaped
out of the lions' den : albeit the story as told
scarcely hangs together, inasmuch as the " Russe
Commonwealth " itself testifies that the then
reigning Czar, Theodore Ivanowich, was " verie
gentle, of an easie nature, quiet and mercyfull."
The ' opposition ' and scare of the Russian Merchants wrought damage : but the Ambassador's
statement of his case and of what had been achieved
and unachieved, is a very masterly Paper.   On
his settlement in London again, he was 'appointed'

---

[1] In the Preface of the admirable "Analytical Indexes
to Volumes II and VIII of the Series of Records known
as the Remembancia.   Freserved among the Archives of
the City of London. A.D. 1580-1664 (1870)" Mr. Overall,
the accomplished librarian of the Guildhall Library, has
furnished interesting extracts relative to the duties of
' Remembrancer' as discharged by Dr. Fletcher.   See pp.
vii-ix.

by direct command of Elizabeth, "Remembrancer" (or Secretary) to the City and one of the "Masters of the Court of Requests." The emoluments do not seem to have been very great, while the duties to be discharged were alike onerous and delicate. This comes out as well as the Embassages and other public services, in a letter addressed by his brother, then Bishop of London, to "the Lord Treasurer" in suit for the office of "Extraordinary Master in Chancery." It is found in STRYPE's Annals of the Reformation (Vol. IV., p. 373) under 159ℐ, and is as follows:

"As I have found your l[ordship's] honorable aide to me in my occasions, so I humbly pray yʳ l[ordship] to give me leave to be a mover and solliciter (hereby) for my brother, Dr. Fletcher, to yʳ good lord[ship]; whom, if he were not to me as he is, I might truly commend to yʳ l[or[ship], to be worthy of regard. But yʳ lord[ship] hath many times signified yʳ h[onour's] respect of him. His service, in place where he is, being of much payne and imployment without intermission, is notwithstanding accompanyed by a stipend very unproportionably to his charge and labours. And yet so obnoxious to a people yᵗ are jelous of all dealing and sollicitation even of their own agents; especeally in matters of expenses and charges imposed, as if their negligence or subornation were the cause thereof. On the other side, there followeth him the mislyke and displeasure of great persons, for y he is enforced oftentimes to deliver unto them many unpleasing and denying messages on the citye's behalf; and to sollicite against the immoderate designes of some noblemen and others of the Court. Wherein he cannot find that moderation, but in very few, to excuse the messenger for the duty of his place.

Y^r l[ordship] also best knoweth his imployments in her Majesty's and his country's service in Scotland with Mr. Randolph, in Germany, Hamburgh, and Stade, with very good effect of that trade, till this day, In Russia, for the repayre of the English intercourse then interrupted and in a manner dissolved, but since greatly increased and in especiall sort continued: the regard of all which toward him, consisteth yet in favour to cum. It hath pleased her majesty, in other matters besyde those, to take knowledge of him, and at his going toward Russia, to admit him extraordinary to the Bequests And if now it may lyke her highnes, that in this infirmity of Mr. Rockbye he might stand as Dr. Cæsar did, and so, upon occasion befalling, to be called farther to that place of service, he would be fownde faithful. Whereunto by y^r l[ordship's] good and favourable word in his behalf, as opportunitye may serve, he shall finde furtherance, y^r l[ordship] shall increase his dutye and service with all faithfulness to y^r l[ordship], and add more to both o^r prayers and observance, which unfaignedly we owe alwayes to y^r honour. Whom I pray God to bless with cheerfulness and comfort of body and minde in all y^r l[ordship's] manifold and great affayres.

From Fulham, the 17th of May.

Your lordship's ever in Christ bownden
Rich. London."[1]
To the right honorable my very
good L. the Treasurer of England,

We have little light on the ' infirm ' MR. ROCKBIE[2]
nor does it appear what was the issue of the
application. But another ' appointment ', probably more lucrative, was obtained in the
Treasurership of St. Paul's. Evidently the
elder and younger brother—RICHARD the Bishop
and our Doctor—were devotedly attached to
each other : and yet very sorrowful, even
tragical was one result of the tie. One

---

[1] See the original in Lansdowne MSS. lxxxii. art. 28. :
our text is the result of a collation of Strype with the
MS. : important blunders are rectified, as ' subornation '
for ' subordination '.

[2] My friend Mr. Clark, as before, sends me these notes
viz., that there was a Ralph Rokeby, Serjeant-at-law
about this period. He was a younger son of Rokeby of
Mortham, the place immortalized by Scott : and had a
son Ralph, who compiled a history of his Family entitled
" Œconomia Rokebeiorum " which is incorporated into
Dr. Whitaker's History of Richmondshire. This younger
Rockbye was a friend of Camden, who wrote some Latin
Verses on the death of his wife Douglas. Possibly the
" Rockbye " of the letter (*supra*) was the Sergeant above
named.

short month after BISHOP FLETCHER penned his
fraternal Letter to the Lord Treasurer, viz, on
15th June, 1596, he died suddenly : and not only
left a widow and ' 8 poore children '—one of them
JOHN FLETCHER the Dramatist, ' *great* Fletcher '
as John Dryden named him in MacFlecknœ—in
painfully necessitous circumstances, but having in-
duced our DR. GILES FLETCHER to become security
for his " debt to the exchequer for his first-fruits
and tenths " involved him in most harrassing
supplications and defences over three years at
least, and ultimately imprisonment.   The pathetic
Letter which the ' prisoner ' wrote has already
been given by us in Memoir of PHINEAS FLETCHER
but it must find place here also, yielding as it
does sad glimpses of the home of the Poets : for
be it remembered, the ' poor wyfe ' was fair Joan
Sheafe of Cranbrook, and two of the ' many children ' PHINEAS and GILES FLTCHER.

" Right Honourable,—

    I humbly thank you for regarding the humble suit
of my poor wyfe.   Her poor estate and great distress and
so many children, do thus force me to mone my case, and
to reveal unto your Honour my present state.   My great
charge and small revenue, with the executorship of my
brother, have made my debt exceed my estate, being un-
doon and worse than nought, by 500 pounds.   For dis-

charging hereof, I have no means but the present sale of my poor house wherein I dwell, and of my office, if I can assign it to some fitt man. At the quarter day I am to pay 200 pounds, upon forfeiture of double bonds. I have yet no means nor liberty to seek for means, for payment of it, and I am infirm through grief of mind for this restraint, and the affliction of my wife and children. How perplexed I am for them and they for me, I beseech your Honour, (who art a father of so toward and happy children) to consider. Touching my fault, what shall I say? I have been abused by those fables and foolish lyes of the Earle's daunger by Sir Walter Raleigh. But my hart is untouched and my hands clear of his wicked practices, which I know not of, nor should discern so great a mischief under such a colour. I will learn wisdom by this folly. My humble suit is that you will be pleased to be a mean for my discharge or if not that, for enlargement of my bonds. To relieve a poor distressed family will please God, and bynde us all, besides other duties, to pray to God to bless you and yowr. So humbly take my leave 14 of March, 1600. Your H[onour's] most humble suppliant.

G. Fletcher ". [1]

The allusion to " the Earle " reminds us that Essex had been his friend : but one is grieved to find the illustrious RALEIGH 'suspect'. There is reason to believe that the Lord Treasurer obtain-

---

[1] Our Phineas Fletcher, Vol. I. pp. viii-ix : Bond's Hakluyt edition of Russe Commonwealth, pp. cxxv-vi.

ed his old College correspondent's "enlargement" and ultimate relief from the pressure of obligations that were purely technical. So far as I have been able to discover by our dim light at this later day, he suceeded in retaining his different offices, the duties of which doubtless occupied him sufficiently from 1600 onward. His last extra service of a public kind, was in his former tried capacity of a 'commissioner' intrusted by the company of 'Eastland Merchants' to treat with DR. JOHN CHARISIUS, the King of Denmark's ambassador, about "the required removal of the trade from the towne of Crimpe (Krempe) by the mediation of John Rolt" dated November, 1610. He was then 'in the shadows': for in a few months he 'slept well' in the Parish Church of St. Catherine Coleman, Fenchurch Street, London, in whose Register I found this entry of burial: "March 11th, 1610, [*i. e.* 1610-11] DR. GYLES FLETCHER"[1]

It was our rare fortune to be the first to notice and recover from Phineas Fletcher's over-looked (posthumous) "Father's Testament", a fine bit

---

[1] By inadvertence Mr. Bond, as before, after noting above commission in 1610, dates his death 1600-1 instead of 1610-11,

of filial reverence and memorial of his father's
death-bed : and I know not that I can more fit-
tingly gather up these imperfect words than by
borrowing my earlier use of them : and so here it
is : In presenting his book to his own children,
the Poet of the Purple Island thus addresses
them : " The great legacy which I desire to confer upon you is that which *my dying Father*
bequeathed unto me, and from him (through
God's grace) descended upon me : whose *last and
parting words* were these, ' My son, had I followed
the course of this world, and would either have
given or taken bribes, I might (happily) [=
haply] have made you rich : but now must leave
you nothing but your education, which (I bless
God) is such as I am well assured rather that I
should dye in peace, than yourselves live in plenty.
But know certainly that I your weak and dying
father leave you to an ever-living and all-sufficient
Father, and in Him, a never-failing inheritance :
Who will not suffer you to want any good thing :
Who hath been my God, and will be the God of
my seed '. Thus he entered into peace and slept
in Christ : leaving behind the fragrant perfume of
a good name to all his acquaintance, leaving to us
a prevalent example of an holy conversation, and
that ' goodly heritage ' where ' the lines are

fallen to us in pleasant places', (Psalm xi. 6.)
and leaving us to His protection Who hath never
failed us. This I desire, and as I am able endeavour to bequeath it unto you' (pp. 1—3)
Radiant words! All honour to such a father! and
such a son! It is clear that Misfortune (which
is not always a ' miss-of-fortune ') had mellowed
the erewhile vehement, and eager, and specula-
tive nature.[1]

Our Worthy must have entered suddenly and
been ' quick' in ' walking' through, the ' valley
of shadows' though his resignation of the Treasurership of St. Paul's seems to intimate conscious-
ness of final ailment.[2] His Will was a noncupative
one : and we have recovered it and would now
present it *verbatim* from the Wills' Office :

" Memorandum, that on the eleventh day of Ffebruarie
one thousand sixe hundred and tenne or thereabouts,
Giles Ffletcher, Doctor of Lawe, late of the parishe of
Sainte Catherine Colman in the Citie of London,
deceased, being of perfect mynde and memorye and
having an Intent to make his last Will, did nuncupatively
declare the same in manner and forme followinge or the
like in effecte, viz., he gave and bequeathed the residue of
all his goods and chattells (his debts that he oughte [=

---

[1] See our Phin : Fletcher, Vol. I. lx-lxii.
[2] *Ibid* Vol. II. pp 256-7.

owed,] being payed or deducted) unto Johane Ffletcher
his wife, or at least he declared his Will, in some other
wordes of the like effect, being then and there present,
William Webb, John Lane, and others."

PHINEAS FLETCHER was in 1610 in his 28th
year : and in his ' Eclogs ' he softly sings—with
tears like thundrous rain, sheathing fire in
them,—of his father. ' THELGON ', as before explained is the Poet's father : ' THOMALIN ' is
TOMKINS of Cambridge : ' Thirsil ' is the poet
himself.

Thomalin.

Ah Thelgon, poorest but the worthiest swain,
That ever grac't unworthy povertie !
How ever here thou liv'dst in joylesse pain,
Prest down with grief and patient miserie ;
Yet shalt thou live when thy proud enemie
   Shall rot, with scorn and proud contempt opprest.
   Sure now in joy thou safe and glad dost rest,
Smil'st at those eager foes, which here thee so molest.

Thirsil.

Thomalin, mourn not for him : he's sweetly sleeping
In Neptune's court, whom here he sought to please :—
While humming rivers by his cabin creeping
Rock soft his slumbering thoughts in quiet ease,—
Mourn for thy self—here windes do never cease ;
   Our dying lif will better fit thy crying ;

He softly sleeps, aud blest is quiet lying.
Who better living dies, he better lives by dying."[1]

The Widow and ' many children ' had a tranquil retreat in RINGWOOD : and her sons PHINEAS and GILES ' won' their way. But I wish I knew where Joan (Sheafe) Fletcher, their mother ' lies '.

Even from the few FACTS that have reached us in the life-story of DR. GILES FLETCHER, it is clear that he was a man of action rather than of words ; and I rather think that if all were known it would be found that this later generation owes much more commercially to him than we are aware. So potential and persistent and open-eyed a Commiss-ioner could not fail worthily to represent his beloved England, when to do so was to give direction to the very spring-flow of the tides of Commerce. While in a period of venality and shiftiness it was a national blessing to have a man of incorruptible integrity as Secretary of the Metropolis. Our documents have shewn how trying the post was. Accordingly his literary work was more bye-play than work and yet

---

[1] I find under a notice of Bayly, Bp. of Bangor,—1610, 7, Febr. Ludov. Bayly, A. M. Admissus ad Thesauarian S. Pauli, per Resign. Egidii. Fletcheri. LL.D. Reg. Lond. Wood. A. O. Bliss.

it abides. His account of his embassage to Russia is vital still : and must remain so. For the " Russe Commonwealth " (1591) is unique, alike historically and biographically. It bears the stamp of a keen intellect, penetrative, alert, intense: and there are many quaint tid-bits for the lover of plain-speaking " Travellers ". SIR JEROME HORSEY is a boor beside Fletcher. Mr. Bond's reprint for the Hakluyt Society is itself a scarce book now. We commend it, and specially its Introduction, to our Readers. Sprung of the same " Travelles," though not given to the world until long after, viz. in 1677, is his Essay on some probable grounds that the present Tartars near the Caspian Sea, are the Posterity of the Ten Tribes of Israel ", edited by Samuel Lee and accompanied by a " Dissertation " of his own on the " Restauration of Israel ". This thoughtful little treatise was furnished to the Editor by " Mr. Phineas Fletcher, his grandson, a worthy citizen of London, together with his kind leave to pass it into publick light ". It struck WHISTON, who has incorporated it in his " Memoirs," from another MS. Besides these prose Writings of our Worthy published by himself and posthumously, as afterwards with FULKE, LORD BROOKE, the world was deprived of a History of ELIZABETH by him. Among the LANSDOWNE MSS.

(65 art 59.) as before, there is an important letter
—never hither-to published—addressed to Lord
Burleigh, which puts the whole scheme before
him. It is as follows :

" My humble duety, remembered I acquainted y^r H. wt^h
my purpose to make trial of my self for writing a Latin
storie of hir Ma$^{tie's}$ time. Yr L. knoweth what is needfull
to make it a storie not a tale, bysides *res gestas* to have
consilia rerum gestarum, wherein I shall fynd great defect except y^r H. vouchsafe y^r help for instructions. I
desire not the very arcana (wch are best when they are
secreatest) but soe much as shalbee necessary to explain
and justifie the actions. To wch pourpose I have sett
downe a briefe of the first book and extracted out of it
the pointes to be instructed in, which I mean to observe in
the course of the whole for beeing over troublesome to y^r
H. and to note only so much at once as may serve for
on [e] book—except it please y^r L. to give order to Mr.
Mainard that I may see at once so much as I need—
whear allso I am most humbly to intreat yor H.L. that it
may be doon under yor patronage.

Y$_r$ H. knoweth what it is to write a storie, especially
de præsentibus and how hard it is to please truth and
the actours. If the idea and generall scope tend to the
honour of hir Ma$^{tie's}$ government, I hope it wilbe borne
withall if I tell truth in occurrent matters. Ffor the
rest I am to speak honour of that which deserveth it
and truth of all, wch wilbee doon wth better discretion

I may have yor H. direction in soom nicer points. As
in the first book, whether I shall deal wth justifying the

marriage betwixt King Henry and hir Matie's mother in soom larger discourse, wch I would think better rather to passe by wth out any toutch, for making a doubt whear the matter is found of so great a sequeal, but for the open and scurrilous sclaunders of ye Popish party allready in print in large discowrses, whereof soom of late have written with more venom than the rest; wch may bear credit hereafter if the truth bee not knowen by soom other discourse of better spirit and credit than theirs. As allso whether I weare better to begin the storie wth her Matie's time (touching only K. Edward and Q. Marie's time) as I have sett down in this brief; or whether I shall begin whear Polydor endeth, viz. at the 30th year of K. Henrie the 8. whear he concludeth with Catherine dowagre's letter, written to him at her death; or ells wth the king's marriage with Q. Anne, whear occasion is offered in both places to make narration and discourse of the lawfulness of that marriage in the very entrance of the storie. Yr H. knoweth Polydore's defects, his stile soomwhat harsh and uneaven and the matter not very iudicial, wch both I would avoyd. I have enfolded hearewth all these scribbled papers that contein a beginning of the storie at K. Edward's time, wch I toutch very briefly, to make an introduction to hir Matie's reign. If I fetch the begining from K. Henrey's marriage wth hir Matie's mother (wch will make a fuller storie) all this of K. Edward and Q. Marie is to be amplified more at large. These scribblings I am bold to offer to yr H. iudgement that may censure the same, wch wilbee more eaven and historicall when it cometh to the full narration. If yr H. allow it and will vouchsafe me yr help and patronage —

God willing, I mean to proceed— Thus humbly I take my leave 7th day of Nov., 1590.

Yr H. most humble

G. Fletcher.

To the right honourable my very good
L. the L. H. Treasurer of England.

The accompanying outline-plan it is not worth-while giving here.

Turning now from his prose writings, there were the following Latin Poems :

(*a*) In the Collection presented by the Eton scholars to Queen Elizabeth at Windsor Castle 1563.

(*b*) Prefixed to Foxe's " Acts and Monuments" 2nd. edn. 1570.

(*c*) An Eclogue on the death of DR. NICHOLAS CARR, Master of Magdalen College and Regius Professor of Greek, inserted in an edition of the *Olynthiacs and Philippics* of Demosthenes, edited in a Latin translation by Nicholas Carr, but not published till after his death (London 1571), with several poetical tributes to his memory in Greek and Latin. This Eclogue is entitled *Ecloga Daphnis inscripta, sive Querela Cantabrigiæ, in obitum doctissimi viri D. Nicolai Carri per Aegidium Fletcherum.*

(*d*) Latin Verses on publication of the Prelections of Dr. Peter Baro : therein 1576.

(*e*) Before Baro's Prelections on Jonah 1579.

(*f*) In the University Collection on Death of Sir Philip Sidney. 1587.

(*g*) Contributions to the *Poematum Gualteri Haddoni Legum Doctoris, sparsim collectorum, Libri Duo*" (*Lond.*) 1592.

There are three Elegies herein by our Worthy, the first noticeable as containing definite allusions to the Elegies published by Dr. DILLINGHAM, as onward. It is headed " *De obitu clarissimi Viri, D. Gualteri Haddoni Elegia per Aegidium Fletcherum.*" *** The widow of Walter Haddon, (Anne, d. of Sir Henry Sutton by Alice, d. of Sir John Harrington) married Sir Henry Brooke, 5th son of George Brooke, Baron Cobham, (Reliquary, Jany. 1868). See next section :

(*h*) Three Eclogues in " Poemata varii argumenti" (1678). They are entitled respectively " *Contra Prædicatorum Contemptum* ", " Querela

---

1 See our Phineas Fletcher, Vol. I. lxiv. Mr. Williams as before, having been appointed to RINGWOOD, most kindly made every possible search for me there : but nothing additional was discovered concerning Dr. Giles Fletcher at Ringwood. Still, the State-Paper shows the widow was granted her petition to hold the land.

Collegii Regalis " "De morte Boneri." DR. DIL-LINGHAM has entered these as " Eclogæ tres Incerti Authoris " : and it is easy to understand that when the DR. GOAD 'rebellion' had been amicably determined by Burleigh, as shewn in this Intro-duction earlier, the Author would have no desire to proclaim his authorship, or to publish. But PHINEAS FLETCHER in his " Piscatory Eclogues " has distinctly assigned them and others to his father, who as ' Thelgon ' thus speaks :

> ...." Whether nature joyn'd with art, had wrought me,
> Or I too much beleev'd the fisher's praise ;
> Or whether Phœbus' self or Muses taught me,
> Too much enclin'd to verse, and musick-playes ;
> So far credulitie and youth had brought me,
>   *I sang Telethusa's frustrate plaint,*
> *And rustick Daphnis' wrong, and magick's vain restraint.*
> *And then appeas'd young Myrtilus, repining,*
> *At generall contempt of shepherd's life."*

This is sufficiently explicit as to our FLETCHER, being the author of these Eclogues, inasmuch as the "frustrate plaint " of Telethusa, and "magick's vain restraint " form the burden of the second Ec-logue, viz., ' *Querela* ' (= plaint or complaining) Colegii Regalis ', wherein he sings of Telethusa, *e. g.*

" Flumenæve movent plangentes littora Nymphæ
Grantigenas quantum nuper Telethusa per undas " :

(p 123, lines 27-8.)

The 'magic restraint' appears in " Et me &c. and
" Esto mihi &c. (p 197 *et seqq*). The '*frustrate*
plaint' comes out in the pathetic '*frustra*' " *In
vain* have we tried magick arts ", and again in
Talia, &c. " Such things *in vain* Telethusa poured
out ". Again, in the first Eclogue we have
Myrtilus " repining at generall contempt of shepherd's life " as the heading shews, " Contra
Prædicatorum Contemptum ". The interlocutors
are Celadon and Myrtilus, and the same are the
interlocutors in the third Eclogue 'De Morte
Boneri ". As already noticed FLETCHER himself
tacitly claims the three Eclogues in one of his
three Elegies for Haddon, wherein he thus addresses his lamented friend, using the same names
of Celadon and Myrtilus :

" Non ego te (*Celadon*) ultra sub tegmine fagi
Teve canam placidas (*Myrtile*) propter aquas."

and again,

" Quid juvat aut reliquas coluisse laboribus artes ?
Jurave vesani litigiosa fori ?
Armaque Barbariem contra, Satyrosque rebelles
Ferre, nec e vulgi pars rudis esse choro."

497

The " Querela" satire and the GOAD disputes are
self-indicated in these lines.   Mr. Williams, as
before, who (mis) applied the " Querela " to the
PHILIP BAKER disputes, in his " Notes" to
"Memoir and Correspondence of Dr. Millington "
has laboriously and successfully proved the
Fletcher authorship of the Eclogues, from internal
evidence and comparison with the others.
Strange to say he seems to have been utterly
unaware of the more distinct evidence in the
" Piscatory Eclogues " or he might have been
saved superfluous labour.

(i) In Holinshed's Chronicles p 1512 are Verses
on the motto and crest of Max. Brooke, eldest
son of Lord COBHAM, who died in 1583, by Dr·
Fletcher (Cole MSS. Addl. MSS. 5808 f. 205).

(j) De Literis Antiquæ Britanniæ, Regibus
presertim qui doctrina claruerunt, quique Collegia
Cantabrigiæ fundarunt. (Cantab. 1633). This
long Poem was edited and published along with
his own *Sylva Poetica* by PHINEAS FLETCHER,
with profound filial reverence and love.   In the
" Piscatory Eclogues " he notices " De Literis "
also, where Thelgon tells he

> ...."taught our Chame to end the old-bred strife,
> Mythicus' claim to Nicias resigning"

as in the outset of " De Literis " :

Mythicus et Nicias (quorum Isidis alter ad amnem
Alter ad irriguas Chami consederat undas)
Certabant, ætate pares."

Intending originally to reprint our Worthy's
Latin poetry, we had translated the "De Literis",
and were much struck with the ingenuity with
which pre-historic or ' mythical' legends are interwoven, and not less with the well-turned praise
of the historic Founders, as ALFRED, EDWARD,
HENRY, ELIZABETH.

We have now reached our present reprint :

(*k*) Licia or Poemes of Love in Honour of the
admirable and singular vertues of his Lady, to the
imitation of the best Latin Poets, and others.
Whereunto is added the *Rising to the Crowne of
Richard the Third*" (1593). The same Eclogue
that determines our FLETCHER to have been the
author of the Eclogues *'incerti Authoris'*, with
equal explicitness asserts his authorship of the
volume entitled "Licia ". For after Telethusa's
' frustrate plaint' and ' Daphnis' wrong' and
' young Myrtilus' repining ', Thelgon says.

[I] *"rais'd my rime to sing of Richard's climbing "*

than which there could hardly be a more definite

pointing out of the "*Rising to the Crowne* of Richard Third". Then, not only do the Epistles-dedicatory to LADY MOLLINEUX and to the Reader, relate to the whole volume and so necessarily include 'Licia', but their allusions harmonize with outward facts brought out in this Introduction. Thus in vindicating his devotion to 'love-sonnets' he boasts of others who had shewn the same fealty, and takes the opportunity of lauding the University (of Cambridge) generally and his own College ('King's') in particular, *e.g.* " I can say thus much, that the Vniuersitie wherein I lived (and as I thinke the other) hath so many wise, excellent, sufficient men, as setting their learning aside, wherein they are most excellent, yet in all habilliments of a gentleman they are equall to any besides. This woulde that worthie Sidney oft confesse, and Harington's Ariosto (which Madame was respected so much by you) sheweth that his abode was in Kinge's Colledge". So that internally and externally the evidence seems absolute. I believe further that if we could get at the facts of the Author's mother-hood, it should be found that if not herself a GERARD or MOLLINEUX, she was in some way related to one or other of these families. And here it is I find a key to Dr. GILES FLETCHER's dedication of " Licia " to Lady

Mollineux. That is to say, as stated earlier, the relationship or friendship between the Fletchers and Nevilles of Liversedge was the probable origin of the warm relationship or friendship with him and the Mollineuxs. The Nevilles of Liversedge intermarried with the Mollineuxs. For by the Visitation of Yorkshire in 1530, Robert Neville of Liversedge, married Ellen, daughter of a Mollineux of Lancashire, and by her had issue Sir John, who married Maud, daughter of Sir ROBERT RYTHER. Then, though the Nevilles of Liversedge, in Yorkshire, and of Leverton in Notts, (the family to which Dr. Thomas Nevile belonged) were only remotely connected in the direct line of descent, it is noteworthy that about the time of Henry the VII, a Neville of the Liversedge stock and one of the Nottinghamshire family married two Yorkshire sisters and co-heiresses named Bosvile. So that the two branches had been brought into very close connection before the Master of Trinity's time : and it is easy to suppose his patronage would willingly be extended to any worthy relation or protege of his Yorkshire cousins, as in GILES FLETCHR (*filius*). These relations of the Neviles, and Fletchers, and Molineuxs, and Gerards go far to supplement our other evidence of the authorship of " Licia ", and as such we

have gladly turned to account the facts communicated very fully to us by Mr. Clark, of West
Dereham (as before).   I have placed below what
I have said elsewhere on the late Mr. Dyce's
remarks on " Licia ".[1]   I find in " Licia " and

---

[1] In my Memoir of PHINEAS FLETCHER (Vol. I., p.
xlvii.) I note the late Mr. Hunter's ascription of ' Licia '
&c., to our Fletcher: and I have since discovered a
further statement among his MSS.   I would here repeat
Mr. Dyce's remarks in his " Beaumont and Fletcher "
with my reply.   Mr. Dyce says " A poem called The
Rising to the Crowne of Richard the Third, which is
appended, with several other short poems, to Licia, or
Poems of Love, &c., *n.d.* 4o. is unhesitatingly assigned
by Mr. Hunter (New Illustr. of Shakeipeare, II. 77) to
the pen of DR. GILES FLETCHER, because in the first
Piscatory Eclogue of his son Phineas, where he certainly
is represented by the person called Thelgon, he is made
to say,

> And then appear'd young Myrtilus, repining
> At general contempt of shepherd's life
> And rais'd my rime to sing of Richard's climbing, &c.

I suspect however that Mr. Hunter is mistaken.   The
volume in question was evidently intended for private
circulation, having neither printer's nor publisher's
name.   I see no reason to doubt that all the pieces in it
are by the same author.   The Epistle-dedicatory to
Licia is dated by the same author " from my chamber " ;

related poems, very much more really than in
the Latin poetry, a ground for that very distinct

---

and assuredly the author of the amatory rhapsodies
so entitled, was not Dr. Giles Fletcher " (Vol. I. pp.
xv-qvi)." So much for Mr. Dyce. His remarks are a tissue
of most uncharacteristic blunders. I thus confute them,
as *supra* : " One must differ from Mr. Dyce with no less
diffidence than reluctance; but his conclusion being
based on errors, falls with proof of these. Had Mr.
Dyce read either of the Epistles prefixed, he would have
seen at once that he was mistaken in pronouncing the
volume to have been " evidently intended for private
circulation." So far from this, there is an elaborate
special Epistle addressed to the Reader, who in the
earlier to Lady Mollineux is called ' the indifferent
Reader (= impartial or general) : and at the close to his
patroness, he says explicitly, in reference to the printing
of his verses, " well, let the Printer looke to grow not a
beggar by such bargaynes, the Reader that he loose not his
labour," &c. So that it is manifest the volume was
designed for any ' reader ' and was published in ordinary
course. But what if it had been intended for private
circulation—printed perchance at the expense of Lady
Mollineux? That should in no wise have mili-
tated against the definite allusion of Phineas. Apart
from this, Mr. Dyce on re-consideration must know well,
that absence of ' printer's ' or ' publisher's ' name, is no
evidence of ' private circulation.' There are hundreds of
volumes of the period similarly issued. As I write this
note ' Christ's Bloodie Sweate ' (1613) is before me as an

recognition contemporarily of our Dr. GILES
FLETCHER as a Poet.   The Sonnets seem to me

instance. Mr. Dyce describes the ' other short poems '
as appended to " Richard's Rising " This is incorrect :
they form part of the ' Licia ' series. Besides, it would
have prevented so dogmatic a judgment on the authorship of the ' Love-sonnets' and so of "Richard's Rising,"
had Mr. Dyce *read* these so called, ludicrously miscalled,
' amatory rhapsodies '. The Epistle to the Reader reveals that the ' Love-sonnets ' were a mere form and veil
for something deeper. ' Amatory ' is out of the question
as addressed to a married ' Lady ', the much-praised
patroness of the poet. ' Rhapsodies ' is an equally unfortunate word. The Verse is laden with thought and
brilliant in no common degree. To evidence the esoteric
meaning take these few lines : " If thou muse what
Licia is, take her to be some Diana, at the least chaste,
or some Minerva, no Venus fairer farre: It may be she is
Learning's image or some heavenlie wonder which the
precisest may not mislike : perhaps under that name I
have shadowed Discipline. It may be I meane that
kinde courtesie which I found at the Patronesse of these
Poems ; it may be some Colledge, it may be my conceit
and pretende nothing." Finally here, Mr Dyce being
ignorant of Phineas Fletcher's allusions to his father's
other writings—for he does not appear to have looked
beyond the brief three lines in Mr. Hunter—was the more
easily misled into rejection of an authorship certainly
indubitable. (Our Phineas Fletcher, Vol. I-, pp. xlvii-l.)

full of fine and subtle thought and tremulous with a delicate emotion. The wording is close to both, as our skin to our body and our blood : and there are 'higher strains ', that tell of genuine poetic faculty. The 'rime' of Richard's Rising has historic interest in relation to Shakespeare, like CHRISTOPHER BROOKE'S. Taken all in all I feel that I am conferring no slight boon in for the first time placing this dainty and quaint Verse within reach of the chosen few who have made themselves my constituents in the Fuller Worthies' Library. And so good Readers ' Good-bye ', [God-be-with-you]

ALEXANDER B. GROSART.

APPENDIX

ON

PHINEAS AND GILES FLETCHER.

I. PHINEAS FLETCHER. In our Memoir of
Phineas Fletcher we were obliged to leave the
date of his death uncertain (Vol. I. pp. cli-liv).
It is our privilege to have recovered his Will,
which shews that he died in 1650. The following
is a *verbatim et literatim* copy from the original.

EXTRACTED FROM THE DISTRICT REGISTRY AT NORWICH,
FROM THE RECORDS OF THE ARCHDEACONRY COURT OF
NORFOLK.

June ye twenty one thousand six hundred
& nine & forty.

I Phinnees Ffletcher Preacher of ye word of God in Hillgay in ye County of Norfolk being at this present (blessed
bee God) in perfect memory doe make & ordaine this my
last will & Testament in manner & forme following. In
primis I bequeath my soule into the hands of Almighty
God my Maker & preserver & Jesus Christe my redeemer
& my body to bee interred in the Churchyard of Hillgay

at the discretion of my Executrix and for my temporall
goods wch it hath pleased God of his mercy to bestow
vpon mee for my comfort & vse in this Lyfe, I give &
bequeath them in manner & forme following vidzt : unto
my sonnes Phinnees & Williā, & to my daughters
Anne, Elisabeth, ffrances & Sarah & to every of them
my sayd sonnes & daughters Twenty shillings to be payd
them within one year next after my decease, Itē I give
& bequeath unto Elizabeth my wyfe all my lands &
tenements whatsoever during the terme of her naturall
lyfe & after her decease to Phinnees ffletcher my sonne &
his heires for ever all ye residue of my goods & Chattells
I give and bequeath unto Elizabeth my wife whom I
make sole Executrix of this my last will & Testament
shee paying my debts (Especially tenne pounds or ther
abouts wch I doe owe unto my daughter Anne) or what
Else I am indebted & allsoe these legacies above written,
& performing this my last will & Testament in Wittnes
whereof I have heerunto sett my hand & seale The
day & yeare above written.
in the presence of

PHINNEES FLETCHER.

JOHN LAMBE &
WILLM LIFE.

Pbatū corā m̄ro Cornelio Cushing
Clici surrōto &c apud Hellgay 13º
die menss Decembris Anno Dni
1650 Juram^{to} Elizabethæ ffletcher
Executricis &c.

508

With reference to the Sheafes (Vol. I. pp. xxxiii-
vi) Rev. J. H. Clark, M.A., of West Dereham, informs me that Thomas Haselrig, of London,
Mercer, a younger brother of the famous Sir
Arthur, married Rebecka, daughter of Thomas
Shefe, preb. of Windsor, and had issue (Additions
to Viz. a ped. of Haselrig, Leic. 1619, published by Harleian Society). I may also add as
another Phineas Fletcher *item* that since our
edition was issued I have been so fortunate as to
secure another MS. (wholly autograph) of the
Locustæ, with an interesting Epistle-dedicatory
to Henry Prince of Wales. I have also come on
still another copy of the Locustæ among the
Sloane MSS (444) with an Epistle-dedicatory to
the Bishop of Bath and Wells (Montagu). I
hope to utilize these in my intended fac-simile
edition of Milton. Finally : In addition on
Phineas Fletcher and his meeting with his future
wife, Elizabeth Vincent, while resident with the
Willoughbys, at Risley, in Derbyshire, (near the
junction of the Derwent with the Trent) it may
not be uninteresting to note that James Duport
(brother to John Duport, Master of Jesus College,
Cambridge, from 1590 to 1618) married a daughter of William Vincent, of Peckleton, county
Leicester. He was I presume either father or

uncle to the Greek professor of the same name.
The note to c. iv. stanza 33rd of the Apollyonists
is also very interesting in this part of the Poet's
life. It is evident that during his residence in
the valley of the Trent he obtained access to that
Library collected by Sir Thomas Hutchinson, at
Owthorpe, which his daughter-in-law tells us was
the "choicest in that part of England", and
which she says, "drew to him all the learned
and religious men thereabouts, who found better
resolutions from him than from any of his books."
(See Memoirs of Colonel Hutchinson : Bohn's
edition pp. 38-9, from which it appears that
school divinity was a very favorite study with Sir
Thomas).

II. GILES FLETCHER. After we had issued our
edition of GILES FLETCHER, while pursuing our
researches at Oxford for our CRASHAW, we were
fortunate enough to come on an unpublished poem
by him among the TANNER MSS. and here reproduce it. It has characteristic touches and is
worthy of the Poet of " Christ's Victorie " :

FROM TANNER MSS., VOL. 465, FOL. 42.

Nisis amore pio pueri, &c.

It was at euening, and in Aprill mild,
Of twelue sonnes, of the yeare the fairest child,

When Night and Day their strife to peace doe bring,
To haue an equall interest in the Spring.
The sunne being arbiter : I walkt to see
How Nature drew a meddow, and a tree
In orient colours, and to smell what sent
Of true perfume the winds the aire had lent.
When with a happy carelesse glance I spy
One pace, a shade : Encolpus cry'd 'tis I ;
And soe vnmaskt, his forehead branch't more faire,
Than locks of grasse, our mother Rhea's haire.
I had mine eyes soe full of such a freind,
That Flora's pride was dim̄d ; and in the end
I askt some time, before I could perswade
My senses it was Spring ; the silken blade
Of cowslips lost their grace ; the speckled pancie
Came short to flatter, though he smil'd, my fancie.
If later seasons had the roses bredd,
I doubt the modest damaske had turn'd redd,
Stain'd with a parallel ; but it was good
They swadled were, like infants, in the bud,
Solsequium, gladd of this excuse, begunne   *sunflower*
To close his blushes with the setting sunne.
Thrice chanting philomel beganne a song,
Thrice had no audience for Encolpus tongue.
This thorne did touch her breast to be rejected,
And tun'd a moane, not heard, she was neglected.
I thought vncurteous Time would wait, but Night
Appear'd, Orion's whelpes had chas'd the light
Into the Westerne couerts ; judge from hence
How farre a beauty com̄ands reuerence.
The neighbour starres in loue were waxen clearer

The farthest shott, me thought, to view him nearer.
My Vranoscopy said, the moone did cast
Faint beames and sullen glimpses; when at last
I spy'd in her a new and vncouth spott,
Doubtles through envy all the rest she gott.
And then she held her palenes in a shrowd,
Borrowing the pleighted curtaines of a clowd.
Flowers, birds, and starres, all to Encolpus yields,
As to Adonis doe Adonis fields.
Oh had some other thus describ'd, and seene!
I came a partiall judge, to praise the screene.

G. FLETCHER.

On the margin, SANCROFT has written that he had obtained the preceding from Mr. Blois, and notes that it was from the Encolpus of Petronius. Every Miltonic illustration is valuable, and so I place beside "*pleighted* curtaines of a *clowd*" the "play is the *plighted clouds*" of Comus, line 300.

I have also been favoured by Mr. W. Aldis Wright, as before, with the following additional notes from the Conclusion Book, Trinity College, Cambridge.

1617. January 24th: Mr. Fletcher and Mr. Kinaston added to Catechise to those already appointed.

These notes too from the Senior Bursar's Book.

1614. Item paid to Mr. Fletcher for a quarter's

allowance at 3s. 4d. the weeke from St. Ladie day to Midsomer for Mr. Gardiner—xliijs. iiijd.

1615. Item spent in carring [*sic*] of letters gratulatory to the King and Prince to Grenwiche by my selfe and Mr. Fletcher, man and horse 5 days vl. xviijs.

The Bursar was in the last case Thomas Fortho. These all refer to Giles Fletcher, Junior. With reference to the first entry it is necessary to explain that Fellows who wished to qualify themselves for College preachers had to expound the Catechism a certain number of times in Chapel. Under the old statutes the College Preachers had certain privileges with regard to livings which they were allowed to hold with their Fellowship. Finally I am indebted to Colonel Chester, as before, for the following information, viz. that Letters of Adminstration were issued 12th November, 1623, in the Prerograrive Court of Canterbury, on the estate of Giles Fletcher of Alderton, county Suffolk, S T. B. to his relict Anne. This gives us the Poet's wife's Christian name.

Licia

OR

Poems of Love

ETC.

𝔑ote.

THE title-page of Licia etc. will be found below.
Our exemplar is the perfect copy in the BODLEIAN.
Throughout, as usual, we have reproduced the original
in integrity of orthography and all, even (in this instance)
to the somewhat arbitrary capitals and punctuation.   G.

LICIA

or

POEMES OF

LOVE, IN HO-

nour of the admirable

and singular vertues of his Lady,

to the imitation of the best

Latin Poets, and others.

Whereunto is added the Rising to the

Crowne of RICHARD

the third.

Auxit musarum numerum Sappho ad-

dit a musis,

Fœlix si sævus, sic voluisset Amor.

On reverse of the title-page are the two following Latin
addresses :

AD AMOREM.

Si Cœlum patria est puer beatum,

Si vero peperit Venus benigna,

Si Nectar tibi Massicum ministrat,

516

Si Sancta Ambrosia est Cibus petitus,
Quid noctes habitas, diesq mecum?
Quid Victum face supplicemq. aduris?
Quid longam lachrimis sitim repellis?
Quid nostræ dape paceris medullæ?
O vere rabidum genus fœrarum:
O domo stige patriaq. digne:
Iam levis sumus umbra, quid lacessis?

TO LOVE: TRANSLATION.

If indeed the heavens adore thee!
If indeed kind Venus bore thee!
If Jove's nectar is thy wine,
And ambrosia divine
Is the food that's found for thee!
Tell me, boy, how can it be
That day and night thou art with me?
Why thy vanquish'd suppliant still
Eager with thy brand to kill?
Why with tears long thirst deceive,
And upon our marrow live?
Seed of fell beasts, fierce and wild,
Of grim Styx the true-born child;
Since a flitting shade we are
Wherefore thus incessant war?

AD LECTOREM.

Non Convitia, nec latrationes,
Nec konchos times, Calumni asue,
Nec ullos obelos severiores,
Non quod judicio meo Poeta

517

Sim tantus, nihil ut queat reprehendi :
Sed quod judicio meo Poeta
Sim tam ridiculus ; parumq, doctus,
Ut nullum fore judicem eruditum,
Meos carpere qui velit labores :
Nam quis Aethiopeni velit lavare ?

TO THE READER : TRANSLATION.

It is not rude abuse, nor envy's bark
Nor empty noise, nor any harsher mark
I am afraid of, nor that I should seem
In my own judgment of such high esteem
As to be faultless : but that I should feel
Myself ridiculous, equipp'd so ill
That to my works no mind of weight and power
Should care to turn aside and pluck a flower:
This I should rue indeed—for what fond man
Would try to wash1 an Ethiopian ?
J. H. Clark, M. A.

---

1 = blanch.   G.

Licia or Poems of Love, etc.

TO THE WORTHIE, KINDE, WISE AND
VERTUOUS LADIE, THE LADIE
MOLLINEUX; WIFE TO THE RIGHT
WORSHIPFULL SYR RICHARD MOLLI-
NEUX KNIGHT.[1]

OWSOEVER in the settled opinions of
some wise heads this trifling labour may
easily incurre the suspicion of two evils;
either to be of an idle subject, and so frivolous:

---

[1] I am indebted for the following information to
'Notes and Queries' in reference to a 'Note' from me:
" Sir Richard Mollineux of Sefton, Lancashire, was in
ward to Sir Gilbert Gerard of Sudbury, Master of the
rolls, and was knighted by Queen Elizabeth, June 24th,
1586, being then in his 26th year.   In 1589 and 1597 he
was sheriff of the county of Lancaster; and upon the insti-
tution of the order of baronets, May 22nd, 1611, was the
second created to that dignity.   He married Frances,
eldest daughter of the aforesaid Sir Gilbert Gerard, and
had six sons and seven daughters.   Lodge's *Peerage* : ed.

or vainly handled, and so odious. Yet my resolute purpose was to proceed so farre, as the
indifferent[1] Reader might thinke this small paines
to be rather an effect then a cause of idlenesse ;
and howsoever Love in this age hath behaved himselfe in that loose manner, as it is counted a
disgrace to give him but a kind looke ; yet I take
the passion in it selfe to be of that honour and
credite, as it is the perfect resemblance of the
greatest happinesse, and rightlie valued at his

1789, iii 254 " (4th S. II., August 15th 1868.) Further,
in an after-communication from Dr. Duffield, Rector of
Sephton,Lancashire, we have these entries in the Register : " 1620: Dna Francisca uxor Richardi Molineux de
Sefton militis et Baronetæ senioris, nono die, ffebruarij
1622. Richardus Molineux de Sefton, Miles et Baronetta
octauo die Martij. 22nd August, 1868. In the present
Epistle onward, the Author names M. Lee and courteous
Mr. Hoghton. The former was no doubt Peter Leigh,
Esq. (sometimes spelled Leigh and Lee) who married
another daughter of Sir Gilbert Gerard, viz. Margaret : the
latter Richard Hoghton, of Hoghton, Esq., near Blackburn, who married still another daughter, Catherine:
both sisters of Lady Mollineux and the ' fair ladies '
celebrated in the extra-poem among the Sonnets (?) It thus
appears that Fletcher's connection was with the Gerards.
See our Memorial-Introduction for the relationship between the Fletchers, Neviles, Mollineux, &c. G.

[1] = impartial. G.

just price (in a minde that is syncerely and truly
amorous) an affection of greatest vertue, and able
of him selfe to æternize the meanest vassall. Concerning the handling of it, (especially in this age)
men may wonder, if a Scholler, how I come by
so much leasure : if otherwise, why a writer. Indeede to say trueth, though I cannot justly challenge the first name, yet I wish none to be writers
save onely such as knowe learning. And whereas
my thoughts and some reasons drew me rather to
have dealt in causes of greater weight, yet the
present jarre of this disagreeing age drive me into
a fitte so melancholie, as I onely had leasure to
growe passionate. And I see not why upon our
dissentions I may not sit downe idle, forsake my
study, and goe sing of love, as well as our Brown-
istes forsake the Church, and write of malice.

And that this is a matter not so unfitte for a
man, either that respecteth himselfe, or is a
scholler, Peruse but the writings of former times,
and you shall see not onely others in other
countryes, as Italie, and France, men of learning,
and great partes to have written Poems and Sonnets of Love ; but even amongst us, men of best
nobilitie, and chiefest families, to be the greatest
Schollers and most renowned in this kind. But
two reasons hath made it a thing foolishly odious

in this age : the one, that so many base companions
are the greatest writers : the other that our
English Genevian puritie hath quite debarred us
of honest recreation ; and yet the great pillar (as
they make him of that cause[1]) hath shewed us as
much witte and learning in this kinde, as any
other before or since. Furthermore for all students
I will say thus much, that the base conceit,
which men generally have of their wants, is such,
as I scarce terme him a scholler, that hath not all
the acomplyments [*sic*] of a Gentleman, nor sufficiently wise that will not take oportunitie in some
sort to shew it. For I can say thus much, that
the Vniversitie wherein I lived (and as I thinke
the other) hath so many wise, excellent, sufficient
men, as setting their learning aside, wherein they
are most excellent, yet in all habilliments of a
Gentleman they are equall to any besides. This
woulde that worthie SIDNEY oft confesse and
Harington's Ariosto (which Madame was respected so much by you) sheweth that his abode was
in Kinge's College. Yet nowe it is growen to

---

[1] Query—CALVIN ? This illustrious man took a larger
part in the sacred song and music of the Church than is
generally known. Like LUTHER he had an intense
sympathy with all harmonies. Or is it Cartwright ? G.

this passe, that learning is lightly respected, upon a perswasion, that it is to found every where; a thing untrue and unpossible. Now in that I have written Love sonnets, if any man measure my affection by my style, let him say, I am in Love : no greate matter, for if our purest divines have not bene so, why are so manie married ? I mislike not that, nor I would not have them mislyke this. For a man may be in loue and not marrie, and yet wise ; but hee cannot marrie, and not be in love, but be a mere foole. Nowe, for the manner; we will dispute that in some other place; yet take this by the waie, though I am so liberall to graunt thus much, a man may write of love, and not bee in love, as well as of husbandrie, and not goe to plough ; or of witches and be none : or of holinesse and be flat prophane. But (wise and kinde Ladie) not to trouble your eares with this idle discourse, let this suffice, I found favours undeserved in such manner as my rude abilitie wantes meanes to make recompence, and therefore in the meane time I request you to accept this : If I had not so woondred at your admirable and rare vertues, that my hearte was surcharged with the exceeding measure of your woorthinesse, I had not written : you are happie everie way, and so reputed : live so, and I wish so you may live long: excuse me, favour me, and if I live, for I am loth to admire without thankefulnesse, ere long it shall be knowne what favours I received from wise Sir Richard, to whome in all kinde affectes[1] I reste bouud.

For the Reader, if he looke for my letters to crave his favour, he is farre deceived : for if he mislike anie thing, I am sorie he tooke the paines to reade, but if he doe, let him dispraise, I much care not : for praise is not but as men please : and it is no chiefe felicitie, for I have hearde some men and of late for Sermons at Paules crosse and for other paines so commended by all (excepting some fewe Cynickes, that commend none that doe well) that you would have thought England would have striven, for their spedie preferment, but lyke a woonder it lasted but nine dayes, and all is quiet and forgotten : the best is they are yong men and may live to be preferred at another time : so what am I worse if men mislike and vse tearmes ? I can say as much by them. For our great men I am sure, they want leasure to reade, and if they had, yet for the most part, the worst speake worst. Well, let the Printer looke he grow not a begger by such bargaynes, the Reader that

---

[1] = affections.　G.

he loose not his labour, and for mine that is past, and who so wiselie after an afternoone's sleepe gapes, and saith, Oh howe yong men spend their time idlie : first, let him spende his tyme better than to sleepe : Secondlie, he knowes not my age : I feared a hot ague, and with Tasso I was content to let my wit blood. But leaving these to their dogged humour, and wishing your Lady-ship all happinesse, I humbly take my leave. From my chamber, Sept. 4, 1593.

TO THE READER.

HAD thought, (curteous and gentle Reader) not to have troubled thy patience with these lines; but that in the neglect thereof I shoulde either scorne thee as careless of thine opinion (a thing savouring of a proud humour) or dispaire to obtaine thy favor, which I am loth to conceive of thy good nature. If I were knowne I would intreat in the best manner, and speake for him, whom thou knewest : but beeing not knowne, thou speakest not against me, and therefore I much care not; for this kinde of poetrie wherein I wrote, I did it onely to trie

my humour : and for the matter of love, it may
bee I am so devoted to some one, into whose hands
these may light by chance, that she may say,
which thou nowe saiest (that surelie he is in love)
which if she doe, then have I the full recompence
of my labour, and the Poems have dealt sufficient-
lie, for the discharge of their owne duetie. This
age is learnedlie wise, and faultles in this kind
of making their wittes knowne : thinking so
baselie of our bare English (wherein thousandes
have traveilled with such ill lucke) that they
deeme themselves barbarous, and the Iland barren,
unlesse they have borrowed from Italie, Spaine,
and France, their best and choicest conceites ;
for my owne parte, I am of this mind that our
nation is so exqasite (neither woulde I overwein-
inglie seeme to flatter our home-spunne stuffe, or
diminish the credite of our brave traveilers) that
neither Italie, Spaine nor France can goe beiond
vs for exact invention ; for if aniething be odious
amongst vs, it is the exile of our olde maners :
and some base-borne phrases stuft up with such
newe tearmes as a man may sooner feele vs to
flatter by our incrouching eloquence than suspect
it from the eare. And for the matter of love,
where everie man takes upon him to court
exactlie, I could iustlie grace (if it be a grace

to be excellent in that kinde) the Innes of
Court, and some Gentlemen like students in
both Vniversities, whose learning and bringing up,
together with their fine natures, makes so sweet a
harmonie, as without partialitie, the most iniurious will preferre them before all others: and
therefore they onelie are fittest to write of Love.
For others for the moste parte, are men of meane
reach, whose imbased mindes praie uppon everie
badde dish: men unfitte to know what love meanes;
deluded fondlie with their owne conceit, misdeem-
ing so divine a fancie, taking it to bee the contentment of themselves, the shame of others : the wrong
of vertue : and the refiner of the tongue; boasting
of some fewe favours. These and such like errours
(errours hatefull to an upright minde) commonlie
by learnlesse heades, are reputed for love's kingdome. But vaine men naturallie led, deluded
themselves, deceive others. For Love is a Goddesse (pardon me though I speake like a Poet)
not respecting the contentment of him that loves
but the vertues of the beloved, satisfied with
woondering, fedde with admiration : respecting
nothing but his Ladie's woorthinesse : made as
happie by love as by all favours, chaste by honour,
farre from violence : respecting but one, and that
one in such kindnesse, honestie, trueth, constan-

cie, and honour, as were all the world offered to
make a change, yet the boote were too small, and
therefore bootles. This is love, and far more
than this, which I knowe a vulgare head, a base
minde, an ordinarie conceit, a common person
will not, nor cannot have : thus doe I commende
that love where-with in these poemes I have
honoured the woorthie LICIA : But the love
wherewith Venus sonne hath injuriouslie made
spoile of thousandes, is a cruell tyrant : occasion
of sighes : oracle of lies : enemie of pittie : way of
error : shape of inconstancie : temple of treason :
faith without assurance : monarch of tears : mur-
therer of ease : prison of heartes : monster of
nature : poisoned honney : impudent courtizan :
furious bastard : and in one word not Love. Thus
(Reader) take heede thou erre not, esteeme Love
as thou ought. If thou muse what my LICIA is,
take her to be some Diana, at the least chaste, or
some Minerva, no Venus, fairer farre ; it may be
she is Learning's image, or some heavenlie woonder, which the precisest may not mislike : perhaps
under that name I have shadowed Discipline. It
may be, I meane that kinde courtesie which I found
at the Patronesse of these Poems ; it may bee some
Colledge. it may bee my conceit, and portende
nothing : whatsoever it be, if thou like it, take it,

and thanke the worthie Ladie MOLLINEUX, for whose sake thou hast it; worthie indeed, and so not onlie reputed by me in private affection of thankefulnesse, but so equallie to be esteemed by all that knowe her: For if I had not received of her and good SIR RICHARD, of kind and wise M. LEE, of curteous M. HOVGHTON, all matchlesse matched in one kindred, those unrequitable favours, I had not thus idlely toyed. If thou mislike it, yet she or they, or both, or divine LICIA shall patronize it, or if none, I will and can doe it my-selfe: yet I wish thy favour: do but say thou ar content, and I rest thine: if not farewel til wet both meete. Septemb. 8. 1593.

To Licia, the Wise, Kinde, Vertuous. and Fayre.

BRIGHT matchles starre, the honour of
    the skie,
        From whose clear shine, heavens vawt[1]
        hath all his light,
I send these Poems to your gracefulle eye :
Doe you but take them, and they have their
    right.
I build besides a Temple to your name,
Wherein my thoughtes shall daily sing your praise :
And will erect an aulter for the same,
Which shall your vertues, and your honour raise.
But heaven the Temple of your honour is,
Whose brasen toppes your worthie selfe made
        proude :
The ground an aulter, base for such a blisse
With pitie torne, because I sigh'd so loude.
And since my skill no worship can impart,
Make you an incense of my loving heart.
Sadde all alone, not long I musing satte,
But that my thoughtes compell'd me to aspire,

---

[1] = vault.   G.

A Laurell garland in my hande I gatte :
So the Muses I approch'd the nyer.
My sute was this, a Poet to become,
To drinke with them, and from the heavens be
      fedde :
Phœbus denyed, and sware there was no roome,
Such to be Poets as fond fancie ledde :
Withthat I mourn'd ; and sat me downe to wee pe,
Venus she smil'd, and smyling to me saide,
Come drinke with me, and sitt thee still and
      sleepe .
This voyce I heard : and Venus I obayde.
That poyson (sweete), hath done me all this
      wrong,
For nowe of love, must needes be all my song.

SONNET II.

Wearie was love, and sought to take his rest.
He made his choice, uppon a virgin's lappe :
And slylie crept, from thence unto her breast,
Where still he meant, to sport him in his happe.
The virgin frown'd, like Phœbus in a cloude,
Go packe sir boy, here is no roome for such,
My breast no wanton foolish boyes must shroude;
This saide, my Love did giue the wagge a tuch,
Then as the foot that treads the stinging snake,
Hastes to be gone, for feare what may ensewe,

So love, my love, was forst for to forsake,
And for more speede, without his arrowes flewe.
Pardon (he saide) for why you seem'd to me,
My mother Venus, in her pride to be.

SONNET III.

The heavens beheld the beautie of my Queene,
And all amaz'd, to wonder thus began :
Why dotes not Iove, as erst we all have seene,
And shapes himselfe like to a seemely man ?
Meane are the matches which he sought before,
Like bloomelesse buddes, too base to make com-
  pare,
And she alone hath treasur'd beauties store :
In whome all giftes and princely graces are.
Cupid reply'd:[1] I posted with the Sunne,
To viewe the maydes that livèd in those dayes,
And none there was, that might not well be
  wonne :
But she, most hard, most cold, made of delayes.
 Heavens were deceiv'd, and wrong they doe
  esteeme,
 She hath no heat, although she living seeme.

SONNET IIII.

Love, and my love, did range the forrest wilde,

---

[1] Misprinted 'relyyd'. G.

542

Mounted alyke, upon swift coursers both :
Love her encountred, though he was a childe,
Let's strive (saith he) whereat my love was wroth,
And scorn'd the boy, and checkt him with a smile;
I mounted am, and armèd with my speare,
Thou art too weake, thy selfe doe not beguile,
I could thee conquere, if I naked were :
With this love wept, and then my love reply'd :
Kisse me (sweet boy) so : weepe (my boy) no
      more ;
Thus did my love, and then her force she try'd,
Love was made yce, that fier was before.
A kisse of hers , as I poore soule doe proove,
Can make the hottest freese, and coldest love.

SONNET V.

Love with her haire, my love by force hath ty'd,
To serve her lippes, her eies, her voice, her hand;
I smil'd for joy, when I the boye espy'd,
To lie inchain'd, and live at her commaund.
She if she looke, or kisse, or sing, or smile,
Cupid withall, doth smile, doth sing, doth kisse,
Lippes, handes, voice, eies, all hearts that may
      beguile,
Bicause she scornes, all hearts but onlie this.
Venus for this in pride began to frowne :
That Cupid borne a god, inthrald should be :

She in disdaine, her prettie sonne threwe downe,
And in his place, with love she chainèd me.
So now (sweet love) though I my selfe be thrale,
Not her a goddesse, but thy selfe I call.

SONNET VI.

My love amaz'd did blush herselfe to see,
Pictur'd by arte, all naked as she was :
How could the Painter, knowe so much by me,
Or Art effect what he hath brought to passe ?
It is not lyke, he naked me hath seene,
Or stoode so nigh, for to observe so much,
No, sweete ; his eyes so nere have never bene,
Nor could his handes, by arte have cunning such :
I showed my heart, wherein you printed were,
You, naked you, as here you painted are,
In that (My Love) your picture I must weare,
And show't to all, unlesse you have more care :
Then take my heart, and place it with your owne,
So shall you naked never more be knowne.

SONNET VII.

Death in a rage, assaulted once my heart,
With love of her, my love that doeth denie.
I scorn'd his force, and wisht him to depart,
I heartlesse was, and therefore could not die :
I live in her, in her I plac'd my life,

She guydes my soule, and her I honour must,
Nor is this life but yet a living strife,
A thing unmeet, ane yet a thing most just :
Cupid inrag'd, did flie to make me love,
My heart lay garded with those burning eies,
The sparkes whereof denyed him to remoove ;
So conquerd now, he like a captive lies,
Thus two at once by love were both undone :
My heart not lov'd, and armlesse Venus sonne.

SONNET VIII.

Harde are the rockes, the marble, and the steele,
The auncient oake, with wind, and weather tost,
But you my love, farre harder doe I feele,
Then flinte, or these, or is the winter's frost.
My teares too weake, your heart they cannot
    moove,
My sighes, that rocke, like wind it cannot rent,
Too Tyger-like you sweare, you cannot love :
But teares, and sighes, you fruitlesse back have
    sent.
The frost too hard, not melted with my flame,
I Cynders am, and yet you feele no heate :
Surpasse not these (sweet love) for verie shame,
But let my teares, my vowes, my sighes, entreat,
Then shall I say as I by triall finde :
These all are hard, but you (my love) are kind.

SONNET IX.

Love was layd downe, all wearie fast asleepe,
Whereas my love his armour tooke away ;
The boye awak'd, and straight began to weepe,
But stood amaz'd, and knew uot what to say :
Weepe not, my boy, said Venus to her sonne,
Thy weapons non can weild, but thou alone,
Lycia the faire, this harme to thee hath done,
I sawe her here, and presentlie was gone ;
She will restore them, for she hath no need,
To take thy weapons, where thy valour lies ;
For men to wound, the Fates have her decreed,
With favour, handes, with beautie, and with eies ;
No, Venus no : she scornes them (credite me)
But robb'd thy sonne, that none might care for
　　　thee.

SONNET X.

A paynter drew the image of the boye,
Swift love, with winges all naked, and yet blind :
With bowe and arrowes, bent for to destroye :
I blam'd his skill, and fault I thus did fynde :
A needlesse taske, I see thy cunning take ;
Misled by love, thy fancie thee betrayde :
Love is no boye, nor biinde, as men him make,
Nor weapons weares, whereof to be affrayde :
But if thou Loue, wilt paint with greatest skill,

A Love, a mayde, a goddesse, and a Queene :
Woonder and view at Lycia's picture still,
For other love, the world[1] hath never seene,
For she alone, all hope, all comfort gives :
Mens hearts, soules all, led by her favour lives.

SONNET XI.

In Ida vale three Queenes the shepheard sawe,
Queenes of esteeme, divine, they were all three :
A sight of worth. but I a wonder shawe,
There[1] vertues all in one alone to be.
Lycia the fayre, surpassing Venus pride,
(The matchlesse Queene commaunder of the goddes,
When drawen with doves, she in her pompe doeth
    ride)
Hath farre more beautie, and more grace by oddes.
Iuno Iove's wife, unmeete to make compare,
I graunt a goddesse, but not halfe so mylde :
Minerva wise, a vertue, but not rare.
Yet these are meane, if that my love but smyl'de.
  She them surpasseth, when their prides are
    full :
  As farre as they surpasse the meanest trull.

---

[1] Misprinted 'wortld'. G.   [2] = Their. G.

SONNET XII.

I wish sometimes, although a worthlesse thing,
Spurd by ambition, glad for to aspyre,
My selfe a Monarch, or some mightie King:
And then my thoughtes doe wish for to be hyer.
But when I view what windes the Cedars tosse,
What stormes men feele that covet for renowne,
I blame my selfe that I have wisht my losse,
And scorne a kingdome, though it give a crowne.
A' Licia thou, the wonder of my thought,
My hearte's content, procurer of my blisse,
For whom a crowne, I doe esteeme as nought,
And Asia's wealth, too meane to buy a kisse.
   Kisse me sweete love, this favour doe for me:
   Then Crownes and Kingdomes shall I scorne
      for thee.

SONNET XIII.

Innamour'd Iove, commaunding did intreat,
Cupid to wound my love, which he deny'd,
And swore he could not, for she wanted heate,
And would not love, as he full oft had try'd.
Iove in a rage, impatient this to heare,
Reply'd with threats: I'le make you to obey:
Whereat the boye did flie away for feare,

---

[1] Misprinted xiii. **G.**

To Lycia's eyes, where safe intrench'd he lay :
Then Iove he scorn'd, and darde him to his face,
For now more safe than in the heavens he dwell'd,
Nor could Iove's wrath, doe wrong to such a place
Where grace and honour, have their kingdome
     helde.
   Thus in the pride and beautie of her eyes :
   The seelie[1] boye, the greatest god defies.

SONNET XIIII.

My love lay sleeping, where birdes musicke made,
Shutting her eies, disdainfull of the light ;
The heat was great, but greater was the shade,
Which her defended from his burning sight :
This Cupid saw, and came a kisse to take,
Sucking sweet Nectar, from her sugred breath :
She felt the touch, and blusht, and did awake,
Seeing t'was Love, which she did think was Death :
She cut his winges, and causèd him to stay,
Making a vowe, hee should not thence depart,
Vnlesse to her, the wanton boy could pay,
The truest, kindest and most loving heart :
   His feathers still, she usèd for a fanne :
   Till by exchange, my heart his feathers wan.

---

[1] = silly or semi-innocent. G.

SONNET XV.

I stood amaz'd, and sawe my Licia shine,
Fairer than Phœbus, in his brightest pride,
Set foorth in colours, by a hand divine,
Where naught was wanting, but a soule to guide.
It was a picture, that I could descrye :
Yet made with arte, so as it seem'd to live,
Surpassing faire, and yet it had no eye :
Whereof my senses, could no reason give.
With that the Painter bidde me not to muse,
Her eyes are shut, but I deserve no blame.
For if she saw, in faith, it could not chuse,
But that the worke, had wholly beene a flame.
 Then burne me (sweete) with brightnesse of your
  eyes,
 That Phœnix like, from thence I may arise.

SONNET XVI.

Graunt fayrest kind, a kisse unto thy friend !
A blush replyde, and yet a kisse I had :
It is not heaven that can such nectar send,
Whereat my senses, all amaz'd were glad.
This done, she fled, as one that was afrayde,
And I desyr'd to kisse, by kissing more ;
My love she frown'd, and I my kissing stayde,
Yet wisht to kisse her, as I did before :
Then as the vine, the propping elme doeth claspe.

Lothe to depart, till both together dye :
So folde me (sweete) untill my latest gaspe,
That in thy armes, to death, I kist, may lye.
 Thus whilest I live, for kisses I must call,
 Still kisse me, (sweete) or kisse me not at all.

SONNET XVII.

As are the sandes (faire Licia) on the shore,
Or coloured flourès, garlands of the Spring,
Or as the frosts not seene, nor felt before,
Or as the fruites that Autumne foorth doth bring ;
As twinckling starres, the tinsell of the night,
Or as the fish that gallope in the seas ;
As aires each part that still escapes our sight :
So are my sighes, controllers of my ease.
Yet these are such, as needes must have an end,
For things finite, none els hath nature done :
Onlie the sighes, which from my heart I send,
Will never cease, but where they first begunne.
 Accept them (sweet) as incense due to thee :
 For you immottall[1] made them so to be.

SONNET XVIII.

I sweare (faire Licia) still for to be thine.
By heart, by eies, by what I held most deare ;
Thou checkt mine oath, and said : these were not
  mine,

---

[1] *Sic :* query immortal ? or it may be = immovable. G.

And that I had no right by them to sweare.
Then by my sighes, my passions, and my teares,
My vowes, my prayers, my sorrowe, and my love,
My griefe,[1] my joy, my hope, and hopeles feare,
My heart is thine, and never shall remoove.
These are not thine, though sent unto thy viewe,
All els I graunt, by right they are thine owne,
Let these suffice, that what I sweare is true,
And more than this, if that it could be known.
   So shall all these, though troubles ease my griefe :
   If that they serve, to worke in thee beliefe.

SONNET XIX.

That tyme (faire Licia) when I stole a kisse,
From of those lippes, where Cupid lovelie laide,
I quakt for colde, and found the cause was this,
My life which lov'd, for love behind me staid,
I sent my heart, my life for to recall :
But that was held, not able to returne,
And both detain'd as captives were in thrall :
And judg'd by her, that both by sighes should
     burne
(Faire) burne them both, for that they were so
     bolde,
But let the altar be within thy heart :

---

[1] Misprinted 'gtief'.   G.

And I shall live, because my lyfe you holde,
You that give lyfe, to everie living part ;
   A flame I tooke, when as I stole the kisse ;
   Take you my lyfe, yet can I live with this.

SONNET XX.

First did I feare, when first my love began ;
Possest in fittes, by watchfull jealousie,
I sought to keepe, what I by favour wanne,
And brookt no partner in my love to be.
But Tyrant sicknesse, fedde upon my love,
And spred his ensignes, dy'd with colour white,
Then was suspition, glad for to remoove :
And loving much did feare to loose her quite.
Erect (faire sweet) the collours thou didst weare,
Dislodge thy griefes, the shortners of content :
For now of lyfe, not love, is all my feare,
Least lyfe and love be both together spent :
   Live but (faire love) and banish thy disease,
   And love (kind heart) both where, and whom
     thou please.

SONNET XXI.

Lycia my love was sitting in a grove,
Tuning her smiles unto the chirping songs,
But straight she spy'd, where two together strove,
Ech one complaining of the other's wrongs.

Cupid did crie, lamenting of the harme :
Ioue's messenger, thou wrong'st me too too
    farre :
Vse thou thy rodde, relye upon the charme :
Thinke not by speach, my force thou canst debarre
A rodde (syr boy) were fitter for a childe,
My weapons oft, and tongue, and minde you tooke ?
And in my wrong, at my distresse thou smil'de,
And scorn'd to grace me with a loving looke.
    Speake you (sweet love) for you did all the
        wrong,
    That broke his arrowes, and did binde his tong

SONNET XXII.

I might have dyed, before my lyfe begunne,
When as my father for his countrie's good,
The Persian's favour and the Sophy wonne :
But yet with daunger, of his dearest blood.[1]
Thy father (sweet) whome daunger did beset,
Escapèd all, and for no other end
But onely this, that you he might beget :
Whom heavens decreed into the world to send.
Then father, thanke thy daughter for thy lyfe,
And Neptune praise, that yeelded so to thee,

---

[1] See our Memorial-Introduction for the biographic
value of these references.   G.

To calme the tempest, when the stormes were
    ryfe,
And that thy daughter should a Venus be.
I call thee Venus (sweet) but be not wroth,
Thou art more chast, yet seas did favour both.

SONNET XXIII.

My love was maskt, and armèd with a fanne,
To see the Sunne so carelesse of his light,
Which stood and gaz'd, and gazing waxèd wanne,
To see a starre, himselfe that was more bright.
Some did surmize, she hidde her from the sunne :
Of whome, in pride, she scorn'd for to be kist:
Or fear'd the harme, by him to others done ;
But these the reason of this woonder mist,
Nor durst the Sunne, if that her face were bare,
In greatest pride, presume to take a kisse :
But she more kinde did shew she had more care,
Then with her eyes, eclypse him of his blisse.
    Vnmaske you (sweet) and spare not, dimme the
        sunne :
    Your light's ynough, although that his were
        done.

SONNET XXIIII.

When as my love, lay sicklie in her bedde,
Pale death did poste, in hope to have a praie ;

But she so spotlesse, made him that he fledde,
Vnmeet to die (he cry'd) and could not staie.
Backe he retyr'd, and thus the heavens he told,
All thinges that are, are subject vnto me,
Both townes, and men, and what the world doth
     hold,
But let faire Licia still immortall be,
The heauens did graunt : a goddesse she was made,
Immortall, faire, vnfit to suffer chaunge :
So now she lives, and never more shall fade;
In earth a goddesse, what can be more strang ?
    Then will I hope, a goddesse and so neare
    She cannot chuse my sighes, and praiers but
      heare.

SONNET XXV.

Seven are the lights, that wander in the skies,
And at these seven, I wonder in my love,
So see the Moone, how pale she doeth arise,
Standing amaz'd, as though she durst not move :
So is my sweet, much paler than the snowe,
Constant her lookes, these lookes that cannot
    change ;
Mercurie the next, a god sweet tong'd we know,
But her sweet voice, doth woonders speake more
    strange :
The rising Sunne doeth boast him of his pride,

And yet my love is farre more faire than he.
The warlike Mars, can weildles weapons guide,
But yet that god, is farre more weake than she.
The lovelie Venus, seemeth to be faire,
But at her best my love is farre more bright :
Saturne for age, with groans doth dimme the aire,
Whereas my love, with smiles doth give it light.
  Gaze at her browes, where heaven ingrafted is :
  Then sigh, and sweare, there is no heaven but
    this.

SONNET XXVI.

I live (sweete love) : whereas the gentle winde,
Murmures with sport, in midst of thickest bowes,
Where loving Wood-bine, doth the Harbour[1] binde,
And chirping birdes doe eccho foorth my vowes :
Where strongest elme, can scarce support the vine,
And sweetest flowers enameld have the ground,
Where Muses dwell ; and yet hereat repine
That on the earth so rare a place was found.
But windes delight, I wish to be content :
I praise the Wood-bine, but I take no joye :
I moane the birdes, that musicke thus have spent :
As for the rest, they breede but mine annoye.
  Live then (fayre Lycia) in this place alone :
  Then shall I joye, though all of these were gone.

---

[1] = arbour. G.

SONNNT XXVII.

The Chrystal streames, wherein my love did
  swimme,
Melted in teares, as partners of my woe :
Her shine[1] was such, as did the fountaine dimme ;
The pearlike[2] fountaine, whiter than the snowe,
Then lyke perfume, resolvèd with a heate,
The fountaine smoak'd, as if it thought to burne :
A woonder strange, to see the colde so great,
And yet the fountaine, into smoake to turne.
I searcht the cause, and found it to be this,
She toucht the water, and it burnt with loue.
Now by her meanes, it purchast hath that blisse,
Which all diseases, quicklie can remoove.
  Then if by you, these streames thus blessèd be :
  (Sweet) graunt me love, and be not woorse to
    me.

SONNET XXVIII.

In tyme the strong and statelie turrets fall,
In tyme the Rose, and silver Lillies die,
In tyme the Monarch's captivee are, and thrall,
In tyme the sea and rivers are made drie :
The hardest flint, in tyme doth melt asunder,
Still living fame, in tyme doth fade away ;

---

[1] Query—skin ?   [2] = pearl-like. G.

The mountaines proud, we see in tyme come
    under;
And earth for age, we see in tyme decay;
The sunne in tyme, forgets for to retire,
From out the east, where he was woont to rise,
The basest thoughtes, we see in tyme aspire,
And greedie minds, in tyme do wealth despise:
    Thus all (sweet faire) in tyme must have an
      end:
    Except thy beautie, vertues, and thy friend.

SONNET XXIX.

Why dy'd I not when as I last did sleepe?
(O sleepe too short that shadowed foorth my
    deare)
Heavens heare my prayers, nor thus me waking
    keepe:
For this were heaven, if thus I sleeping weare.
For in that darke there shone a Princely light:
Two milke-white hilles, both full of Nectar
    sweete:
Her Ebon[1] thighes, the wonder of my sight,
Where all my senses with their objectes meete:

---

1 = ivory, not 'ebony' (black): a noticeable occurrence
of the word.   G.

I passe those sportes, in secret that are best,
Wherein my thoughtes did seeme alive to be ;
We both did strive, and wearie both did rest :
I kist her still, and still she kissèd me..

  Heavens' let me sleepe, and shewes my senses
    feede :
  Or let me wake, and happie be indeede.

SONNET XXX.[1]

When as my Lycia saylèd in the seas,
Viewing with pride, god Neptune's stately crowne,
A calme she made, and brought the merchant ease,
The storme she stayed, and checkt him with a
    frowne.
Love at the sterne, sate smiling, and did sing :
To see howe seas, had learnd for to obey :
And balles of fire, into the waves did fling.
And still the boy, full wanton thus did say :
Both poles we burnt, whereon the world doeth
    turne,
The rownd of heaven, from earth unto the skies :
And nowe the seas we both intend to burne :
I with my bowe, and Licia with her eyes.

  Then since thy force, heavens, earth, nor seas
    can move,
  I conquer'd yeeld ; and doe confesse I love.

SONNET XXXI.

When as her lute is tunèd to her voyce,
The aire growes proude, for honour of that sound;
And rockes doe leape, to shewe how they rejoyce,
That in the earth, such Musicke should be found.
When as her haire, more worth, more pale, then
    golde,
Like silver threed, lies waffting in the ayre :
Diana like she lookes, but yet more bolde :
Cruell in chase, more chaste, and yet more fayre.
When as she smyles, the cloudes for envie breakes,
She Jove in pride encounters with a checke :
The Sunne doeth shine for joye when as she
    speakes :
Thus heaven, and earth doe homage at her becke.
    Yet all these graces, blottes not graces are :
    Yf you my love, of love doe[1] take no care.

SONNET XXXII

Yeares, months, daies, houres, in sighes I sadlie
    spend,
I blacke the night, wherein I sleeplesse tosse :
I love my griefs, yet wish them at an end ;
Thus tyme's expence, encreaseth but my losse,
I musing stand, and woonder at my love :

---

[1] By inadvertence 'doe' is twice printed.   G.

That in so faire, should be a heart of steele :
And then I thinke, my fancie to remove:
But then more painfull, I my passions feele.
Thus must I love (sweet faire) untill I die,
And your unkindnesse, doth my love encrease :
I conquer'd am, I can it not denie :
My lyfe must end, yet shall my love not cease.
  Then heavens, make Licia faire, most kind to
    me :
  Or with my life, my losse may finisht be.

SONNET XXXIII.

I wrote my sighes, and sent them to my love,
I prais'd that faire, that none ynough could praise :
But plaintes, nor praises, could faire Lycia moove,
Aboue my reach, she did her vertues raise.
And thus reply'd : False Scrawle, untrue thou
    art,
To faine those sighes, that no where can be found :
For halfe those praises, came not from his hart :
Whose faith and love, as yet was never found.
Thy maister's lyfe (false Scrawle) shall be thy
    doome :
Because he burnes, I judge thee to the flame,
Both your attempts, deserve no better roome :
Thus at her word, we ashes both became.

Beleeve me (faire) and let my paper live :
Or be not faire, and so me freedome give.

SONNET XXXIV.[1]

Pale are my lookes, forsaken of my lyfe,
Cynders my bones, consumèd with thy flame,
Floodes are my teares, to end this burning stryfe,
And yet I sigh, for to increase the same,
I mourne alone, because alone I burne ;
Who doubts of this, then let him learn to love,
Her lookes, colde yce into a flame can turne :
As I distressèd in my selfe doe prove.
Respect (faire Licia) what my torments are,
Count but the tyth, both of my sighes and teares,
See how my love, doeth still increase my care,
And cares increase, my lyfe to nothing weares.
　　Send but a sigh, my flame for to increase,
　　Or lend a teare, and cause it so to cease.

SONNET XXXV.

When as I wish, faire Licia for a kisse :
From those sweet lippes, where Rose and Lillies
　　　　strive,
Straight doe mine eies, repine at such a blisse,
And seeke my lippes, thereof for to deprive ;

---

[1] Printed XXXIIII. as before. G.

When as I seeke, to glut mine eies, by sight,
My lippes repine, and call mine eies away :
Thus both contend, to have each others right :
And both conspire, to worke my full decay.
O force admyr'd, of beautie in her pride :
In whose each part, such strange effects there be,
That all my forces, in themselves devide :
And make my senses, plainlie disagree.
If all were mine, this envie would be gone :
Then graunt me all (faire sweet) or grant me
none.

SONNET XXXVI.

Heaie how my sighes, are ecchoed of the wind,
See how my teares, are pittied by the raine :
Feele what a flame, possessèd hath my mind,
Taste but the griefe, which I possesse in vaine.
Then if my sighes, the blustering windes sur-
passe :
And watrie teares, the droppes of raine exceed,
And if no flame, like mine, nor is, nor was :
Nor griefe like that, whereon my soule doth feed :
Relent (faire Licia) when my sighes doe blowe,
Yeeld at my teares, that flint-like, droppes con-
sume :
Accept the flame, that doth my incense showe,
Allowe the griefe, that is my heart's perfume.

Thus sighes, and teares, flame, griefe, shall
    plead for me,
So shall I pray, and you a goddesse be.

SONNET XXXVII.[1]

I speake (faire Licia) what my torments be :
But then my speach, too partiall doe I finde :
For hardlie words can with those thoughts agree :
Those thoughtes that swarme, in such a troubled
    mind.
Then doe I vowe, my tongue shall never speake
Nor tell my griefe, that in my heart doth lie :
But cannon-like, I then surcharg'd, doe breake.
And so my silence, worse than speach I trie.
Thus speach, or none, they both doe breed my
    care :
I live dismay'd, and kill my heart with griefe :
In all respectes, my case alyke doth fare :
To him that wants, and dare not aske reliefe.
    Then you (faire Licia) soveraigne of my heart :
    Read to your selfe, my anguish and my smart.

SONNET XXXVIII.

Sweet, I protest, and seale it with an oath :
I never saw, that so my thoughtes did please :

---

[1] Misprinted XXXVIII. G.

And yet content displeas'd I see them wroth,
To love so much, and cannot have their ease.
I tolde my thoughts, my soveraigne made a pause,
Dispos'd to graunt, but willing to delay :
They then repin'd, for that they knewe no cause,
And swore they wisht, she flatlie would say nay.
Thus hath my love, my thoughts with treason fild :
And gainst my soveraigne, taught them to repine :
So thus my treason, all my thoughts hath kill'd,
And made faire Licia, say she is not mine.
  But thoughts too rash, my heart doth now
   repent :
  And as you please, they sweare, they are
   content.

SONNET XXXIX.

Faire matchlesse Nymph, respect, but what I craue,
My thoughts are true, and honour is my love :
I fainting die, whome yet a smile might save :
You gave the wound, and can the hurt remove.
Those eyes, like starres, that twinkle in the night,
And cheeks like rubies pale, in lilies dy'd,
Those Ebon[1] hands, that darting have such might,
That in my soule, my loue and life[2] deuide,
Accept the passions, of a man possest ;

---

[1] = ivory, as before. G. [2] Misprinted (?) 'live'. G.

Let Love be lov'd, and graunt me leave to live :
Disperse those clouds, that darkened have my rest:
And let your heaven, a sun-like smile but give.
   Then shall I praise, that heaven for such a
      sunne,
   That saved my life, when as my griefe begun.

SONNET XL.

My griefe begunne (faire Saint) when first I saw,
Love in those eyes, sit ruling, with disdaine :
Whose sweet commandes, did keepe a world in
    awe :
And caus'd them serve, your favour to obtaine.
I stood as one enchaunted with a frowne,
Yet smilde to see, all creatures serue those eyes :
Where each with sighes, paid tribute to that
    crowne :
And thought them gracèd, by your dumme re-
    plyes.
But I, ambitious, could not be content :
Till that my service, more than sighes made
    knowne :
And for that end, my heart to you I sent :
To say, and sweare, that (faire) it is your owne.
   Then greater graces (Licia) doe impart :
   Not dumme replies, unto a speaking heart.

SONNET MADE VPON THE TWO TWINNES, DAUGHTERS OF THE LADIE MOLLINEUX, BOTH PASSING LIKE, AND EXCEEDING FAIRE.[1]

POETS did faine, that heavens a Venus
    had :
    Matchlesse herselfe, and Cupid was her
      sonne,
Men sew'd[2] to these, and of their smiles were
    glad.
By whome so manie famous were undone.
Now Cupid mournes, that he hath lost his might :
And that these two, so comelie are to see :
And Venus frowns because they haue her right.
Yet both so like that both shall blamelesse be.
With heavens two twinnes for godhead these may
    strive,
And rule a world, with least part of a frowne :
Fairer then these two twinnes are not alive :
Both conquering Queenes, and both deserve a
    crowne.
    My thoughts presage, which tyme to come shall
      trie :
    That thousands conquerd, for their love shall die.

---

[1] This Sonnet is oddly enough inserted between XL.
and XLI. G.   [2] = sued. G.

SONNET XLI.

If (aged Charon) when my life shall end,
I passe thy ferrye, and my wafftage pay,
Thy oares shall fayle thy boate, and maste shall
    rend,
And through the deepe, shall be a drye foote-way.
For why my heart with sighs doth breath such
    flame,
That ayre and water both incensèd be :
The boundlesse Ocean from whose mouth they
    came,
For from my heate not heaven it selfe is free.
Then since to me thy losse can be no gaine :
Avoyd thy harme and flye what I foretell.
Make thou thy love with me for to be slaine,
That I with her, and both with thee may dwel.
  Thy fact thus (Charon) both of us shall blesse ;
  Thou save thy boat, and I my love possesse.

SONNET XLII.

For if alone thou thinke to waft my love,
Her cold is such as can the sea commaund,
And frozen Ice shall let[1] thy boate to move,
Nor can thy forces rowe it from the land.
But if thou friendly both at once shalt take,

---

[1] = hinder. G.

Thy selfe mayst rest, for why my sighes will
    blowe.
Our colde and heate so sweete a thawe shall make,
As that thy boate without thy helpe shall rowe.
Then will I sitte and glut me on those eyes,
Wherewith my life, my eyes could never fill.
Thus from thy boate, that comfort shall arise,
The want whereof my life and hope did kill.
    Together plac'd so thou her skorne shalt crosse,
    Where if we part, thy boate must suffer losse.

SONNET XLIII.

Are those two starres, her eyes, my life's light
    gone?
By which my soule was freèd from all darke :
And am I left distres'd, to live alone?
Where none my teares and mournefull tale shall
    marke.
Ah Sunne, why shine thy lookes, thy lookes like
    gold,
When horseman brave thou risest in the East.
Ah Cynthia pale, to whome my griefes I told,
Why doe you both rejoyce both man and beast?
And I alone, alone that darke possesse
By Licia's absence brighter then the Sunne,[1]

---

1 Misprinted 'snune'.   G.

Whose smyling light did ease my sadde distresse
And broke the clowdes, when teares like rayne
    begun.
    Heavens graunt that light, and so me waking
    keepe:
    Or shut my eyes, and rocke me fast a-sleepe.

SONNET XLIIII.

Cruell fayre Love, I justly do complaine,
Of too much rigour, and thy heart unkind,
That for mine eyes, thou hast my bodie slaine,
And would not graunt that I should favour find.
I look'd (fayre Love) and you my love lookt fayre,
I sigh'd for love, and you for sport did smyle.
Your smyles were such as did perfume the ayre,
And this perfumèd did my heart beguyle:
Thus I confesse, the fault was in mine eyes,
Begun with sighes, and ended with a flame :
I for your love, did all the world despise,
And in these poems, honour'd have your name.
    Then let your love, so with my fault dispense,
    That all my parts feele not mine eyes offense.

SONNET XLV.

There shone a Comet, and it was full west.
My thoughts presagèd, what it did portend:
I found it threatned to my heart unrest,

And might in tyme, my joyes and comfort end.
I further sought, and found it was a Sunne:
Which day, nor night, did never use to set:
It constant stood, when heavens did restlesse run,
And did their vertues, and their forces let,[1]
The world did muse, and wonder what it meant,
     A Sunne to shine, and in the west to rise,
To search the trueth, I strength and spirits spent,
     At length I found, it was my Licia's eyes:
Now never after, soule shall live in darke,
That hath the hap, this westerne Sunne to marke.

SONNET XLVI.

If he be dead, in whom no hart remaines,
Or livelesse be, in whome no lyfe is found:
If he doe pyne that never comfort gaines,
And be distrest, that hath his deadlie wound.
Then must I dye whose heart els where is clad,
And livelesse passe the greedie wormes to feed:
Then must I pine, that never comfort had,
And be distrest, whose wound with teares doth
     bleed.
Which if I doe, why doe I not waxe cold?
Why rest I not lyke one that wants a hart?
Why moove I still, lyke him that lyfe doth hold?

---

[1] = hinder, as before.   **G.**

And sense enjoy both of my joy and smart.
Lyke Nyobe Queene, which made a stone, did
    weepe,
Licia, my heart dead and alive doth keepe.

SONNET XLVII.

Lyke Memnon's rocke, toucht with the rising
    Sunne,
Which yeelds a sownd, and ecchoes foorth a
    voice :
But when it's drownde in westerne seas, is dunne,
And drousie lyke, leaves off to make a noice.
So I (my love) inlightned with your shyne,
A Poet's skill within my soule I shroud,
Not rude lyke that which finer wittes declyne,
But such as Muses to the best allowde :
But when your figure, and your shape is gone,
I speechlesse am, lyke as I was before :
Or if I write, my verse is fill'd with moane,
And blurd with teares, by falling in such store.
    Then muse not (Licia) if my Muse be slacke,
    For when I wrote, I did thy beautie lacke.

SONNET XLVIII.

I sawe (sweet Licia) when the spydar ranne,
Within your house, to weave a woorthlesse web :
You present were, and feard her with your fanne,

So that amazèd, speedilie she fled.
She in your house such sweete perfumes did smell,
And heard the Muses, with their notes refin'd:
Thus fill'd with envie, could no longer dwell,
But straight return'd, and at your house repin'd.
Then tell me (spidar) why of late I sawe
Thee loose thy poison, and thy bowels gone :
Did these enchaunt, and keepe thy limmes in awe,
And made thy forces, to be small or none?
　　No, no, thou didst by chaunce my Licia see,
　　Who for her looke, Minerva seem'd to thee.

SONNET XLIX.

If that I dye (fayre Licia) with disdaine,
Or hartlesse live, surprisèd with thy wrong,
Then heavens and earth shall accent both my paine,
And curse the time so cruell, and so long.
If you be kinde (my Queene) as you are fayre,
And ayde my thoughts, that still for conquest
　　　　strive,
Then will I sing, and never more dispayre,
And praise your kindnesse, whylst I am alive.
Till then I pay the tribute of my teares,
To moove thy mercie and thy constant trueth.
Respect (fayre love) howe these with sorrowe
　　　　weares
The truest heart : unlesse it find some ruthe.

Then grace me (sweet) and with thy favour
  rayse me,
So shall I live, and all the world shall praise
  thee.

SONNET L.

A' Licia sigh, and say thou art my owne,
Nay be my owne, as you full oft have sayd.
So shall your trueth unto the world be knowne,
  And I resolved, where now I am afrayd.
And if my tongue æternize can your prayse,
Or silly speech increase your worthy fame.
If ought I can, to heaven your worth can rayse,
The age to come shall wonder at the same.
In this respect, your love (sweete love) I told,
My faith and trueth I vow'd should be for ever.
You were the cause, if that I was too bold,
Then pardon this my fault, or love me never.
  But if you frowne, I wish that none beleeve me,
  For slayne with sighes, Ile dye, before I greeve
    thee.

SONNET LI.

When first the Sunne, whome all my senses serve,
Began to shine upon this earthly round,
The heav'ns for her, all graces did reserve,
That Pandor-like, with all she might abound.

Appollo plac'd his brightnesse in her eyes,
His skill presaging, and his musicke sweete.
Mars gave his force; all force she now defyes.
Venus her smyles, wherewith she Mars did meete.
Python a voyce, Dyana made her chaste,
Ceres gave plentie : Cupid lent his bowe :
Thetis his feete : there Pallas wisdome plac't.
With these she Queene-like kept a world in awe.
   Yet all these honours, deemèd are but pelfe,
   For she is much more worthie of her selfe.

SONNET LII.

O sugred talke, wherewith my thoughts doe live :
O browes love's Trophee, and my senses shine :[1]
O charming smyles, that death or life can give :
O heavenly kisses from a mouth devine :
O wreaths too strong, and tramels made of hayre :
O pearles inclosèd in an Ebon[2] pale :
O Rose and Lillyes in a field most fayre,
Where modest whyte, doth make the red seeme
     pale.
O voyce whose accents live within my heart,
O heavenly hand, that more than Atlas holds,
O sighes perfum'd, that can release my smart.
O happy they, whome in her armes she folds.

---

[1] Query—shrine ? G. [2] = ivory, as before. G.

Nowe if you aske where dwelleth all this blisse,
Seeke out my love, and she will tell you this.[1]

AN ODE.

LOVE I repent me that I thought,
    My sighes, and languish, dearely bought.
    For sighes and languish both did prove,
That he that languisht, sigh't for love.
Cruell rigour, foe to state,
Lookes disdainfull, fraught with hate :
I did blame, but had no cause,
(Love hath eyes, but hath no lawes)
She was sadde, and could not chuse,
To see me sigh, and sitt, and muse.
We both did love, and both did doubt,
Least any should our love finde out.
Our heartes did speake by signes most hidden,
This meanes was left, all els forbidden.
I did frowne, her love to trye,
She did sigh, and straight did crye.
Both of us did signes beleeve,
Yet either grievèd friend to greeve.
I did looke, and then did smyle ;

---

[1] There are in all 54 Sonnets, _i. e._ the first consists of
two though numbered as one only, and that between xl
and xli is not reckoned in the numbering. Hence other
mistakes in the numbering (corrected by us). G.

She left sighing all that whyle.

Both were glad to see that change ;

Things in love that are not strange.

Suspicion, foolish foe to reason,

Caus'd me seeke, to finde some treason.

I did court another Dame,

(False in love, it is a shame)

She was sorrie this to vewe,

Thinking faith was prov'd untrewe.

Then she swore, she would not love,

One whome false, she once did prove :

I did vowe I never meant,

From promise made, for to relent.

The more I said, the worse she thought,

My othes and vowes were dem'd as nought,

(False) (she sayde) how can it be,

To court another, yet love me.

Crownes and Love no partners brooke,

If she be lyk'd I am forsooke.

Farewell false, and love her still,

Your chaunce was good, but mine was ill.

No harme to you, but this I crave,

That your newe love, may you desave.

And jeast with you, as you have donne,

For light's the love, that's quickely wonne.

Kinde, and fayre-sweete, once beleeve me,

Jeast I did but not to greeve thee.

Court I did, but did not love,
All my speach was you to prove.
Wordes and sighes, and what I spent,
(In shewe to her) to you were ment.
Fond I was your love to crosse,
(Jeasting love oft brings this losse.)
Forget this fault, and love your frend,
Which vowes his trueth unto the end ;
Content (she sayd) if this you keepe :
Thus both did kisse, and both did weepe.
For women, long they cannot chyde,
As I by proofe in this have tryde.

A DIALOGUE BETWIXT TWO SEA-NYMPHES DORIS AND GALATEA CONCERNING POLYPHEMUS ; BRIEFELY TRANSLATED OUT OF LUCIAN.

HE Sea-Nymphes late did play them on
  the shore,
   And smyl'd to see such sport was new
  begunne :
A strife in love, the like not heard before,
Two nymphes contend, which had the conquest
  wonne,
Doris the fayre, with Galate did chyd.
She lik't her choyce, and to her taunts replyd.

Doris.

Thy love (fayre Nymph) that courts thee on this
  plaine,
As shepheards say, and all the world can tell,
Is that foule rude Sicilian Cyclop-swayne,
A shame (sweete Nymph) that he with thee should
  mell.[1]

Galatea.

Smyle not (fayre Doris) though he foule doe
  seeme,
Let passe thy wordes that savour of disgrace,
He's worth my love, and so I him esteeme.
Renownd by birth, and come of Neptune's race,
Neptune that doth the glassye Ocean tame,
Neptune, by birth from mighty Iove which came.

Doris.

I graunt an honour to be Neptune's chyld,
A grace to be so neere with Iove allyde.
But yet (sweete Nymph) with this be not beguyld
Where nature's graces are by lookes descryde.
So foule, so rough, so ugglye as a Clowne,
And worse then this, a Monster with one eye.
Foule is not gracèd, though it weare a Crowne,
But fayre is Bewtie, none can that denye.

· = match. G.

Galatea.

Nor is he foule, or shapelesse as you say,
Or worse, for that he clownish seem's to be,
Rough, Satyr-like, the better he will play,
And manly lookes the fitter are for me.
His frowning smyles are gracèd by his beard,
His eye-light, Sunne-like, shrouded is in one.
This me contents, and others makes afeard.
He sees ynough, and therefore wanteth none.[1]

Doris.

Nay then I see (sweete Nymph) thou art in love,
And loving, doates; and doating, doest commend
Foule to be fayre; this oft doe lovers proove,
I wish him fayrer, or thy love an end.

Galatea.

Doris, I love not, yet I hardly beare,
Disgracefull tearms, which you have spoke in
    scorne.
You are not lov'd: and that's the cause I feare:
For why, my love of Iove, him selfe was borne.
Feeding his sheepe of late, amidst this plaine,
When as we Nymphes did sport us on the shore,
He skorn'd you all, my love for to obtaine;
That greev'd your hearts: I knew as much before.

---

[1] On margin here ' with one eye.' G.

Nay smyle not Nymphes, the trueth I onely tell,
For fewe can brooke, that others should excell.

Doris.

Shoud I envie that blinde did you that spite?
Or that your shape doeth pleease so foule a
groome?
The shepheard thought of milke, you look'd so
white,
The clowne did erre, and foolish was his doome;
Your looke was pale, and so his stomach fed.
But farre from faire, where white doth want
his red.

Galatea.

Though pale my looke, yet he my love did crave,
And lovelie you, unlyk'd, unlov'd I view:
It's better farre one base, than none to have,
Your faire is foule, to whome there's none will
sew:
My love doth tune his love unto his harpe,
His shape is rude, but yet his witt is sharpe.

Doris

Leave off (sweet Nymph) to grace a woorthlesse
clowne.
He itch'd with love, and then did sing or say:
The noise was such, as all the Nymphes did
frowne,

And well suspected that some Asse did bray.
The woods did chyde, to hear this uglie sound,
The prating Eccho scorn'd for to repeate;
This grislie voice did feare the hollow ground,
Whilst artlesse fingers did his harpstrings beat.
Two Bear-whelps in his armes this monster bore,
With these new puppies did this wanton play,
Their skinnes was rough, but yet your loves was
      more:
He fouler was and farre more fierce than they,
I cannot chuse (sweet Nymph) to thinke, but
      smyle,
That some of us thou fearst, will thee beguyle.

Galatea.

Scorne not my love, untill it can be knowne,
That you have one that's better of your owne.

Doris.

I have no love, nor if I had, would boast,
Yet wo'd have been, by such as well might
      speed:
But him to love, the shame of all the coast,
So uglie foule, as yet, I have no need.
  Now thus we learne, what foolish love can doe,
  To thinke him faire, that's foule and uglie too.

To heare this talke, I sate behind an oake,
And mark'd their wordes and[1] pend them as they
  spoke.

AD LECTOREM, DISTICHON
cujusdam de Autore.

Lascivi quæres fuerit cur carminis autor :
Carmine lascivus, mente pudicus erat.

A LOVER'S MAZE.

TREWE are my thoughts, my thoughts that
  are untrue,
  Blinde are my eies, my eyes that are not
  blinde :
New is my love, my love that is not newe,
Kinde is that faire, that faire that is not kinde.
  Thus eyes and thoughts, that fairest faire, my
    love,
  Blind and untrue, unkind, unconstant prove.

True are my thoughts : because they never flitte,
Vntrew my thoughtes : because they me betraide,
Blinde are my eyes : because in cloudes I sitte,

---

[1] The printed word here is 'to' : but it is crossed
out and 'and' written over it. G.

Not blinde my eyes : because I lookes obeyed.
  Thus eyes and thoughtes, my dearest faire may
      vewe :
  In sight, in love, not blinde, nor yet untrew.

Newe is my love : because it never dies,
Olde is my love : because it ever lives.
Kinde is that faire : because it hate denyes,
Vnkinde that faire : because no hope it gives.
  Thus newe my love, and still that faire unkinde,
  Renewes my love, and I no favour finde.

Sweete are my dreames, my dreames that are not
      sweet,
Long are the nightes, the nightes that are not long:
Meete are the panges, these panges that are unmeet:
Wrong'd is my heart, my heart that hath no wrong :
  Thus dreames, and night, my heart, my pangs,
      and all
  In taste, in length, conspire to worke my fall.

Sweet are my dreames : because my love they
      showe :
Vnsweet my dreames : because but dreames they
      are.
Long are the nights : because no helpe I know,
Meete are the nights because they end my care,

Thus dreames, and nightes wherein my love take
    sport
Are sweet, unsweet, are long, and yet too short.

Meet are my panges : because I was too bolde,
Vnmeet my panges; because I lov'd so well.
Wrong'd was my heart; because my griefe it
    tolde :
Not wrong'd : for why? my griefe it could not
    tell.
    Thus you my love, unkindlie cause this smart
    That will not love, to ease my panges and heart.

Proud is her looke : her looke that is not proude,
Done all my dayes, my dayes that are not done,
Lowd are my sighes, my sighes that are not lowd,
Begun my death, my death not yet begunne,
    Thus looks and dayes, and sighs and death might
      move :
    So kind, so faire, to give consent to love.

Proud is her looke : because she scornes to see.
Not proud her looke : for none dare say so much.
Done are my dayes : because they haplesse be.
Not done my dayes : because I wish them such.
    Thus lookes and dayes, increase this loving strife,
    Not proude, nor done, nor dead, nor giving life.

Loud are my sighes, because they pearce the skie,
Not loud my sighes, because they are not heard,
My death begunne, because I artless crie,
But not begunne : because I am debard
 Thou sighes, and death, my heart no comfort
  give :
 Both lyfe denie, and both do make me live.

Bold are her smiles, her smiles that are not bold,
Wise are her wordes, those words that are not
 wise.
Cold are her lippes, those lippes that are not colde.
Ise[1] are those hands, those handes that are not ise.
 Thus smiles, and wordes, her lippes, her handes,
  and she,
 Bold, wise, cold, ise, loves cruell torments be.

Bold are her smiles, because they anger slay,
Not bold her smiles : because they blush so oft.
Wise are her wordes : because they woonders say,
Not wise her wordes; because they are not soft.
 Thus smiles, and wordes, so cruell and so bold :
 So blushing wise, my thoughts in prison hold.

Colde are her lippes, because they breath no
 heate,
Not colde her lippes, because my heart they burne.

---

    [1] = ice. G.

Ise are her handes : because the snow's so great.
Not ise her handes, that all to ashes turne.
    Thus lippes and handes, cold ise my sorrowe
        bred,
    Hands warme-white-snow ; and lippes, cold
        cherrie red.

Small was her wast, the wast that was not small :
Gold was her haire, the haire that was not gold,
Tall was her shape, the shape that was not tall :
Folding the armes, the armes that did not folde :
    Thus haire, and shape, those folding armes and
        wast :
    Did make me love, and loving made me waste.

Small was her wast, because I could it spanne,
Not small her wast : because she wanted all.
Gold was her haire : because a crowne it wanne,
Not gold her haire : because it was more pale.
    Thus smallest waste, the greatest wast doth
        make :
    And finest haire, most fast a lover take.

Tall was h   shape : because she toucht the skie,
Not tall her shape : because she comelie was.
Folding her armes : because she hearts could tie,
Not folded armes : because all bands they passe.

Thus shape, and armes, with love my heart did
    plie,
That hers I am, and must be till I die.

Sad was her joy, her joy that was not sadde,
Short was her staie, her staie that was not short:
Glad was her speach, her speach that was not
    glad :
Sporting those toyes, those toyes that were not
    sport :
    Thus was my heart, with joy, speach, toyes,
      and stay,
    Possest with love, and so stollen quite away.

Sadde was her joy : because she did respect,
Not sad her joy : because her joy she had.
Short was her stay : because to smal effect,
Long was her staie : because I was so sadde.
    Thus joy, and staie, both crost a lover's sporte,
    The one was sadde, the other too too short.

Glad was her speach : because she spake her mind,
Not glad her speach : because affraid to speake.
Sporting her toyes : because my love was kinde,
Not toyes in sport : because my heart they breake.
    Thus speach, and toyes, my love began in jest :
    (Sweet) yeeld to love, and make thy servant
      blest.

Tread you the Maze (sweet love) that I have
      run :
Marke but the steppes, which I imprinted have:
End but your love, whereas my thoughtes begun,
So shall I joye, and you a servant have.
  If not (sweet love) then this my sute denie :
  So shall you live, and so your servant die.

AN ELEGIE.

DOWNE in a bed, and on a bed of doune,
      Love, she, and I to sleepe together lay :
      She like a wanton kist me with a frowne,
Sleepe, sleepe, she saide, but meant to steale away ;
  I could not choose, but kisse, but wake, but
      smile,
  To see how she thought us two to beguile.

She faind a sleepe, I wakt her with a kisse :
A kisse to me she gave, to make me sleepe :
If I did wrong (sweete love) my fault was this,
In that I did not you, thus waking keepe :
  Then kisse me (sweete) that so I sleepe may
      take,
  Or let me kisse, to keepe you still awake.

The night drew on, and needs she must be gone :
She wakèd Love, and bid him learne to waite :

She sigh'd, she said, to leave me there alone,
And[1] bid Love stay, but practise no deceit.
  Love wept for griefe, and sighing made great
      mone,
  And could not sleepe,[2] nor staie, if she were
      gone.

Then staie (sweet love) : a kisse with that I gave,
She could not staie : but gave my kisse againe :
A kisse was all that I could gett or crave,
And with a kisse she bound me to remaine.
  A' Licia still, I in my dreames did crie,
  Come (Licia) come, or els my heart will die.

ELEGIE II.

DISTANCE of place, my love, and me did
      part :
      Yet both did sweare, we never would
      remove ;
In signe thereof I bid her take my heart :
Which did, and doth, and can but chuse but love.
  Thus did we part, in hope to meete againe :
  Where both did vow, most constant to remaine.

---

[1] Misprinted 'Add'. G.   [2] Misprinted 'slaepe'. G.

2 A She there was that past betwixt us both,
   By whom ech knew how others cause did fare.
   For men to trust men in their love are loth :
   Thus had we both of love a lover's care.
      " Haply he seekes his sorrowes to renue,
      " That for his love doth make another sue.

3 By her a kisse, a kisse to me she sent,
   A kisse for price more worth then purest gold.
   She gave it her, to me the kisse was ment,
   A she to kisse, what harme if she were bold ?
      Happy those lippes, that had so sweet a kisse ;
      For heaven itselfe scarce yeeldes so sweet a
      blisse.

4 This modest she, blushing for shame of this,
   Or loth to part from that she lik't so well,
   Did play false play, and gave me not the kisse ;
   Yet my love's kindnesse could not chuse to t ell.
      Then blame me not, that kissing sigh'd, and
      swore,
      I kist but her, whome you had kist be fore.

5 Sweete, love me more, and blame me not (sweet
      love)
   I kist those lippes, yet harmlesse I doe vowe,
   Scarce would my lippes, from off those lippes re-
      moove,

For still me thought (sweet fayre) I kissèd you.
And thus kinde love, the summe of all my blisse,
Was both begunne, and ended in a kisse.

6 Then send me moe, but send them by your
      friend,
Kisse none but her, nor her, nor none at all.
Beware by whome such treasures you doe send,
I must them loose, except I for them call.
    And love me (deare), and still still kissing be,
    Both like and love, but none (sweete love) but
    me.

ELEGIE III.

F sadde complaint would shewe a lover's
      payne,
      Or teares expresse the torments of my
hart,
If melting sighes would suth and pitty gaine,
Or true Laments but ease a lover's smart.

2 Then should my plaints the thunder's noyse sur-
      mount,
And teares like seas should flowe from out my
      eyes,
Then sighes like ayre should farre exceede all
      count,
And true laments with sorrow dimme the skyes.

3 But plaintes, and teares, laments and sighes I
    spend,
  Yet greater torments doe my heart destroy ;
  I could all these from out my heart still send,
  If after these I might my love enjoy.

4 But heavens conspyre, and heavens I must obey,
  That seeking love I still must want my ease.
  " For greatest joyes are temperd with delay,
  " Things soone obtain'd do least of all us please.

5 My thoughtes repyne, and think the time too
    long,
  My love impatient, wisheth to obtaine,
  I blame the heavens that do me all this wrong,
  To make me lov'd, and will not ease my payne.

6 No payne like this, to love and not enjoye,
  No griefe like this, to mourne and not be heard.
  No time so long, as that which breeds annoy,
  No hell like this, to love and be deferd.

7 But heaven shall stand, and earth inconstant flye,
  The Sunne shall freese, and Ice inconstant burne,
  The mountaines flowe, and all the earth be drye,
  Ear time shall force my loving thoughtes to turne.

8 Doe you resolve (sweete love) to doe the same,
  Say that you doe, and seale it with a kisse.

Then shall our truthes the heav'ns unkindnesse
    blame,
That can not hurt, yet shewe their spyte in this.

9 The sillye prentice bound for many yeeres,
  Doeth hope that time his service will release,
  The towne besieg'd, that lives in midst of feares,
  Doeth hope in time the cruell warres will cease.

10 The toyling plough-man sings in hope to reape,
  The tossèd barke expecteth for a shore;
  The boy at schoole to be at play doeth leape,
  And straight forget's the feare he had before.

11 If those by hope doe joye in their distresse,
  And constant are, in hope to conquer tyme.
  Then let not hope in us (sweete friend) be lesse,
  And cause our love to wither in the Pryme.

Let me conspyre, and time will have an end,
So both of us in time shall have a frend.

𝔉𝔦𝔫𝔦𝔰.

THE RISING TO THE CROWNE OF RICH-ARD THE THIRD.   WRITTEN BY HIM-SELFE.[1]

HE Stage is set, for Stately matter fitte,
   Three partes are past, which Prince-like
     acted were,
To play the fourth, requires a kingly witte,
Els shall my muse, their muses not come nere.
  Sorrow sit downe, and helpe my muse to sing,
  For weepe he may not, that was cal'd a King.

Shore's wife, a subject, though a Princesse mate,
Had little cause her fortune to lament.
Her birth was meane, and yet she liv'd with State,
The King was dead before her honour went.
  Shore's wife might fall, and none can justly
    wonder,
  To see her fall, that useth to lye under.

Rosamond was fayre, and farre more fayre than
   she,
Her fall was great, and but a woman's fall.
Tryfles are these, compare them but with me,

---

[1] = as if spoken by himself.   G.

My fortunes farre, were higher then they all.
 I left this land, possest with Civill strife,
 And lost a Crowne, mine honour, and my life.

Elstred I pitie, for she was a Queene,
But for my selfe, to sigh I sorrow want;
Her fall was great, but greater falles have beene;
"Some falles they have, that use the Court to
  haunt.
 A toye did happen, and this Queene dismayd,
 But yet I see not why she was afrayd.

Fortune and I (for so the match began)
Two games we play'd at tennyse for a Crowne :
I play'd right well, and so the first I wan:
She skorn'd the losse, whereat she straight did
  frowne.
 We playd againe, and then I caught my fall,
 England the Court, and Richard was the ball.

Nor weepe I nowe, as children that have lost,
But smyle to see the Poets of this age :
Like silly boates in shallowe rivers tost,
Loosing their paynes, and lacking still their wage,
 To write of women, and of womens falles,
 Who are too light, for to be fortunes balles.

A King I was, and Richard was my name,
Borne to a Crowne, when first my life began.
My thoughtes ambitious, venterd for[1] the same,
And from my nephewes I the kingdom wan.
   Nor doe I think that this my honour stayn'd,
   A crowne I sought, and I a kingdome gayn'd.

Tyme-tyrant fate, did fitte me for a Crowne,
My father's fall did teach me to aspire :
He meant by force his brother to put downe,
That so himselfe might hap to rise the higher.
   And what he lost by fortune, I have wonne,
   A Duke the father, yet a king the sonne.

My father Richard, duke of Yorke was call'd ;
Three sonnes he had, all matchlesse at that tyme,
I Richard yongest, to them both was thrall'd,
Yet two of us unto the crowne did clyme.
   Edward and I this realme as kinges did holde,
   But George of Clarence, could not, though he
     would.

Sad Muse set downe in tearmes not heard before,
My sable fortunes, and my mournfull tale :
Say what thou canst, and wish thou could say
   more,

---

1 Misprinted 'fot.' G.

My blisse was great, but greater was my bale.
  I rose with speed, and so did fall as fast,
  Great was my glorie, but it would not last.

My brother George did plot for to be king,
Sparkes of ambition did possesse us all :
His thoughts were wise, but did no profite bring,
I fear'd his rising, and did make him fall.
  My reaching braine, did dout what might ensew,
  I scorn'd his lyfe, and so he found it trew.

My brother George, men say, was slaine by me,
A brother's part, to give his brother wine,
And for a crowne I would his butcher be,
(For crownes with blood the brighter they will
    shine)
  To gaine a kingdome still it me behoov'd :
  That all my lettes[1] full soundly were remoov'd.

Henrie the sixt depriuèd of his crowne,
Fame doeth report I put him to the death,
Thus fortune[2] smyl'd, though after she did frowne.
A dagger's stab men say, did stop his breath.
  I carelesse was both how, and who were slaine,
  So that thereby a kingdome I could gaine.

---

[1] Obstacles. G.
[2] Misprinted 'fottune' as before 'fot' for 'for'. G.

Clusters of grapes full rypenèd with the heat,
Nor smaller timber builded up on height,
Fall not so fast as persons that are great :
Loosing their honours, bruisèd with their weight.
  But fewer means, the faster I did rise,
  And to be king, I fortune did dispise.

My thoughts ambitious spread, began to flie,
And I a Crowne did followe with full wing,
My hope was small, but yet I thought to trie,
I had no right, yet long'd to be a king.
  Feare or respect amaz'd me not at all,
  If I were crost, the worst was but to fall.

The Lyon fearce dispoylèd of his praie,
Runnes not with speed so fast as did my thought :
My doubtfull minde, forbad me long to stay ;
For why a kingdome was the thing I sought.
  Now was the tyme when this was to be done,
  Or blame my thoughts, because they it begun.

My brother dy'd, and left two Sonnes behind,
Both under age, unfitte to guyde the land,
This right fell out according to my minde,
For now these two were rulèd with my hand.
  England's great Lord the subjects did me call,
  And I was made protectour over all.

But as the Wolfe defends the harmelesse sheepe
Whose bloodie mouth can hardlie be content,
Vntill he spoile what he was set to keepe,
And sillie beast be all to peeces rent.
   So still a crowne did hammer in my head,
    Full of mistrust, till both these two were dead.

The elder sonne with speed to London came,
And walles forsooke where he had liv'd before :
London the place of greatest strength and fame,
The Island's treasure and the English store.
   For him Lord Rivers was appoynted guyde,
    The king's owne uncle by the mother's side.

Rivers was wyse, but him I could not brooke,
I well forsawe what harme there might ensew,
This to prevent with speed I counsell tooke,
And as I thought, so did I find it trewe.
   For if that Rivers should obtaine his minde,
    My heart's desire, then hardlie could I finde.

Rivers and Graie of treason I accus'd,
And tolde the Prince, what both they did intend:
My tale was false, and I the king abus'd :
Thus both their lives unjustlie did I end.
   The King was yong, the greater was the griefe,
    And needs my words did urge him to beleefe.

Not long this past, but hasting to the Queene,
A post was sent to shew what did befall ;
And who the actors of this fact had bene :
That Lord protector was the cause of all.
   The Queen amaz'd, did woonder at this newes,
   And skarse did think it, yet she could not choose

Possest with feare, foure daughters and her sonne
She thence convayd into a sacred place :
Supposing true, the harme but now begun,
And that I thought to murther all her race.
   She York's Archbishop did entreate for aide,
   Who in the Abbay not far distant laide.

The Bishop came, and mourning found the Queen e
Who did lament the fortune of her sonne :
The realmes distresse, the like before not seene,
Her own misfortune, and the state undone.
   Thus sigh'd the Queene, and wisht her state
      were lesse,
   And prayde that heavens would give the king
      successe.

My Lord (she said) my thoughts presage some ill,
And mournfull sorrowe seazeth on my heart :
This suddaine newes with griefe my soule doth fill,
And I for feare doe quake in everie part.
   In this distresse we cannot hope to live,
   Except this sacred place some safetie give.

He then reply'd : dread Soveraigne, doe not faint,
A causelesse feare, in wisdom doe withstand :
Yeeld not to[o] soone, with griefe to make com-
    plaint,
When no such cause approaching is at hand.
    " For feeble mindes through weaknes coyne new
      feares,
    " When stronger hearts true griefe more wise-
      ly bears.

And if they crowne, some other, not your sonne,
A thing unlyke (yet feare what may befall)
Then shall the same, unto this child be done,
Whom brothers right by dew a king shall call :
    But tyrant's force, will hardly be so bold :
    During the tyme, the other is in hold.

Then more advis'd, he told her what he thought,
She and her sonne some causes had to feare,
And England's seale he therefore with him
    brought,
Which by his place he customd was to beare.
    Thus he resolv'd to leave the Seale behind,
    Till wiser thoughts straight alterèd had his
      mind.

The Bishop home returnèd in all haste,
And sadly sate, suspecting what might fall.

But then my comming made them all agast,
And for the Bishop I did straightway call.
    I knew his deede, and blam'd him to his face,
    And for the Seale, another had his place.

Thus tyrant hate possest me for a Crowne,
My minde the anvill of a thousand harmes.
I rais'd my friendes, my foes I cast them downe.
This made the subjects flocke to me in swarmes.
    My will was strong, I made it for a Lawe,,
    " For basest mindes are rulèd best by awe.

I cal'd the Counsell, and did straight perswade
From mother's side to fetch the other Sonne.
My drift was further then they well could wade;
I gave them reasons why it must be donne.
    The king a play-mate wanted for his yeeres,
    And could not well be fitted with his Peeres.

The Cardnall went on message to the Queene,
And us'd perswasions for her other chyld,
He plainely sayd, her feare had causelesse bene,
Nor neede she dout by me to be beguyld,
    I was Protector chosen by consent,
    With counsell grave all treason to prevent.

And I protest (quoth Cardnall) on my life,
(For so indeede the Cardnall did suppose)
Your Sonne with safetie shall cut off this strife,

And you, nor place, nor land, nor Sonne shall
    loose.
  Dread soveraigne graunt, and let your Sonne
    be free,
  If he have harme, then set the fault on me.

The Queene was mov'd and quaking did reply,
A mother's love doeth breed a mother's feare,
And loth I am those mischiefes for to try,
With doutfull hazard of a thing so deare,
  I doubt (my Lord) the neerest of his blood,
  In true intent scarce wisheth any good.

The lawes doe make my Sonne his mother's ward,
Religion bids I should not slacke my care,
And nature bindes mine owne for to regard,
These and his health (my Lord) good reasons are,
  To make my feare no smaller then it is,
  Whylst feare perswades what harme may come
    of this.

Yet take my sonne, and with my sonne take all.
Come kisse me (sonne), thy mother's last fare-well
Thy yeeres (sweete boy) suspect not what may
    fall ;
Nor can my tongue for teares thy fortune tell.
  But hardly crownes their kindred will discerne,
  As you (sweete child) I feare yet long shall learne.

God blesse thee (sonne) and I my sonne thee blesse,
Thy mother's comfort, and thy brother's life.
Nay weepe not (sonne) God send thee good successe,
And safe defend thee from that tyrant's knife.
  (Cardnal) farewell, be carefull of my sonne,
  For once I vow'd, this never to have done.

I and the counsell in Starre-chamber weare,
To whom the Cardnall did in haste resort,
Who brought the child which ended all my feare,
The mother's care he briefely did report.
  I kist the child, and tooke it in my arme,
  Thus none did think I meant it any harme.

Then as the Wolfe halfe famisht for his pray,
Or hungrie Lyon that a lamb hath got:
My thirstie minde, I ment his blood should stay
And yet the wisest not perceive my plot.
  To' the Towre in haste I sent him to his brother,
  And there with speed, I both at once did smother.

Nowe two there was, but living in my way,
Buckingham and Hastings both, to crosse my
    mind,
The one was headed[1] straight without delay,
The other, favours did unto me bind.

---

[1] — be-headed. G.

To match our children, I did him perswade,
And Earle of Herford he him selfe be made.

Nowe as the Sea before a storme doeth swell,
Or fumes arise before we see the flame ;
So whispering Brute[1] began my drifts to tell,
And all Imparted unto babbling fame.
 I dem'd it danger, speech for to despice,
 For after this I knew a storme would rise.

London's Lord Major, I used for my turne,
And caus'd him speake what treason had bene
  done,
I by these meanes the peoples hearts did turne,
And made them eye me as the rising sunne.
 Thus whilst I ment the Iland to bring under,
 The peoples heads on newes I set to wonder.

Then at the crosse I caus'd a Doctor preach,
To tell the subjects what I wishd them know ;
The man was cunning, and had skill to teach,
Out of my braine I made his Sermon flow.
 Thus every where I did such notice give,
 As all did crie, Heavens let King Richard
  live.

---

[1] = bruit or rumour. G.

So did I live, and call'd was a king,
Friendes swarm'd so fast, as Bees unto the hive,
" Thus basest meanes the highest fortunes bring.
The crowne obtaind did cause my thoughts
    revive ;
  I scornd my friends, and those did most des-
  pyse
  That were the means, by which I did aryse.

Blood and revenge did hammer in my head,
Vnquiet thoughts did gallop in my braine :
I had no rest till al my friends were dead,
Whose helpe I usde the kingdome to obtaine.
  My dearest friend I thought not safe to trust,
  Nor skarse my selfe, but that perforce I must.

Nor speake I now, as if I did repent,
Vnlesse for this a crowne I bought so cheap.
For meaner things men wittes and lives have spent,
Which blood have sowne, and crowns could never
    reap.
  Live Richard long, the honour of thy name,
  And scorne all such as doe thy fortune blame.

Thus have I told how I a crowne did win,
Which now torments me that I cannot sleep.
Where I doe end, my sorrow did begin,

Because I got which long I could not keep.
My verse is harsh, yet (reader) doe not
    frowne,
I wore no garland but a golden Crowne.

𝔉𝔦𝔫𝔦𝔰.

TO THE READER.

OURTEOUS Reader for my owne fault I referre thee to my Preface; but for the Printer's, I crave pardon. The excuse is just, if thou knew the cause. I desire thee therefore to correct the greater, thus; the lesse, of thy selfe; and to pardon all.

Thue to the read pag. 3, lin. 20 : Thus.
Gracelesse, pag. 1, lin. 3, Gracefull.
You, pag. 3, lin. 6, Such.
O. pag. 8, lin. 14, Sonne.
Hands, pag. 4, line 7, O.
My, pag. 17. line 12. Thy.
Make, pag. 36. lin. 12. O.
Singers pag. 58. lin. 20. fingers.
Feiend, pag. 69. lin. 19. friend—this *is corrected with ink in book.* [These all made. G.]

ADDITIONAL NOTE.

I HAD reason to hope for fruit from further local researches being made for me at Bishop Stortford while the
preceding pages were passing through the Press.   But I
regret to say that nothing bearing on the paternal
RICHARD FLETCHER's incumbency there has resulted beyond
the fact recorded in our Introduction from NEWCOURT, (II.
896) that he held Bishop Stortford from 1551 to 1555. I indulged the hope that some register-entry would give the
family-name of MRS. FLETCHER.   Besides this disappointment, my friend Mr. Clark, as before, found in Hunter's
South Yorkshire, that a (blank) Fletcher had married a
MARGARET BOSSEVILLE or BOSVILE (inter-related with the
Nevilles and Mollineuxs): and all the outward circumstances seemed to identify her with the 'fair ladye'
sought by us.   But on COLONEL CHESTER's kindly examining a genealogical MS. at Herald's College (Brook
Collection I. C. B. Vol. 92. fol. 79.) it proved that the
blank Fletcher while tantalizingly also a Richard Fletcher,
was of Campsall, and that his family by Margaret Bosvile
shews none of our Richard Fletcher's known sons or daughters through several generations.

I omitted in the Introduction to state that among other
Fletcher entries sent me by Colonel Chester from
the Parish Registers of St. Luke's, Chelsea, is the following :

1596 [Buried] June 12. Nehemias son of Giles Fletcher
Dr of Laws.

There is also the entry of Maria filia Rici. Fletcher,
Bristol. Epi. buried 1592 Oct. 15. and 1592 (blank, but
after Dec. 16) Elizabetha uxor Rici. Fletcher, Bristol,
Epi. sepultus in Cācillo. subta mensā.   These were sister
and mother respectively of John Fletcher, the Dramatist ;
and as such I could not with-hold the entries.   Finally, as
bearing on the birth-place of our Worthy and his brother
at Watford, I note that in Bishop Fletcher's Will, among
other legacies, is the following, "to the poor of Watford,
Herts, £10, and £5 to Cranbrooke, Rye, Chelsea, and
Peterborough—Watford coming first, and being double
the others.   G.

The End.

MISCELLANIES

OF

The Fuller Worthies' Library.

I. A CRUCIFIXE, OR A MEDITATION UPON REPENTANCE AND THE HOLIE PASSION.

II. QUEENE ELIZABETH'S TEARES, OR HER RESOLUTE BEARING THE CHRISTIAN CROSSE.

(1607).

BY

CHRISTOPHER LEVER.

Edited with Introduction and Notes:

BY THE

REV. ALEXANDER B. GROSART,

ST. GEORGE'S, BLACKBURN, LANCASHIRE.

PRINTED FOR PRIVATE CIRCULATION.

1872.

156 COPIES ONLY.

Contents.

Introduction.

HAD thought to have connected our present Worthy—CHRISTOPHER LEVER— with the LEVERS of Lancashire and so with the pungent and wise as witty Preacher of the (early) Reformation and the scholarly and renowned Master of ST. JOHN's (Cambridge) and of SHERBURNE. But notwithstanding the co-operation of the first living authorities in such matters, I have failed to do so—failed, after wearying research, to come on anything whatever regarding him beyond what his own title-pages and Epistles-dedicatory give.

The un-commonness of the name and the dedication of his quaint and matterfull "Holie Pilgrime leading the Way to Heaven, or a Divine Direction in way of Life, containing a familiar exposition of such secrets in Divinity as may direct the simple in the way of their Christian Pilgrimage" (1618)—"to the worshipful Master Newton, tutor to the Prince and Dean of Durham, :

603

Master Murray, tutor to the Duke of York and Master of *Sherborne* House, and to the reverend Society of the Church of Durham "—suggested some link of relationship with ' *Sherburne* ' through its illustrious Master (' Lever '), only to be disappointed in trying to trace it. In his title-pages he gives nothing more than his name. In his Epistles, as *supra*, and to the ARCHBISHOP of Canterbury (Bancroft), he informs us he held no ' place' in either Church or State, although in the ' Epistle' to ' Queene Elizabeth's Teares ', he seems to intimate that in some way or other the Archbishop had shown him kindness and had respect to his ' profession '—whatever that might be. His words are lowly and touching *e. g.* " The reason of my vndertaking, is the duety of Christian conscience, which bindeth euery man to some profitable performance. And because God hath not yet beene pleased to giue me particular place of seruice, wherein I might employ His talent with more aduantage.............. I be the meanest in respect both of nature and fortune " (" Heauen and Earth " 1608). Later (1618) even more pathetically and meekly he writes in the Epistle of "Holie Pilgrim ":— " Though I am yet vnprofest in any particular place of charge, eyther in the Church or State, whereby I might imploy (my little) to more aduantage, yet my very being Christian, doth challenge from me the best performance I can for the common good."

Besides the present Poems and the 'Holie Pilgrim' (which by the way deserves a place in the bibliography of the immortal ' Pilgrimage ') our Lever published at least other two considerable quartos in prose, viz., " Heauen and Earth. Religion and Policy. Or, the maine difference betweene Religion and Policy" (1608) and " The History of the Defenders of the Catholique Faith, viz., King Henry VIII. Edward VI. Queen Mary, Queen Elizabeth and King James. (1627)." I have no doubt that the latter is the work mentioned in his Epistle to the ' Holie Pilgrim' as delayed by ' the powers' that were.

I have found a good many well-put things in these several books, especially in the " Holie Pilgrim " and " Heauen and Earth "—thought original and originally worded so as to arrest attention of the most cursory Reader. But our present reprints of his Poems, present CHRISTOPHER LEVER, at his humble best : and I will venture to promise if the Student will exercise *'patience'* he will not go unrewarded from these two old Poems. In the " Holie Passion "—the Author's own

favorite abbreviation of the title when naming
it in "Queen Elizabeth's Teares" —he will
come upon such epithets as these of Life
and of the Sun: '*glassie* liues', 'the *resplendent* eye', 'the *ever-burning* eye' : and lines that
the Memory takes hold of instantly *e. g.*

> ' If we to heauen, we must as pilgrims goe '
> ' ......old men are stepping to their grave '
> ' With the smoothed face of a faire pretence '
> ' The parchèd land that gaspes for rain '
> ' Here is verture which they cannot naile '.

Then WORDSWORTH's 'the boy is father of the
man' has a dim preluding utterance thus :

> ' Children's first aptitudes doe well expresse
> Whither the progresse of their liues intend,
> For like beginning, often hath like end.'

Occasionally an unusual use of a word occurs, as
'*sanctimonious* tree' and 'O place most *sanctimonious*' and '*affectation*' for 'affection' and 'induments' for 'endowments' and 'holy *Maudlen*'
i. e. Mary Magdalene—the last telling of the sad
degeneracy of 'maudlin' in our day from its
primal pathetic memorial-allusion to Mary's
white tears of penitence. The last stanza of the
'Holie Passion' has a fine yearning in it, such as
CRASHAW or SOUTHWELL would not have disowned :

' Now (holy Joseph) help me to interre
This sacred corse : my hart's a fitting place,
Wherein thou maist His sepulchre prepare.
Digge deepe (old man) this graue will not disgrace
My willing hart, but dignifie the place,
  (Lord Iesu) if this resting place may please,
  Not three daies (Lord) but rest here many
    threes.'

" Queene Elizabeth's Teares " is less poetical as
a whole, than the " Holie Passion " but is of no
common historical value for its self-revealing
utterance of the natural feeling of the " hidden
ones " all through the dolorous reign of Mary the
Bloody. There are sketches of familiar incidents
in the great Queen's early life that assure us of
first-hand observation. But beyond this historical
interest, there are unquestionable poetic touches
and gleams of elevated sentiment. ROBERT
BURNS's sun-eyes should have flamed over this
stanza :

" The name and place of honour may be given
As please the prince in fauor to dispose :
But true deriuèl honor is from heauen
And often loues a mean estate, with those
That to the courts of princes neuer goes :
  How vainly proud are such as would get fame
  Yet get no more of honour than the name."

Now and again you discover that the good man had his eyes open on Nature *e. g.*

> '.........Beautie's but a floure
> Which being pluckt it fadeth in an houre."

Again :

" Looke, as the Earth bedeckt with beauteous flowres
(*The pretty children of the Earth and Spring*)
Warm'd with the sun and fed with heavenly shoures
Have but a little time of tarrying :
So, when the winter of our age shall bring
 Our fading time, our beauty like the floure
Cannot the winter of our age endure."

Once more, of the Queen's startled and timid ' maid ' :

> ' Shivering she stoode, *as doth the aspine leafe.*'

Then—judging by myself—the Reader will very often find himself marking tersely-put sayings of an aphoristic type. I had selected at least fifty, but can't spare space for them. Take these, which THOMAS FULLER would have fathered :

> "They runne the best to euill that runne last."
> " Exceeding wealthy, the contented are
> That with their little have but little care."
> " And there (as often when it goes by voyce)
> The worse (and not the better) had the choice."

" Such reuerence in the seely men appeares
Their hands haue weapons though their eies haue
         teares " (in conducting the arrested Princess.)
' Our loue is in our heart, not in our phrase '.
' No light apparant, where no light m⁊y shine :
    And but the fires of martires that gaue light,
    All had been blacke, and in eternall night.'
' The cuckooes sing not where colde winters be '.
' When this life setts, a better doth arise '.
' Vncertaine dayes, yet full of certaine griefe '

This tribute euen to MARY is significant :

' You that haue nothing holy but your name,
That did incence this Marie vnto blood ;
Be it to you, your euerlasting shame,
So to corrupt her nature that was good ;
O had she had the spirite to withstoode
    You, that did hearten her to her disgrace,
    She had deseru'd preheminence of place.'

Every Miltonic word ought to be recorded, and
hence I give the following use of one of his most
unusual substantives, ' *bright* ' (' dark with excess
of *bright*' P. L. B iii. line 380).

" Much like a showre upon a summer day :
    For though her face be ouerwasht with teares
    The *bright* of her great majesty appeares "

The title-pages of LEVER cover 1607 to 1627 : and
it is disappointing that of one so truly ' worthy ',

609

lowly, patriotic, so very little should be known. There will be a resurrection of memories as well as of bodies, some day, said dear old RICHARD SIBBES.

ALEXANDER B. GROSART.

P.S. It may be as well to add here the only verses that occur in LEVER'S prose books viz., these Lines from his "Holie Pilgrim":

O happy life when vaine affections die
And when our hearts can holy works desire:
And when our soules with meditation flie,
To God, who did them in our flesh inspire,
How base is earth to heauen that is aboue!
How vilde we value all, when God wee loue!
Potest miser dici, qui non potest esse.

I.

A Crucifixe:

OR

Meditation on the Holie Passion,

(1607.)

NOTE.

—

The following is the original title-page :

A CRUCIFIXE:

OR

A MEDITATION VPON REPENTANCE

AND

THE HOLIE PASSION,

WRITTEN BY CHRISTOPHER LEVER.

Nocet indulgentia nobis.

AT LONDON,

Printed by V. S. for John Budge, and are to be sold
at his shop at the great south doore of
Paules. 1607.

Collation : Title-page, Epistle, and Poem occupy 21
leaves in quarto. G.

TO THE READER.

HE writings of men, as they are divers, so they are diuersely affected: yet euer in this inequalitie; that mo to the bad than to the better, be disposed. The reason is, corruption in iudgement, dulnesse of vnderstanding, blindnesse in election, and a deprauednesse in the whole frame of nature : whereof it commeth that many deceiue themselues in their choise, neglecting what is of neerest consideration, yet embrace that (with strong appetite,) which is most pernitious and pestilent. I write not this to offend any one, but to remember all: for I had rather profite than please : and to giue friendly admonishment is better than silence. That great Apostle Saint Paule, desired to 'know nothing but Iesus Christ, and Him crucified,' and dooth detest to reioyce in aught save in the crosse and sufferings of his Lorde and Maister. A lesson woorthy so great a doctour, and worth our immitation. This is that 'one thing' which is onely necessary ; whereof who hath true knowledge, hath all knowledge. This Crosse, this Crucifix, and this Passion, I present thee (gentle Reader) not in their exact formes, for that exceedes the power of mortalitie) but in a little resemblance : wishing thee to reade, not for mirth, but for matter ; and with holy Paul, faithfully to apply to thy soule, the glorie and reioycings of the Holy Passion.   Farewell.

EPISTLE-DEDICATORY.

To the most Reuerend Father in God, Richard
(by diuine prouidence) Archbishop of Canterbury, Primate and Metropolitane of England.
My singular good Lord and Patron.

RIGHT REUEREND LORD.

HERE is a disease in the natures of men,
most powerful in the vulgar and base
multitude, to mis-interpret, (yet to
interpret) all men's proceedings : Therefore the
best cause doth most neede protection, lest otherwise, it receiue wrong in their iniurious and false
constructions.   For this particular; the frame
and disposition is my owne, and therefore I
willingly submitte that to a mercifull iudgement.
The Subject is not mine, but God's, being extract
from sacred Authorities; and therefore of itselfe
able to resist all opposition.   Here hence I deriue
my comfort, that the worthinesse of the Subject

Richar d Bancroft : born 1544, died 1610.   G.

may giue supplyment to my verse, that wants
woorth ; and that in the opinion of good men, I
shall be thought to have done more, in giuing a
religious matter this poore forme, than others
(that with much industry and arte) haue painted
the deformed face, of profane and idle Inuentions.
The reasons (my good Lord) that moue me to
this dedication, are these ; First, the many testimonies I haue of your Lordship's gratious res-
specting me, which earnestly presse me, to
returne this little demonstration of thankes, where
I haue receiued so much fauor. Next, your
Lordship's trauell, to continue the body of
Religion vnited ; or rather, to make vp the rent
and diuision. Wherein God hath made you
prosperous, giuing you spirite to enterprise, and
victory to finish a care of that religious importance.
And because the Crucifix I present, is a meditation of the sufferings and death of Christ, represented to vs in the ceremony of the Crosse, (in
the holy vse whereof, your Lordshippe hath fortunately trauelled). I haue therefore thought
this Dedication (of right) to belong unto your
Grace, assuring myselfe, that where the shadow,
there the substance ; where the figure, there the
trueth ; and where the crosse, there the Christ,
shall finde gratious and glad acceptance. The

616

which, with all respects of duty and humblenesse,
I offer vnto your Lordship : beseeching God to
giue you to support the reputation of learning,
helpfull to both the States of Church and kingdom : and after this life perpetuity with the holy
angells and saints.

    Your Grace's
      in all duety and seruice.
        CHRISTOPHER LEVER.

A Crucifix

OR

A Meditation vpon Repentance, and the Holy Passion.

THERE is a griefe, which farre exceedes
the skill
Of many learnèd spirits to define :
And this deriuèd is from doing ill ;
Yet doth it rectifie, and much refine,
The blurrèd image, of that power diuine,
   Which in our purer souls, at our creation,
   Made vs belouèd, and of estimation.

Such is the terrour of a wonnded soule,
Stretchèd vpon the painefull racke of tryall,
Presented with that blacke accusing scroule,
The register of sinne, the Lord's espiall ;
Authorities that n'er admit denial.
   For when our conscience doth display our sinne,
   Then true affected griefe, doth first beginne.

It were in vaine, I labour'd to expresse,
The just proportion, and the qualitie
Of horred griefe; nor what amazednesse,
Attends this court of lawe, and equitie ;
The soule, must here implead impietie
    Against the soule. The Iudge that here pre-
      ceedeth
    Against himselfe, himselfe the law impleadeth.

In this Assise of soules, there is no plea,
Receiues his strength, by mis-interpretation :
No craftie lawyer, for his double fee,
Findes errour, in the writ of condemnation ;
Here needeth not the twelue, for approbation :
    For here the conscience, that recordeth all,
    Can well distinguish just and criminall.

Here, canst thou not, in fauour of thy cause,
Produce perfidious knight-postes to contest :
Here, no prouiso, or exceptiue clause,
By forgèd exposition canst thou wrest :
These mony trickes, thy conscience will detest.
    What needeth all these probates to be scan'd,
    Whereas the fellon doth condemnèd stand :

You that haue had contrition for your sinnes,
And bath'd your soules in your repentant teares :
You, when your reformation first beginnes,

In your rebellious harts, tell me what feares,
What horrednesse, remorsefull conscience beares :
  Or rather, doe confesse, as doth my verse ;
  There is no power of words, can it reherse.

The father-iudge, that sits his sonne to trie,
Cannot resist the torture of his minde,
When he denounceth sentence ('thou must die') :
Examples may be fitted to this kinde,
But to resemble ours no like we finde :
  For here the Iudge, that giues the dying word,
  Condemnes himselfe : euen of his owne accord.

The eye, condemnes the sight ; the sight the eye ;
The power of speach, our much-offending tongue :
All qualities, their instruments envie,
And say, their aptnesse to offence and wrong,
Impels the sence ; the weaker by the strong,
  Is captiuate : and sinne that hath the reynes,
  The commonwealth in man, to sinne constraines.

Like as that bull, Perillus[1] fram'd of brasse,
To be a wond'rous instrument of woe :

---

1 The maker of the bronze bull of the tyrant Phalaris.
As with the Scottish ' maiden ' (so called) and the French
' guillotine' and other inventors of instruments of death,
Perillus is said to have become one of the victims of his
own 'bull'. G.

Within whose wombe, when the offender was,
In brutish sort, he as a bull did lowe :
The organe of the beast, did cause it so.
    Right so our bodies, beastlie by our sinne ;
    Doe bestifie the soule, that lives within.

In opposition to this formall plea,
The body, to the soule againe replyeth :
The state of sinne, hath his estate in thee :
Our soules without, sinne in our bodies dyeth ;
Nature to liuelesse things, all act denyeth.
    For as the ayre is mov'd with the wind,
    So are our subject bodies, by the mind.

Who euer yet accus'd the murderous knife,
As actor of that horrible effect ?
The agent must be somewhat that hath life,
It is the liuing hand, that doth direct
The mortall blade : nor is there had respect,
    To instrumentall causes of offending :
    For in the agent, guilt hath his depending.

Thus in the lists of hot contention,
This man of sorrow doth himselfe diuide.
In euery part, a fearefull apprehension,
Of guiltinesse ; which judgment hath descride :
For who against the conscience aught can hide ?

And in this state of wretchednesse doth dwell,
A state more wretched, then my verse can tell.

O you that gull the poyson'd cup of pleasure;
And spend your time, in nothing but expending!
You, in whose lap, if lust let fall his treasure,
You entertaine vile shame with much commending,
And thinke your glassie liues, shall ne're haue
    ending.
  Let the remembrance of repentant teares,
  Diminish sinne; but much inlarge your feares.

Be not secure, when death is eminent;
The bubble of this life, cannot secure thee;
There is an after-state most permanent,
That will in honour, or in death assure thee;
If then to honour, now to die inure thee:
  For he, whose life will mortifie no sinne,
  Shall finde the gate of Mercie shut to him.

Thy life is truely by resemblance said
To be a shadowe : shadowes from the sun
Deriuèd be : for sure there is no shade,
Where Phœbus doth not guild our horizon :
So we may say, the pride of life is done
  When as the sunne of glorie shall denie,
  To giue the beames of his resplendent eye.

Change your corrupt opinions of delight ;
Sometime delight in teares, in bitter woe ;
To launce and cut, oft heales the wounded knight,
If we to heauen, we must as pilgrims goe :
It is a christian pleasure to doe so :
    For he that doth appoint al times for pleasure;
    To his repentance can admit no leisure.

Were it, that he that over-loads the sense,
In surffetting the much forbidden tree,
Could with the habite of his sinnes dispense,
Whilst he might view his soule's enormitie,
And with the judgement of Discretion's eie,
    Sentence his vaine, exorbitant delight,
    And all his pleasures that doe sinne invite :

Then might he see the powre of much offending,
The little powre of him that so offendeth :
That warre of soules that never can haue ending,
Where sinne in opposition, death intendeth,
To him that (prodigall) in sinne expendeth,
    His very selfe, and like a traitor thiefe,
    In his owne treason makes himself a chiefe.

Who-ever saw a generall in armes,
When as the day determineth the warre ;
To be imprison'd in the treacherous armes
Of such as neerest to his person are,

Vnto himselfe may make a like compare :
  For such are we when our delightfull pleasure,
  Vpon our soules (like traitors) make a seasure.

Or like, as when the man reported horned,
Was chasèd by the seruants of his pleasure :
So, when by monstrous sinne we are deformed,
We find offensiue what we held our treasure :
Our vaine affects (like dogges) doe make a seasure,
  Vpon our soules : and like the hunted deere,
  Of our loud yelping sinnes, we stand in feere.

When we can truelie thus suruey our sinne
Our state of death, our death in our offending :
The warre intestine, that we haue within ;
The infinite of griefe, thereof depending ;
The little powre we haue, of our amending.
  When this we know, we know our stat's not
    well :
  As doth the sicke, that heares his passing bell.

Then in the ballance of suspence we lay,
Our little hope, the mountaine of our care.
The scale of feare, by much doth ouersway,
Our owne assurances, that nothing are :
Which makes this sicke man of his health despaire.
  And were it not that grace did vs auaile,
  We should not stand the triall of the scaile.

Now had I neede, a new to inuocate,
That All Sufficient to direct my verse :
Myselfe much sinfull, cannot sinne relate,
Whose largenesse dis-inables my rehearse.
O giue me power to beautifie the hearse
  Of Penitence: which then is said to die,
  When men liue most in their securitie.

If euer thing of greatest admiration,
Could draw the vulgar eye, for to admire it ;
Then let the subiect of this poor relation,
Be powerfull in their harts, that shall desire it :
It is a heauenly act, for to inspire it.
  For though onr penance, be a crabbèd tree,
  Yet is the fruit, of rare proprietie.

Suppose thyselfe arraignèd at the barre,
Laden with fetters of thine owne offence ;
Thy crying sinnes, thy aduerse lawyers are,
The diuell doth his action here commence,
And for his witnesse, hath thy conscience.
  Suppose this court-house, in thy soule to be,
  Thy selfe to plead, thy selfe to answere thee.

That part, which best remembers, plaies the clarke,
Who, when the word of silence is proclaim'd,
Intreates, that great assemblie well to marke
Th' inditement of that traytor : who asham'd,

Stands at the barre of death : and being nam'd,
　　Holdes vp his guilty hand.　The clarke then
　　　readeth,
　　Those treasons, which my vtterance much
　　　exceedeth.

Yet as I may : This I suppose was said :
(Traytor) thou art more ancient in thy sinne,
Then in thy dayes : It cannot be denai'd,
But when thy first fore-father did beginne,
To listen to his wife's solliciting :
　　Thou in him then, didst with him giue consent,
　　To further that his treasonous intent.

For like as he that for his murtherous fact,
Must satisfie the offended law, by dying ;
Although one little part, perform'd the act,
Yet doth the correspondence, and relying
Among the parts, force such a naturall tying,
　　As no particular can doe that thing,
　　That in his generall hath not warranting.

So though thou hadst not in the first creation,
The act of sinning in particular ;
Yet hadst thou then thy habitation
In Adam's flesh, who whenas he did erre,
Did then partake with all that with him were :

Who did so taint the purity of nature,
As he thereby hath tainted euery creature.

In this estate thy parents did produce thee,
Blind-folding thee, yet in thy soule more blinde,
Thy birth wants innocence for to excuse thee,
Depriu'd of light, deprauèd in thy minde :
Neither of soule or bodie, canst thou finde
    Integrity.   Thy Father's generation,
    Inlargeth sinne, not giues it limitation.

And as thy yeares, so doe thy sinnes augment :
Nay, they out-strip thy time in forwardnesse.
For long before thy childishnes be spent,
Thou wilt be agèd in thy wickednesse :
Childrens first aptitudes doe well expresse,
    Whither the progresse of their liues intend :
    For like beginning, often hath like end.

What though thy parents in their prouidence,
Couet to better thee, by education.
Yet is their trauell, but a vaine expence,
Thy time of youth, will giue an intimation,
How much vnlike thou art thy first creation.
    Neuer could any precepts from the wise,
    Ere rectifie a man's infirmities.

Thus dost thou make gradation in thy sinne,
Till thou attaine the vtmost step of life ;

And like report, when it doth first beginne,
Is then the least ; yet when it waxeth rife,
It doth inlarge it selfe ; so sinfull life.
    By custome, and continuance in sinning,
      Men are much worse, then in their first be-
      ginning.

For when the time doth bring them to that state,
That makes a man ; the strength of nature then,
Doth their injurious parts corroborate.
The length of yeares, doth euer giue to man,
Habilitie in wickednesse ; and whan
    Depraued man, hath meanes of doing ill,
    He makes them serue, his much depraued will.

Like as the neighbour riuers to the sea,
Cannot support vpon their shallowe backes,
The huge proportion of an argosie,
Because the little currant water lackes :
Yet when the sea (that all resistance wrackes)
    Shall fill the emptie channell with his tide ;
    The greatest vessell with great ease may glide.

So are the first vnable yeares of man,
Too weake, in moouing the huge bulke of sinne :
Yet when the tide of yeares approcheth, than
Men grow more impudent in their committing ;
And will receiue the mightiest vessels in,

To harbour in their little streams of Time ;
Till fatall end shall cut their little twine.

It were a wondrous taske to make relation,
Of euery grieuance in particular :
Thy sinnes of blood, of wanton agitation.
How infinite in euerie kind they are,
Hearts may suppose, but speech cannot declare.
　For when that man in nature is most strong ;
　He is most powrefull then in doing wrong.

See, if thy time grow agèd with expence
Of many yeares, be lesse in thy offending :
Time is the giuer of experience :
Old age will preach to youth, their youthe's
　　offending ;
Yet youthfull sinnes in youth haue not their
　　ending.
　For when old men are stepping to their graue,
　In youthful sinning, strong desires they haue.

Old age (though colde) can neuer quench the fire
Of lustfull youth.   Though age be in thy flesh,
Yet in thy thoughts, thou dost maintaine desire ;
Which in performance, thou canst not expresse,
By reason of thy bodie's feeblenesse.
　Yet know, that when Desire is in thy hart,
　It is as much, as thou an actor wert.

This thy desire, incends the noble parts
Of reason, and blunteth thy discretion.
Makes a combustion in obdurate harts ;
Depraues the sence, and blindeth thy election ;
Dries vp repentant teares, (thy soule's refection) :
   And sure that man eternallie shall die,
     Whose hart will not giue water to his eye.

Thus (O thou worst of God's creation !)
Thou dost reuerse the ordinance of Nature.
All other beings, keepe their ordination,
Obedience liues in euery other creature ;
Only in him, that hath the goodliest feature,
   He that from God, most blessings hath deriued ;
     He against God, most treasons hath conspired.

Search the immence circumference of Earth,
The many wondrous mouers in the Sea,
The element of ayre, wherein we breathe,
The regiment[1] of heaven, and sympathy
Of moouing orbs, and starrie deitie.
   In all the parts of this circumference,
     No one like man in disobedience.

If God command the seas to patience :
They still their noise, and smooth their horrid face

---

[1] = government. G.

Let him againe be moovèd to offence,
The raging wind, the swelling billowes chase,
Vnto the daring rockes that doe imbrace
    Their violence, and there doth bound the seas,
    Vntill a calme their troubles doe appease.

If God command the clowdes to teare the ayre,
And blast the hopefull haruest in the blade,
By fearefull thunder; they obedient are.
If God command the Earth, the Earth is made,
With fearefull trembling, to make men afraide.
    These elements, that haue no law but Nature,
    Yet haue more dutie, then thy selfe (O traytor !)

God hath commanded Time, to giue the yeare,
Months, daies, and houres, for her distinction.
Both daies, and houres, by Time well ordered were,
They vnto Time, and Time to ordination,
Giue their performance vnto God's creation.
    (Traytor) men say, that times vnconstant are ;
    Yet, than thy selfe, they are more certaine
        farre.

The mightie fish, the sea-deuouring whale,
Waites for to waft poore Ionas to the shoare.
The little flies of Ægipt doe auaile,
To wage victorious warre ; nay more,
Lice, durst presume the priuie-chamber dore,

And sease the person, of a mightie king,
Because from God they had a warranting.

Hath God bestow'd His sacred breath on thee
To countervaile the angels that erst fell :
Giuing thy soule of His eternitie ;
Yet thrust thy betters, for lesse sinne to hell ?
Did God refuse those spirits that excell
 In holy worship ; to partake thy nature ?
 He did, for thy redemption this, (O traytor !)

If God command let this or that be done ;
The little creature, that is bid to doe it,
Is wondrous quicke in execution :
Yet vnto man that hath the power of wit,
And in the verie place of God doth sit,
 Is giuen a law, the which was neuer kept,
 By any one : (the Sonne of God except.)

Now to inlarge the huge proportion
Of thy offence (traytor !) thou didst attempt,
That treason, which exceedes comparison :
Whose horrour did bedimme the element :
Both Heauen and Earth in wonders did consent ;
 To point it out, for greatest admiration,
 Which farre exceeds the power of all relation.

This little out of much : God to redeeme,
The lost integritie of man, His creature,

Did His defacèd image so esteeme,
As He inuested in thy humane nature,
The Sonne of God, (the Word that made each
      creature)
  Eternall Christ, Who in His flesh did merit,
  Eternall life, for each beleeuing spirit.

See how thou dost returne Him recompence :
Thou gau'st Him pouertie that was a king :
Iustice it selfe, yet blam'st His innocence :
Great majestie, had but the poore attending :
Nor had thy treasons, in these wrongs their
      ending.
  But didst with (wicked Iewes) conspire His
    death
  That first did giue, thy first forefather breath.

And didst preuaile.   Thy tongue did sentence
    Him ;
Thy hands (O wicked instruments of sinne !)
Bound the most free, and tortur'd euery lim ;
Not so content, labour'd to vex within
His sacred spirit, with most vile profaning :
  And last, to please the spirits of thine eye,
  The Holy Lambe betweene two thieues must
    die.

Was this enough, or art thou still more great
In thy offence?   O still thou dost augment it;
Thou want'st not sinne, but I wordes to repeate
Thy infinites; thy soule cannot repent it;
For thy delight is euer to augment it:
  Witnes thy horred customary swearing,
  Wherewith each day His body thou art tearing.

¶ Here let the conscience make one little pause,
Whilst that the Diuell that intends the plea,
Produceth witnesses to prooue the cause;
Shewing large recordes of impietie:
And with a wondrous skill in sophistrie,
  Giues a proportion to his sinful state,
  Hoping to make the guiltie desperate.

Hoping to make the guiltie desperate,
He doth augment the volume of our sinning,
Adding inlargements to exasperate
The Iudge, that stands to sentence our offending:
Euen from our birth, to these our days of ending.
  It hath, and will be still his exercise,
  Against our happy beings to deuise.

Witnes his enuy at our first creation,
That did deny our state of innocence,
A little breathing-rest from his temptation;

But with the smoothèd face of faire pretence,
Suggests into our natures his offence :
  Witnes againe this time of our repentance,
  How he incites the Iudge to cruell sentence.

No one (howeuer skilfull in his art)
Can giue more fit expressing formes to sinne.
He makes a priuie search within the heart,
And laies that open that was hid within ;
And with most curious workemanship doth limme
  The vgly formes of our impieties ;
  And then presents their terror to our eyes.

This, and much more this enemy of man,
And then the conscience doth againe beginne ;
(Traitor) how is't, this thy accuser can
Produce these certaine probats of thy sinne ?
Speake ; can'st thou cleare thyselfe of guilt
    heerein ?
  Thy cause will not finde help in thy deniall,
  For in the court of conscience is thy triall.

Like vnto him, that in a mighty throng,
Labors to hasten to some businesse,
With heate and sweate doth vex himselfe among
The mouing multitude, that in their prease,
Arrest his haste, and stoppe his forwardnesse :

So doe our sighes, our teares and griefe within,
Arrest our words, when gladly we beginne.

(Alas!) what else but guiltie in the weake!
Which he, in broken accents would relate.
He puffes it out in sighes that cannot speake;
The sence of sinne doth so examinate
Those faculties, that on our soules doe waite:
   As with a lawfull warrant, may be said,
   In this estate, our verie soules are dead.

Our reason then, demands our guilty spirit,
What for our justice we can argument.
Whether our iudgement correspond our merit,
Or if corruption in this parlament,
Heere in thy owne free-holde, we doe conuent;
   The jurie, that doth sentence what thou art,
   Are of thy tenants, dwelling in thy hart.

Nothing (alas!) the conscience can replie,
Nothing (indeede) nor no word to excuse vs;
Where all is sinne, there's no integrity.
All our euasions, in this case refuse vs;
Nothing in vs can comfort, but accuse vs.
   For he that hath this sorrowe in his flesh,
   Hath least of joy, and most of heauinesse.

The judgement then (for judgement must be just)
Denounceth sentence of our condemnation.

(Traytor) thy flesh, shall first returne to dust;
(The matter of thy first formation)
Thy soule transported to that strange vexation;
    Whereas the soules of damnèd doe beginne,
    To act the wofull parts of tragike sinne.

This is the law, and thus we sentence thee;
Our power extends not for to moderate;
This court is Iustice, Iustice we decree.
The seate of mercie is predominate,
And liues in God, He that did first create
    Thy innocence.   To Him thou must appeale,
    If this our condemnation thou repeale.

¶ Thus farre the Law: Now to our worke of Grace
To wash this moore, and giue him innocence:
To reobtaine what er'st he did deface,
Integritie: To cancell his offence;
In lieu whereof, to giue him excellence.
    To make that glorious, that before was base;
    (Doubt those that list) it is a worke of grace.

Of Grace me thinkes th' ingratious will replie,
I rob God's image of his worthinesse:
Because to sinfull man, I doe denie
Innatiue power to worke his holinesse.
Will you (O men deceiuèd)? I confesse,

That God will share the glory of His name,
With man, whose liues dishonour most the same.

Here is the world, in great dispute and strife,
Whence doth arise, this penitentiall fire,
That purgeth sinne, and rectifies the life.
Some will deriue it from their owne desire,
Others, the blessed angels doe inspire ;
   Some in their friends, and many in their priest :
   In errour all, in God they place it least.

When God did giue a spirit vnto man,
He did but gently breathe it in his flesh ;
But if He once call backe the same againe,
He speaketh loud, and groanes with painfulnesse :[1]
Adam, and Lazarus doe well expresse,
   That He that can determine sinfull strife,
   Doth somewhat more, than He that gaue vs life.

It were a well-deseruing worke, to set
The kirnell that's a prisoner in the shell :
Which, when the sunne doth warme, and heauens
    wet,
Receiues a life, yet doth it farre excell
In curious art, to make that prosper well ;

---

[1] Adam : Genesis ii. 7 : Lazarus : St. John xi. 38. G.

Which (like a rotten member of a tree)
For fewell fit, for Grace vnfit to be.

Methinkes I heare the mutinous repine,
And blame the hard construction of my verse :
And to the fire condemne this discipline ;
Or wish, my recantation to reuerse,
The doome I censure on this vniuerse.
    (Thus these repiners) God should wrong our
        spirits,
    To giue vs lawes, and take away our merits.

Thus may your earthern vessels make dispute,
And aske, how hap the potter made them so ?
Do you not know, that God is absolute ?
Nor giues a reason for His doing so ?
Shall God out of Himselfe for wisedome goe ?
    How dar'st thou argument with God maintaine ?
    Being His vassaile, He thy soueraigne.

To make it best, thus I compare thy state,
Like to a candle, wel-prepar'd for light :
The reason why I thus doe estimate,
Is thy discourse, thy reason, and delight,
To vnderstand each cause.   But the insight
    Of that which neerest doth concerne thy minde,
    In this thou art not sighted, but starke blinde.

Suppose ten thousand torches in the night,
They give no light, vnlesse thou giue them fiere :
So is thy reason, and thy judgement's sight,
Blinde in it selfe, if Grace giue not desire.
It is the God of Spirits, doth inspire
   Thy soule with Grace ; for when it wants His
     light ;
   It is more blacke, then is the darkest night.

And in this darknesse, this our man of griefe,
(Whome we proportion) is in darknesse placed.
Within himselfe, he cannot finde reliefe :
What was diuine in him, is now defaced.
The pride of his deseruings is disgraced.
   And when a man in this dejection lyeth,
   He wastes in sorrow, and in teares he dyeth.

And die he must, in his repentant teares,
Before his reformation can beginne :
The graine must die, before the blade appeares,
New birth is gotten, by the death of sinne :
When thus we die, our spirit that's within,
   Respires a life, that neuer will deceiue vs ;
   Whereof, nor Time, nor Enuie can bereaue vs.

The manner how : This out of my report.
When man is ouer-chargèd with the cares
Arising from the judgement of this Court.

And when within himselfe he much despaires ;
The Holy Spirit, then to him repaires,
   And brings his pardon, testified good,
    With this subscription (IESVS) writ in blood.

And thus (this sacred instrument of life)
(Poore man) we adde not to thy heauinesse,
To speake in anger or contentious strife :
Mercie is only in our businesse :
We come to make thy much affliction lesse,
   And offer to thy neere despairing spirit,
    The psalme of Mercie : Mercie best can merit.

See here, the booke of life I do present thee ;
Wherein thou maist Eternitie behold.
Thou canst not reade, before thou first repent thee;
Thou must first know thy selfe, and then vnfold
This sacred volume.   The Spirit then doth hold,
   Before the darkned spirits of his eye,
    A representment, how His Christ did die.

Said I, a representment, and no more ;
It is much more, then in my wordes can be.
My soule conceits, a verie Christ before ;
Spreading His sacred bodie on the tree :
Me thinkes, His verie torments I doe see.
   This Crucifix is that most sacred booke,
    Wherein each happy spirit needes must looke.

And this the Holy Ghost presents the eye,
And bids vs reade our penitentiall verse :
If we can (clarkely) reade this mystery,
He promiseth, our judgement for to trauerse,
And all our condemnation to reuerse :
 But Sinne (alas) so darkned hath the minde,
 As in this holy learning we are blinde.

Like when th' vnlearnèd fellon hath his booke,
Without a prompter, he no letter readeth,
Although with mnch desire, he thereon looke;
Euen so our soules, as much (vnlearnèd)
  needeth,
The helpe of that sweete comfort that proceedeth.
 For if that God assist vs not the better,
 We vnderstand, no sence, no word, nor letter.

In this condition, this our man of sinne,
Cannot reade mercie in these misteries,
Before God's Holy Spirit doe beginne,
To cleanse the soule of his impieties.
To mooue the hart, and cleere the darkned eyes :
 When once this grace, in vs hath but a being,
 In holy secrets, we haue perfect seeing.

The leaprous man, to heale his filthinesse,
Must seauen times water his contagious skinne.
Is holy water of that worthinesse ?

Then with repentant teares let vs beginne,
To wash the leaprous body of our sinne.
　　Seauen times is nothing, multiply thy seauen:
　　We must wash cleane, ere we can enter heauen.

This is our first degree of holinesse;
Which at the first, (as all beginnings are)
Little (in trueth) but large in hopefulnesse.
He that beginnes this sorrow with a teare,
Vnto a better worke doth but prepare.
　　And when in vs this grace hath but beginning,
　　We live to hope, and die vnto our sinning.

Take for an instance him whom we proport:
No more of sinne, but now the childe of Grace:
As he wastes teares, his benefits resort;
The bad thrust out, the betters haue the place,
What was delightfull now he doth deface:
　　When thus he hath a new begotten minde,
　　His eyes are open that before were blinde.

No sooner open, but with eagernesse,
They gaze vpon that sanctimonious tree,
The Holy Crosse, (O sacred worthinesse!)
That beares the fruit ot immortalitie:
And with a greedy appetite doth eie,
　　This Crucifix, this Christ that's nailde thereon,
　　This God, this man, this our redemption.

Not form'd in mettle, or with curious paint,
Nor hallowed with earthen sanctitie;
We estimate not much a woodden saint,
Nor can a painter learne the mysterie,
To make a Christ, or giue diuinitie.
   Thus then of all I would be vnderstood,
   This Crucifix, nor mettle, paint, nor wood.

But very Christ, which with a faithfull eie,
This sonne of Grace reuiews with good affection:
In euery part he earnestly doth prie
For sacred bloud, which is the soule's refection;
For without bloud we seale not our election,
   Now giue him wordes, or else we doe him wrong,
   To giue him much desire, and not a tongue.

¶ Sacred (he saith) most glorious, most diuine;
Thou Word that mad'st, Thou Christ that sav'dst
    all;
Thou Sonne that euerlastingly dost shine,
Coequall God, and consubstantiall;
Thou Gate of mercy, Way to life eternall:
   O sith Thou giv'st me sorrow for my sinne,
   Open thy Mercy-gate, and let me in.

Thou art that foode, and euer-liuing spring,
Whereof who tastes, shall neuer thirst againe.
O I am thirst, with my much sorrowing;

Euen as the parchèd land that gaspes for raine :
Do not Thy heauenly droppings then detaine.
   If that my soule, this holy water want,
   What thriueth it, I set, I sowe, or plant ?

But want I cannot, if I but desire it ;
Thy mercy doth preuent my forwardnesse :
Thou giuest grace before we can require it.
If in our hearts there be but willingnesse,
Thou com'st vnto vs, ere we can expresse
   What we determine.   In this, scarce one
   Of mortall race, loues imitation.

This, and tenne thousand testaments of loue,
T'vnworthy men are daily multiplide,
Which might their blunted vnderstandings moue
To loue and honor, whom they crucified :
Their King and Sauiour Iesus is denied.
   For euer be it hatefull in the Iewes,
   To choose a villaine, and the Iust refuse.

Pilate, thou canst not wash in innocence,
Nor Cayphas, how e're in holy place,
You give a monstrous sinne, a faire pretence,
Your greatnes cannot countenance the case :
Both prince and prelate, and the vulgar base
   Conspire in one.   These discords can agree
   To plot, and practise this conspiracie.

Traitors, hold off your blacke and treasonous
    handes,
Touch not His pure, and neuer-tainted flesh.
Villaines, your King, must He be lockt in bands ?
How prodigall you be in wickednesse !
To buffet, binde, and whippe His sacred fleshe.
    Let me my sinfull body interpose,
    The sinne was mine, let me beare off the
      blowes.

See how His bloud spirts from their cruell stripes ;
(O sacred blood ! O sacred body bleeding !)
These Iewes have lesse compassion than their
      whippes,
To spill that blood, which is the holy feeding,
Of blessed soules. O cruelty exceeding !
    Traitors, you little know one drop of blood,
    Would be enough to do all sinners good.

(Sweete Iesu,) may Thy seruant begge this grace,
To be a vessell, to receiue this spilling :
The earth my Lord's a farre vnworthy place ;
A place of bloud, a slaughter-house of killing.
Sith I haue woundes, O Iesu be thou willing,
    That some of this, these Iewes shed on the
      ground,
    I may reserue, to cure a mortal wound.

In this aray, their God, our Christ they bring,
Vnto the place of execution ;
His enemies entitle Him a king ;
Yet that is done in their derision.
The stage is Caluerie they act vpon ;
  A place of skulles ; the moral may be this :
  We are but rotten bones without His blisse.

Looke, as a pyrate roauing at the seas,
When by aduenture hitting on a prise ;
Doth first vpon their stoage make a sease,
Then on their victor'd liues doth tyrannise :
These hel-houndes so their envie exercise.
  First, they doe strippe our Sauiour of His
    cloathing,
  Then of his life, and thus they leaue Him no-
    thing.

Is it not wonder this rebellious rout
Trauells in sweat, to worke their fatall woe ?
See, with what painefulnesse they goe about
This horred act ; herein they are not slowe,
That to a worke of grace could neuer goe.
  They dragge, they binde, they naile, they
    fasten on ;
  Our holy life, but their damnation.

Betweene two malefactors they did place Him ;

In scorne of His most perfect innocence.
These theeues there set, of purpose to disgrace Him.
Yet did these varlets faile in their pretence:
Their neerenesse could not giue Him their offence.
  For that is said to be the vertuous meane,
  That on each hand, hath neighbour'd the ex-
    treame.

Now they haue rearèd vp this Crucifix,
See how their resting time they entertaine.
Some, vinegre and gall togither mix;
Others deride, and all of them disdaine.
In scorne they call Him Lord, and soueraigne.
  The souldiers, that aboue the rest doe raue,
  Doe cast the dice, who should His garment haue.

My Lord is now in other businesse,
Building the frame of man's saluation:
These drops of bloud and water doe expresse
His inward griefe: He giues a demonstration
Of torment, that exceedeth all relation.
  For, He that would bring merit vnto man,
  Must suffer more than any other can.

O what is man whome Thou regardest so!
A staynèd cloath, a beauty witherèd.
Yet did my Lord His greatnesse humble so,
As He inuests our nature that was dead;

He brings againe what erst was perishèd.
  Now by His bloud, and euer by His grace,
  He makes vs worthie that before were base.

What though they heape iniquitie on sinne ?
He layeth not His sauing worke away :
He helpeth most, when they most torture Him ;
To giue vs life, He doth His owne defray.
(Lord Christ) Thou didst for Thy tormentors pray,
  Father forgiue them, (thus Thy innocence)
  Forgiue them (gratious Father) their offence.

The horror of this act did blind the sunne,
Remoue the Earth, the holy temple rend :
Dead bodies from their sepulchers did runne,
And preach to many how these Iewes offend:
All things reprou'd, and nothing did commend.
  The sunne, the earth, the temple, and the grave,
  Haue more of grace then these tormentors haue.

The sunne doth hide his euer-burning face,
Abhorring to suruey their damnèd fact.
The earth did shame it, as her owne disgrace ;
Because vpon her body they did act.
The graues disclaime, and dis-alowe the fact,
  The holy temple doth it selfe diuide,
  Because a holier they haue crucifide.

Now giue me breath (O sacred-breathing Spirit!)
With faithfull affectation to applie,
This death, this Christ, this compotence of merit
Vnto my soule; that in itselfe would die,
If not supported by the hand of Mercie.
   How helpeth it the hurt man to be sound,
   Vnlesse the salue be plasterd to the wound.

And as the holy prophet that did spread,
His liuing body on the liuelesse corse,
And so brought backe, the spirit vanishèd,
And made a contract, where there was diuorse:[1]
So, when our soules are mantled with this crosse;
   That life of grace, we erst had lost with sinning
   Hath then a second time in vs beginning.

And to make fit for good digestion
This bread of life, we must the loafe diuide;
Our faithfull soules in morsels feeds thereon,
So by degrees my Lord was crucified.
In ciuill fellowship it is denied,
   To gobbet vp a supper at a bit,
   When we have time and leisure for to sit.

It were good order we beginne the lowest,
When we this Iacob's ladder would ascend;

---

[1] 2 Kings c. iv.   G.

In happie progresse we attaine the rest,
And then we giue our trauells happie end.
This only counsaile I doe recommend,
   That he that would ascend these holy staires,
   Must to his footing first direct his cares.

Then with His blessed feete let vs beginne,
That now are stainèd with the streaming bloud
That issues from the nails, that stickes therein.
O that my eyes would doe my hart that good,
To be as moist as is the swelling floud !
   For holy Maudlen[1] doth instruct my teares,
   To wash and then to wipe them with my haires

These holy passengers doe neuer haste,
To guilty bloud, nor vnto lustfull fire.
No little minute of a time they waste,
To minister to any vaine desire.
In enuy therefore did the Iewes conspire,
   To raile these holy moovers vnto wood,
   That were such forward instruments of good.

Their trauell was, to trauell to the weake;
Bring comfort to the vnrespected poore;
To giue the lame to goe, the dumbe to speake,
And fit applyments vnto euery sore;

---

1 Magdalene. See our Introduction. G.

A greater yet than what was saide before:
   They brought the newes of peace vnto our
      spirite,
   And therefore our acceptance they doe merite.

See how His sacred knees be markt with praire!
A demonstration of His sanctitie.
To adulation they vncustomd are
Nor fawne they with officiall flatterie.
Giue me (sweete Lord) these merites to apply :
   These markes are no disgrace vnto my skinne;
   Better be marked with holy prayer, than sinne.

Now let me reach my meditation higher,
And touch my Lord's most blessed heart that
      bleedeth :
This bloud cannot extinguish holy fire,
That in this holy principall exceedeth :
He warmes with zeale, and with His blood He
      feedeth
   Our spirites that are cold and hunger-starued,
   Wanting the grace we men haue not deserued.

This heart is not the nursery of pride,
Of murther, lust, of mammon, and debate :
Within His secrets there is none implide,
The new inuention to equiuocate.

The heart must thinke what ere His wordes relate.
  Lying is sinne, all sinne is from the deuill :
  The art of reseruation then is euill.

No sin had ere admittance in this place,
(O place, most sanctimonious, most diuine !)
The presence-chamber and the seat of Grace,
Whereas His soule in majesty did shine.
How can it be The Holiest should incline,
  To entertaine into His chaire of State,
  The least of euills we can estimate ?

May I (sweet Iesu) view in euery part,
The secret closet of Thy thoughts within ;
The speare hath made a passage to Thy heart,
The entrance then is open ; let me in
To see the merite that hath vanquisht sin.
  Do not Thy mercy-gate against me locke,
  For I will euer at Thy Mercy knocke.

See, here is nothing that presents my eie,
But loue, but fauour, and compassion :
In euery quarter Mercy I espie ;
Mercie's the briefe of all I looke vpon ;
Mercie the cause and meanes of my saluation.
  O, sith there is such mercy in Thy hart,
  (Sweete Iesu) giue my grieuèd soule a parte.

Like to a prince that in his royall throne,
Bethinkes what may his people benefit ;
Sends this his good determination,
To such as at his counsaile-table sit,
That by their wisedomes they may order it:
   So dooth the heart determine first the deede,
   Then sends it to the counsaile in the head.

Let me a little higher now ascend,
Whereas my Lord His holy armes doth spread,
This moralles how His Mercy doth extend :
Inuites to saue what would be perishèd:
Come vnto me all ye that are wearièd,
   I will support your life, vnloade your cares,
   Infuse My grace, and wipe away your teares.

Then sith I am inuited to this grace,
(Sweete Iesu) giue my spirite entertaine ;
I would vnloade this burthen in this place,
Whose weight is more than I can well sustaine :
(Lord Iesu) ease Thy seruant of this paine :
   Take off the heauy bondage of my sinne ;
   Thy yoke is easie, let me liue therein.

These hands (O sacred instruments of health !)
That neuer failèd yet in any cure ;
The sicke man's comfort, and the poore man's
      wealth :

Whose holy vertue euer shall indure,
And euer for to help will them inure :
   Why do the Iewes the holy helpers wound,
   Whose very touch made the diseasèd sound.

These mercifull and free bestowing hands,
Are euer reaching their benevolence :
He giueth aught to any that demands ;
Neuer respecting gainefull recompence ;
His bounty is not wasted with expence.
   For as the springs supply the wasting streames,
   So hath His grace supplyment from the heauens.

His flesh they wound, and mortise it in wood,
T' vnfit my Lord from healing any more ;
As they strike in, out starts the sacred blood,
That cureth more than did His hands before :
One dramme of this will helpe the greatest sore.
   These people in their purpose (then) did faile,
   For here is vertue which they cannot naile.

This holy vertue (might my Lord be pleasd),
T' infuse my soule, all hackt with mortall sinne,
Wounded and sore, in euery part diseasd ;
I should my restauration then beginne.
My hands haue blood, that ouer-spreads my skinne
   With sinfull guilt ; O let Thy blood diuine
   Expell my guilt, and then my guilt refine !

Now I arriue my much desirèd port ;
The orbe wherein all holinesse doth moue,
The place whereto all wisedome doth resort,
The court of mercy, majestie, and loue,
Furnisht with all acquirements from aboue.
   Such is my Lord's most sacred holy head,
   With all these rich induments furnishèd.

This is that one and vniuersall head
That ouer all hath true preheminence ;
Who seekes a second, from the first is dead :
Two vniuersals haue no excellence.
Who can corriuall Christ without offence ?
   (Lord Sauiour Christ) it doth my soule content,
   To be a member in thy regiment.

From this first head deriuèd is all grace,
That giues the members life, and holy being.
The head is said to be the fittest place,
Where our immortall spirits be decreeing,
How to repaire this house of flesh ; then seeing
   The lower parts to reason are but dead,
   They must repaire for wisedome to the head.

See how these Iewes this head doth dignifie ;
His temples with a crowne they doe adorne.
They call Him king, yet this their king must die ;
They giue Him state, but that is done in scorne.

657

A diadem they fashion Him of thorne,
  Yet know (you traytors !) when it toucht His
    head,
  Neuer was crowne so richly garnishèd :

A crowne of thorne ! O let their great offence,
Re-eccho backe my indignation !
Were ye (good people !) at this great expence,
To solemnize His coronation,
That was the King, that gaue all kings creation ?
  See you these drops, that trickle from the
    thorne ?
  They damne your deede, but doe His grace
    adorne.

His holy eyes, (O sacred lamps of light !)
The busie searchers of all mens distresse :
Whose seeing is not lettèd by the night,
In naked formes they all things can expresse ;
They haue all knowledge, and all holinesse.
  These planets that are mouers in this Heauen.
  Haue better constellation then the Seauen.

(Lord Iesus) let Thy holy eyes reflect,
Their influence, vpon my earthen state :
Thy heauenly presence is a faire aspect
There doth my soule delight to speculate.
For by those starres, I best can calculate

My lot of grace : which neuer is deni'd
To him that viewes this Christ thus crucifi'd.

But O the organe of His holy speech,
That breatheth life to euery faithfull eare !
This holy one, His holy word did preach :
He giues for nothing what would cost vs deare,
And makes assurance, where before was feare.
  (Lord Iesu) giue me knowledge in Thy teaching,
  I shall lesse neede these times contentious
     preaching.

His breath He formeth into holy prayer,
Which doth ascend the throne of majestie.
For vs poore men, all His petitions were ;
He aduocates for vs perpetuallie.
Thinke ye, the Father will His sonne denie ?
  What neede I for more Intercessors' care,
  When holy Christ doth interceede His prayer.

Thou splendor of Thy Father's majestie !
Thou God of God, thou man, all men's Redeemer !
Thou King of Iewes, thou Christ they crucifie !
Thou one, wherein all graces treasur'd are !
Thou mercifull, Thou all, Thou euery where !
  To Thee (O Sauiour Iesus) I repaire ;
  Exhibite (Lord) my pardon in Thy prayer.

Pardon my youthfull sinning, and my old ;

Pardon my secrets, and reuealèd ones ;
Pardon my errours, that be manifold,
Pardon committings, and omitions,
Pardon my nature staynèd with corruptions,
   (Lord) pardon all, in all I haue offended :
   Thy pardon's free, to all be it extended.

Now (holy Ioseph) helpe me to interre
This sacred corse : my hart's a fitting place,
Wherein thou maist His sepulchre prepare.
Digge deepe (old man) this graue will not disgrace
My willing hart, but dignifie the place.
   (Lord Iesu) if this resting-place may please,
   Not three daies (Lord) but rest here many threes.

God forbid that I should reioyce, but in the
Cross of our Lord Iesus Christ, whereby the world
is crucified vnto me, and I unto the world. GALAT.
6. 14.

The End.

II.

Queene Elizabeth's Teares.

1607.

Note.

The following is the original title-page of " Queene Elizabeth's Teares " :

QUEENE ELIZABETHS

TEARES :

OR

Her resolute bearing the Christian
Crosse, inflicted on her by the persecuting
hands of Steuen Gardner Bishop of Winchester,
in the bloodie time of Queene
Marie.

Written
By Christopher Leuer.

Nocet indulgentia nobis.

Printed at London by V. S. for *Mathew Lownes*
dwelling in Paules Churchyard.

It is a thin quarto of 31 leaves un-numbered. Our exemplar, by the kindness of John Small, Esq., M.A., principal Librarian, is that in the Library of the University of Edinburgh in the Drummond of Hawthornden collection. G.

EPISTLE-DEDICATORY.

To the right honorable Lord, ROBERT, ERLE OF
SALISBURIE, VICOUNT CRANBORNE, Baron of
Essingdon, principall Secretarie to the king's
most excellent Maiestie, Maister of the Courtes
of Wardes and Liueries, Chancellor of the
famous Vniversitie of Cambridge, Knight of the
most noble order of the Garter, and one of his
Maiestie's most honorable priuie Counsell.[1]

RIGHT HONOURABLE LORDE;

HE gratious and well deseruing, when
they die, leaue behind them a reputation that can never die. I instance
this in QUEENE ELIZABETH of blessed memory: a
lady beyond example, beautifyed with the orna-
ments of Grace and Nature (the two hands of

---

[1] This was Robert Cecil, youngest son of William,
Lord Burleigh, Queen Elizabeth's renowned high-trea-
surer, by his second wife Mildred, daughter of Sir
Anthony Cooke. He was knighted in 1601, and in the

God) whose name (like the aire) is spread ouer
All the Earth, whereby this our little world (the
English nation) is made famous to all posteritie :
and because I my selfe haue seene many, the
admirations of her time, and haue with many
others shared in participation of those blessings
which God did giue her most gratious and fortunate gouernment; I haue therefore (willingly)
forced my endeuours to this demonstration of
thankes, hauing euer vowed my selfe a seruant
to her honourable remembrance. The reasons
(my good L.) of dedication are these : First, your
Lordship's honourable deseruing, in being a
principall supporter of the leaning State of
Learning, the MÆCENAS and patron of the
learned (in what deseruing qualitie soeuer :)
wherein (though I be but meanely profest) yet
your Lordship's zealous regard to the profession I
beare, shall euer binde me in the most approued

---

reign of Elizabeth was of the privie Council, Secretary
of State, and Master of the Wards.   King James created
him 13th May, 1603,   Baron Cecil, of Essendine, co.
Rutland : 26th August, 1604, Viscount Cranborne of co.
Dorset, and 4th May, 1605, earl of Salisbury. He finally
became Lord High Treasurer. He married Elizabeth,
sister of the unfortunate Henry Brooke, Lord Cobham,
He died 24th May, 1612.   G.

bonds of duetie and thankefull seruice. Againe, that honourable testimony of your Lordship's regarde, euen to the very name of your late Soueraigne, approued by the generall applause and acclamation of all good people : by which act, your Lordship hath proceeded to the highest degree of good opinion, and by giuing honour to her that best deserued it, deseruedly made your selfe much honoured.

And therefore (my good Lord) haue I ventured on your Lordship's gratious acceptance, humbly requesting your Honor, that my particular (howsoeuer unworthy to trauaile in so honourable an argument) may (notwithstanding) haue gratious acceptation, being presented in the name of QUEENE ELIZABETH, to whose honourable remembrance your Lordship is so much deuoted, and to whose name I haue principally dedicated this seruice : beseeching Almighty God to deriue uppon your name and House, a perpetuall succession of honour and good fortune.

> Your Honour's
> in all duetie and
> humble seruice.

CHRISTOPHER LEUER.

Queene Elizabeth's Teares :

OR

Her resolute bearing the Christian Crosse.

THAT haue reacht my meditation hie,
    And versd the holy suffrings of my Lord,
    Still doe I mooue in that emperiall skie,
Where saints and holy angels doe afford
Subject that may diuinest wit accord :
   I glory then that to my verse is giuen,
   This care, to set their holy cause from heauen.

Among the number of those holy saints,
A happy Lady, where all happie are,
Whose name Report in euery place acquaints,
Who like the beauty of the fairest starre,
In beauteous name exceedes all other farre :
   And but we doe except the virgin-mother
   We reach her praise as high as any other.

Thus I conceiue her image in my thought,
Clad in the virgin ornament of white ;

Within that white her innocence was wrought,
Vnspotted with the touch of vaine delight ;
Her habite is all day, and nothing night :
   And in that white (as my remembrance saith)
   Was writ this motte, 𝕯𝖊𝖋𝖊𝖓𝖉𝖊𝖗 𝖔𝖋 𝖙𝖍𝖊 𝕱𝖆𝖎𝖙𝖍.

Her presence could expresse what she had beene,
Humble, yet full of princely maiestie,
A constant martire, yet a royall queene ;
Before her State went much aduersitie :
In all proportions iudgement might descry
   What holy motions moouèd in her hart ;
   For holy signes of prayer did mooue each part.

Vpon her head a coronet of golde,
To intimate her eminence of place ;
But in her royall presence I beholde,
The image both of maiestie and grace ;
The heart of State was grauen in her face :
   Let him in iudgement be reputed blinde,
   That in the face sees nothing of the minde.

Within one hand she had an armèd blade,
(Whereon was writ her many victories ;)
The other with much reuerence she laide
Vpon the Booke of heauenly mysteries ;
As if that God in wisedome did deuise,

To giue this ladie that victorious sword,
To guard the passage of His Holy Word.

Before her feete a globe of earth was cast,
Scepters, and crownes, and markes of high estate;
Yea kings themselues and potentates were plac't,
In humble ranke before this magistrate ;
Their fortunes on her victories did waite :
    For when that she would fauour or cast downe,
    The bad had warre, the better had the crowne.

These trophies doe erect eternal name,
That euer liues in honour of this queene ;
That giue occasion vnto busie Fame,
To make report what her deserts haue beene :
My selfe that haue these admirations seene,
    In humble verse her suffrings doe relate,
    That dare not meddle with her time of State.

This cogitation of this princely one,
Is often entertainèd in my minde ;
Waking, or not, I oft reuise thereon,
And often in my thoughts this queene I finde,
And oft her glad remembrance hath inclinde
    To heart my verse, that writ the Holie Passion,
    Of her religious teares to make relation.

O Thou that dost inspire with holie flame,
The moouing spirits of deepe Poesie ;

Giue me to adde some honour to her name,
That wants her due of holy memorie :
For Time will rot our best mortallitie.
   And sith that she all vertuous ones did cherish,
    It pittie were her vertuous name should perish.

O let my verse mooue indignation,
And stir the blood of better ablèd wit :
Enuie, or shame of this relation,
May hap beget the meanes to better it :
Howere my shame, it doth my liking fit,
   By anie meanes to adde vnto her praise :
   Our loue is in our heart, not in our phrase.

¶ When holy Edward's[1] spirit did exspire,
Borne on the wings of angells into blisse,
The earth grew cold and wanted holy fire ;
When this diuine defendor parted is,
Blacke Night did then succeed this Day of his :
   For then the glory of the day is done,
   When interposèd earth bedims the sunne.

O the exceeding wisedome in the heauen,
Whose prouidence protecteth euery care :
To seely[2] men the licence is not giuen,
To see forbidden secrets what they are ;

---

    [1] Edward VI. G.   [2] = silly, weak. G.

In vaine vpon the face of heauen men stare,
　To know the hidden cause of that effect,
　Which in God's secret will is hidden kept.

Tell me, thou wisest in iuditious arte,
(Or if thou canst not tell, I silence thee)
Why God remou'd this holy king apart,
And left His Church to open tyrranie :
You reade not in the starres this secrecie :
　He that all futures can discerne afarre,
　Within His breast these secrets hidden are.

Now Time had set this glorious sonne of grace,
To darknesse he his Empire did resigne ;
Darknesse that long had ouerspread the face
Of holy truth and vertuous discipline ;
No light apparent where no light may shine :
　And but the fires of martires that gaue light,
　All had been blacke, and in eternall night,

You that haue nothing holy but your name,
That did incence this MARIE vnto blood ;
Be it to you your euerlasting shame,
So to corrupt her nature that was good ;
O had she had the spirite to withstoode
　You that did hearten her to her disgrace,
　She had deseru'd preheminence of place.

To saue a world of sinners you pretend,
But you intend another by pretence :
Religious duties often you commend,
Yet interdict you our obedience,
You bid speake truth, but in a double sence :
    How can your teaching many spirits saue,
      When words and works such contradictions
       haue.

These instigators fill her hands with blood,
(In all respects saue this a vertuous queene)
What they made vitious would haue prooued good:
Had not their powrefull prouocations beene,
Vpon her name this blood had not bin seene :
    And men of holy place be sure of this,
      Where you touch blood, the marke apparent is.

This Ladie (in the number of the rest)
Indur'd the storme of persecution :
Highest in griefe, and in her name the best,
And with the best maintain'd her resolution :
She (like the lamb prepar'd for execution)
    Doth still expect by loosing of her breath,
      To giue her holy cause a holy death.

And reason hath she of this iust suspect,
(So strange was alteration in the State)
Within her sister's face she found neglect ;

And friends doe euer faile th' vnfortunate.
The present State, men onelie estimate :
   For as the wind transports the flying aire,
   So, as times alter, men stil fliers are.

Her house in EDWARD's time, a little court,
Full of the fawning seruice of the knee :
But MARIE now cuttes off this full resort
And men fall backe in their apostasie ;
The cuckooes sing not where colde winters be :
   And Time the lady of her port[1] bereaues,
   As winter frosts nip off the falling leaues.

These were the first beginnings of her care,
Which (like the heads of little rising springs)
Runne to a larger bignesse than they were :
So Time that fauours not this ladie, brings
Still fresh supplies vnto her sufferings ;
   Like flouds that with their swelling tides are
      fed,
   Till falling seas doe make their waters ebbe.

Here might she spend her holy meditation,
(As sure she did much holier than I write)
She alters not with Fortune's alteration :
Resolue had made her sufferings her delight,

---

   [1] = refuge or house, G.

673

Her holie cause did giue her holie might :
   To beare the indignation of their spleene,
   That made her sister her offended queene.

O Thou eternal Spirite (thus she saies)
Without Whose pleasure nothing hath euent :
Before we be, Thou numbrest all our daies,
And preordainest euerie accident ;
To Thee all things that be, themselves present.
   And I, that for Thy holy name must die,
   Imbrace the cause, and thanke Thy maiestie.

Whatere I suffer is in Thy decree,
Which limits all the purposes of men :
My selfe, my cause I consecrate to Thee,
Let them cut off vncertaine life, yet then
Ile breathe it in Thy sacred hands ; and when
   My sister MARIE offers vp my blood,
   Ile offer vp my heart to make it good.

My Sauiour Iesus sufferèd more than I,
And for my sake, that Lord He sufferèd,
The righteous One did for the sinnefull die,
And giue His life for ours that perishèd.
Thy seruant is by Thy example led,
   To die for Truth, sith Truth did die for me,
   For thus to die, is life's eternitie.

What is my life the world should enuie for?
(Alas) a little puffe of breathing aire;
Death hath ten thousand meanes to let it goe,
And flie this wearie body of my care:
Vncertaine I to lose it when or where.
　　Ther's somewhat else than breath they care for
　　　　than,
　　For breath is common vnto euery man.

It is for conscience and religious cause,
That I indure the burthen of their hate;
Howere guiltlesse, yet the wrested lawes
Must correspond in iudgement with the State,
For that is lawe our gouvernours relate:
　　And though by Law my innocence be proou'd,
　　The case wil alter, if the prince be moou'd.

Be it that God's preuenting eie should sleepe,
And that their purpose haue desirèd end:
That soule they take from me they cannot keepe,
Which to a mighty Lord I recommend;
His right He can against all claimes defend:
　　How fruitles is the harvest which they make,
　　That cannot keepe the treasure which they take.

Men are iniurious that report of Death,
To be the highest of extremities;
Whenas we die, what loose we else but breath,

And many numbers of our miseries?
When this life setts, a better doth arise :
   And when to Death a holy cause is giuen,
   Death is the gate by which we enter heauen.

Within our life these sorrowes we containe,
Vncertaine daies, yet full of certaine griefe :
In number few, but infinite in pain :
O're chargde with wants, but naked of reliefe :
In ruling it our euill partes are chiefe :
   And though our time be not cut short of Death,
   Olde age will creepe to stop vncertaine breath.

Yet to the much affliction of the minde,
This of the body is a scant compare;
Wherein so many, and so much I find,
As would astonne[1] my spirits to declare ;
Triall can onely tell vs what they are :
   For we whom custom hath with griefe ac-
      quainted,
   By vs her sad proportion best is painted.

The griefe of mind in that intestine warre,
That stirres sedition in the state of man ;
Where, when our passions once commaunders are,

---

[1] = astonish : a-stony or (metaphorically) turn to stone, after the old Medusa myth. G.

Our peacefull dayes are desperate, for than
It[1] stirre's more hate, than when it first began;
 For heady passion's like an untam'd beast,
 That riots most, when we desire it least.

This violence exceedes his vertuous meane,
Like swelling tides that ouerrunne their shore,
Leauing the lawfull current of their streame,
And breake their bankes that bounded them before:
Yet griefe in her great violence is more:
 For if that reason, bound not griefe with lawes,
 In our destruction griefe will be the cause.

Griefe should be borne with much indifference,
Not much regarded, yet regardlesse neuer;
Not much affected, yet we must haue sense,
To feele our griefe and apphrehend it euer;
Yet let the grieuèd ouer this indeuer,
 To make his burthen ease full as hee may,
 And so his griefe with ease is borne away.

So much of griefe we onely doe sustaine,
As in our choice our selues doe apprehend:
Griefe may present itselfe, but not constraine
That we imbrace what it doth recommend.
Beare it but lightly then; for to that end

---

[1] Misprinted ' The '. G.

Is patience giuen, by whose resolued might,
  The heauieste loade of griefe is made but light.

This is the most of happinesse we haue,
That with our patience we support our cares ;
Not we our selues, but God the vertue gaue,
Which our vnworthy life right well declares ;
To loose my life, is for to loose my cares.
  Then what is death that I should fear to die,
  Death is the death of all my miserie.

What then is that that doth beget desire
In humane flesh to linger out long daies ?
Is it because to honor men aspire ;
Or, for their name in beautie hath a praise ?
Or, i'st their greedy auarice them staies ?
  Honour, beautie, nor desire of golde,
  Cannot the certaine of their death withhold.

Honour is nothing but a very name,
Often conferd to men of little merite ;
In euery place, as common as is fame,
Commonly giuen to euery common spirite ;
So little worth, as any one may weare it.
  Then why should that be thought of estimation
  That giues to base deseruings high creation ?

The name and place of honour may be giuen,

As please the prince in fauour to dispose ;
But true deriuèd honour is from heauen,
And often liues in meane estate with those,
That to the courts of princes neuer goes.
   How vainely prowd are such as would get fame,
   Yet get no more of honour but the name.

Be it, thy honour as the glorious sunne,
Exceede the rate of common expectation ;
Thy prince displeasèd once, thy honour's done :
In rising to this pitch men use gradation,
But at one fall they loose all estimation :
   For he whose powre is euer absolute,
   His angry breath can puffe thy glorie out.

Where is the honour of great MACEDON,
That measur'd his large empires with his sworde ?
Great JULIUS is with many CÆSARS gone,
Leauing no more of honour than the word ;
And but the pennes of schollers that record,
   Old Time would bring their honour to that
      shame,
   As Cæsar and the rest would haue no name.

Who is't that now to CÆSAR bends the knee,
Or frames the sweete of wordes to please his eare ?
Who is't that now regardeth his decree,
Or his offended countenance doth feare ?

Cæsar in's graue, his honour is no where:
  If honour thus doe perish in the best,
  What may be then expected in the reste?

He that from enuious eie, and full resort,
Liues priuate, with a little state content;
Little desires the honour of the Court,
Where emulation stirres a discontent.
Men shoote at him that is most eminent:
  And whom the prince with highest grace doth
    crown,
  Enuy brings many hands to pull him downe.

See here the glorie of mortallitie
Which we with infinite of care pursue;
Painefull to get, but lost at libertie;
Fatall to many, fortunate to few,
Whereto so many miseries insue,
  As filles our time with cares; then why
    should I
  For this respect of honour feare to die?

Is Beauty then of that high consequence,
Wherein I may disswasiue reason finde?
Is that faire shadow of that excellence,
That for the face I should exchange the minde?
Beauty that blindeth many, cannot blinde

My reason so; for Beautie's but a flowre,
Which being pluckt it fadeth in an houre.

What though the world with Admiration's eie,
Gaze at the wondrous pleasure in the face;
Wherein the greatest vse great industrie,
Watching each little fauour to imbrace,
And prowd themselues to be in Beautie's grace:
   Yet when the best of Beauty men haue got,
   (If not old age) the graue will make it rot.

Where are those Beauties which the world
     admirde,
That with attraction slau'd the hearts of men?
Within their graues these ladies are retirde,
And all their beauty is decay'd with them;
What is't in beautie we should value then?
   For those that were of most admirèd face,
   Are now confinèd in a rotten place.

Beautie is like a comet in the aire,
Which being lighted by the burning sunne,
Seemes to the strange beholder wondrous faire,
But when the matter of the light is done,
The fire goes out: in like comparison,
   Let Beautie like the fairest starre be bright,
   Beauty will set, and be as blacke as night.

It well befits the spirit of great blood,
To loue that least which is of common vse;
Then why should beauty be esteemèd good,
Which many commons commonly abuse?
For where in wisedome Nature doth refuse
   To giue to many beautie of the face,
   A little arte will couer that disgrace.

Looke, as the Earth bedeckt with beauteous
      flowres,
(The pretty children of the Earth and Spring)
Warm'd with the sun, and fed with heauenly
      showres,
Haue but a little time of tarrying :
So, when the winter of our age shall bring
   Our fading time, our beauty like the flowre,
   Cannot this winter of our age indure.

This nothing of desert cannot perswade,
That I should feare this image of my death ;
The beauty of the minde will neuer fade,
Which I must value deerer than my breath :
Who would aduenture heauen for little Earth?
   The beauteous name of Truth for which I die,
   Exceedes the beautie of the fairest eie.

If these respects haue not the powre to moue,
That haue beene powrefull in great potentates;

For many great ones haue desirèd loue,
And for their loue haue wasted great estates,
And for their loue haue oft prou'd desperates.
  But for the base desire of hauing much,
  Neuer was any of the princely such.

He that of wealth desireth any more,
Than may suffice an honest compotence ;
Fills to a vessel that is full before,
Which ouerrunnes with prodigall expence,
What care put in with greedy diligence.
  Exceeding wealthy the contented are,
  That with their little haue but little care.

Among great euills Auarice is chiefe,
Attended on by many miseries,
Whose like is well resembled in the thiefe,
Who thriueth most by many robberies :
So he that would by greedie Mammon rise,
  Must like a thiefe by some deuise or other,
  Make himselfe rich by taking from another.

And hence it is that men in euery trade,
Haue secret art to raise a wealthy state ;
Whereby their base beginnings oft are made,
To large possessions wondrous fortunate :
Yet righteous God that doth iniustice hate,

Oft giues to wealth thus gotten such an heire.
As freely spends what Auarice did spare.

Desire of much doth oft beget desire,
To rob the orphane and the widdow mother ;
Makes, that in bloud we many times conspire,
Against the very bosomes of our brother ;
The couetous doe feede one of another;
   For when men's heart on this desire are set,
   They care not what the meanes be, so they get.

And therefore is't that Law hath many cases,
And euery case wrapt vp in double sense ;
And euery sense so traueld in law places,
As the professour for his diligence,
Must weare the case that is in difference.
   Desire of wealth is then an euill cause,
   That thus corrupts the tenor of good lawes.

What should I number up these euills more,
Where repetition grieues my better minde ?
Crœsus is gone with all his heapèd store,
Leauing no more than euill name behinde ;
Who can one penny of his treasure finde :
   Then Honour, Beauty, and Desire of gaine,
   Are pleasures that but little time remaine.

God is my honour, God's the beauteous face,
Which I with greedie appetite beholde ;

He is my treasure that I would embrace,
To purchase Him, all others I haue solde.
He is my honour, beautie, and my gold:
   Sith I am God's, and God is mine, then I
   Make it my (all) for this my God to die.

Thus did this Ladie with herselfe dispute,
And to herselfe she framde such argument,
As in her purpose made her resolute,
To beare what ere those euill times present.
Griefe is not felt by one so patient;
   For what though men lay all their euills on vs,
   A little patience beares their euills from vs,

(Good Ladie) she had only this one care,
(So holy MARY had but onlie one)
How she for happie death might best prepare;
For this she spends her cogitation,
Her houres in prayer, her time in meditation:
   When Death comes thus to our preparèd daies,
   We honour God, and get eternall praise.

Such was the saint, the sinner was not so;
Such was the lambe, the butcher different,
Such was the larke, the bussard that's below,
Mounts to a pitch to sease the innocent;
The good, the bad, the base, the eminent:

So opposite, as she in euiles least,
Suffers the prowd controlement of a priest.

(*Steuen*)[1] it was thy contriuement and thy care,
To persecute the cause for which STEUEN[2] bled.
Betwixt two STEUENS what differences are ;
Yet both of you with blood were sprinklèd,
Thou martiredst many, he was martirèd.
    How ill it fittes thee to be callèd STEUEN,
    Thy nature is from hell, thy name from heauen.

Thou hadst the name and place of *gardner*,
To dresse the vintage thou commaundest o're ;
But by thy hand, the hedges broken were,
Which holy Church had fencèd in before ;
And thou thyselfe (prowd GARDNER) like a bore,
    Rootst vp the flowre, and fruitfull bearing tree,
    That in God's holy gardens fairest be.

The reuerend name of bishop that was giuen,
Ill sorted with thy strong desire of blood ;
Those hie deseruings were not found in STEUEN,
That correspond the name of fatherhood ;
Where all is euill, there is nothing good :

---

[1] Stephen Gardner, bishop of Winchester : born 1483 :
died November 12th, 1555. G.

[2] Stephen the proto-martyr of the " Acts of the Apostles." G.

And so thy names and nature disagree,
As opposites in their extreamitie.

Bishops (if they would correspond their name)
Must be composde of mercifull respect ;
For God is such whence their creation came,
Who hath from many numbers them select,
To patterne holie life to God's elect :
   And sith to princes, God hath giuen the sword,
   Let them be princely onely in God's Word.

What is't they be inuested in their white,
And weare the holy orders of their place ?
If vnto fonde offence they haue delight ;
That will their whited vestiments disgrace,
Pride, and ambition in a prelat's face,
   Are vglie formes ; nor is their priesthoode good,
   That wash their hands in holy martires blood.

If any thinke I speake with enuious breath,
And wrong the iust deseruings of this man,
He is deceiu'd : it is ELIZABETH,
Whose tribulation she indurèd then,
Stirres vp more angrie bloud than Enuie can :
   (And if the trueth in stories be recorded)
   He was the worst of men those times afforded.

Witnes this Ladie of deseruèd praise,
Witnes the much affliction she indur'd,

Witnes the number of her greiuèd daies,
Witnes the prisons where she was immure'd,
Witnes himselfe these euills that procur'd,
   Witnes the saints that perisht in that fire,
    Which STEUEN (like bellowes) kindl'd with
      desire.

When she (good Ladie) is in holie prarie,
Or in the heauen of holy meditation ;
The Macheuillian doth his plots prepare,
How to incence the queene with indignation :
And to that end he makes a large relation ;
   Which though the truth be not in stories reade,
   This for a truth may be imaginèd.

(My Soueraigne, thus his enuy can begin)
I that haue place in your affaires of State,
And detestation of heretique sin,
Am therefore bolde for to expostulate,
And giue aduise vnto your high estate ;
   In matter of most weighty consequence,
   Faithfull aduise is our best diligence.

ELIZABETH (O may I not offend)
Your sister (gratious Soueraigne) is not true
Vnto your State, nor to your life a friend ;
She is the head of that rebellious crue,
That mooues sedition in the residue.

When Faction get's a head that's neere the
    crowne,
Wisedome would beat the head of Faction
    downe.

Our Sister (saith the much offended queene)
(Bishop) be well aduisèd what you saie ;
We to our sister haue right gratious beene,
How is't that she in loue should fall away ?
We cannot think our sister will betray.
    The priest replied, If so your grace will heare,
    Ile giue you instance, both of when and where.

When WYAT[1] with the mutinous in KENT,
Moou'd a commotion in your quiet State,
So dangerous that WYAT did present
His rebell troopes before your princely State ;
Whoome, though the heauens were pleased to
    ruinate,
    Yet let it be within your princely care
    To know the cause from whence these rebells
    were.

WHAT (alas) a priuate gentleman,
Whose reputation neuer reacht so hie,
As to be mark'd in State ; could WYAT than

---

[1] Sir Thomas Wyatt, the Younger: born 1520: died
April 11, 1554. G.

With his weake credite raise a companie,
So warrelike as to match your maiestie ?
  (Madame be sure) a greater was the head,
  Although the body WYAT gouernèd.

In great attempts it's weighty pollicie,
That whom the practise doth most neere respect,
With false appearance they dissemblèd be,
That if their bad designes haue bad effect,
They may auoyd the danger of suspect ;
  But if the practise haue desirèd end,
  The plotters then the practise will commend.

Your sister learnèd in this subtle arte,
(Be pleasd to pardon plainenesse in my speach)
Would not the secret of the plot impart,
Saue unto WYAT, whom her art could teach,
To silence how ambition made her reach :
  And though the traitor to his death denie it,
  The truth of circumstance will verifie it.

What other curse, saue LUTHER's discipline,
Begat this ciuill discord in your State ?
Nor can your kingdome's holy Church resigne,
Whilst that your princely selfe is magistrate.
Then sure these rebells she did animate,
  Your sacred life (by treason) to depriue,
  That she and LUTHER might the better thriue.

Who is't but you that weares the princely crowne,
With which Ambition would adorne hir head ?
She cannot rise before your Grace be downe,
Nor can she rule before your state be dead :
This tricke of State would be considerèd.
   The Queene replide, (and saist thou so good
      priest)
   Who then desireth all, she shall haue least.

The times that followed, were good testament,
How much the prelate did the queene incence ;
For presently commissioners were sent
To Ashbridge-house, to set the lady thence,
With strict command to haste their diligence :
   So forcible was his perswasiue tongue,
   To make one sister doe another wrong.

These ministers (in silence be their name)
Posted their iourney with a greedie harte ;
For Euill is like double-wingèd Fame,
That looseth breath by flying ouer-fast ;
They runne the best to euill that runne last.
   And these that now (to please Queene Marie)
      flie,
   Will runne for Elizabeth, if Marie die.

A maiden that attended on her Grace,
By them demaunded how the princesse did ;

A reuerend feare brought palenesse to her face,
And in her heart she was astonishèd,
And with a fearefull voice deliuerèd
   This answere; Lords, my Ladie is not well,
   Please it your Lo : your occasions tell.

They answer, No, and with a sterne aspect,
Threaten the fearefull spirit of the maide ;
Those spirits from her outward parts were crept,
To cheere her heart, with terrour much afraide :
And still, when she could get a word, she said :
   My Mistris (Lords): Hir words then stopt with
      feares,
   The rest that wanted were supplide with teares.

Goe tell thy Mistris (thus they make reply)
That we are sent to bring her to the Court ;
Our haste is greate, stay not to aske vs why,
Our estimation it doth much import,
That dead or liuing she with vs resort.
   The maide whose heart their very words did
      breake,
   Would haue replide, but that she could not
      speake.

But in she runnes with much amazèd haste,
As those that are transported with their griefe ;
Close by the princesse' bed hereself she plac'd,

Shiuering she stoode, as doth the aspine leafe ;
And oft she would begin, and oft her griefe
    Draws back hir words, that in hir troubled
      breast,
    Heaue vp her bodie with their much vnrest.

The Princesse when she sees her so dismaide,
Raiseth her sickly bodie in her bed ;
And fearlesse she demaunds her fearefull maide,
How she with griefe became so alterèd ;
It's ease (she saith) to haue it vttered :
    (If for my sake) I prethee shed no teare,
    We that are princely-minded cannot feare.

(As griefe would giue her leaue) the maiden saide,
Madame, your Grace is sent for to the Queene.
(The Ladie then) Why art thou so afraid ?
Would God this let[1] of sickenes had not beene :
I haue not of long time my sister seene.
    And though for much affliction I be sent
    My God hath taught me to be patient.

Returne againe vnto the Lords, and say,
My sickenes is at this time violent ;
Please it them rest their trauells heere to day,
To-morrow they their message may present ;

---

[1] Hindrance. G.

We to our prince must be obedient.
   Pray them to giue deferment to my sorrow:
   What they giue not to night, thei'l giue to
      morrow.

The maide, whose dutie was obedience,
Hastes to acquaint them with her Ladie's pleasure
But rudely they with much vnreuerence,
Whose pride would not attend the Princesse leasure,
Rush (vndesir'd) where lay this heauenly treasure.
   Which their presumption so offends her Grace,
   As she confronts them with au angrie face.

(Sirs) you are not aduisèd what you do,
(Thus their abuse stirres up her princely fire,)
That your audacious footings enter so
Into our priuate, where we doe retire;
Is it Ambition makes you thus aspire;
   You ill remember what your dueties beene,
   Nor that my selfe is sister to your Queene.

Is my great father's name with you forgot,
Or the remembrance of my princely brother?
There is no graue can make our names to rot,
That in their kingly state exceede all other:
I haue not giuen my name vnto another;
   I tell you true, howe'r we greeuèd be,
   We can not tho forget our dignitie.

Thus had she said, and then she made a pause,
And then begins in milder phrase againe ;
Say on (she saith) what is your earnest cause ?
Came you from Court, how doth my soueraigne ?
Then she commaunds a sernant to sustaine,
 Her much infeeblèd bodie in her bed,
 Whilst their commission they haue vtterèd.

They all make answer with a prowd neglect ;
(Madame) the Queene hath sent vs for your
   Grace,
Of our commision this is the effect :
Then presently you must forsake this place,
And goe with vs. Within the Princesse' face,
 One might perceiue, their words thus vtterèd,
 To giue her sickely pale, an angry red.

Thus she (vnto my soueraigne Ladie Queene)
I yeelde my selfe in all obedieuce ;
My God He knowes that I haue faithful beene,
And He in heauen records my innocence ;
I haue not learn'd to hide with faire pretence :
 For whatsoe'er my soueraigne shall present,
 Euen vnto death I am obedient.

Surely, this addes vnto my sicknesse, paine,
That presently I cannot make repaire
Vnto the presence of my soueraigne ;

So violent my fittes of sicknesse are:
Yet that I may expresse my duteous care,
　　I will contend with death, and this disease
　　Ere I offend: so much I loue to please.

This onely fauour (it's a little one)
That for a day or two I may repose:
This sure exceedes not your commission,
Wee'l iourney hard to get the time we lose:
(I tell you sirs) my heart before me goes,
　　Will you to me this fauour then deriue?
　　They rudely answer in the negatiue.

Th' allowance of our time is not so large,
Nor we so bold to disobey the Queene;
We must be strict to execute the charge,
That to vs strictly hath committed beene:
For to our care this hard commaund is giuen
　　That if pale Death should beare your soule away,
　　To bring the bodie where the spirit lay.

Must you haue one? then take them both (she
　　　saies)
Am I (alas) so great in my offence?
(If needes you must) what is't me vse delaies?
Would God your haste with one day might dis-
　　pence.
They answer, No.　Then beare my body hence;

It is in vaine I thus expend my breath,
Mercy liues not in messengers of death.

Yet this alone all other griefe is highest,
That so my soueraigne sister is offended ;
Neerest in blood and to my loue the nighest,
To whose protection I am left commended :
How is't this loue of sisters should be ended?
   Sure I suspect you doe my sister wrong;
   She cannot be so cruell as your tongue.

How ere it be, my comfort is in heauen,
That makes me powrefull to support my griefe ;
God that is iust, to my iust cause hath giuen
Patience by which the wrongèd haue reliefe :
Among the patient I my selfe am chiefe.
   (I tell you true) it is of much import,
   That God will helpe my sorrowes to support!

Thus she had saide, and then she bids, prepare
To satisfie th' important messengers :
Who on the morrow all preparèd were,
And all set forward with their busie cares ;
Their haste their euill diligence declares,
   For all their haste was but to haste her death,
   Whom God would giue a manie yeeres of breath.

To tell her weary iourney to the Court,
Her sicknesse, and their much discourtesie ;

The few of friends that to her Grace resort,
The many griefes, and much aduersitie,
That had bedim'd her late prosperitie :
   To tell you all I should but tell too much,
   Such was this Ladie, and their vsage such.

Being arriu'd at Court, her entertaine
Sorted the rest of her affliction :
She in a priuate chamber did remaine,
Barr'd from the free accesse of any one ;
And (but for God and angels) she alone,
   (Good Lady) in her priuate spent her prayre,
   Whilst STEUEN and others in contriuing were.

Vnto this saint the Queene a diuel sent,
Who (with some others of the Counsel) came,
With suttle speach to sift and circumuent,
Her innocence.   Be it eternall shame
To brand with blacke the record of thy name :
   For as the hownds pursue the flying chace,
   Thy doggèd thoughts, (O STEUEN) pursue her
      Grace.

Thus he begins to open his vile breath:
(Madame) we come authoriz'd from the Queene ;
That Queene whome you had destinate for Death,
Ha l not the powre of God's resistance beene ;
But He that hath your secret practise seene,

Layes open all your treason in the light,
Which you haue long concealèd from our sight.

(Madam) Nay stay, (the grieuèd Princesse saies)
We haue enough to make a large reply ;
You do not well report vs in your phrase,
And for the name of treason I defie ;
O that in you should be such iniurie !
   It ill befits your reuerend place (my Lord)
   To brand your honour with so foule a word.

But for my soueraigne sister you present,
I in my silence will my selfe containe ;
Onely let this be thought indifferent,
That from the word of treason you refraine.
(I tell you true) I must that word disdaine.
   Then say the rest (my Lords) how vntrue soe'r,
   I will inforce my patience for to heare.

This iust reproofe incenc'd the prelate more,
Kindl'd the fire of Enuy in his flesh :
And made him more bitter than before,
Breathing foorth words of much vnworthinesse,
Which for they would but grieue me to expresse,
   I silence them, and tell you of the rest ;
   The least of euills, is of euills best.

(Thus he) Howe'r you smoothe with faire pretence,
And hide your guilt with resolute deniall ;

The eie of Iudgemnet can discerne offence ;
Nor want we powre to bring you to a triall,
We haue intelligence for our espiall :
    And when you thought all was in priuate kept,
    The eye of State did wake, you thought t'had
    slept.

COURTNEY,[1] and you did not conspire in one ?
(You thinke we know not that you did conspire)
To stirre the people to rebellion,
Whereby you might vnto the crowne aspire ;
And to that end breath'd your ambition's fire
    In WYAT's breast, that by he his attempt,
    Might make a way for your new gouernement.

Which if you should aspire (which God forbid)
How would these kingdomes ruine in your rise ?

---

[1] The Courtenay implicated with Wyat was, Edward
Courtenay, second Earl of Devon, and first Marquis of
Exeter, by his second wife Gertrude, dau. of Wm.
Blount, Lord Mountjoy. His father was beheaded on
Tower Hill, 9th Jan., 1539-40, when he was committed a
prisoner to the Tower and detained there until the ac-
cession of Q. Mary, who restored him to liberty and to
his father's titles and estates. Q. Mary again sent him
to the Tower, but he was subsequently released, and
died at Padua 4th Oct., 1556, it was supposed from
poisoning. He died unmarried. G.

Religion would in banishment be hid,
And LUTHER then must be in exercise.
Do not you thus within your heart deuise ?
  I know you do ; for how should you be other,
  Being deriuèd from so bad a mother. *Anne Boleyn.*

(Madam) you haue too much your father's blood,
And much too much his blinde opinion.
Thinke you your father did his kingdomes good,
To set himselfe in opposition,
Against the Church and true religion ?
  (Though gyantlike) he fought with little oddes,
  To raise seditious warre against the gods.

Such as was he, such your deceiuèd brother,
Treading the path his father went before.
And you, (if that you might) would be another,
To make the holy Church to suffer more.
But God, Whose hand hath cur'd what they made
      sore,
  Hath giuen Religion and the State a friend,
  Whose hopes cutte off the euilles you intend.

Religious MARIE, whose obedience
Vnto the holy seate of Peter's chaire,
Receiues from heauen such large beneuolence,
As if Religion and the kingdomes were
By prouidence committed to her care :

It is in vaine you then with her contend,
Whome God and holy angels will defend.

(Bishop) I record heauen that you do me wrong,
(The Princesse saide) I haue no such intent ;
My heart hath not resemblance with your tongue,
Nor do I hate my sister's gouerment :
My God He knowes that I am innocent.
   If for my conscience thus you do enuie,
   I for my conscience am content to die.

She would haue said much more, but that the
     Lords,
(To haste the execution of their care)
Doe interrupt the passage of her words
Adding more griefe to them that grieuèd were,
Telling her Grace, she must her selfe prepare ;
   For that the Queene gaue strict commandment,
     that
   Shee to the Towre. The Towre (alas) for what ?

(So she made hastie answer, and then wept ;
And then begins in grieuèd words againe.)
What neede a woman in the Towre be kept ?
I in a lesser prison may remaine :
Alas my sister, and my soueraigne,
   How should these wrongs of me be vnderstood,
   That thus receiue them from my neerest blood ?

Recall your euill words, and say not so,
Do not a seely woman so confound,   *innocent*
Vnto the Towre none but offenders goe ;
If then offence within my life be found,
Then (like a traytor) let me enter bound :
    If not, intreate my sister that I die.
    Rather than traitor-like in prison lie.

The Lords made answer, that it could not be,
So much the Queene was moouèd to offence,
As she would not reuerse that her decree,
Nor durst they stand with her in difference :
And then they counsaile her to patience,
    And to the mercy of the Queene submit ;
    Who (for submission) would most fauour it.

Thus they had said, and then they left the place,
And in the place, left many cares behind :
All which (like robbers) did assaile her Grace,
And breake the treasure of her quiet minde ;
So much of grief in one I cannot find :
    And (sure) if God should not supply to such,
    N o woman in the world could beare so much.

(Although I would) I cannot make report,
How much this Ladie is in her distresse ;
Nor how by prayer she maketh her resort,
Vnto the presence of God's holinesse :

Neither can I in liuely formes expresse,
  How God takes vp her holy praire to heauen,
  And all the griefe that to her Grace was giuen.

Nor can I tell you all their busie care,
That had begirt her lodging round about :
How many numbers in their armors were,
Nor how in manhood they were resolute :
What watch and warde, what running in and out :
  Nor how in warlike sort they doe prepare,
  Against a ladie that intends but praire.

The night thus spent, the next succeeding day,
Brought to this lady new supply of wrong :
The Queene hath sent to bid her haste away :
Her stay made people in great numbers throng
Vnto the court. The Towre (she saith) is strong :
  And though the people in her fauour rise,
  Yet being there, she can vs not surprise.

The messengers that brought this hard command,
Saide that a barge did for her Grace attend ;
And that, nor time, nor tide would euer stand,
And therefore did desire she would not spend
The time that made the tide to be her friend.
  The princesse (with a grieuèd smile) replide,
  I am not friended with your forward tide.

Will you but length my time a little more,
And stay the fortunes of another tide :
God may in little time my selfe restore,
And fauour whome the times indignifide ;
Will you my Lords ? The Lords then thus replide :
  Madame, we are but seruants to the State,
  Seruants must euer on their maisters wait.

Is there no mercie ? Then be strong my heart,
To beare the sorrowes of a wearie breath ;
I haue a God, that will from heauen impart
Patience, that makes vs ioyous in our death ;
My God, be such to thy ELIZABETH.
  Sith that the Queene all mercie doth denie,
  I to the King of Heauen for mercie flie.

Yet will I with my duteous care attempt
To purchase fauour from my sister's eie ;
For by my letters to my soueraigne sent,
Her gratious acceptation I shal trie :
(Saue but the Lord of Sussex[1]) all denie,

---

1 Queene Elizabeth's Lord Sussex was Sir Thomas
Ratcliffe, K.G., fourth Lord Fitzwalter and third Earl of
Sussex. He was born in 1526, eldest son of Sir Henry
Ratcliffe, second Earl of Sussex, by his first wife, Lady
Elizabeth Howard, daughter of Thomas Duke of Norfolk.
He was lord-deputy of Ireland 2 and 3 Philip and Mary,
and Lord Lieutenant 3 Elizabeth. In 12 Elizabeth he

To beare the written message she would send,
So much they feare the bishop to offend.

This noble Lord (the heauens record his name),
Kneeld with an humble reuerence to her Grace ;
Swearing he would his honour first disclaime,
And lose the reputation of great place,
Ere he would so denie her princely Grace.
     If so (he saith) your princely griefe be writ,
     Ile pawne my honour to deliuer it.

(See here the diffrence in the mighty ones,
The chancellor STEUEN, whose place was eminent,
Had not as SUSSEX had, these motions :
For why, his birth from basenesse had discent :
But SUSSEX is in honour different.
     For when that honour is deriu'd in blood,
     That honour makes the honourable good.)

The ladie glad she had a meanes to send,
Raiseth him from the seruice of his knee ;

---

was Lord President of the North. He married Lady
Elizabeth Wriothsley, daughter of Thomas, Earl of
Southampton, and secondly, Frances, daughter of Sir
William Sidney, Knight (foundress of Sydney-Sussex
College, Cambridge), but had no surviving issue by
either. He died June, 1583, at his house in Bermondsey,
and was buried at Boreham in Sussex.   G.

And she in teares his honour did commend,
That hath respect to her extremitie.
And then she craues, a little libertie,
   That to hir soueraigne sister she may write:
   Griefe hath a tongue, but cannot well indite.

My soueraigne and my sister (thus she saith)
I haue no griefe but that your Grace is grieu'd,
And that you haue suspition of my faith,
And that I am not of your Grace beleeu'd,
(Alas) who hath my treasure thus bereeu'd;
   Please it your Grace my innocence to trie,
   If I be guiltie, let the guiltie die.

This letter did this faithfull Lord present
Vnto the Queene: but yet with such successe,
As still she is to her maleuolent.
STEUEN had resolu'd her in her bloodinesse,
She therefore blames the Earle's forwardnesse,
   That he would thus expend his industrie,
   In fauour of her greatest enemie.

Away (Shee saith) conuey her to the Towre,
Is our commaund so little of respect?
We will not you deferre it off an houre,
You do dis-honour vs in your neglect:
We tell you SUSSEX, she had neede be kept,

And kept secure, whose pride makes her aspire
To reach her state aboue our selfe much higher.

The Earle thus ill-fortun'd in his hope,
Would not reply vnto the Queene's offence,
Lest he against himselfe might her prouoke,
But backe returnes with his lost diligence,
And telles the Princesse how he did commence
  Her humble sute, and of the Queene's reply,
  That did all fauour to her Grace denie.

(Alas she saies) Why do I then contend,
To help the euill fortunes I endure ?
It must be death must giue my sorrowes end,
In death I shall my quiet best assure,
Death can more happines than I procure.
  Then to the Towre, sith mercy you deny,
  It's better once than euer for to die.

And on the morrow to the Towre she went,
Guarded with bands of manie armèd men :
The time was in the holy time of Lent
And on the day of holy Sabbaoth, when
Religious dueties were performing, when
  Did STEUEN (almost agreeing in the day)
  Most JUDAS-like this holy one betray.

What should I tell you of the much resort,
Of running vulgars that vpon her gaze ?

Or of the strange constructions of the Court,
Nor how the newes the better sort amaze,
Nor what the murmure of the people saies :
    But for to tell the sorrowes in her breast,
    To tell you that, is more than all the rest.

What is't her Grace with griefe should teare her
      mind ?
Or that the giddie people for her pray :
Except in God she can no comfort finde.
What, is't the tide inforce her for to stay
Hulling vpon the riuer where she lay ?
    For when the tide a little time had spent,
    The tide then seru'd for her imprisonment.

Being arriuèd at the place of woe,
They offer to the staires where traitors land :
Her Grace desir'd she might not enter so,
Praying the Lords that they would so command.
Some doe accord, but others do withstand :
    And there (as often when it goes by voyce)
    The worse (and not the better) had the choice.

Then with a grieuèd (yet a princely) grace,
She steppes vpon that ill-arriuing shore :
And here (she saith) now enters in this place ;
As true a subject to my Gouernour,
As ere this heauy passage went before.

And you my Lords, beare witnes what I say,
A loyall heart may enter in this way.

In these our present fortunes you may reade,
The fickle change of all mortallitie;
You know (my Lords) how princely we are bred,
And now you see our great extreamitie;
(Alas) in vs there is no certaintie;
   For though we be the neerest to the crowne,
   A little tricke of Fortune pulles vs downe.

When this was saide, she thence was led away,
Into the circuite of the inner court;
The way she went was marshall'd in array,
A many country swaines in warrelike sort.
These warriors that sawe the princely port,
   Such reuerence in the seely men appeares,
   Their handes haue wepons, but their eies haue
      teares.

Terrour in euery place presents her eie,
And that so much as might examinate,
A heart of well resolued valiancie;
Much more a ladie so vnfortunate,
To loose the pleasures of so high estate:
   For (sure) then Griefe is many doubles more,
   That comes to one that knew it not before.

To see the men of warre to be her garde,
The dismal place she was to enter in ;
The heapes of ammunition in the yarde,
The noyse of fetter'd prisoners from within,
To see these marks of warre and prisoning,
   Were much vnfitting obiects for the sight :
   Ladies (not loue but) feare to be in the fight.

The numbers of her griefe do so oppresse,
The much enfeebled bodie of her Grace,
As she sits downe with her much wearinesse,
And on a stone she makes her resting-place ;
Who (though the clowds did fall vpon her face)
   Lifts vp her hand vnto the weeping skie,
   That onely mournes for her extremitie.

(And thus she said) O Thou eternall eie,
That sees the very secrets of my hart :
I doe report me to Thy Maiestie,
That I am not as foule in my desert ;
Thou art my comfort, and my Iudge Thou art.
   Sith here on earth no iustice will be giuen,
   I for my iustice will resort to heauen.

This humble place (my Lords) you enuie not,
Enuy shootes not at any one so lowe :
The winde beates most vpon the cedar top,
And neuer mooues the vndergrowth below ;

They stand the safest that the lowest grow.
  And if you still your enuious thoughts will
      haue,
  Ere long Ile beare your enuie to my graue.

A gentleman that on her Grace attended,
(So deepely did her sorrowes apprehend)
As prodigall his teares he then expended ;
Which when the grieuèd ladie did intend,
She friendly thus his sorrowes reprehend ;
  Commaund thy eies (I pre thee) to forbeare,
  Our griefe will not be medcin'd with a teare.

See'st thou (and then she poynted vnto heauen)
In yonder spatious court we haue a friend ;
He hath our weakenesse His supportment giuen,
To Him myselfe in prayer I recommend ;
Vpon His becke the angells do attend.
  And when religious griefe bedims our eie,
  The angells come to wipe and make them drie.

The Constable desires she would make haste
Vnto her lodging, for the day grew olde ;
And saith her Grace is there but meanely plac'd,
And that he feares the stone may giue her colde,
And many another circumstance he tolde.

(Her Grace stoode vp and saide) We do not
    feare,
Sith we must die, it is no matter where.

Then was she led into a priuate roome,
Farre from the neighbourhood of any one,
Where to the sunne (till now) did neuer come.
The lights that were, were little, almost none,
A place most fit for tribulation:
    The doores and windowes all were made so fast.
    As if that world should for euer last.

It is not possible I should relate,
How she the powre of sorrow could appease,
Nor how with patience she could moderate,
The griefe that on her spirits made a sease.
She calmes the raging of her troubled seas:
    For when the storme of sorrow doth arise,
    She stilles it with her heauenly exercise.

Often her princely spirit would refraine,
And checke her griefe, and beare her teares away;
Yet would her teares returne to her againe,
And Griefe would pull her on her knees to pray,
Much like a showre vpon a sunnie day:
    For though her face be ouerwasht with teares.
    The bright of her great Maiestic appeares.

As thus her griefe vnrested had her Grace,
To euery place she casts her searching eie,
Fearing some hidden danger in the place,
Where in the hangings wrought, she did espie,
How DANIELL in the lyon's denne did lie ;
   Which counterfet of griefe she stands to see :
   Griefe is best pleas'd with like societie.

The worke did well expresse the workeman's arte ;
For that which should haue life did seeme to haue it :
He could no more then seeming life imparte,
And that was done so well as arte could haue it :
So exquisite the lustre that he gaue it,
   The artist had so much of arte in giuing,
   As she did feare the lions had beene liuing.

In midst of them sate DANIEL at his praire,
His eies, his hands, his heart, he lifts to heauen :
His armèd garde, the kingly lions were,
And vnto him were many angells giuen ;
Some do restraine, the lions that are keene,
   Others vpon his breath attending are,
   To carry vp the message of his praire.

Nor in this holy storie was forgot,
How ABACUC[1] was carried from his men :
Nor how the angell set him on the top,

---

[1] 'Abacuc' of the Apocrypha.   G.

Nor how he called to DANIEL in the Den :
But (sure) some wit was in the workman, when
   He makes the angell beare him by the haire ;
   Yet makes his head be bald, and almost bare.

The princesse on this obiect spends her sight,
And freely spends it with intentiue eie :
The grieuèd doe in grieuèd things delight,
And this well sorts with her extremitie :
Here is (she saith) a friendly company,
   We are not then alone, why grieue me thus?
   For DANIEL and the lyons be with vs.

As I, so DANIEL was of noble blood,
Both I, and DANIEL haue like holy cause ;
As I my selfe, so DANIEL hath withstood
To yeelde obedience vnto wicked lawes ;
Daniel and I are enuièd both, because
   We giue that honour to the King of heauen,
   Which others vnto images haue giuen.

God sends His angells to His holy man,
And bindes the force of lions for his sake ;
If God restraine, what enuie is there than,
That can from any any little take?
The eie of prouidence doth euer wake.
   Then sith that we so like to DANIEL are,
   God will as well for vs as Daniel care.

I am (alas) into this prison cast,
And (God He knowes) without deseruing cause;
And I among such lions now am plac'd,
As watch to seaze my body in their pawes;
Lorde binde the powre of their deuouring lawes,
　And though among these lions be a priest,
　Yet being bloudie, he is a bloodie beast.

This apprehension of another's griefe,
Doth somewhat ease the furie of her owne;
And she from DANIEL can receiue reliefe,
Because to him such fauour God hath showne:
She knowes that God hath all her sorrowes knowne·
　And He that could the furious lions tame,
　Will fauour her that suffers for His name.

Thus (and much better than I can report)
Was this good ladie in her griefe affected;
But much unequall was the care at Court,
Where STEUEN and others other cares respected;
With them there was no tricke of wit neglected:
　They vex themselues with ouer studious care,
　To malice her, so much they enuious were.

With their prepar èd subtilitie they came,
Vnto the Towre, to sift her innocence;
And when the bishop did the princesse blame,
And imputate hir other mens' offence;

Saying she causèd disobedience :
  And those that were rebellious in the State,
  Were only such as she did animate.

Then he a number of the names recited,
Their seuerall plottes and euery circumstance,
And how her Grace was thought with them vnited,
And that from hir the warre had maintenance :
He left not ought vnsaide that might aduance
  His euill drift, which for they were so many,
  And euill ones, I will not write of any.

The princesse to his many words replide
(Alas) What is't you would afflict vs more ?
Are not our griefes enough yet multiplide ?
That still you wrong whom you haue wrong'd
   before,
I haue enough of griefe, what neede I more ?
  And for my answer to your euill tongue,
  I doe protest (my Lord) you doe me wrong.

I neuer had that high aspiring minde,
To pull my sister from her royall throne ;
In my religion I could neuer finde,
Licence or warrant for rebellion.
Rome neuer gaue me dispensation :
  Nor euer learn'd I in my tuterings,
  To merite heauen by murthering of kings.

This sharpe reply the bishop so offended
As he reanswers in a bitter phrase :
(Madam,) against the Church you haue contended,
And still contend (the angry prelate saies)
This disobedience is your great dispraise :
　　If you betray the Church which is your mother,
　　How can you then be true to any other ?

How is't your Grace should thus contend with
　　　heauen,
With God, with angells, and with holy saints ;
How is't that thus to LUTHER you haue giuen
Your soule, which he with blackenesse all de-
　　　paints ?
Who is't this heresie with you acquaints ?
　　(Alas good ladie) LUTHER doth not well,
　　To draw your Grace and many moe to hell.

O giue me leaue a little to aduise,
(I doe not know how fortunate I may)
To leaue the danger of your heresies ;
Let LUTHER beare them with himselfe away ;
Sith you are lost I will direct your way
　　And will you follow but as I direct,
　　You shall arriue the place of God's elect.

What is the new religion you professe ?
(Religion saide I, O it is not so !)

An opposite to antient holinesse ;
A way that leades to damnèd ones below ;
Wherein your wise forefathers would not goe :
    And those that loue this new-begotten lore
    Do damne their fathers that haue liu'd before.

ROME is not so as your new discipline ;
Antient in time, and happy in successe ;
Being assisted with a powre diuine,
That giues to it successe in holinesse ;
Ladie (would God) you had the happinesse,
    With holy teares to wash away your sin,
    ROME hath the keyes to open and let in.

The princesse made the bishop this reply,
I am not cunning for to make dispute ;
I thanke yourselfe, but not your sophistrie,
In my religion I am resolute ;
Yet here is one your learning can confute ;
    (And then she points whereas her Bible lay)
    Here's one (she saith) will teach me what to
       say.

This telles me, that ambition in a priest,
Is that which God with detestation hateth ;
That God will giue the couetuous the least,
And makes that he vpon the humble waiteth,
That with aspiring pride himselfe instateth,

And sith that ROME in pride exceedeth all,
Assure yourselfe, that ROME, and pride will fall.

Christ vnto CÆSAR (not a Christian king,)
Exemplifies a duetifull respect ;
But bloodie ROME would to confusion bring,
All empire and command, her selfe except ;
Her greatnesse is with bloodie practise kept ,
Vnlike to Peter his successors are,
That haue with christian blood distain'd his
chaire.

And much she would haue said, but that the lords
Did interrupt the office of her tongue ;
They say she is too bitter in her words,
And therein to her selfe she offers wrong ;
STEUEN saith, she is in euill ouer strong.
With this their enuious speach they went their
way,
And she (as was her custome) went to pray.

It farre exceedes the powre of any tongue,
To tell you all the sorrowes of this place,
How both her seruants, and her selfe they wrong,
With what neglect and scorne they vse her Grace,
What bloodie men about her they did place.
Their names I silence, for it is not good,
To brand the children with the father's blood.

720

Nor how she was remoouèd from the Towre,
The country being armèd to conuey her
To WODESTOCKE-house, where she expects each
      howre,
The bloodie hand of treason to betray her :
So many griefes, so many feares dismay her,
   As would with griefe my spirits ouercharge,
   To enter in a sea of griefe so large.

What should I speake of PERRIE[1] who was sent,
To short her life with his base treacherous hand ;
Or yet of him, who with the like intent,
Came to surprise her with an armèd band,
Or how with fire she did in danger stand.
   There are both these, and many more behinde,
   Whose repetition would but grieue my minde.

Yet can it not in my remembrance die,
How Spanish PHILIP did this ladie friend ;
That he could pittie hir extremitie,
That he his louing fauour did extend,
That he would praise ; that he hir gifts commend :
   By this we see their malice was but vaine,
   Mercie will come, although it come from SPAINE.

---

[1] Or Perry, notorious in Elizabethan history. G.

So well the king's perswasion could preuaile,
As that the queene did for her sister send ;
The message did with feare her heart assaile,
And sure she thinkes some euill they intend ;
How ere it be (she saith) I recommend
   Into Thy hands, (O sacred Lord of heauen)
   My selfe, and all that to my selfe is giuen.

And thus prepared, she iournies to the Court,
Wherein her chamber, prison-like retirde,
She liues shut vp from any one's resort.
The bishop that this ladie's bloud desirde,
To quench his heart with burning enuy firde ;
   Comes to her, furnisht with his studious care,
   Hoping with craft the princesse to insnare.

GARDNER, it is in vaine thou her assaile,
Whom God protects with His almighty hand;
Canst thou against the liuing God preuaile ?
Or canst thou His all-able powre withstand ?
Or canst thou God and holy heauen command ?
   (Bishop be sure) they are deceiuèd farre
   That thinke (with God) to make preuailing
     warre.

Therefore thy euill had but bad euent,
How ere made strong with thy contriuing wit,
Because thy euill to the good was meant,

And God would not be pleasd to fauour it ;
Though earth and hell in busy counsell sit,
   God countermaunds what euer they deuise,
   And makes them foolish that are iudgèd wise·

And WINCHESTER,[1] we instance this in thee,
Whose howres in studious care were euer spent,
To bring this ladie her extreamitie :
Yet for that God did see thy heart's intent,
He blunts thy edge (O bloudie instrument !)
    And (bellows-like) He makes thy enuious
      breath,
    To make hir liue, thou wouldst haue blowne
      to death.

Thus God can mocke the subtilities of man,
Letting them runne the passage they propose ;
Seeming regardlesse, yet regardfull then,
His eie their hidden secrets can disclose ;
For Prouidence in euery passage goes,
   That howsoere men's pollicies doe plot,
   They haue bad issue if God fauour not.

So God was pleasd with prouidence and care,
This vertuous holy lady to defend.

---

[1] Gardner still, who was Bishop of Winchester. G.

To binde their force, and breake their hidden
    snare,
That euill men for euill did intend.
And now the queene doth for her sister send;
  Where when she was presented on her knee,
  She thus protesteth her integrity.

(Dread soueraigne) I your seruant here present
My selfe as true vnto your life and state,
As is the spirite of an innocent ;
And as let God my griefe extenuate,
As I doe wish you to be fortunate :
  And let the heauens their benefits denie
  To all that enuy at your maiestie.

The queene with angry maiestie then saith,
You stand too much vpon your innocence,
Too confident in your suspected faith ;
It would be better to cast off pretence,
And plainely to acknowledge your offence.
  (The princesse saide) The guiltie shall confesse,
  And so would I, if I had guiltinesse.

But God that sees the very secret thought,
Knowes in my heart there is no guiltines ;
That there was neuer any treason wrought,
Or any thought of such vnworthines.
If then I should against myselfe confesse,

I bring my selfe an euerlasting shame,
To brand the reputation of my name.

O let it please your princely maiestie.
That I your seruant may receiue this grace ;
That Law it selfe my innocence may trie,
That Law may be impartiall in this case :
And if that Law doe quit me of disgrace,
    Then let your seruant haue a gratious eie ;
    If not, let Law and Iustice make me die.

If you be then so righteous (saith the queene)
Belike you'l say, that we vnrighteous are ;
And that your troubles haue vnrighteous beene,
And so the guilt on vs you doe transferre,
And make them righteous that vnrighteous are :
    And so to make your owne purgation,
    You lay on vs the imputation.

The ladie then : let not my soueraigne
Haue that construction of my duetous heart ;
Long may your reputation God maintaine,
And much may He inlarge your high desart :
And (if I may my secret heart impute)
    (I do protest) it doth my spirit good,
    To see such honour in my neerest blood.

And for the sorrowes that I doe indure,
I know the cause is not your owne desire ;

But that some other did the hurt procure,
And stirr'd your anger with their enuious fire;
Against your Grace and me, they doe conspire,
   That would the neerest of our loue diuide,
    Whome God and Nature haue so neerely tide.

Nature (euen in the queene) was powrefull strong,
And makes her spirit haue a feeling sense;
And now she thinkes her sister hath had wrong,
And in her heart she blames their diligence,
That causlesse thus did cause this great offence:
   (And to her selfe she saith) I doe offend,
    Are we not sisters? why should we contend?

Yet would she not expresse her inward heart,
Nor then giue demonstration of her loue;
Nor did she then to any one impart,
What she in her intention did approue:
But (sure) she had a purpose to remoue
   The fire of indignation from her breast
    Which STEUEN had kindl'd with so much vnrest.

The sequell did approue the good intent;
For now the beames of mercie doe appeare,
The queene doth free her long imprisonment,
Remoues her gailer whome she most did feare.
And now she giues her licence to repaire

Vnto her home ; where when she did arriue,
A peacefull quiet doth her griefe depriue.

Now I haue runne the passage I intended,
(I do not know how fortunate I runne ;)
My verse is done now that her griefe is ended.
And she at rest, my busie care is done ;
The cloudes do vanish that bedimm'd this sunne.
    And God that in her sorrowes did protect her,
    Now in her rise He labours to erect her.

GARDNER (the worst of all her enemies)
The heauens cut short his ill-attempting breath,
And made him perish with his subtilities,
But when that Time had giu'n Queene Marie
        death,
The heauens then smil'd on ELIZABETH.
    And now those great ones that enui'd her Grace
    Haue left to her the greatnesse of their place.

When (like the sunne) she was most glorious
        bright,
Casting her beames of mercie euery where ;
And euery where she giues a glorious light,
All other lights to her but little were ;
So matchlesse was she, and so wondrous rare,
    As to her verse her glories I refuse
    Leauing that labour for a better Muse.

I neuer toucht PARNASSUS with my sight,
Nor did the Muses euer teach me rhyme,
Only in humble verse I take delight :
Nor doe I loue the higher straines to clime ;
This plainenesse makes me t' vnfit the time :
   But if that arte vnto my verse were giuen,
   She then should liue in verse, that liues in
     heauen.

Finis.

USA crucem cecinit dudum quæ carmine
    Christi
    Ælizæ varias iam canit illa cruces
Ælizæque cruces crucifixi nomine passas :
    O quam te memorem Virgo, virago, dea,
O nullus laceret liuor LEVERE labores,
    Pergat at in studiis casta MINERUA piis.

HE generous Reader, whose free honest
    soule,
    Did loue the honour'd subiect of thy
    booke,
Will for her sake (whose loue liues in the soule
Of datelesse Memorie) lend a friendly looke.
As other gardens haue bestowed flowres,
To decke her garlands, and to strew her herse ;
So thy graue Muse doth tell her grieuèd houres,
And sings her sorrowes in a sollemne verse :
That though deuouring Time did to bereaue her,
Of palme, and pittie, with her foes conspire ;
Yet thy loue Leuer lets not Honor leaue her,
But by the heate of kind poetike fire
Reviu'd, giu'st virtue her deseruèd hire.

                         R. K.[1]

---

[1] Query—RALPH KNEVET ? See Hazlitt's Hand-Book,
s. n. G.

MY LOUE TO THE ARGUMENT AND
THE AUTHOR.

HE times are now malevolent to verse,
 (To verse that trauells in graue argu-
  ment,)
Yet thy graue Muse adornes the sable hearse
Of her, whose glories were most emiuent.
In this thy art hath well deseru'd of Fame,
That thou ELIZAE's glories dost command,
And that in verse she hath a liuing name,
And that her teares (in verse) by thee are pen'd.
O the deprauèd pleasures of vilde men,
That haue no pleasure in this moouing arte !
And O those spirits, whose licentious pen
Haue made these trauells of so small desert !
When men were better, then the times were so,
And verse had then their high deseruing praise :
Now Time is old, he doth in weakenesse goe
All things (in worth) doe alter as their daies.
Let not the faults of men and euill time
Dishearte thy spirite from poetike fire :
Thy verse is free from all dishonest rhyme,
And from the tract of Cupid's idle fire.
This is thy glorie that thy Muse doth sing
The holie secrets of the Holie Crosse ;
And of this saint, and of her suffering,

In which expence of time there is no Crosse.
Then sith that thus thy trauells doe indeuour,
I do not see but LEUER may liue euer.

ROBERT POSKET.[1]

---

[1] I have not met with this name elsewhere.   G.

TO THE READER.

HE name of Queene ELIZABETH is sufficient argument to perswade a friendly
acceptation; and from the better disposed (whome I couet principally to please) I shall
doubtlesse receiue that reasonable and honest
construction. As for those who haue their tongues
dipt in the poyson of Enuie, I write not to please
them who wil neuer be pleasd with that which is
most deseruing; it being the nature of Enuie, to
depraue that which doth deserue the highest
fauour of loue and good opinion. I may example
this in the wrong offered to the name of Queeue
ELIZABETH, who (though she were the most
admired of her time) hauing extraordinary induments and a gouernment, much more in the
degrees of honour and prosperitie than any of her
predecessors; yet want there not malitious and
base deprauers, who (like dogges that barke
against the sunne) couet to bite her honourable
name, whome God hath made more glorious than

the sunne, giuing her a place of glorie, in fellowship with His holy angelles and saints. For this
double respect haue I therefore taken these
paines : First to plesse the well-affected, in
honouring her whome all that haue honesty will
honour : Next, in giuing Enuie and her sonnes a
morsell to bite vpon; wishing that all the deprauers of her princely name may either reduce
themselues to some degree of honestie, or else
perish with their enuious and euill breath.
Accept then (I pray thee) these my voluntarie
trauells; and honour her remembrance, whome
all the best in the world do honour with admiration, which thou also wilt doe, if thou beest
either honest, or truely English.

¶ AD FŒLICEM HUIUS ELIZABETHÆ PROGRESSUM.

IBER in lautam liber ibis vrbem :
Liber in latum liber ibis orbem :
Liber in lœtas liber ibis vlnas
                    vrbis et orbis.

Paruus est, hinc non liber, est libellus :
Bellus est, hinc non liber, est libellus :
Duplici prodis titulo libellus,
                    belle libelle.

Parue, spem magni retinens honoris ;
Belle, rem magni retinens decoris,
Vade, par natæ cerebro Mineruæ
                    nate cerebro.

I. C.